Indian Alchemy: Soma in the Veda

The book is an epoch-making work—a paradigm-shift in Vedic studies—which identifies *soma* as electrum (gold-silver metallic compound). *Soma* is referred to in the *Ṛgveda* as the soul of the *yajña* (*ātmayajñasya*). The path-breaking identification is based on textual evidence and a penetrating analysis of the Indian alchemical tradition, spanning nearly five millennia.

The author is also the discoverer of the integrating role played by the mighty Sarasvatī river adored in the *Ṛgveda* as the best of mothers, best of rivers and best of goddesses. Sarasvatī and *soma* are no longer mythology but relevant to present-day children, respectively, as the repository of groundwater sanctuaries in north-west India and the metallurgical tradition starting with the Bronze Age civilization, *c.* 3000 BC.

Sarasvatī and *soma* are the symbols of the great Indian traditions of *devī* worship and personification and deification of natural, material phenomena. The *tīrthas* along the rivers are reminders of the critical nature of water management problems all over India and *soma* as an integral part of the *yajña* process, is the embodiment of the scientific, technological and materialist temper of ancient India.

Dr. S. Kalyanaraman, is an Indologist and has contributed to the *History of Science and Technology in Ancient India* (collaborating with Dr. Debiprasad Chattopadhyaya), compiled a multi-lingual comparative dictionary for twenty-five Indian languages. He has also designed and maintained the websites.

Indian Alchemy: Soma in the Veda

S. Kalyanaraman

Munshiram Manoharlal
Publishers Pvt. Ltd.

ISBN 81-215-0880-0
First published 2004

Typeset, printed and published by
Munshiram Manoharlal Publishers Pvt. Ltd.,
Post Box 5715, 54 Rani Jhansi Road, New Delhi 110 055.

Contents

Preface

Focus of the Ṛgveda

Soma is the very soul of the *yajña* elaborated in the *Ṛgveda.*

> The *adhvaryu* takes the skin (*carma* or *tvac*) and puts on it the filaments or shoots of the *soma* (*aṁśu*). He then takes two boards (*adhiṣavaṇa*), puts one on top of the *soma* shoots, and beats them with the stones (*grāvāṇa*). Then the *soma* is put between the two boards, and water is poured on them from the *vasatīvarī* pot. *Soma* is then shaken in the *hotā* cup (*camasa*), wetted again with *vasatīvarī* water and put on a stone. Grass is laid on them, and they are beaten so that the juice runs out. The juice is allowed to run into the trough (*āhavanīya*), then strained through the cloth (*pavitra* or *daśāpavitra*) which is held by the *udgāta.* The filtered *soma* is caught in another trough (*pūtabhṛt*). Libations are poured from two kinds of vessels: *grahas* or saucers, and *camasas* or cups. [Adapted from Haug's notes from Sāyaṇa's commentary on *Aitareya Brāhmaṇa.*]

Soma as electrum and soma as a process (yajña)

Soma is meant for the gods; thus, gods in the *Ṛgveda* are an allegorical personification of the purifications processes (of *soma*), just as Soma is an *āprī* deity, together with other materials and apparatus (ladles and vessels) employed in the *yajña,* accompanied by *ṛcas* (or, *agniṣṭoma*).

If *soma* is electrum and *indra* is burning embers (such as charcoal, *indha,* used in a furnace), the *yajña* can be interpreted, at the material level, as a process of reduction (or, *paritram,* purification), using *kṣāra,* of a metallic ore compound (*mākṣikā* or quartz or pyrites) to yield the shining metals: potable (*pavamāna, rasa-raso varjraḥ,* cf., *ṚV,* 9.48.3, i.e., *rasa,* vigorous as a thunderbolt) gold and silver (*hiraṇyam* and *rayi*), after oxidising the baser metallic elements (in the unrefined pyrite ores) such as lead (*nāga* or *ahi* or *vṛtra*) and copper (*śulba*).

Reducing agents include alkaline as well as combustible materials—vegetable and animal products—such as: herbs (*kṣāra*), barley-grains and cooked *piṇḍa*, milk, curds, clarified butter, viands (animal fat), bones (used in cupellation processes, and for making crucibles, during the Bronze Age), sheep's hair or wool (reminisced as golden fleece).

For e.g., *soma* is described as *parvatāvṛdhaḥ* in a verse, that the pyrites are from the mountain slopes: 9.46.1. Begotten by the stones the flowing (*soma*-juices) are effused for the banquet of the gods' active horses. [Begotten by the stones: or, growing on the mountain slopes.]

The exchange value of gold and silver in Vedic times, is elaborated in metaphorical terms related to wealth and lineage: such as food, cattle, rain, and progeny.

The *vedi* (altar) is the earth and as the *agni* (fire) raises towards the heaven, the poetic imagination of the *ṛṣis* (priests) expands into realms of cosmological thoughts, unparalleled in recorded history of early human civilizations. Thus, at a cosmic level, the *Ṛgveda* raises profound philosophical questions which have been the fountain-head of Indian philosophical traditions.

In such a perspective, the entire *Ṛgveda* can be viewed as an allegory, the human quest for achieving material which has exchange value, in transcending the material level to realms of philosophical explorations, and in expanding the semantic and morphological limits of language to attain new insights into the very concept of "meaning," using language, through metrical, chanted *mantras*, as a means of understanding the *ātman* and the *paramātman*, thereby, attaining *svarga*, or bliss.

All the *sūktas* are thus, governed by a framework of four principal metaphors, rendered in scintillating, ecstatic, spiritual poetic resonance: word, prayer, gods, material well-being. An epitomy of this framework may be seen from the following selections:

9.63.25 The brilliant purified *soma*-juices are let fall amidst all praises.
9.63.27 The purified (juices) are poured forth from heaven and from the firmament upon the summit of the ground. [The summit of the ground; i.e., the raised place, the place of divine sacrifice, or *yajña*.]

Locus

The locus of the *Ṛgveda* is the Sarasvatī river basin.

Sarasvatī river is adored in the *Ṛgveda* as: *ambitame, nadītame, devitame* (best of all mothers, best of all rivers, best of all goddesses). She is a mother because she nourished a civilization on her banks. She is a river which had flowed from the Himalayas to the Arabian Sea carrying the glacier waters which are today carried by the Sutlej and Yamunā rivers. Over 1200 of the 1600 archaeological sites of the civilization unearthed during the last 70 years have been found on the Sarasvatī river basin. For e.g., sites of Ropar, Rakhigarhi, Kunal, Banawali, Kalibangan, Ganweriwala, Kotdiji, Chanhudaro, Dholavira (Kotda), Rojdi, Lothal, Bet Dwaraka where the typical civilization artifacts such as seals with inscriptions, Bronze Age metal weapons and tools, beads, jewellery, weights and measures, water-management systems have been found.*

She is a goddess adored ever since all over India as the goddess of arts and crafts, as the goddess of learning. The civilization nourished by the Sarasvatī had transformed the chalcolithic (copper and stone) age into the Bronze (copper-tin, copper-arsenic alloys or bronze and brass) Age resulting in a revolutionary way to relate to the material phenomena of the world, using hardened metal tools and weapons. She is a goddess of the Saptasindhu region; her *vāhana* is a peacock or a *haṁsa.* She carries a *vīṇā* (lute, string-instrument) on her hands. As Mother Goddess, she is also depicted as Durgā who is adored with weapons in her multiple hands, as Mahiṣāsura-mardinī (the killer of the demon, Mahiṣa, of the bull form).

The river was desiccated due to a number of geological reasons: Yamunā (called Chambal earlier) cut a deeper channel and captured the tributary of Sarasvatī (Tons river) at Paonta Sahib (Himachal Pradesh, a famous Sikh pilgrimage centre). Hence, the cherished memories of the people of Triveṇī Saṁgam at Prayāg (Allahabad) where Yamunā brought in the waters of the Sarasvatī to join the Gaṅgā river. Sutlej (which originated from Mansarovar lake in Mt. Kailas, Tibet) which was a tributary of Sarasvatī river, joining the latter at Shatrana (Punjab), took a 90-degree turn at Ropar (due to tectonic disturbances) and migrated away from the Sarasvatī and joined the

*For a veritable encyclopaedia indica related to the millennium 2500 to 1500 BC, including the text of the *Ṛgveda,* in Devanāgarī and Roman scripts including an English translation based on Sāyaṇa's commentary, cf., the website on the internet: http:/ / sarasvati. simplenet.com, Sarasvati Research Centre, 5 Temple Avenue, Chennai 600 015, India; kalyan99 @ netscape.net.

Sindhu (Indus) river. The phenomenon called *āṁdhī* (sand-storms) which is common even today, resulted in the build-up of sand-dunes on the bed of the Sarasvatī in the areas close to Jaisalmer (Thar or Marusthali desert, also called Cholistan in Pakistan area). Thus Sarasvatī river got choked up and lost the perennial waters coming from the Har-ki-dun glacier (Bandarpunch massif, W. Garhwal, Himalayas). When the river got desiccated, many people moved towards the Gaṅgā-Yamunā doab and moved south towards the Godāvarī river (there is an archaeological site called Daimabad, on Prāvarā river, a tributary of Godāvarī, near Nāsik).

Sarasvatī has been found using scientific techniques: satellite images, carbon-14 dating, tritium analysis of water samples from deep-wells all along the palaeo-channels shown on the satellite images. These have helped in establishing that the river was a mighty one prior to 3000 BC and was desiccated around 1500 BC.

Balarāma, elder brother of Kṛṣṇa goes on a pilgrimage alone the Sarasvatī river from Dwārakā to Mathurā, after visiting Plakṣapraśravaṇa and Yamunotrī (Kārāpacava). During the pilgrimage, he offers homage to his ancestors. (Even at this time, the river was navigable of a distance of 1600 miles from Paonta Saheb to Lothal/ Dwārakā.) The pilgrimage is described in great detail in the Śalyaparva of the *Mahābhārata*. So, our epics contain valuable historical, geographical information of ancient Bhārata.

The evidence from archaeology has firmly established the continuity and substantially indigenous evolution of the civilization right from *c.* 3000 BC to today. So, we have to rewrite the history of our ancient civilization.

Bronze Age Civilization and the fire/metal-workers

Ṛgvedic times are a transition from the neolithic to the Bronze Age. The inscriptions found from hundreds of archaeological sites along the banks of the Sarasvatī and Sindhu rivers have been interpreted elsewhere as lists of Bronze Age weapons.

Ṛgveda is a documentation of the processes of the fire-and metal-workers of the Bronze Age, with particular reference to the most valuable process: *soma*, the purification of the electrum, gold-silver quartz or pyrite ores, the *mākṣikā*. It is notable that the term *śulba* connotes copper (perhaps, pyrite mineral ores); hence, Śulbasūtras are metallurgical manuals elaborating the process of transmutation of minerals to yield the transformed, purified metals: gold and silver.

The book was written while the author was collaborating with the late Prof. Debiprasad Chattopadhyaya for the latter's *History of Science and Technology in Ancient India.*

A remarkable development has been the announcement by the author in the Tenth World Sanskrit Conference held in Bangalore in January 1996, that the most expansive civilization of *c.* 2500 BC was sustained on the banks of the Sarasvatī river which was a mighty and perennial river, which emanated from the Bandarpunch massif, W. Garhwal, Himalayas and which had carried the waters currently carried by the rivers Yamunā and Sutlej. Another remarkable development is the announcement in November 1998 through the Sarasvatī web that the inscriptions of the civilizations have been deciphered as lists of Bronze Age weapons, using a comparative lexicon of Indian languages.

The discovery of the Sarasvatī river is the discovery of the millennium between *c.* 2500 to 1500 BC, which heralded the Bronze Age civilization in India.

Sarasvatī river was indeed *hiraṇyavartanī*, the carrier of potable, placer gold; there are frequent references in the *Ṛgveda* to the *vasatīvarī* waters taken from the Sarasvatī river, in the processes related to the Soma *yajña*.

The identification of *soma* as electrum in this book is consistent with the later-day developments in Indian alchemical tradition and with the discoveries of the Bronze Age artefacts of necklaces made of gold-and silver-discs (*niṣka*) found in Kunal and Lothal (*c.* 3000 BC and 2300 BC respectively)—two archaeological sites on the banks of the Sarasvatī river, separated by a distance of over 1200 kms and united by the bonds of cooperative society (*samāna ūrve, ṚV*, 7.76.5), sustained and nourished by a mighty, navigable river which facilitated commerce and trade by the people of *marutam* (=fertile plain, Tamil) or *marusthalī*. The people are the ancestors (*pitṛs*) of the present-day India—the ancestors to whom Balarāma offered homage on his pilgrimage along the Sarasvatī river.

S. KALYANARAMAN

Chennai
September 2002

Abbreviations

ACI — *Ancient Cities of the Indus*, ed., G.L. Possehl, New Delhi, 1979.

AV — *Atharvaveda.*

BIHM — *Bulletin of the Institute of History of Medicine*, Hyderabad, vol. 1, 1963.

BSOAS — *Bulletin of the School of Oriental and African Studies*, London.

CDIAL — *A Comparative Dictionary of Indo-Aryan Languages.* R.L. Turner, London, 1966.

DED — *Dravidian Etymological Dictionary*, sec. ed., T. Burrow and M.B. Emeneau, Oxford, 1984.

EH — *Excavations at Harappa*, M.S. Vats, Delhi, 1940.

EIP — *Essays in Indian Proto-history*, ed., D.P. Agrawal and D.K. Chakrabarti, New Delhi, 1979.

ER — *Encyclopaedia of Religion*, ed., Mircea Eliade, New York.

ERE — *Encyclopaedia of Religion and Ethics*, ed., James Hastings, Edinburgh.

FEM — *Further Excavations in Mohenjo-daro*, E.J. Mackay, 2 vols., Delhi, 1938.

FIC — *Frontiers of the Indus Civilization* (Sir Mortimer Wheeler Commemoration Volume), ed., B.B. Lal and S.P. Gupta, Delhi, 1984.

HC — *Harappan Civilization: A Contemporary Perspective*, ed., G.L. Possehl, Delhi, 1982.

HCAMI — *History of Chemistry in Ancient and Mediaeval India*, ed., P.C. Ray, Calcutta, 1956.

HSTAI — *History of Science and Technology in Ancient India*, Debiprasad Chattopadhyaya, Calcutta, 1986.

HT — *A History of Technology*, Charles Singer et al., 7 vols., Oxford, 1954.

IHQ	*The Indian Historical Quarterly*, Calcutta.
IJHM	*Indian Journal of History of Medicine*, New Delhi/ Madras.
IJHS	*Indian Journal of the History of Science*, New Delhi.
JASB	*Journal of the Asiatic Society of Bengal*, Calcutta.
JRAS	*Journal of the Royal Asiatic Society of Great Britain and Ireland.*
MASI	*Memoirs of the Archaeological Survey of India*, New Delhi.
MIC	*Mohenjo-daro and Indus Civilization*, ed., J. Marshall, 3 vols., London, 1931.
PIHC	*Proceedings of the Indian History Congress.*
RCIA	*Radiocarbon and Indian Archaeology*, ed., D.P. Agrawal and A. Ghosh, Bombay, 1973.
ṚV	*Ṛgveda.*
SBE	*Sacred Books of the East*, ed., F. Max Muller, reprinted, Delhi, 1972.
SHSI	*Studies in the History of Science in India*, ed., D.P. Chattopadhyaya, 2 vols., New Delhi, 1982.
SHSIA	*Symposium on the History of Sciences in India, Abstracts of Papers*, New Delhi, October 1968.
SSAI	*Science and Society in Ancient India*, Debiprasad Chattopadhyaya, Calcutta, 1979.

Introduction

The argument: Ignis fatuus—alchemy and the "universal" lust for gold

"I am about to give in this little work the history of the greatest folly, and of the greatest wisdom, of which men are capable." These are the opening statements of Lenglet Dufresnoy in his *Histoire de la Philosophie Hermetique,* 1742. Alchemy is perhaps the fiercest passion (*ignis fatuus*) which the world of science has ever known.

This work follows in the footsteps of the pioneering work of P.C. Ray, *A History of Hindu Chemistry* (vol. I, sec. edn., 1903 and vol. II, 1909), which is a unique contribution to the study of chemistry from the earliest times to the middle of the sixteenth century AD. For references to manuscripts, P.C. Ray's work continues to be the principal sourcebook; in this work, there will be little elaboration of chemical substances, preparations and tonics; the principal objective is to update P.C. Ray's work with some historical information based on researches done since 1909 and to highlight those pieces of evidence which have been ignored in the revision of P.C. Ray's work carried out in 1956.

This is, therefore, a tribute to P.C. Ray; it is apposite to invoke the eloquence of P. Masson-Oursel's review in French, of the original work by P.C. Ray:[1]

> *Isis* est heureuse de saluer en ect ouvrage non seulement un des rares exemplaires de serieuse etude critique faite par un savant non European sur l'historire de la science dans sa proper patrie, independent des distinctions de langue et de race. Decteur es-sciences, profeseur de chimie a Presidency College (Calcutta), depuis de longues annees, l'auteur reunit toutes les conditions pour s'acquitter excellement de sa tache, puisqu'l joint a la competence scientifique et a une connaissance approfondie de l'histoire ces naturelles affinites si utiles a la comprehension des doctrines, et qui resultent de la communaute de culture entre le chercheur et les theories qui font l'object de la recherche. . . .

The contribution made by P.C. Ray is so grand that the best tribute that the historian and scientist communities can pay to him is to continue the work he has started. He has enriched the discipline of history of science with profound insights and perspectives, relating the evolution of sciences to the socio-political context.

The focus is restricted and is on only one component of protochemistry or a pseudo-science called alchemy. It should be noted that modern chemistry did not develop from alchemy alone.

Substantial, scholarly work has been done on the alchemical traditions of contemporary civilizations of China, Etypt, Greece, and Islam. In recent years, the Indo-Tibetan alchemical traditions have also been outlined, based on translations of texts from Tibetan. Many Tibetan texts trace their sources to almost all contemporary civilizations, in general, and to India in particular. Tibet may, therefore, like Arabic, prove to be the conservatory of texts of antiquity which are reportedly lost in their places of origin. Since alchemy has progressed across millennia and across civilizations with almost identical objectives not only of aurifiction but also of esoteric alchemy with concepts of elixirs of life and material or spiritual immortality, the alchemical traditions of these civilizations have been used as touch-stones to seek parallels or contrasts with the Indian experience. Quotations from the works related to the alchemical traditions of these civilizations have, therefore, been used liberally to underscore the universal nature of this pseudo-scientific discipline.

The first task attempted was, therefore, to prepare a bibliography of alchemical literature which may have relevance to the Indian traditions. The bibliography includes references to subjects which have spun-off from or are closely allied to the pseudo-science of alchemy, for example: Āyurveda and Siddha medicine, metallurgy, magic, yoga, and tantrism. Since the pseudo-science focuses on gold-making, a background note on the importance of gold has been included. Only a few of the references have been read and evaluated for the purposes of this essay. The objective of this bibliography is to provide a reference base for further explorations on this complex, inter-disciplinary area of research which will call for multi-lingual expertise, and hence, a team of researchers who are proficient in Tibetan, Arabic and Tamil.

The major limitations of this work is that it does not succeed in isolating (and does not even provide milestones in the chronology of) the Indian tradition from the alchemical traditions of other contemporary civilizations spanning from *c.* 2500 BC. At the present state of research, many questions are raised and a few are answered.

The questions are raised in the hope that they may provoke more detailed research work. But, one point is apparent: it would be an impossible task to write alchemical history without writing a social history or evaluating the political economy within which alchemical concepts and practices evolved. The subject of alchemy is shrouded in texts using bizarre techniques of secrecy. The danger of excessive reliance on texts has also to be guarded against since the texts [other than mythologies] generally written by the elite are likely to represent only a fragment (and even, distortion) of reality. In fact, in many cases, the texts shrouded in allegorical and mystical terms are a hindrance to the delineation of reality. On the contrary, the plebeian traditions encapsulated in popular etyma, icons and in the potsherds unearthed by the archaeologist's spade provide reliable evidence. However, the problem becomes tougher since reality has to be reconstructed based on non-textual material, subject to varying degrees of reliability and the unresolved problems of dating.

The impetus

This work would not have been written but for the impetus provided by the late Prof. Debiprasad Chattopadhyaya. A brief outline based on this work appeared in his *History of Science and Technology*, vol. II and the author is overwhelmed by the special reference made by Prof. Chattopadhyaya in his introduction to this work.

He provided the principal philosophical premises that alchemical tradition is an integrating tradition of science potentials; that the tensions between science and its opposite called "counter-ideology" can be reconstructed from the transactions of tantrics in the ale-houses and those who were driven underground; and that, citing Hipocrates, if the historian fails to be understood by the layman, reality may be missed. Success in this litmus test of effective communication is not easy for a subject which by definition is obscure.[2] [To a large extent, "learned" references are relegated to the footnotes, to satisfy the testing and experimental needs of the academic and scientific community.]

It is indeed tough to analyze the devastating impact of an ideology which has resulted not only in a hierarchically classified society but which has excluded a class of people as outside the pale of society. In this ideology which carried within itself the seeds of tension and conflict, science was casualty. It is indeed beyond the scope of this work to go to the roots of this tension or even to analyse the "colour-consciousness" of Indian antiquity; but repeated references to this tension will be made in the alchemical context of the fundamental importance of manual operations, using essentially chemical and metallurgical processes [e.g., pottery, baking, brewing, brick-making, stone-cutting, tanning and dyeing which are perhaps, the oldest arts]. These are operations which were in the field of expertise and competence of the so-called "excluded" classes. These manual operations had the potential for technological advancements, *in an industiral culture* [i.e., simply working with minerals and metals, as distinct from an agrarian culture; an industrial culture which is governed by *lokāyata* or materialism]; the potential was totally suffocated because of the "exclusion" of the "untouchables."

Working definition of alchemy

As a preliminary, working definition, alchemy will be interpreted as "the art of liberating parts of the cosmos from temporal existence to achieve perfection,[3] which for metals, was gold, and for man, longevity, immortality and finally, redemption."[4] As we explore the Indian alchemical tradition and its science potentials, it will be necessary to transmute and solidify this fluid definition which uses some "tough" metaphysical words. In the Indian context, alchemy gets embroiled with the diabolical inequity of social humiliation of the proponent of manual operations who had science potentials—the *caṇḍāḷa* (untouchable).

In effect, the task is to identify the basic components of Indian alchemy as a proto-science with perceptions from the natural order based on observations, and results of manual operations or experiments.[5]

Alchemical tradition provides a number of general hypotheses on natural philosophy: the material unity of the world explaining the origin and evolution of metals; and the possibility of achieving material transformations.

The theoretical premises with which alchemy was started, were sound: the universal characteristics of matter and the convertibility of matter. What was detrimental to science was the way experiments were formulated to test these premises. The creative activity of the artisan could have provided the correct formulation and the correct *design of experiments,* which is fundamental to scientific advancement; the sad story of Indian alchemy is that such an artisan, for instance the *caṇḍāla* (untouchable), was kept outside the pale of "organized" society.

While the task of data-gathering in a complex linguistic era—ancient India—is daunting in itself, and of course, time-consuming, the real task of sifting through the evidence and anecdotes and weighing the material in a historical, philosophical[6] perspectives bristles with problems, "beclouded by a mass of mysticism and misunderstanding."[7] The Indian alchemical context, spanning perhaps from beyond *c.* 2500 BC, the rise of the Indus valley civilization through the Ṛgvedic technology, to the complex tantric traditions, say, upto the fifteenth century AD is a challenge of an extraordinary order.

To quote a great writer of the history of alchemy, Hopkins:[8] "...this preliminary labour (of fact finding and confirmation) has been so difficult and time-consuming that no real history of alchemy has yet appeared...our historians of alchemy may be said to have given us that with which we have had to be content, an enumeration in chronological order of certain important events in this subject.... But still the questions would not down!... Why did the earliest alchemists have to write so obscurely that they are quite incomprehensible to the modern reader? And why, a thousand years later, was their strange collection of terms preserved and continued as if it were an indispensable sign-manual of the initiated? In fact what was it the ancient alchemists were writing about? What also was the cause of their enthusiasm and their staccato language? What was the central penetrating thought and whence did it come?...knowing that alchemy at that time (fourteenth and fifteenth centuries AD) was about a thousand years old, how shall we explain this sudden recrudescence of alchemy in a hysterical form—like the tantric rites in India—'The strangest myth that ever troubled the mind of man'?" To unravel the glimpses of alchemy amidst "the strangest myth" of tantrism, we have to hark back to the texts of antiquity, archaeological and etymological evidence and parallels with alchemical traditions of contemporary civilizations.

Hopkins[9] to whom alchemy begins with Egypto-Greek, and to whom Chinese and Indian alchemic traditions are virtually non-existent, makes a casual statement, appended as a footnote: "The suspicion that the art of alchemy might have been introduced in very ancient times from India is now dispelled."*

This work will endeavour to dispel the misunderstanding created by both Hopkins and Hopkins' misreading of P.C. Ray, two of the most outstanding historians of alchemy, while drawing from brilliant insights provided by them on the socio-philosophical milieu within which alchemists struggled to establish a scientific-materialist temper.

The refrain is that it is impossible to write alchemical history without delineating historical socio-politico-economic contexts within which the alchemist-artisan advanced his manual operations and proto-scientific/technological experiments and endeavours. Indian alchemical tradition, as cultural phenomena, need to be humanized by studying the history of alchemy, within a framework of political economy.

The traditions can be traced to the artisans working in metals, faience, stone and in the dyeing of cloth in a variety of colours, red, blue and yellow in particular. Without mining and without the technology to extract minerals from the earth, which involved manual operations, no technological advancement would have been possible. The rise of an industrial culture and civilization itself is coterminous with the knowledge of mining.

As a junction among contemporary civilizations of Egypt, China, Mesopotamia, Greece, and Islam, the Indian tradition represents a fusion of alchemical concepts of all these great civilizations. It is extremely difficult to isolate the traditions of any one civilization to the exclusion of others. Across civilizations, gold was considered the perfect metal, because it was lasting, resistant to rust and was easily worked with for creating jewellery, its lustre was alluring to the royalty and plebeian alike. It became the standard of value, a currency medium, together with silver, another lustrous (second-ranking) desirable metal, for economic transactions; the state of antiquity sustained their power-base by accumulating gold in their treasuries. May be because of its lasting quality, a religious belief arose that gold-making techniques could be extended to avoid bodily corruption and death and to attain "immortality" for the body and spirit.

The blending of alchemy with medical and chemical sciences, metallurgy, pseudo-sciences of astrology and magic, religion and

*See P.C. Ray, *Hindu Chemistry.*

even social organization (as it seems to have happened in India) is a characteristic feature in the alchemical traditions of all civilizations. What started as a study of nature and evolved into technical accomplishment of transformation (or "union," *yoga*, in one offshoot; the "Great Work," in another) of matter assumes extraordinary dimensions and sometimes, degenerates into metaphysics, occultism and orgies.

Another common characteristic is that the alchemical tradition is kept a closely guarded secret within laboratories or "workshops" and family-lineages. Apart from the use of cryptic language [with bizarre phrases such as the bile of the tortoise, unreleased semen, etc.; confusion caused by merging scientific and artistic, even metaphysical concepts; use of *sandhyā-bhāṣā* (twilight language), in the Indian tantric tradition, for instance], allegories,[10] mythology[11] and special symbols, the key techniques and processes were required to be transmitted only orally.[12]

Joseph Needham,[13] whose magnum opus will be frequently invoked for Chinese alchemical parallels vis-à-vis the Indian alchemical tradition, underscores the extraordinary problems faced by the historian of alchemy: "The facts indeed were much more difficult to ascertain, and also more perplexing to interpret, than anything encountered in subjects such as astronomy or civil engineering. And in the end, one must say, we did not get through without cutting great swathes of briars and bracken, as it were, through the muddled thinking and confused terminology of the traditional history of alchemy and early chemistry in the West. Here it was indispensable to distinguish alchemy from proto-chemistry and to introduce words of art such as aurifiction, aurifaction and macrobiotics[14]...that crucial Chinese distinction between inorganic laboratory alchemy and physiological alchemy, the former concerned with elixir preparations of mineral origin, the latter rather with operations within the adept's own body.... A fruitful comparative history of science would have to be founded not on the counting up of isolated discoveries, insights or skills meaningful for us now, but upon 'the confrontation of integral complexes of ideas with their interrelations and articulations intact'."

The techniques evolved during alchemical processes such as distillation, sublimation (evaporation and condensation), filtration, combustion, means for assaying, purifying and alloying metals, soldering,[15] dyeing and pigmenting, and the knowledge acquired about the properties of matter (organic and inorganic) did, however, (contain the potentials and) provide the foundations for the ultimate evolution of a scientific temper. What happened in India is quite another social story, governed as the class structure was by a diabolical hierarchical *varṇa* and *jāti* (class and caste) order which contained within itself the seeds of destruction of any science potentials and the debunking of manual operations as undesirable activities which the gods do not live. If "truth" had already been delivered and all the "truth" was already enshrined in a special orally transmitted document to the specially-born few, the very process of alchemic experiment advocated by such a school was *ab initio* false, anti-science and militated against rationality. The recipe advocated by this school was simple: Say this, you will get it; do not ask questions.

References

1. *Isis*, III, 1920, pp. 68-73.
2. Cf., for example: *śulva* which connotes copper, mineral-veins in mines and also geometry; *rasa-karpūra*, camphor, also sublimation, synonym: *puṭa-pāka; tarkṣya*, synonym for *yavākṣāra*, saltpetre which is also called *nitre* represented as a dragon; *tarkṣya* may also connote a snake. So is arsenic a snake; toad or crow symbolizes putrefaction; seed of venus is "verdigris;" realgar (*sindhura*, lit. elephant, also cinnabar, also red-lead) and orpiment (red—*rakta dhātu*; yellow—*tālam, pītakam, alam*) are two brothers; lead is *sīsam, nāgam* (cf., Śeṣa, serpent); *vaṅgam*, tin is also *vaṅgam, piccatam, tapu*; mercury is the clearest water, a dove, an eagle, a green lion, also a serpent; gold is a red-lion. Masculine is mercury and feminine is sulphur. A philosopher's stone was a stone (solid) which was not a stone (volatile). Alchemy is remarkably pictorial, and abounds in enigmatic figures and diagrams: wolf (antimony) devours the king (gold) referring to the purification of gold by fusion of metallic oxides with antimony.
3. Pseudo Roger Bacon in the *Mirror of Alchemy* (thirteenth century): "Nature has always had for an end and tries ceaselessly to reach perfection, that is gold;" A.J. Hopkins, *Alchemy, Child of Greek Philosophy*, 1967, p. 58.
4. W.F. Bynum, E.J. Browne, and Roy Porter, *Dictionary of the History of Science*, pp. 9-10.
5. Cf., the article on "Alchemy" by Mircea Eliade, in *Encyclopaedia of Religion* (*ER*), pp. 183ff. "Where the early Greek mind applies itself to science it evinces an extraordinary sense of observation and argument.

Yet the Greek alchemists show an inexplicable lack of interest in the physico-chemical phenomena of their work. To cite a single example, no one who has ever used sulphur could fail to observe 'the curious phenomena which attend its fusion and the subsequent heating of the liquid. Now, while sulphur is mentioned hundreds of times [in Greek alchemical texts], there is no allusion to any of its characteristic properties except its action on metals' (Sherwood Taylor, quoted in Eliade, 1978, p. 147). As we shall see presently, the alchemist's quest was not scientific but spiritual."

6. A.J. Hopkins, op. cit., pp. 2-3, 38: "In the beginning, alchemy was far from being philosophical. It was just an ordinary art like that of the carpenter or blacksmith. It was on this primitive side of its character that it derived from ancient Egypt ... alchemy—a form of philosophy applied to technique.... In that it applied these theories (of Plato and Aristotle) to observations, the proper scientific sequence was followed.
7. Ibid., p. 3.
8. A.J. Hopkins, op. cit., pp. iv ff.
9. Ibid., p. 6.
10. Cf., an example in a Latin alchemical work (AD 1546), Pretiosa Margarita Novella, or "The New Pearl of Great Price," a version of an introduction to alchemy written by Petrus Bonus of Pola in 1330: "A crowned king (gold) is approached by his son (mercury) and his five servants (silver, copper, iron, tin, and lead), who beseech him to change them into kings also. The king maintains a diplomatic silence, whereupon he is killed by mercury. After passing through a series of remarkable vicissitudes, representing alchemical operations, the king rises from the dead and is at last able to accede to the original position.... The final woodcut shows a royal flush of crowned kings, from which, however, there is an unexplained absentee—possibly lead, which was always regarded with a certain amount of suspicion in alchemical circles." J. Read, *Prelude to Chemistry*, p. 58. The parallel to Indian legend of Soma and his son called Budha, mercury is astonishing, reinforcing the universal characteristics of alchemy, across civilizations. Even more remarkable is the occurrence of seven personages on one Indus seal; and six on another, interpreted as *kṛttikā* or *mātṛkā*. This provokes a question: were some signs and pictorial motifs on Indus seals and tablets alchemical messages?
11. Michael Maier advanced a startling thesis that classical mythology from the beginning was subservient to alchemy; cf., J. Read, *Prelude to Chemistry*, p. 160.
12. For this reason alone, one should not discount as "worthless" the work, *Rasajalanidhi* by Budhadev Mukherjee, 5 vols., Calcutta, 1926, though the book may not be acceptable as "historical evidence."

13. Needham, *SCC*, vol. 5, part II, pp. xviii, xxii.
14. Needham defines it as the "belief that it is possible to prepare, with the aid of botanical, zoological, mineralogical and above all chemical knowledge, drugs or elixirs (*tan*) which will prolong human life beyond old age...the adept can endure through centuries of longevity, finally attaining the status of eternal life and arising from the etherealised body as a true Immortal. Such was the Taoist concept of material immortality...." *SCC*, vol. 5, part II, p. 11. Cf., the parallel concepts of Indian *yakṣa* and *siddha/yogī*.
15. Pliny says (XXXIII, p. 94): "For gold, chrysocolla is used; for iron, alumina; for large pieces of copper, calamine; for copper sheets, alum; for lead with marble, resin, with which also lead is joined to tin; for tin with tin, oil; and the same for the union of crude lead with bronze or crude lead with silver." This parallels the solderable list given in *Chāndogya Upaniṣad.* Chrysocolla is interpreted as malachite, i.e., a basic copper carbonate which might have been a constituent of gold solder described by Dioscorides (v. 92): verdigris is mixed with a boy's urine in a copper mortar. Soda is then added. Probably malachite, i.e., chrysocolla is a substitute for verdigris. Cf., the urination mentioned in the Ṛgvedic account of *soma* filtering process. Verdigris is a copper acetate.

1

Gold and the Grammar of Money in Antiquity

The argument

In the march of economic and social history, the dazzle of gold (and silver) resulted in an elitist passion. The passion led to the use of state-power to accumulate gold and silver in the state treasuries. A devastation of incalculable proportions occurred when the concept of "value" (which was merely an arithmetic of proportions in exchange transactions) was distorted. The very possession of a scrap of gold leaf or a gold button (*hiraṇyapiṇḍam*) was considered to be possession of "value." This devastating distortion of the concept of "value" (which in antiquity was synonymous with *māna*, the extension of the labourer's personality into the artefact created by him; in fact, there is no value but value in labour) in the march of capitalism results in a commodity fetishism—in particular, gold-fetishism. This fetishism which ruins social equilibrium, contains also the seeds of alchemy, another passion in search of techniques to "make" gold, the state-dictated "standard of value," called *akṣa* (gold cowrie).

Sacred myth of gold

It is against the backdrop of the evolution of the monetary system of India that the alchemical tradition governed by a craze for acquiring gold, *qua* gold, or alchemical techniques of aurifaction and aurifiction have to be evaluated not only in terms of the state-managed alchemy but also of plebeian[1] alchemy, in the junkets of *yakṣas* (cf., *Manu*[2]). The emergence of the sacred myth of gold under the dictates of the sacerdotal priesthood (with the imprimatur of the conqueror-king, an Indian analogue of the Roman *pontifex maximus*) is, in effect, coterminous with the emergence of the pseudo-science of alchemy with a passion for "gold-making" and the emergence of the slavery of the mining classes.

Unanswered questions

In the alchemical tradition of a Greek civilization, the Greek Corpus from Pseudo-Democritus (*c.* from first century AD to eighth century AD) says again and again: "Thus you will obtain gold," "in this way gold will be made." Nothing this, some great questions are posed by Needham,[3] questions which have to be posed, even if not fully answered (given the tentative corpus of knowledge), in the context of the Indian tradition also: "The great question is (and it signified for aurifaction in all civilizations), how could it be that the philosophers could believe that they were making 'gold,' when the artisans were quite sure that they were successfully imitating it? How did technical aurification generate mystical aurifaction? How was it possible that the idea of the transmutation of base to noble metals could arise in a world which had known the refiner's fire and the test of cupellation for a thousand years already?" ...it is curious that Pseudo-Democritus and the Leiden papyrus X both refer with respect to Pammenas or Phimenas, a great artist in chrysopoia...both texts deal with such matters as the doubling or augmentation of gold and silver by alloying them with claudianum[4] a fermented drink are not intoxicants; but the fermented product gains the power to intoxicate.[5]

Historical alchemical perspectives: metals

Multhauf[6] notes that the awareness of the transformation of matter as a particular art resulted from the inventions in the field of metallurgy. In this field, it was possible to produce artificial metals through a chemical transformation, by heating certain minerals with reducing agents, usually obtained in contact with the fuel. He cites the conclusions drawn by Aitchison (1960) about the historical sequence of the production of metals: gold, before 5000 BC; electrum 3800 BC; native copper, before 5000 BC (which may contain an impurity of tin of upto 2 per cent); smelted copper, 4300 BC; bronze, 4300 BC; lead, 3500 BC; silver (gold free), 2500 BC; tin, 1800-1600 BC; iron, 1400 BC; brass, or copper-zinc alloy, *c.* beginning of Christian era.

Gold for the "elite"

"It is surprising, for instance, that on the archaeological record Mesopotamia (Tepe Gawra XII=end of Ubaid),[7] where deposits of metal and ore are meagre, became familiar with gold before Anatolia which has its own reserves. Moreover, the occurrence of a twisted gold wire at Ur (Ubaid period)[8] is the earliest example of any metal in Southern Mesopotamia.... The rise of gold metallurgy in Central Anatolia coincides with the establishment of what may be described as an elite society at Alaca, and this is a case which is similar to that of *varṇa,* though much later in time...tomb material created for a chosen few and that their demands in terms of imagery, religious symbolism and metal quality were quite sophisticated.... These priorities may have been social in character, as Professor Renfrew suggests."[9]

Professor Renfrew[10] suggests, based on *varṇa* gold finds in Turkey, Anatolia that a social structure based on class distinction or a "chiefdom" may have determined the development of precious metals, to meet the needs of particular societies. The morpheme *varṇa* connoting the site is of interest in the context of Indian alchemy which has to contend with a compound term for gold, *su-varṇa* interpreted as of yellow/green colour or "desirable" colour.

The dazzling metal is desired, with extraordinary passion, by the elite and the ruling classes; they take possession of the resource-bases and use it as a standard measure of value and impose this standard on the society. The ornaments made of this metal is for the gods, the royalty and the priests. Many plebeians try to climb the social ladder and the craze for gold assumes epidemic proportions; and changing metaphor, a cancer enters the body politic with incalculable social impact.

The dazzling head-dress of Queen Shub-ad of Ur (Mesopotamia) had interlacing gold rings and *aśvattha* (*pīpal*) gold leaves, exquisitely veined, both rings and leaves strung on bead-chains of lapis lazuli and red carnelian, like diadems of pendants over her forehead. Above these was a third tier of gold willow leaves betwixt golden flowers inlaid with lapis lazuli and white calcite. Towering these tiers was an arrangement of upright golden flowers with lapis lazuli in the centres. Dated to *c.* 2700 BC; a difficult question is raised and answered by Sutherland:[11] there was no gold in Mesopotamia; whence did the Shub-ad's gold ornaments come and how? "Their nearest gold sources were not very near...southern India contained rich deposits in and around the area of Kolar[12] (west of Madras). . . . In the Hindukush area between Peshawar and Tashkent, at the head of the Oxus valley, gold was to be found in rich supply, together with lapis—itself, like gold, non-existent in Mesopotamia.

Farther north again the Ural-Altai area of Central Asia held immense quantities of gold, which were certainly destined in the course of time to have an impact on the gold economy of the Near East...a coast-wise trade might even now have existed between Arabian gold sources on the Red Sea and the Lower Euphrates valley...a world in which individual civilizations and economies absorbed gold, or were injected with it, gaining or losing their wealth by increasing conquest or trade, or by sudden subjection, while all the time the total quantity of gold in existence mounted steadily and massively."

The gold-leaf on Queen Shub-ad's diadem is veined like the *aśvattha* leaf on the Indus pictorial motifs on seals; Indus lapidary had worked with all the materials used in Shub-ad's head-dress. In the over-all context of Indus seals found in the Tigris-Euphrates valleys, it is a plausible hypothesis that the gold ornaments came from the Indus artisans. The evidence of gold and silver ornaments and beads from Indus sites and the ornaments on Mother Goddess figurines attest to the Indus lapidary's expertise.

A necklace of gold cowries was found at Dashur, Egypt *c.* 1850 BC.[13] The magico-religious symbolism of cowries in ancient civilizations is related to their use as life-giving amulets. Shaped like the mouth of the womb, or like the opening of the eye (coming alive; in one etymon stream, *akṣa* also means an eye), cowries reproduced in gold—an indestructible metal—attain the power of immortality. The golden cowrie becomes the emblem of Egyptian Mother Goddess Hathor, the personification of life-giving shells and the guardian deity of the sea where cowries were obtained. [In the Indian religious-iconographic tradition, *akṣamālā* on one of the many hands of a *yakṣa*-type image is a recurrent symbol.] In Indian history, the gold cowrie is the *akṣa*, the unit of account for the state treasury. When gold became very valuable, and became inaccessible to the plebeians, the real cowries themselves became the unit of currency in the transactions among plebeians.

Doctrines of economic "value," gold and alchemy

Since alchemy is concerned with gold-making, it is relevant to understand the importance of gold in antiquity. It was a currency medium; it was a standard of value in economic transactions controlled or regulated by the state. Its possession assured access to economic resources.

What is value? Is it not mere arithmetics of proportions?

"Value is not a thing, nor an attribute of things; it is a relation, a numerical relation, which appears in exchange. Such a relation cannot be accurately measured without the use of numbers, limited by law, and embodied in a set of concrete symbols, suitable for transference from hand to hand. It is this set of symbols which, by metonym, is called money. In the Greek and Roman republics it was called (with a far more correct apprehension of its character) *nomisma* and *nummus*, because the law (*nomos*) was alone competent to create it."[14]

This technical abstraction may be related to conditions of antiquity in the Indian subcontinent. A gold cowrie, a unit of account for the state treasury, was called *akṣa*. A seal, *accu* was used to record the revenue in books of account of the treasury. Only one concept of value was known in a society which was initially governed by a social compact of shared living: that was *māna*, an extension of the personality of the artisan which enters into the artefact he creates, say a lapidary creating a steatite or chert weight or a faience seal or a gold-beaded necklace. A gold cowrie was only a symbol of value for exchange of commodities. A natural cowrie or sea-shell from the sea could as well have served this purpose, if the concept of the "state" had not intervened. In fact, it was used as a currency unit of account in ancient India even after the metals took over the functions of a currency in the six or seven centuries before the Christian era.

That a symbol could be used to measure value represented a big leap in social organization; it became a necessary tool in the sustenance of capitalism in its evolutionary days. The material used for the symbol was altered: sometimes it was gold, sometimes it was silver or copper. The combined denominations, and capitalist functions of the symbols have remained unchanged to the present day. Money is, therefore, a measure, *māna*.

In this process of symbolizing, a disaster occurred—a disaster which was ultimately to result in incalculable social[15] devastation and the birth of a pseudo-science called alchemy. A fallacy was created. A symbol called *rūpya*, or simply form[16] was made synonymous with silver and value; *kācu*, glass or perhaps, glazed steatite of the proto-Indus era, yielded place to *akṣa*, the gold cowrie; the gold[17] in the cowrie was equated with value.

The metal used to create the symbol was mistaken to be the measure of value. It was somehow forgotten that only numbers measured value, not metal. It was somehow forgotten that the numbers which could help in organizing produce into groups for "sharing," say, using a balance and weights created by the proto-Indus artisan, are the true measure of value in social exchange.

The disaster was that money was equated with value and value was equated with metal. [Though scarce, relative to other minerals, gold was easily acquired from alluvial deposits in rivers or as placer gold; it was an easy metal to work with on a crucible and on an anvil with a hammer, it could be beaten on an anvil to a thin plate; most importantly, it was easily divisible into fractions of sizes and weights (cf. the binary division of weights in proto-Indus from a standard 27.2 gms); and it had some lasting lustre and hence, it was chosen as a symbol, a cowrie, *akṣa* of value.]

Arthaśāstra (*c.* third century BC) devotes a chapter and more to the *akṣa-śālā* or a workshop for manufacturing *akṣa*, dealing primarily with gold and silver metals. This level of importance attached to two metals, reveals a historical situation of fundamental import in the political economy of antiquity. The state-power was sought to be sustained by monopolizing the control of gold and silver mineral resources and by controlling the production of refined gold and silver to build up the treasury. A devastating concept of value was put in place and enforced by state-power, equating a unit of weight of metal with value itself.

Yet another link to the proto-Indus mercantile legacy may be related to the frequently occurring pictorial motif on Indus seals: *svastika* (treated as a compound: *su+vastika*). *Arthaśāstra* (2.7.35) uses a technical term—*vastuka* to connote an item of entry in the ledger. "For one writing down an item (in the accounts) without any order or in a wrong order, or in an illegible manner, or twice over, the fine is twelve *paṇas.*" The right-and left-handed *svastika* symbols used in Indus script messages may, therefore, somehow, be related to this later-day practice; hence, the signs may perhaps be interpreted as: accrual (*pūrvam siddham*) and realization, or *deyam* and *dattam* (what is due and what is given) to use book-keeping terms to connote trade-contract execution status. The symbol *svastika* has an important diagnostic value for the alchemist: if an ore in earth or rock shows spots or *svastikas* of fine sand (apart from other characteristics mentioned), *Arthaśāstra* recommends that such ore is a gold-ore, to be used for insertion, as transmuters of copper and silver (2.12.5). The phrase used is: *pratīvāpārthaḥ* interpreted by commentators as an "ore in powder form inserted in copper or silver while boiling."[18] The symbol *svastika* is also used by *pautava-adhyakṣa*, superintendent of standardization (of weights and measures).[19] He is responsible for making a *yantra*, the balance beam (*yantram ubhayataḥśikyam vā*) with scale-pans on the two sides of the fulcrum or a pan (on one side only; *yantra* as a steelyard type of balance; *ubhayataḥśikya* denoting the pair of scales; *śikyam* "chains for cups"). Archaeological evidence of the Indus two-pan balance is vividly recalled as a continuing legacy. He is responsible for markings on a *samavṛttā* balance, lit. "even-rounded," possibly a steel-yard type; markings intended to indicate units of weight in *karṣa* and *pala*, going upto 100 *palas*, starting with a zero on the beam's end. In this context, a phrase is used which are important in explaining the *svastika* and *akṣa*, two terms which are important in the financial and economic transactions: *akṣeṣu nāndīpinaddham.* The morpheme *nāndī* is a synonym for *svastika* or a mark of the crow's foot, or a mark of the wedge, according to the commentators. "*Pinaddha* then would mean 'covered,' i.e., marked, perhaps even carved, engraved. The reading *naddhrī* would mean 'a strap,' *pinaddha* would then be possible in the sense of 'tied' and *akṣa* in the sense of 'the pivot.' But it is not easy to see pivots, straps, etc. in the balance described here. For *tulā*, cf.: 'The balances with which the Hindus weigh things are charistones, of which the weights are immovable, while the scales move on certain marks and lines. Therefore, the balance is called *tulā*. The first line means the units of the weight from 1 to 5 and further on to 10; the following lines mean the tens: 10, 20, 30, etc.' (*Alberuni's India*, I, 164-65.)"[20] The commentator goes on to interpret the morpheme *akṣa* as a multiple of five: 5, 10, 15, etc. This re-inforces the interpretation of *akṣa* as a standard unit of account used for the treasury and all financial and economic transactions of the state.

Where had the *mana* gone—*mana*, that magnificent proto-Muṇḍa concept of a material as the extension of a manual operation? Where had the *ṛta* gone—*ṛta*, that magnificent Ṛgvedic concept of an order in nature? Seeds of social conflict can be sown by a mere slip; mixing metaphors, it takes but a drop to poison the social distillate. [If the proto-Indus practice of recording value in script symbols on mere clay or faience[21] seals and tablets had been continued—similar to the present-day credit cards—his disaster of using metal and imputing value to that metal might have been avoided; perhaps, the history of capitalism (and certainly, the history of alchemy) might have been changed; oh, it is one of those sad "ifs" in history!]

Tracing back the story of gold through the maze of Brāhmaṇa and Vedic texts and the proto-Indus, Chinese, Mesopotamian, Egyptian and Greek archaeological finds, it may be possible to perceive the origins of alchemy across civilizations of antiquity. To overcome the problems of wading through the allegories and mysticism of the literary texts, it will often be necessary to depend upon more straightforward, hence trustworthy, references or parallels in contemporary civilizations. Sophocles, a contemporary of Herodotus, makes Creon say in *Antigone*, "Go, and buy if you will, the electrum of Sardis (Lydia) and the Indian gold." Thucydides places the era of Creon to sixty years after the Trojan war; hence, del Mar infers that the gold coins of India alluded to by Creon relate to the eleventh century BC.[22]

Variations in the relative "value" of the metals used for coins was sought to be remedied by Greek states of the fifth century BC, at first issuing coins with both metals—gold and silver—together (called electrum[23] coins). By combining different proportions of these metal coins, state-power was invoked to confer a "value" which was stabler than the "value" inhering in the metal-content as commodities. The struggle continued to extricate "commodity" from "measure of value;" the blunder was in the commodities used: both silver and gold were used for making ornaments. The state restricted the use of these metals in the arts. "To secure permanency in the ratio (between relative proportions of silver and gold, subjected to vicissitudes of natural gold-silver alloy finds), it was subjected to sacerdotal authority; and we shall find that, as a result of this regulation, it remained fixed for centuries...."[24]

Slave-mining and foreign conquests in search of gold and silver are the social sagas of savagery driven by the lust to acquire these "measures of value" which had gained the attribute of "value" itself, paralleling Marx's profound insight on commodity fetishism. Indeed, it may be postulated that the concept of "fetishism" of the product of labour may have been influenced by sacerdotal dicta, imputing magical power to the "owner" of a commodity such as gold,[25] a material to be regarded with awe, superstition and magical potency, almost a cult of gratification.

When sacerdotalism combines with state-power, the impact on the plebeians[26] is stunning; the plebeians are told that the particular commodity has "power" and at the same time, they are prevented from possessing it, except by permission from those in authority. The plebeian is bottled up from all sides. When he has no access to the gold *akṣa*, he revolts using the real *akṣa*, the plentiful cowries or shells[27] from the shores of the high-seas in his inter-personal transactions and exchanges.

Ant-gold

For Yudhiṣṭhira's coronation, the king of Kulindas presents ant-gold.[28] This is legend. Megasthenes associates it with Dards, living in the Himalayas.[29] A geological perspectives is provided by Rawlinson and Schiern[30] whose view is that a tribe of Tibetan Himalayas were diggers of gold, particularly during winter to avoid problems of ground water. While the miners remained underground, tents were pitched at the portals of the pits. The tents made of yak fur gave the appearance of a pack of dark hairy animals. The bluff advanced by the miners, to keep the mining operations secretive, was to spread the story that the earth-digging ants were excavating the gold. From the general area of modern Bokhara, Afghanistan, Kafiristan and Dardistan north of the Himalayas, the Persian empire received over 20,000 lb. of probably alluvial gold a year in the fifth century BC. Herodotus called it gold-dust from the Indians, produced by ants, smaller than dogs but larger than foxes... "these ants dwell under the ground, and turn up the sand; and the sand which is brought up contains gold.... The Indians come to the place with bags and fill these with sand, riding away as fast as they can; for the ants, as the Persians say, detect them by smell and begin to chase them...so that, unless the Indians got away with a start while the ants are gathering, not one of them would escape."[31]

Alexander, accompanied by an expert mining prospector, took over 2,000,000 lb. of gold and silver in the form of ingots and 500,000 lb. of gold coins from the royal treasure of Susa.[32] As elucidated by Needham, in Sumer, a distinction was made between two sorts of loss in gold refining: litharge volatilization and the absorption of the base metal oxides by the cupel; two stages of refining were called *tubbu* and *pataaqu*.[33]

The scarcity caused perhaps also by the expeditions of Darius, Alexander and Seleucus might be related to the revival of mining and the installation of Aśoka's edicts intriguingly near gold-mines, despite the Buddhist Vinaya commandment against possession of gold.

Allchin[34] suggests that the town of Suvarṇagiri mentioned in the Brahmagiri edict may be identified with the golden hill of Maski and provides an insight into the political dynamics of the lure for gold:

"The minor Rock Edict at Maski is actually on the gold field; the two Koppal edicts are no more than 30 miles from the Gadag band of gold-mines; the three at Brahmagiri are equally near to several mines in north Mysore and Sandur; while the other two sites of inscriptions at Yerragudi and near Pattikonda are in the centre of country long famous for diamonds. Viewed in this light the Aśokan edicts of the south reflect a very material interest in the area, and though they may also proclaim the sincere Buddhism of their author they tempt us to ask whether this was not rather a case of the banner of Dharma following the prospectors than vice versa?"

A deeper evaluation of socio-economic facets and class-conflicts resulting from an exploitation [by ruling classes expanding their span of regional control], of mines which would have been earlier worked by *pāṣaṇḍas* and *caṇḍālas*, is a task of great importance to be pursued by historians of Lokāyata.

The need to recover the plundered gold is also seen in the later-day acquisition of 50 to 100 million sesterces of silver per annum from Rome in Pliny's time, paying for this metal in merchandise and also gold, "at a rate for silver that yielded the Romans nearly cent per cent profit."[35] This was the time when cowries, the shells, were used for small change; cf. the finds in Manikyala tope (*c.* eighth century AD) of cowries mingled with Roman and Sassanian moneys. Very soon, the cowries had to be counted in lakhs (cf. the inclusion of *-akṣa* morpheme in the word: *lakṣa* = one lakh or 100,000), not merely in *paṇas* or handfuls, to equate them to the silver coins, putting the lid on any opposition by plebeians to the state-orchestrated introduction of commodity fetishism for gold and silver.

Gibbon's review of the Byzantine empire (chap. 17) includes a legal declaration that the imperial taxes during the dark ages were payable in gold coins alone, presumably because the oriental trade had gone. Theodosius's reign had an officer entrusted with gold coinage called *Comes Sacrerum Largitionum*, or Count of the Sacred Trust, one of the 27 greatest nobles of the empire; comparable to the *ṛtvij* of *Arthaśāstra*; under whom, perhaps, was the *ākara-adhyakṣa* responsible for the mines whence gold was extracted, the mints for coinage and the revenues payable in *akṣa* gold coins into the treasury kept for the service of the sacred emperor or in exchange for silver. All these bureaucratic functions are analogous to the those of the Theodosius's Count of the Sacred Trust.[36] The priest alone, apart from the king's treasury possessed gold, as *dakṣiṇā*; stealing his gold would incur severe punishment, under the law.[37]

"Kings maintained royal priests and gave them lavish gifts (*ṚV*, VII.18.22-24). Kings were elected by the people (*viṣ*) (*AV*, III.4.2), i.e., the man chosen from the royal family by the "king-makers" was acclaimed *rājā* by the assembled clansmen. He was then consecrated. Standing on a tige-skin, a 'tiger on a tiger-skin' (*AV*, IV.8.4), the priest sprinkled (*abhiṣeka*) on him water consecrated with mantras (*AV*, IV. 8.5) and recited prayers for the king's long life and prosperity (*ṚV*, X.173).... Pieces of gold (*rukma*) (*AV*, IX.5.14) and lumps of gold (*ṚV*, VI.47.23) were used in place of coins; besides in *ṚV*, VIII.67.2, there is a reference to the golden *māna*, an old semitic measure of coin.... Demands for priestly fees (*dakṣiṇā*), exaggerated accounts of royal liberality to Brāhmaṇas in the *dānastuti* hymns (*ṚV*, V.7.8; X.107 et seq.), peremptory injunctions like, 'distribute treasure to Brahmans' (*ṚV*, X.85.29) occur constantly in the Mantras."[38] From this snap-shot of the 'Age of the Mantras,' it would appear that the consortium between the ruling and priestly classes was in place even in the Ṛgvedic days. Sacerdotalism had paid homage to the state-power, to ensure its share of the desirable metal, of glorious colour, *su-varṇa*. [*Suh* in Sumerian meant yellow/ green; as referred to anything hard, hence stone. Cf., Ṛgvedic *ayas* connoting metal.]

There was an ideological underworld[39] where some autonomous actions were possible, outside the control or even patronage of the royal-priestly consortium. There were those who said that "if professionally paid for we can cure maladies caused by spirits *(yakṣa)*, orges *(rākṣasa)*, ghosts *(bhūta)*, goblins *(gaṇa-piśācāḥ)*, etc." and there were others who loved "to be a stumbling-block among the believers in Veda by the tricks of futile reasoning and observation of facts." Of course, from the ideological point of view of the Upaniṣad which identifies these people, one should not associate with these people, even though there may be learned people even among the Śūdras *(śūdrāḥ ca śāstra vidvāṁsaḥ)*. A reconstruction of this underworld which had also pursued an alchemical tradition is a *sine qua non* to unravel the reality of Indian alchemy which operated in a total environment of the passionate search for gold.

Amṛtam āyur hiraṇyam: Gold is immortality

The operating environment of the alchemist across the millennia, starting, perhaps, with the Indus valley civilization, and certainly, with the Ṛgvedic hymns, evolved to be a complex milieu of conceptions of *ṛta, āyuḥ, soma, amṛta,*[40] *mokṣa, yakṣa,*[41] *yoga, siddhi* or *bhūti/bhasma.*[42] The extraordinary hierarchical classifications (*varṇa*) of men and material, of the Brāhmaṇa periods, is exemplified by the term *suvarṇa.*[43] [In the Egypto-Greek-Islamic alchemic traditions, the spirit of metallicity was colour.][44] Lokāyata of antiquity had to contend with an ideology which had moved the alchemical tradition from lapidary crafts, metallurgy and aurifaction to aurifiction summarized by the quintessential phrase: *amṛtam āyur hiraṇyam.*[45]

It should however, be noted that the phrase, *amṛtam āyur hiraṇyam,* is not of artisans who endeavour to perfect metallurgical techniques, not of merchants who intend to deceive, but of "chemical philosophers" who either believe or intend to deceive that gold has really been produced in their operations of *yajña.*[46] The import of the phrase, almost the very *raison d'être* for the ritual complex built around the inviolability of the Vedic legacy, is clear: the goal is aurification. Gold has to be made. It is its own justification. It is not merely the path to long life. It is immortality. The goal of aurification is vividly portrayed in *Śatapatha Brāhmaṇa* with a detailed procedural manual for the assemblage of the *agni* or the fire-alter using a variety of substances in multiple layers.

Without the assistance of and active involvement of the artisans, what in fact was left of the proto-Indus metallurgical, possibly alchemical, legacy was *dakṣiṇā* or gift of gold, *hiraṇya piṇḍa* (gold-lumps), form the *yajamāna* (sacrificer, or the "capitalist" for whom the priest was organizing the smelting operation). [*Gārhapatya* is the nuptial fire; *dakṣiṇā* is the ceremonial fire; *āhavanīya* is the sacrificial fire (*Manu,* II.231).] The Ṛgvedic allegory and the grand proto-philosophical conception of *ṛta* get transformed into a ritual, justified by a Dharmaśāstra, the origins of which (and incorporation as a cancer in to the body politic) alone may fully explain the dark periods of ancient Indian history, for example the eleven centuries between *c.* 1700 BC and *c.* 600 BC. The devastating effects (and effects which have lasted to the present day) of hierarchical classification of people frozen into social organization as a pernicious caste system, is another story. One direct effect of the loss of *ṛta* has been that the alchemists who had the potentials to develop true natural science, were driven undergrounds. For alchemy, as an art of "improving" metals, could flourish and develop only among people who laboured, were proud of their skill, developed practical arts and were not afraid of dirtying their hands in a hard day's work.

In the Babylonian Talmud (second century AD), *asemon* is a commonly used word referring to bullion (gold, silver or mixed). Leiden X papyrus (*c.* third century AD) says: "No. 8. It will be *asem*, (i.e., electrum, an alloy of gold and silver) which will deceive even the artisans (a tin-copper-gold-silver alloy); no. 12. Falsification of gold (a zinc-copper-lead-gold alloy)...."[47] Soma *yajña* as a ritual, can be interpreted as an elaborate justification for the memories of processing *asemon, asem,* electrum (cf. phonetic concordance with: *ayas* metal). A Tamil lexicon of Winslow (1862) provides a philological trace; *soma maṇal,* is interpreted as meaning *veḷḷi maṇal,* sand containing silver ore! *Soma, soma maṇal, asenon, asem,* electrum may perhaps denote the same substance that dazzled and drew travellers of antiquity in search of Indus gold. It may perhaps be the same substance [contained in the *kamaṇḍalu* symbols in the icons of the *yakṣa* legacy] said to be *amṛtam* which was considered to be the elixir of life, of immortality. It may perhaps be the same substance reffered to as *amṛtam āyur hiraṇyam.*

Soma! The very justification for the Vedic hymns; the quintessence of the only technological process elaborated in magnificent poetry and philological excursus in the grand allegory, the *Ṛgveda.*

References

1. To steal sacred gold is the highest of crimes, *Manu,* VIII.99; IX.237. The Buddhists made it unlawful to mine for, or even to handle gold, probably because the Brahmins had used it as an engine of tyranny. According to Mr. Ball, this superstition is still observed in some parts of remote India. It is possible that, in some instances, the sacerdotal character attached to gold by the Brahmins belonged only to such of it as had been paid to the priests, or consecrated to the temples, and that when the priests paid it away it was no longer sacred; but the texts will not always bear this reading. For example: "He who steals a *suvarṇa* (a gold coin) dies on a dung-hill, is turned to a serpent, and rots in hell until the dissolution of the universe," vide Brahmanical

inscription found on copperplate dug up at Raiwan, in Delhi, *JASB*, VI, 118.

Herodotus relates that "in the reign of Darius, 521 BC, he reserved the coinage of gold to himself absolutely...Greek...coinages...were conducted in the temples and under the supervision of priests. Upon these issues were stamped the symbolism and religion of the State, and as only the priesthood could correctly illustrate the mysteries of their own creation, the coinage—at least that of the more precious pieces—naturally became a prerogative of that order." A. del Mar, *History of Monetary Systems*, pp. 120-21.

2. *Manu*, XI.96: "Those liquors, and eight other sorts, with the flesh of animals, and *āsava*, the most pernicious beverage, prepared with narcotic drugs, are swallowed at the junkets of *yakṣas, rākṣasas,* and *piśācas*: they shall not, therefore, be tasted by a Brahman, who feeds on clarified butter offered to gods." This injunction is strange and self-serving, to put mildly; *Śatapatha Brāhmaṇa* elaborates the preparation of *soma* in exactly the same terms, using the flesh of animals, etc. The rationale is bizarre; if done by a Brahman "for the gods," it was permissible; if done in the "junkets of *yakṣas*," it somehow became "bad" in law!
3. Joseph Needham, *SCC*, vol. 5, part II, p. 20.
4. Needham cites Aristotle who viewed gold as an example of mixis. Berthelot noted the confusion of nomenclature between alloys and pure metals. The gold-silver natural alloy had one name, Greek, Latin: *asem, electrum*; while Latin *aes* applied to bronze (Cu/Sn) as well as copper, and as did Chinese *thung*. Claudianum was a debased copper (Cu/Pb). In Chinese, too, *chin* meant any metal, though very often applied to gold, especially if preceded by the adjective yellow, *hunag chin* (cf., *ṚV*, I.122.2, *hiraṇya*, pl. ornaments of gold).

It seems that *thung* was originally a word for bronze.... (An onomatopoeic use of word whose sound suggests a sense.) The parallels to the Indian philological perspectives are striking: *DEDR*, 3013, Tamil: *taṅkam*, pure gold, of great worth; Malayalam: *taṅkam*, pure gold; Sanskrit: *ṭaṅka*, a stamped (gold) coin. *CDIAL*, 5426-28, 5437, Prākṛta: *ṭaṅka*, a stamped coin; *ṭaṅka*, stone-chisel, sword; Kashmiri: *tang*, projecting spike which acts as a bolt at one corner of a door; Nepali: *ṭani*, measuring rod (cf. the Kalibangan and Banawali evidence of central stele in the so-called "fire-altars)." Sanskrit: *ṭaṅgaṇa*; Khotanese: *danākāra*; Oriya: *ṭāṅgaṇā*; Sinhalese: *ṭagara*, borax, an ingredient in the gold-smelting process! In the *Ṛgveda*, the car-seat of Mitra and Varuṇa is *ayosthuṇa* (*ṚV*, V.62.8 with pillar of *ayas*), Agni is *ayodaṁṣṭra* (*ṚV*, I.88.5; X.87.2 with the teeth of *ayas*). What is Vedic *ayas* which parallels the Latin *aes*? Later-day compounds such as *lohayas* (red metal?;

bronze), *śyāmāyasa, kārṣṇāyasa* (black metal), seem to define *aes* as any metal. In another context, Needham states (*SCC*, vol. 5, part II, p. 51): "Shuo Wen lexicon, compiled by AD 121, gives the word *thang* as an ancient and almost obsolete synonym for gold, adding that a second antique word, *lu,* meant the 'best' gold.... *Lu* was soon replaced by simpler expressions such as *sh c.*" To rationalize the transmutation process, an alchemical analogy is presented: the constituent.

5. Cf., B.K. Matilal, "Cārvāka," *Encyclopaedia of Religion* (hereinafter cited as *ER*), pp. 105ff.; and the references cited.
6. Robert P. Multhauf, *The Origins of Chemistry*, New York, 1965, pp. 20ff.
7. A. Tobler, *Excavations at Tepe Gawra,* II, Philadelphia, 1950, p. 193.
8. L. Woolley, "Excavations at Ur, 1930-31," *Antiq. J.*, 11, 1931, pp. 343-81.
9. Prentiss S. de Jesus, "Varṇa and Early Metallurgy," *Antiquity*, 54, no. 212, 1980, pp. 215-16.
10. C. Renfrew, "Varṇa and the Social Context of Early Metallurgy," *Antiquity*, 52, 1978, pp. 199-203.
11. C.H.V. Sutherland, *Gold—Its Beauty, Power and Allure,* p. 47.
12. The ancient working at these mines are upto 100 yards deep.
13. Sutherland, op. cit., p. 6, pl. 4.
14. Alexander del Mar, op. cit., p. vii.
15. "Every truth or error which the word value introduces into men's minds is a social one," Bastiat, "Harmonies of Political Economy," op. cit., p. xxxiii.
16. Cf., the early "punch-marked" coins in silver (*c.* sixth century BC) with upto five symbols stamped on bent-bars. Wilson, Marsden and Thomas believe that these are even older than the Vedic writings. The term *karṣāpaṇa* mentioned by Hesychius (cf. A. Cunningham, *Coins of Ancient India*, p. 2) may be related to the *karṣa* antelope symbol or to *kāca*, glazed steatite and *pana* to a unit of weight (= 10 silver *sikkal* or *śakula)* little fish, proto-Indus symbol! Also mentioned in an erotica hymn in *Atharvaveda* and *Yajurveda*: The refrain is, *gosaphe śakulāviva*, like a little fish between the cow's cleft-hoof relatable to the Mediterranean *mīna* (27.2 gms, Indus standard weight) of silver or electrum, the earliest metal which was perhaps used for the earliest coins of India. The later coins of Argos and Lydia in Greece are of the same metal, which was given a name derived from its amber colour. Another interpretation for *sikkal* is knife-money; cf. the form used in ancient China; the semantic radical may also be related to sickle, scissors, chisel and other cutting instruments and hence to symbols such as the right-or left-handed *svastikas* (which also mean surgical instruments in *Suśruta-saṁhitā*). The two forms of *svastika* may relate to the number of cupellations or "conversions" or "movements"

(*ayana*) to which the *galena* ore or *electrum* ore is subjected to.

17. Cf., *rāma-ṭaṅkas*; the morpheme *ṭaṅka* is from *ṭaṅkaṇa*, gold. These may belong to the Brāhmaṇa epoch: "...the archaic coins stamped with the figure of the Sun [a proto-Indus symbol], countermarked by Buddhic emblems *caitya, svastika,* cross, Bodhi-tree, elephant, bull, etc. [all proto-Indus symbols], are certainly older than Buddhism; while those originally stamped with the *caitya, svastika,* tau, cross, crook, and lamb (or dog), and other Buddhic emblems, are certainly of pre-Grecian date...ample basis for the conclusion that coins of the precious metals were used in India at epochs far more remote than can be attributed to any coins of the West." A. del Mar, op. cit., p. 2; the parenthetical references to proto-Indus have been added, extending the hypothesis that numismatics of antiquity may be traceable to proto-Indus era.
18. R.P. Kangle, *Kauṭilīya Arthaśāstra,* part 2, p. 106; 2.12.5.
19. *Arthaśāstra,* 2.19.1-46.
20. R.P. Kangle, op. cit., part 2, p. 135; 2.19.14.
21. Cf., the devices used in the states of Ionia, Byzantium, Sparta and Athens (*c.* tenth-fifth centuries BC) of a limited and publicly known number of counters, belonging to and issued by the state—commonly discs of purposely rotted sheet-iron or bronze—having no value as pieces of metal, but possessing great and definite value as a public measure...the concept of value was therefore, simply an arithmetical relation. The key problem of the use of counters was, however, that the system's efficiency depended upon the autonomy of the State and the nefarious trade of the forger. A. del Mar, op. cit., pp. xxxiv ff.
22. A. del Mar, op. cit., p. 46. Athenians struck no gold coins before the time of Herodotus.
23. Pliny described artificial electrum.
24. A. del Mar, op. cit., p. xxxvii.
25. Cf., *Atharvaveda* hymns on gold amulets.
26. "Plebeian" concordant with plumbum, lead, which in alchemical lone is symbolized as snake and black-lead is declared a less-desirable metal; generally of the lowest rank, after gold, silver, copper.
27. A. del Mar, op. cit., p. 4: "It is to the epoch following the Mahābhārata wars (1650 BC, Pococke; 1367 BC, Prinsep) that must be ascribed that severe dearth of the precious metals in India, which is evinced by the use of cowries and other commodity-moneys of illimitable supply, and of the practice of that strange abstention from the employment of precious metals which is enjoined by the Buddhist Ten Commandments of the Vinaya."
28. *Mahābhārata,* loc. cit.; J.W. McCrindle, *Ancient India as Described by Ptolemy,* p. 110.
29. J.W. McCrindle, *Ancient India as Described by Megasthenes,* pp. 94-96.
30. V. Ball, *Manual of Geology,* vol. I, Economic Geology, p. 203.

31. Sutherland, *Gold*, p. 70.
32. Ibid., 71.
33. J. Needham, *SCC*, vol. 4, part II, 1974, p. 39: "...the process of cupellation having a longer continuous history than any other quantitative chemical process still surviving. Men weighed what went in and weighed again what came out.... Already in the early-fourteenth century (corresponding to Shang times), Burraburiash, king of Babylon, was complaining to Amenophis IV of Egypt about the poor quality of the gold which had reached him—'of 20 minas only 5 remained after being put in the fire.' Yet the purity of the -4th millennium Mesopotamian gold reaches as high as 91%, and deliberate alloys of gold and copper are mentioned in Ur III texts (-19000). Evidence from inscriptions suggests that gold was being refined in Egypt from at least -1200, and by -500 a figure of 99.8% purity was attained, well above any possible naturally occurring product...(there is) even a Sumerian distinction between the two sorts of loss (litharge volatilization) and the absorption of the base metal oxides by the cupel), for there are two stages in the refining (*tubbu* and *pataaqu*)."
34. F.R. Allchin, "Gold mining in ancient India," *Journal of Economic and Social History of the Orient*, vol. 5, part II, 1962, Leiden, pp. 195-210.
35. A. del Mar, op. cit., pp. 6, 22, 26. The relative values of silver and gold were estimated as proportions of weight content of the metals: Vedic epoch, 4:1; Brahmanical epoch, 5:1; Buddhic epoch, 6:1. "But these are inferences which as yet rest upon slight foundations, and, therefore, which must only be held tentatively until more certain light can be thrown on the subject. With more assurance it may be believed that from the time of Darius Hystaspes to the twelfth century of our era, the Eastern ratio centred at about $6^1/_2$...until the East India Company began to coin, when it was suddenly enhanced to $16^1/_2$ for 1...." The cent per cent profit made by the Romans is relatable to Herodotus's estimate that the Persian ratio of value between silver and gold was 13:1, with 20 silver shekels or darics going for one daric, the weights of the two being dissimilar. The term, "daric" may be relatable to the effigy of the kneeling archer, *dhanuṣ*.
36. A. del Mar, op. cit., p. 131: "It is not to be wondered that Justinian I rebuked Theodorat the Frank for striking heretical gold coins, nor that Justinian II proclaimed was against Abd-el-Malik for presuming to pay his tribute in other heretical gold...; the sovereign-pontiff alone enjoyed the prerogative of coining gold throughout the Empire."
37. *Manu*, VIII.314: "The stealer of gold from a priest must run hastily to the king, with loosened hair, proclaiming the theft and adding: 'thus have I sinned; punish me.' He must bear on his shoulder a pestle of stone, or a club of *khadira-wood*, or a javelin pointed at both ends, or an iron mace...the king, if he punish him not, shall incur the guilt of

the thief." How does the priest come to possess gold?

38. Srinivasa Iyengar, *Life in Ancient India*, reprint, Delhi, 1982, pp. 20, 41, 43.
39. Cf., Debiprasad Chattopadhyaya, *SSAI*, pp. 286 ff.; *Maitrāyaṇī Upaniṣad*, VII.8.
40. Cf., synonyms: *nirjara*, not aging, hence linked to geriatrics; *pīyūṣa*, the juice. The legend of an intoxicating nectar of immortality, sought by the gods and *asuras*. All treasures of heaven and earth emerged from this. Dravidian etymon: *maṭṭu*, honey (*DEDR*, 4662), Sanskrit *madira* and *madya* are wines; in tantric *cakrapūja* rites, *madya* connotes an intoxicant, a drug as well as the magical juices of internal secretion.
41. In Mesopotamia, the Ashipu was a priest and exorcist; also concerned with diagnosis and prognosis. Asu was not a priest but used empirical methods to treat acute symptoms; he was a craftsman employing techniques whose efficacy was enhanced by limited use of incantations or prayers. Both healers did not compete and at times worked together to cure a patient. In Egypt, *swnw* was identical to *asu* and *sau* was comparable to *ashipu* though *sau* also employed, drugs occasionally. The third type of healer in Egypt was *wabw*, a priest of the goddess of healing, Sekhmet. In addition to mediation between the patient and the goddess, he would employ drugs and minor surgery. Cf., article on "Medicine and Religion in Western traditions" in *ER*, 1987, pp. 319-20.
42. Cf., A.J. Hopkins, op. cit., p. 110; Berthelot, *Collection des anciens alchimistes grecs*, III.18.1; IV.1.6, 9; from Mary, the Jewess-alchemist of Greece: "When they are in the solid state they cannot tint. They ought at first to be pulverized [fine powders being considered equal to vapours] and made into spirits in order to tint in the condition of spirit.... Now the sulphur water at first reduces them to powder and then later crysolith [gold ferment?] spiritualizes them;" "He calls 'substances' matters which resist the fire; and 'nonsubstances' those which do not resist the fire;" and "Although in this process the body of the metal is destroyed, the spirit is not destroyed but permeates the body."
43. Cf., Greek alchemic tradition; A.J. Hopkins, op. cit., 1967, p. 58: "The fire spirit of gold was its pure colour and it was toward this pure colour that all metals were tending. The task of the alchemist was to assist nature in this upward course. By demonstrating that this assistance could be successfully brought to bear upon the course of nature, alchemy first acquired the prestige of being identified with philosophy...."
44. A.J. Hopkins, op. cit., 1967, p. 123.
45. *Śatapatha Brāhmaṇa*, III.8.2.27; *Aitareya Brāhmaṇa*, VII.4.6; *Maitrāyaṇī-saṁhitā*, II.2.2.

46. Cf., Debiprasad Chattopadhyaya, *Lakāyata—A Study in Ancient Indian Materialism,* pp. 65ff.: "...the *yajñas* were originally thought of as means or aids to the productive activity of the early Vedic people...the process of *yajñas* and the process of sexual union were often inextricably mixed up; the very images with which *yajñas* was understood and explained were often the images of the sexual union." In the tantric tradition, the metaphors themselves become the reality, perceiving a parallel with the alchemical transmutation processes; "...the Lokāyata tradition retained the same belief as forming part of the agricultural-matriarchal ideas. Tantrism must have had some significance other than mere perversity."
47. Cited in Joseph Needham, *SCC,* vol. 5, part II, pp. 18-21.

2

Indus: Roots of Alchemy

Pūrve yājikāḥ

Yāska's Niruktam (VII.23) refers to "old ritualists" or the cosmic school[1]:

athā sāvāditya iti Pūrve yājikāḥ.

This is the only reference in the text to those who identified the Vaiśvānara Agni with the sun who pierces the cloud and breaks the stasis. The solar symbolism in the Indus valley civilization is vivid and definitive. (Cf., an Indus seal depicting the sun symbol on the obverse and the unicorn on the reverse; a unique depiction of six-spoked circle sign on the neck of the "unicorn" in Field Symbol 3 in Mahadevan.[2]) The link of the sun with Agni[3] is the key which takes the trace to the proto-Indus metallurgist-lapidary.[4]

There are hundreds of Indus seals which depict a so-called "cult object" in front of the "unicorn." It will be argued in another section that the "cult object" was sublimation apparatus, antedating Mary's *keratokis* of the Greek tradition by nearly a millennium, and that the sublimate was used in the *soma* smelter-filter. Hence, the link with Agni. It will also be argued that the so-called "fire-altars" in Kalibangan and Banawali Indus sites were the goldsmiths' hearths and the central clay stele or stake in these hearths were the supports or *sthūpa* for the smelter-filters of the proto-Indus lapidary-goldsmith. [Vedic *dehya saṅkhu* is interpreted as *vṛtra saṅkhu* or a stony peg, spike or nail (*saṅkhu*); *deyhī* (*ṚV*, VI.47.2) is interpreted as a rampart or mound—*navatim nava ca deyhyo' han digdhā upacitā āsurīḥ purīḥ.*]

In a retrospective reconstruction, let us start with the description of the Indramaha festival in *Bṛhatsaṁhitā*[5] and trace the *mātṛkā* symbolism. The Śakra festivities begin with obtaining a tree-trunk (*arjuna, ajakarṇa* or *udumbara*). It is chiselled and fixed onto a pedestal—*yantra.* Five or seven smaller staffs (*śakra-kumārī*)[6] are placed near the main *dhvaja.* Wooden pegs or *mātṛkā* or *toraṇa* are kept on both sides of the staff to tie it with eight strong ropes. An adorned arch at the bottom of the staff is fastened with tight nails, *argala*. Hymns accompany the erection ceremony and devotees offer clarified butter, rice, flowers, honey. The *dhvaja* is taken down on the fifth day.

Suma Chhien describes six or seven normally visible pin-points of light, the star-cluster, Pleiades (*mao*) as *mao thou*—the hairy-head—to which he adds the words "the white-robed assembly" (*pai i hui*). Needham[7] adds: "... (the ancient Chinese) astrological-calendrical series begins with the curious term *she-thi-ko....* Some Chinese historians of astronomy (e.g., Ting Wen-Chiang; Chu Kho-Chen) have believed that this and some of the other terms are transliterations of the Indian names for the years of the Jupiter cycle...and it seems unconvincing. . . . Chu Kho-Chen sees in (*she-thi-ko*) the *nakṣatra* Kṛttikā where the full moon was in the month Kārtika corresponding to the year Mahākārtika of the Jupiter cycle. He would also derive in a parallel way *ta-tuan-hsien* from the *nakṣatra* Dhaniṣṭha corresponding to Mahāśrāvaṇa. But there are no other equation even plausible." We submit that *mao thou* (hairy-head, white-robed assembly) corresponds to *mātṛkā* and the seven-robed persons on Indus seals; *she-ti-ko* parallels Kṛttikā, six or seven stars visible on the sky in a cluster, as pin-points of light. The parallel with the Indramaha symbolism of *mātṛkā* five or seven pegs around the staff is striking. In this, is it unreasonable to see a legacy of constructing a smelter-filter structure around a central clay stele? The mythological stream links Kārttikeya, six-headed, also called Skanda, and the planet Mars, as the son of Rudra or Śiva and born without the intervention of a woman. Śiva's seed cast into the fire was later received by the Ganges bringing forth Kārttikeya; hence is *agnibhu* or *gaṅgā-ja*. Archaeology finds Kārttikeya on the ancient punch-marked "tribal-coins" and on the coins of Kuṣāṇa emperor, Huviṣka. It is highly relevant to recall an insight of J.N. Banerjea:[8] "...Vedic traits of (images of various Hindu gods and goddesses), especially in the case of some of the cult divinities, were really superimposed on their primitive pre-Vedic core...the conch-shell with wheel and other emblems (on Bhit and Basarh seals and clay sealings)... when appearing alone may sometimes denote the *śaṅkha nidhi* of Kubera, a very appropriate symbol for merchant guilds and bankers." Extending the retrospective reconstruction further, many symbols may indeed refer to the porto-Indus alchemical, manual operations of the lapidary working on the forge and the crucible and on alchemical compounds or substances.

The pit in Kalibangan containing bones

The bones found in a pit near the Kalibangan hearths were essential ingredients in the smelting process of the proto-Indus, *tvaṣṭṛ*, gilder-plater.[9] (Cf., Tamil *taṭṭān*, goldsmith; Mt. Tattha. Buddha Prakash endorses the views of P.R. Deshmukh that the god on the so-called proto-Śiva seal was Tvaṣṭṛ.)[10] In the *Rasahṛdaya* of Bhikṣu Govinda, an important use is indicated for animal bones: to make cupels for refining gold and silver: "A cupel made of bone-ash (goat's) and lined internally with borax, etc...."[11] It is, not therefore, necessary to postulate animal sacrifices, etc. in Kalibangan and Banawali where the circumstantial evidence clearly points to the use of the hearths by lapidary-goldsmiths.

The characteristic peforated pottery may be interpreted as a part of the smelter apparatus to extract the *rasa.* The proto-Indus metallurgical repertoire may be summarized; unfinished castings and hoards of small copper objects were found at Chanhu-daro.[12] A metal workshop was excavated at Lothal with finds of slag, a copper sheet, a clay crucible and some tools, apart from a mould used for casting needles.[13] At Harappa, sixteen furnaces of various sizes and shapes were found crowded in a small area, apparently used for copper smelting.[14] An analysis of bronze and copper objects of Harappa and Mohenjo-daro reveals: pure unalloyed copper of 98.5 per cent; bronzes with variable tin context (2 to 26 per cent), arsenical copper (2 to 6.58 per cent), copper-nickel alloy (upto 9.38 per cent) and copper-lead-tin bronzes (upto 14.9 per cent).[15] This is a very impressive metallurgical legacy which indicates that the metals alloyed with copper exceeded 2 per cent and hence, the inference that the alloys were not naturally occurring minerals (which normally have only upto 2 per cent alloys) but were deliberately produced alloys of copper with tin, arsenical compounds, lead and nickel.

Alchemical technique: distillation

Hopkins and Hammer-Jensen believed that alchemy rested on the discovery of distillation and properties of sulphur (arsenic sulphides regarded as varieties of sulphur?), first revealed in distillatory processes.

Multhauf[16] refers to distillation apparatus: Discorides (Bk. 5.70) describes the condensation of mercury from cinnabar in an inverted cup, compared to which Maria's variety of retorts are revolutionary indeed. Her most complex apparatus was a tribukos, a three-beaked alembic for making the sulphur water, but the most important was the *kerotakis*, a sublimatory. The *kerotakis* was a closed vessel containing a sort of shelf as a diaphragm. On that shelf a solid material could be subjected to an atmosphere of distilled or sublimed vapour. It enabled the alchemists to convert cementation processes into distillatory processes.... Zosimos speaks of the spirits mercury, sulphur and arsenic, and emphasizes their distinction from soul....The term Xerion had been used for a medical powder (Aetius Medicus 6, 12, late second century AD), a substance which acted like a medicine or like a ferment, and was to be the parent of the Arabic word, *al-iksīr* (elixir).

Is it a reasonable conjecture that sulphur or divine water may indeed be *amṛta* carried by the *yakṣa*, the genii or the proto-alchemist? Hopkins (1934, 69, 92ff.) explains the critical colour sequence in the operation: the alchemist began with a black alloy of the imperfect metals (lead, tin, copper, and iron), known as the *tetrasoma* (four-membered body).[17] The next step if whitening (on the surface) of the alloy with mercury or arsenic. Next, it was yellowed with gold or sulphur water. The final step was to purple it. Hopkins adds that the violet bronze colour of alloys contain a fraction of gold which may explain the purple colouring.

The archaeological evidence of distillation in the Indus valley civilization is of interest in a search for the beginnings of the alchemical tradition.[18] Greek alchemic tradition records the alembic for simple distillation and the reflux fitted with the *kerotakis* for treatment of the metals; and with alembic and *kerotakis* all the processes of the alchemist inventions, there was firmly established the fundamental thesis alchemistic philosophy:

> All sublimed vapour is a spirit and such are the tinctorial qualities.... The vapour is a spirit...the Spirit which penetrates into the Bodies [of the matals].... Above, the things celestial and below the things terrestrial.... Such is the useful thing; the tinctorial element. [This is to be understood as the kinetic colouring principle, not the colour but the ability to impart colour, in analogy to the dye....] The spirit...has not been destroyed but it has penetrated into the depths of the metal when

the operator has accomplished his work.... And when the preparation is coloured then it, itself, colours in its turn.[19]

This may indeed be deemed a precis of the Ṛgvedic Soma *yāga* in Greek alchemical terms.

Distillation is defined[20] as a process which combines the volatilization of a substance by heat with the cooling of the product(s) to cause condensation. The current view among historians of science is that the first distillery apparatus is traceable to Mary, the Jewess of the school of Alexandrian protochemists and alchemists of the first-third centuries. This may have to be revised in view of the proto-Indus evidence. The alchemical overtones of the churning of the ocean resulting in the separation of *amṛta,* separation of the heavy from the light, the sublime from the gross, is a metaphorical use of distillatory terms. The "water of life" symbolism reverberating through the Varuṇa, Brahmā and Yakṣa traditions vividly portrayed in the *kamaṇḍalu* symbols on icons is also a metaphor relatable to distillation.

Allchin[21] and Mahdihassan[22] refer to the possibility that the art of distillation might perhaps have been the ancient (*c.* 500 BC) gift of India to the world. In the context of alchemic traditions, the most significant aspects of the evidence may be summarized: Distillation was a technique for purifying liquids and hence was perhaps the oldest alchemical technique. Taylor[23] states: "...a sort of sublimation of liquids was occasionally practiced. Thus sea-water was heated in covered cauldrons and the drops condensed on the lid were collected and used as drinking water." *Ṛgveda* (VII.86.6) refers to *surā,* an intoxicating drink, perhaps made from fermented barley. Suśruta refers to *madya,* a fermented liquor. From the excavations at Taxila, John Marshall[24] has reconstructed a condensation unit made of pottery components: a boiler, a hood to re-direct vapours, a hollow leading tube; a receiver kept cool in a basin. Marshall was hesitant to attribute a specific use for this apparatus (*c.* first century BC). Allchin notes that this type of still is described in Vāgbhaṭa's *Rasaratna Samuccaya* as a *tiryak patana yantra,* the oblique falling apparatus. Mahdihassan reconstructs a vertical still made of three pots set on top of one another; the middle pot has a small pot which acts as a receiver of condensed liquid from the base of the uppermost pot. Brown's Telugu lexicon provides the Telugu morphemes for distillation: *baṭṭi peṭṭu,* literally putting across. *CDIAL,* 11360, Pāli: *vaṭṭi,* circumference, rim; *DEDR,* 5395, Tamil: *viṭṭam,* crossbeam, anything put across; Kodagu: *buṭṭu*, ceiling joist. These etyma provide a proto-Dravidian synonym of the Sanskrit *śuṇḍa* (lit. elephant's trunk), both connoting the technique of putting something across—to receive the distilled liquid.

At Shaikhan Dheri, Charsada (old name: Puṣkalāvatī, capital of Gandhāra region), Cambridge-Peshawar University excavations of 1963 found a large number of "characteristic receivers" (from *c.* 150 BC) which have also been found in Begram, Damkot, Bala Hisar, Taxila, Tulamba, and Rang Mahal west and east of the Indus. The most significant aspect of these receivers was that, from the first century BC, they were marked during manufacture with a stamped impression. One of the early marks had the form of a wine jug. "With the arrival of the Kuṣāṇas (first century AD), the stamped marks are generally monograms similar to those found on the Kuṣāṇas' coins and generally regarded as a royal insignia.... The custom of stamping pottery with decorative or auspicious marks, and more rarely with royal marks, goes back in India to the third century BC, but no comparable series has hitherto been recorded. One is at once reminded of the common practice of stamping the handles of the amphorae used in the Mediterranean world for the carriage and export of wine from Rhodes and elsewhere during Greek and Hellenistic times.... Reviewing the evidence from Shaikhan Dheri we conclude that it is consistent with the yard having been used as a small scale distillery and drinking shop, where the receivers, both marked and unmarked, were used in the production, storage and subsequent sale of spirits...(Ayurvedic scholars) identify a group of Sanskrit words, including *pariśrut* and *pariśravaṇa*, having meanings associated with trickling, with distillation. European Vedic scholars have generally favoured a different meaning for these words, involving the straining or filtering of wine."[25] The archaeological evidence is not adequate to conclusively establish the correct meaning. Suryakanta[26] interprets: *pariśrut* (*ṚV*, IX.1.6; *Taittirīya Brāhmaṇa*, II.6.10) flowing around, foaming (*AV*, III, 12.7; *Mantra Brāhmaṇa*, II.3.15), fermented liquor; *pariśrut*, wine-goblet, decanter. A cognate morpheme: *parisvaj* (*AV*, I.2.3) embracing from all sides, closely embracing. Allchin adds that the pipe of the Taxila still resembles the head and trunk of an elephant, *śuṇḍa*; an early nineteenth century dictionary refers to *śuṇḍa yantra* as an alembic or retort. Suryakanta interprets *śuṇḍā-mukha* (*Satyāṣāḍha Śrautasūtra*, XXIII.1.9): an implement for distilling spirituous liquor. Allchin notes the general reluctance to specify details of processes involved and the general pattern of secrecy may be due to the crafts being regarded as of questionable respectability and due to the ritual and sacramental aspects associated with consumption of alcohol.

Arthaśāstra provides recipes for a number of fermented drinks using rice, sugarcane juice, grapes, and spices. Caraka and Suśruta refer to medicinal, fermented preparations which are intoxicants. These texts do not indicate if the ferments were distilled and concentrated.

Two points may be added to these insights of Mahdihassan and Allchin: The custom of stamping pottery is seen in the early Indus valley civilization itself. The signs on these proto-Indus vessels do not resemble the examples of Kuṣāṇa monograms [fig. 6] of Shaikhan Dheri pottery receivers (first to third centuries AD) referred to by Allchin. The proto-Indus pottery vessels with stamped inscriptions are, generally, not narrow-mounted and do not bear any resemblance to the Shaikhan Dheri receivers which seem to have characteristic narrow mouths to fit the *śuṇḍa* hollow tube and round bottoms, to float in a basin of water. The proto-Indian stills may be considered the *ambix* and reflux condenser *kerotakis*[27] of antiquity.

However, it is noteworthy that the stylized monogram of two concave vessels may be compared with the so-called "cult object" generally found in front of the "unicorn" on many Indus valley seals. A reconstruction of the process depicted in these "cult objects," the archaeological evidence of knobbed and perforated pottery, and the so-called "fire-altars" with characteristic central stakes will be elucidated. This ancient monogram of two concave vessels is comparable to two ancient Chinese glyphs for *chu*, red colour; and *chhing*, blue-green, indigo. (Cf., Karlgren, nos. 128 and 812 c, d; *Grammata Serica.*[28]) If the production of indigo can be postulated in the few centuries before the Christian era, it is not unlikely that the monogram on the pottery may have connoted the collected indigo, as a bill of lading for the merchandise. The four-pronged "fork" symbolism is also paralleled by a "harrow" Indus script sign with five or six prongs.

Alchemical technique: perforated pottery and lapidary hearths

Paddayya[29] of the Deccan College, Pune, provides a new

perspective on the use of shallow, open-mouthed perforated bowls (with perforations varying from 5 to 8 mm. in diameter) and with round bottoms, commonly found at the Neolithic sites of the southern Deccan. He cites an analogy from a process recorded in a village near Guntur in Andhra Pradesh using a round-bottomed bowl (20 cm. dia. and 6 cm. depth). In this process, great millet cereal paste is used. The perforated bowl[30] is placed over a vessel containing milk. The cereal paste is pushed through the perforations to fall down as tubular, macaroni-like pieces into milk. The product, a delicacy, is called *pālatalikalu* milk tubes. Paddayya also notes that these bowls contrast sharply with the perforated vessels found at the Harappan sites.

The proto-Indus perforated vessels have characteristic, tall cylindrical bodies and bear a large circular hole in the centre of the base. The vessels have been found at Mohenjo-daro and at several sites including those in southern Baluchistan, notably, Suktagendor and Kulli. Marshall,[31] however, notes that dish-like specimens comparable to the Neolithic examples also occur at Mohenjo-daro, rather infrequently, alongside the cylindrical-bodied perforated vessels.

Mackay[32] believed that the vessels were used chiefly for pressing curds, though they could equally well be used as braziers. "They were always wheel-made, of a light red paste sometimes coated with a cream clip. The holes were made by pushing a stick through the sides while the clay was still damp.... There is always a large hole in the base, which suggests that these vessels were supported on a stick." A stick! Kalibangan and Banawali Indus sites provide evidence of a clay stele or stake in the middle of the lapidary's hearths!

"Berthelot has reproduced the drawing of this apparatus (*kerotakis*; from the MS. St. Marc, eleventh century) in his *Collection* (Introduction, pp. 143, 146), and he has shown very clearly the derivation of this 'sieve' [perforated clay bowl] from the painter's palette, on which in the old days colours were mixed in wax, softening by gentle heating. The Greek word for wax gave the name *kerotakis* to the derived form.... When the mercury, like wax, made the metals into a soft alloy or amalgam, the technical term was 'softening of the metals.' Tin which preceded mercury as the most fusible metal figures largely for this purpose in the recipes of the Leyden papyrus. At the moment of softening, the amalgam, like the wax on the painter's palette, assumed a new colour."[33] This description of the origins of the *kerotakis* is a possible pointer to the use made of the perforated pottery bowl and vessel by the proto-Indus lapidary who had worked with tin and with cinnabar. The proto-Indus "cult object" may indeed be explained as the earliest sublimation apparatus of the lapidary who could "tint" not only faience but also metals. Tvaṣṭṛ who may perhaps be the so-called "proto-Śiva" on some Indus seals, was, the earliest gilder-plater recorded in the Ṛgvedic text. Tvaṣṭṛ could as well have been the proto-Indus lapidary's image of an artificer par excellence.

That the perforated pottery were made with the base flat, tapered, or rounded, indifferently finds a remarkable parallel with the variations in shapes of the bases of the top vessel depicted in the so-called "cult object" on the Indus seals. The tapered vessels so characteristic of Indus pottery which could have been kept standing only on a stand are also paralleled by the tapering imagery of the top vessel depicted in the so-called "cult object."

The diameter of the bottom hole ranged from 0.05 in. to 1.2 ins. and the height from 1.4 ins. to 6.45 ins. The specimens found in Chanhu-daro had heights of: 1.23, 1.3, 1.84, 2.1, 2.43, and 4.53 ins. Two vessels were not cylindrical, but were shaped like pottery jars.

The "cult object" also depicts a central stake running through the bottom holes of the two vessels of the "cult object." The central stake may be related to the spike found in the so-called "fire-altars" in the Indus sites.[34] At Kalibangan, in the southern half of "the citadel," an enclosed area was found with five or six massive platforms of mud bricks, "each separate from the other and intended to be used perhaps for a specific purpose by the community as a whole.... All these platforms were found to be oriented along cardinal directions.... Access to the working floor of the platforms was by means of steps which rose from the passage. At one place the passage fronting the platform was found to be paved. Through the passage also ran baked-brick drains...the available remains do indicate that some of these might have been used for religious or ritual purposes (pl. XVII). While on the one with the known complete outline, besides a well and a fire-altar, a rectangular pit (1.24 x 1 m.), lined with baked bricks and containing bones of a bovine and antlers, representing perhaps a sacrifice, were found (pl. XVIII), atop another was noticed a row of seven rectangular 'fire-altars' aligned beside a well."

B.B. Lal[35] underscores the fact that there were no residential houses within the southern rhomb which had these series of mud-brick platforms. He adds: "The 'altars' were in fact clay-lined pits, each measuring 75 x 55 cm. Within each pit were noted ash, charcoal and the remains of a clay stele as well as of what are known as terracotta cakes. Of the last-named item, complete examples were found in some of the 'fire-altars' in the residential houses of the Lower Town. The clay stele, as seen from the relatively more intact examples in the Lower Town, stood vertically up, was either cylindrical or slightly faceted, and measured about 30-40 cm. in height and 10-15 cm. in diameter. It would even appear that it occupied the focal position in the complex.

"...to the west of the row, but within easy reach of the 'worshipper,' was the lower half of a jar, partly embedded in the ground and full of ash and charcoal. Perhaps in it was kept some ready fire to be used for the ritual."

"... a short distance away from these altars, were a well and the remains of a few bath-pavements with attached drains...for the construction of the well, bath-pavements and drains, kiln-burnt bricks were used, so that the mud-brick platform on which these stood did not get slushy. The drains from the top of this platform, as also from the tops of others, discharged into the bigger drains, often covered, that ran through the streets in-between the platforms."

B.B. Lal reiterates the observation that the bovine bones and antlers were found in a rectangular, kiln-burnt-brick-lined pit which was separate from the "fire-alter." This leads him to surmise two possible sacrifices, one of animals and another related to fire. "...the 'fire-altars' do not seem to have been associated with any kind of animal-sacrifice, since no bones were found in or around them." If a religious connotation to the term "fire-altar" is excluded, the entire description given by Thapar and Lal may indeed relate to a metallurgical-smelting complex in the so-called "Upper Town" of Kalibangan.

Commenting on the overall likeness of Banawali finds with Kalibangan, Bisht[36] highlights a noteworthy structure: "...a partially uncovered house complex with several hearths, ovens and fire-pits in the room (pl. 10.4). Excessive fire activity in this area has reddened house floors there. Surely, it should be a workshop, plausibly that of a metalsmith. One more interesting feature is the presence of precisely circular pits, both large and small, neatly cut deep into the house floors. In one case, a pit rim was lined with mud bricks and its walls were thickly plastered. Most of these pits yield fine bluish ash, occasionally mixed with charred grains; although the pits themselves show no sign of firing. These might be the storage silos or bins. The paucity, or near absence, of large storage jars lends further credence to this surmise...characteristic clay bangles...beads of gold, semiprecious stones, steatite (including disc beads), faience, shell, bone and clay; bangles of shell, faience and copper; animal figurines of terracotta...."

"(Period II: Mature Indus Culture)...the house (pls. 10.11 a and b) belonged to a rich merchant as it has yielded more than one seal, a few weights and a large number of jars half embedded in the house floor. Another large house (pl. 10.12) may have belonged to a jewelry dealer.... A house was generally provided with a room containing a square fireplace, with or without bricklining, but with a longish cone of clay placed in the center. This was also noticed at Kalibangan.... One of the rooms had a platform constructed against a wall. It also had a curious fireplace with thin, vertical mud walls...ten steatite seals and one terracotta sealing (pl. 10.16)...these seals were generally recovered from houses which on the basis of their contents (noted elsewhere in the paper) have been tentatively attributed to a trader or jeweler. It is also important to note that the site is very rich in lapis lazuli and gold. Gold-plated terracotta beads were also found."

Elaborating on the clay stele referred to earlier and also by Lal at Kalibangan, Bisht observes: "...Another diagnostic, yet curious artifact, is a clay object that gradually tapers upwards from the square base and ultimately turns towards a side terminating into two short, horn-like prongs. It is usually found placed in the centre of a hearth. This object has been found widely distributed at cognate sites. At times, the lower body of a vessel or a roughly straight-sided pottery stand is found to have been placed in a fire pit."

The evidence unearthed by Bisht at Banawali and Dholavira is vivid and definitive (apart from explaining the use of ring-stones as supports for buildings): the clay stele had prongs which might have been used to support a pottery vessel with a hole in its base or to directly insert a pottery vessel with a stand into the prong. The crucible or vessel complex or *yantra* is ready for alchemical processes of the lapidary-metallurgist of the proto-Indus Civilization!

Proto-Indus perforated pottery, hearth, clay stele, smelter-filter apparatus

Aurel Stein[37] found a remarkable specimen of the proto-Indus type cylindrical vessel at Firoz Khan-damb near Awaran, Makran. The vessel was filled with ashes and charcoal. Aiyappan[38] extended the conjecture related to the possible use of these types of vessels as braziers or heaters, using the analogy of globular-bodied perforated pots used to burn camphor by devotees in temples of the Madras state. Mackay suggests the substitution of incense in this analogy. Jaggi[39] suggests that the perforated cylindrical pottery might have been used to strain fluids or perhaps were used as heaters to contain in the fire and let the warmth penetrate out. The latter use may be more appropriately related to the fact that the Indus perforated pottery had perforations not only on the sides but had a big hole at the bottom. The hole at the bottom might have been used to insert the pottery on to the clay stele embedded in the centre of the so-called fire-altars of Kalibangan and Banawali, Indus sites. Such a reconstruction leads to the possibility that the Indus lapidary/goldsmith had used the clay stele and perforated pottery as parts of a *somanāla yantra,* a smelter-filter apparatus. Such an apparatus may, indeed, be something similar to the so-called "cult object" depicted on the Indus seals. This object may also be interpreted as "ligaturing" of a drill and a portable furnace.

Needham cites the description of a cupellation furnace from *Huang Ti Chiu Ting Shen Tan Ching Chueh* (Explanation of the Yellow Emperor's Canon of the Nine-Vessel Spiritual Elixir), dated *c.* second century AD:

> How to make the cupel (*phei*) that stands within the muffle (*huo wu*). Earth is packed together to form a trough (*tshao*) 3 ft. deep and any convenient length; within this place the moulds (*mo*) must be, in each of which a cupel is to be made. Take finely sifted and purified ashes and fill up the moulds, adding some water so that the stuff is neither wet nor dry...take a knife and scrape it out so as to make it into a cup-like (*phei*) or crucible shape. Spread a thin layer of salt over the cupels, and put in the crude silver (with some lead). Cover up with yellow earth, and pack all round and above with charcoal; when this is done make a roof for the furnace of sun-dried tiles, arranging a hole directly above each cupel to allow the escape of the copious vapours.... After some time the fire penetrates all through, and the lead and silver begin to boil, swirling round in violent motion; eventually the lead disappears (lit., separates) and the silver moves no more. Beautiful colours of purple, green and white and then to be seen....

This description is important because, it is accompanied by a small diagram (fig. 1305 in Needham). The remarkable featuré of this diagram, though somewhat abstract and the textual description is that they parallel the "cult object" on the Indus seals.

The Sanskrit texts which contain methods of preparation of mineral compounds quite often refer to the final product as gold. One conjecture, following Needham,[40] is that the product might have been stannic sulphide, SnS_2, which is "easily made from tin filings, mercury, sulphur and ammonium chloride, and its non-tarnishing flakes, which have the colour and lustre of gold, are used as 'bronze powder,' the basis of some modern gold paints. We are more and more inclined to think that this product played a larger role in Ko Hung's elixir preparations than has generally been suggested...."

Alchemical technique sublimation

Taylor's[41] pictorial reconstruction and copies provided by Partington,[42] of the ancient *ambix* (alembic) and *kerotakis* may be compared and contrasted with the sublimation device of the Bower Manuscript[43] and the sublimation device depicted (the so-called "cult object") on the Indus seals. The process of sublimation is vividly portrayed on the pictorial motif on the Indus seals.

Mahadevan provides a path-breaking reconstruction of the motif as a filtering device, drawing parallels from the Ṛgvedic Soma *yajña* and Wasson's interpretation of *soma* as a mushroom, fly-agaric.[44] In view of the substantive importance of the insights and perspectives provided, Mahadevan's thesis is summarized. After surveying the views that the Harappan cult object was an incense burner (Marshall), a bird-cage (Mackay), a crib and stable rack (Freiderichs), a calendar system of the Jovian cycle (Knorozov et al.) and a superb analysis of the orthographic variations depicted on over 1015 seals, sealings and tablets, Mahadevan has prepared a composite diagram of the "Harappan Sacred Filter." That it is a filter is surmised from the flow symbolism, drops of liquid symbolism and perforations on the sides of the lower vessel. Using Wasson's identification of *soma* as mushroom juice, Mahadevan finds remarkable parallels with the Soma *yajña* of Ṛgvedic hymns and reconstructs the components of the Ṛgvedic filtering process composed of *pavitra* (strainer), *aṇvi* (sieve), and *pavamāna* (flow). Mahadevan under-scores the depiction of the cult object as a ceremonial standard.

There are a few points which may need a review in this reconstruction by Mahadevan:

1. The smoke emanating from the bottom vessel may indeed be smoke or fire;
2. the circle-with-dot symbols appearing on the bottom vessel may not be drops of juice; since they are used independently to constitute field-symbols on other seals and since this symbolism also occurs on punch-marked coins, they may denote gold or silver pellets (cf. Vedic morphemes connoting value: *mṛḍa, pṛḍa* > *pēḍa,* pellets) or droplets of mercury resulting from a process of sublimation from cinnabar;
3. the top vessel may contain multiple layers of metallic pyrite ore (*electrum*) or cinnabar; some orthographic variants do indicate fire symbolism extending beyond the dome of the top vessel;
4. the conical shape of the top vessel inserted into the bottom vessel may connote the flow of molten metal after sublimation; or may represent a drill (part of a goldsmith's lathe) with zig-zag lines on the top-vessel denoting churning motion; and
5. the entire apparatus firmly anchored around a spike may be linked to the context of the lapidary-goldsmith's hearths with a central clay stele and separate pits containing animal bones reagents: Kalibangan and Banawali Indus sites, the so-called "cult object" may indeed be a representation of the lapidary's sublimation device or goldsmith's instrumentation-furnace complex.

A hypothesis may be that the circle-with-dot denotes mercury; the *svaslika*'s (both right-and left-handed versions) represents *pon*[45] gold and *veḷḷi* silver, or the number of *puṭam* (refining or sublimation) processes to which the metal has been subjected. [It is notable that in ancient Tamil *poṅgaḍi* means an elephant or a lion. On an Indus seal, an elephant is seen pushing a *svastika.* According to the Tamil lexicon, *puṭam* means the refining or sublimating vessel or cup; cover; calcination in fire or in the sun; concavity, bend; true daily motion of a heavenly body; celestial longitude; purity. In Sanskrit, *sampuṭa* is a hemi-spherical bowl (cf. the top bowl on the Indus "cult object"); Suśruta uses it to cannot a round casket (*CDIAL,* 12941). Pāli: *sampuṭa,* hollow of the hand; Prākṛta: *sampuḍa,* collection, mass; Gujarati: *sāpaḍ,* cavity formed by two bowls placed together.][46] The so-called "cult object" may perhaps be a representation of: *kampaṭṭam* (> Greek *gammadium*, a Greek cross symbol), smelter-filter, sublimation apparatus, pre-dating the Greek *keratokis* by almost three millennia.

The *Ṛgveda* and the Brāhmaṇa texts do not provide substantive information on an apparatus which may stand comparison with the proto-Indus sublimation apparatus. The Śrauta rituals of the Brāhmaṇa days however contain the names of a number of vessels and ladles and cups used during the *yajña* operations. Analogous to the *Śulbasūtra* which provided the geometry of the *agni* hearth (and perhaps, also the science of mining or extraction of minerals and metals), there may have been specific technical *sūtras* explaining the construction of the apparatus. Since the Ṛgvedic artisan was perhaps not fully aware of the techniques and since the priests of the Brāhmaṇa days had alienated the metallurgist-lapidary, relegating him to a lower-caste status, the memories of the proto-Indus lapidary techniques had been lost for the officiants of the Soma *yajña.* It is a reasonable inference that the manual operations involved in preparing a pottery-sublimation apparatus of such exquisite elegance could only have been performed by the lineage of the proto-Indus lapidaries. It is likely that this tradition is preserved among later-day alchemists, physicians, potters, goldsmiths, and blacksmiths.

The search for the continuity of the alchemical tradition which dates back to the proto-Indus lapidary has, therefore, to be continued by tracing the traditions of manual operations, even in the symbolisms of the inconographic art and not in the texts of a class of priests who had to make do with a mere symbolism of a sacrifice, like an alchemist's children playing with metallurgical toys, not knowing what to do and how to do it. The "it" may be defined as the "art of making gold and the laboratory complex, substances and apparatus needed." In one ancient myth for instance, what remains is only *hiraṇya-kacipu,* the spill-over demon of (or dross from) molten gold!

Proto-Indus "cult object": a lapidary's alchemical yantra

The so-called "cult object" in front of the so-called "unicorn" on hundreds of Indus seals, the pictorial motif constituting the veritable symbol par excellence of Indus civilization may also be explained as a "distillation or sublimation tower."

The pictorial motif vividly portrays ascending hot vapours, the descent or the flow of a liquid and the collection of condensates [drops or pellets] in the bottom, at times knobbed, vessel. The symbolism is an alchemical representation of purification, possibly enrichment (if some regents may be conjectured on the top domed vessel) of the sublimate.

Since *Śulbaśāstra* related not only to geometry of the fire-altars but also to mines and mineralogy (e.g., metallic veins in rocks), according to *Arthaśāstra,* and since the back-brick technology of the *Śulbasūtra* are traceable to the proto-Indus legacy of practical production of baked-bricks, it is reasonable to extrapolate the Ṛgvedic Soma *yajña* as a metallurgical legacy of the proto-Indus lapidary. The archaeological evidences are the chert weights used for weighing precious metals, smelting furnaces, the fire-altars with central clay stele (Kalibangan and Banawali), pits containing animal bones and significant quantities of bronze, copper, gold and silver artifacts with clear indications that some metals were deliberately alloyed. The proto-Indus "cult object" may indeed be a smelter-filter or a proto-*kerotakis,* sublimation apparatus, paralleling the *soma pavamāna* and close affinities between *soma* and gold in Vedic, Brāhmaṇa texts. Soma *yajña* in the *Ṛgveda* may be explained as the earliest recorded alchemical allegory, interpreting *soma* as electrum, gold-silver pyrite ore and the *yajña* as a smelting process, yielding *rasa* or *amṛtam hiraṇyam.* In the *dakṣiṇāgni* portion of the fire-altar, what is produced is *hiraṇyapiṇḍa* (from out of *hiraṇyagarbha,* the golden womb), the gift for the alchemist-priests—*amṛtam,* according to Manu, something that is given unasked.

Earliest use of the touchstone in India

The use of the touchstone in sixth century BC in Greece is attested by Pindar and Bacchylides.[47] Needham[48] states that "the touchstone was probably a far later introduction (fourteenth century AD)" to distinguish false from true natural gold. Use of the touchstone is attested in *Arthaśāstra* (2.13.17-18) which is dated at least fourteen centuries earlier: *suvarṇam pūrvam nikaṣya paścādvarṇikām nikaṣayet; samarāga lekhamaṇimnonnate dese nikaṣitam...,* after first rubbing the gold (to be tested) on the touchstone, he (*suvarṇika,* Superintendent of Gold) should afterwards rub the standard gold (on it). That with a streak of the same colour (as the standard) on places (on the stone)...(he should know as perfectly tested). Further in 2.13.20:

sakesaraḥ snigdho mṛdur bhrājiṣnuśca nikaṣarāgaḥ śreṣṭaḥ. The streak (of the gold) on the thouchstone, that has filaments, is smooth, soft and lustrous is best. The artisans, therefore, knew not only the technique of cupellation but also the use of the touchstone to call the bluff of aurifaction. How then could the *pammena* get away with the deception? One reason that will be evident from a survey of the ancient Indian policy is that the *pammena* had royal patronage; indeed, there was a royal-priestly consortium headed by an *ākarādhyakṣa*, directing the *rasapāka*, as an alchemical state enterprise.

Valentine and Makaradhvaja

The fifteenth century frescoes of Nicolas Flamel in the churchyard of the Innocents in Paris were reportedly endowed with a twofold alchemical and religious significance.[49] In a remarkable parallel, the icons in the tantric tradition embellishing hundreds of temples of medieval India can be interpreted in tantric and alchemical terms in a continuing metaphor of "union."

A crystalline red sulphide of mercury is named *makaradhvaja* or *svarṇasindhura* in alchemical trantric texts extolling the substance as a panacea for all diseases of the human flesh.[50] Black sulphide of mercury is called *kajjali*; mercuric chloride is *rasa-karpūra*.[51] That the proto-Indus "cult object" was carried in a procession as a standard evokes the symbolism of a *-dhvaja*; and if, as hypothesized elsewhere, this indeed was a sublimation device to prepare mercury from mercuric sulphide, or cinnabar or *svarṇasindhura*, the *dhvaja* may indeed have been the *makaradhvaja*. (Cf., Varāhamihira's account of Indramaha festival and later-day flock traditions of Kāma-dahana, the god of love who had the *makaradhvaja*. In iconography, Varuṇa has *makara* as his *vāhana*, described as a fabulous sea-monster.] One other standard is discernible from a tablet depicting the procession: the "unicorn" carried as a standard. This might have been the "gold"-standard. In seals and tablets of Harappa, the crocodile, *makara*, is a dominant pictorial motif, at times depicted holding a fish in its snout, suggesting the possible evolution of an alchemical symbolism of a term *sindhuvara* which is relatable to the waters of the sindhu river and hence, explaining the use of water animals, crocodile, and fish. The crocodile may be a pictorial metaphor and symbolize a homonymous morpheme, *sindhu(ra)*. A synonym for the elephant, *nāga* is *sindhura*; elephant is also a pictorial motif on Indus seals; it may be symbol for *nāga*, lead; or *sindhura*, mercuric sulphide or cinnabar.

Nicolas Flamel (1330-1418): His Exposition of the Hieroglyphical Figures is an English translation of the Frenchman's famous work. His interpretation of the Greak work, as depicted in the frescoes known as the figures of Abraham the Jew is relevant in any alchemical tradition. The interpretation is taken from Read, to underscore the importance of symbolism in alchemy:[52] "The white and red flowers of this picture represent the white and red stages of the Greak Work.... The dragon is sophic mercury; the griffin, a combination of lion and eagle, that is, of the fixed an the volatile. [Cf., the Indus pictorial motifs of the so-called fabulous animals.] The old man with the scythe, representing Saturn or Kronos cutting off the feet of Mercury, signifying the fixing if mercury. The adepts identified sophic mercury with the 'essence' of silver. Now when silver is cupelled with lead, its original impurities sink into the material of the cupel, and the residual silver becomes 'fixed,' or unalterable. Thus the pure 'essence' of silver, or of quicksilver (regarded as a baser form of silver), has been obtained: Saturn has cut off the feet of ordinary mercury or quicksilver, and rendered it immobile. The fountain of heavy water is the Hermetic stream, symbolic of sophic mercury. As Flamel eventually discovered, to his great relief, infants' blood signified merely the mineral spirit of metals, 'principally in the *sunne*, *moone*, and *mercury*,' that is, in gold, silver and mercury." The parallels, not only with Indus motifs, but also with the icons, the symbol carried on the multiple hands, in the Hindu, Buddhist and Jaina traditions are too vivid to be ignored as accidental concordances.

Basil Valentine's emblem

Read[53] adds that the emblem is accompanied by the Latin epigram *Stolcius' Viridarium Chymicum.* This epigram states that "the wandering planets are beheld in the sky; earth is equal to them with her yield of metals. The sun is father to the stone, wandering Cynthia (moon) its mother, Wind bore the child in its womb, Earth gave it food." This is reportedly the direct allusion to the percepts of Hermes and the design is often associated in alchemical works with the Emerald Table of Hermes. The epigram is remarkably concordant with the *Śatapatha Brāhmaṇa* text, treating the *lokam-pṛṇa* bricks as the food for the nobility, the *svayam-ātṛṇṇa* perforated brick. The two-headed eagle and the lion represent Wind and Earth, the star the seven metals corresponding to the seven planets. The parallel symbol of *śyena*, the falcon is significant. It is also said that the cross was a symbol attributed to Thoth, denoting the four elements proceeding from a common centre. Snakes were the male and female or the fixed and volatile principles around the central stem denoting gold of the philosophers. The *svastika* symbol and snake pictorial motifs are concordant with these Graeco-Egyptian alchemical symbols. The sun and serpent can be traced back to Babylonia to connote sun-workship and phallism. Shedding of the skin is likened to rejuvenation and linked to concepts of immortality; the idea of regeneration is linked to phallism and hate renovation of seasons attributed to the sun.

In another alchemical design titled, "The Whole Work of Philosophy" from *Viridarium Chymicum* (1624), the geometrical designs of square, triangle and circle are used together with the acrostic, "Vitriol." Numbers and symbols are used to denote heavenly bodies and metals; Saturn is darkened cubic stone, surrounded by five stars suggesting five planets. King Sol (Apollo) is seated on a lion, associated with earth and fire. Queen Luna (Diana) riding upon a dolphin, is associated with water and air. [Cf. comparable *vāhana* in Hindu iconography of Durgā and lion; Varuṇa and *makara.*] A dragon perhaps signifies sophic mercury. A circle with a dot denotes gold. [Cf., dotted circle motif on the bottom bowl of the Indus "cult object" and as independent pictorial motif on seals.]

Symbols have always fascinated the alchemists of all ages, all civilizations and all traditions of antiquity. One of the best-known alchemical designs is the summary of twelve emblems in what has been called the Twelve Keys of Basil Valentine purporting to convey the secrets of the Great Work. The emblem reproduced from the *Chambers's Encyclopaedisa* (p. 234) may be explained by a quotation from the accompanying article: "...the First Key shows Sol and Luna, or the king and queen, representing gold and silver of exoteric alchemy and sophic sulphur and sophic mercury of the adepts. The adept is told to cast the body of the king to a fierce grey wolf and burn him in a great fire. This cryptic direction indicates the purification of gold by fusion with stibnite (*lupus metallorum*, or "wolf of the metals"), thus leading to "philosopher's gold," "our gold," or "sophic sulphur." Similarly the queen, or Luna, is purified by cupellation so as to yield sophic mercury. The ensuing conjunction of the masculine and feminine principles leads to the Stone, often depicted as an infant. Similarly, the fourth precept of Hermes tells us that "its father is the sun, its mother the moon, the wind carries it in its belly, its nurse is the earth" and fifth precept adds, "it is the father of perfection throughout the world." Another emblem found in works ascribed to Basil Valentine and also linked with the Emerald Table (*tabula smaragdina,* said to have been engraved by Hermes with thirteen precepts and regarded by generations of alchemists with superstitious reverence), shows the conjunction of Sol and Luna in association with a cup or chalice, suggestive of the Holy Grail, an allegorical fount of physical and spiritual life. The five other metals and associated planets proceed from iron (Mars) through the darkened symbol of lead (Saturn) to quicksilver (Mercury), tin (Jupiter), and copper (Venus). The lion and double-headed eagle represent the fixed (masculine) and volatile (feminine) principles. The Latin words of the legend from an acrostic, "vitroil" (a shiny crystalline body), and direct the searcher to "visit the inward parts of the earth; by rectifying thou shalt find the hidden stone." Basil Valentine was the pseudonym of a writer who seems to have flourished in the late seventeenth century.... The crucial and final phase of the operations of the Great Work consisted in heating the prepared materials in the "philosopher's egg" or sealed vessel of Hermes, mounted in an athanor or alchemical furnace. During this process a series of colours was supposed to appear in the sequence of black, white, yellow and red; 'red is last in works of Alkimy,' wrote T. Norton of Bristol in 1477."

This quotation admirably summarizes the accumulated tradition as perceived during the dying phases of the alchemical tradition in the seventeenth century of the Christian era. While it is hazardous to extrapolate this tradition and compare it with the origins which go back almost four millennia into the mists of history, some alchemical, almost "universal" principles of alchemy may be gleaned only as a framework for further, detailed historical evaluation of the Great Tradition.

If the proto-Indus hearth can be interpreted as the lapidary's furnace and if the central stele found in such hearths of Kalibangan and Banawali (Indus sites) is linked to the central stem of the so-called "cult object" on the Indus seals, it is permissible to interpret the cult-object as a sublimation apparatus, paralleling the "sealed" vessel or apparatus of Hermes. The centre-piece of the emblem of Valentine depicting the Great Work is a remarkable evocation of the proto-Indus sublimation device rendered in splendid lapidary iconography on Indus seals.

A Lydian electrum coin of *c.* sixth century BC depicts the Indus unicorn facing a lion; are they symbols of gold and silver, the constituent elements of the electrum coin? The proto-Indus "unicorn" symbolized the sun; may be, sun was the proto-Indus symbol of gold. The cult-object almost always found in front of the unicorn is relatable to the primary apparatus of the lapidary which yielded this purified metal. If it was a sublimation device to prepare mercury from cinnabar, the proto-Indus lapidary might indeed have known the techniques of using the *upa-rasa,* a metallic oxide or sulphide, using it as a reducing agent, to extract gold from a mineral, *soma,* which may be electrum or some type of *mākṣika,* pyrite ore.

The opposition between the "lion" and "bull" symbol can be traced to the early dynastic period of Mesopotamian civilization (*c.* 3000-2340 BC) and linked to the proto-Indus civilization. A design occurs on a steatite vase from Khafaje reproduced by Henri Frankfort.[54] The design contains a pair of humped bulls, of the Indian zebu breed; the same bulls which are depicted in some magnificent Indus seals with pronounced humps, also called the Brāhmaṇī or zebu bulls. These bulls are not native to Mesopotamia and are uniquely Indus. Frankfort notes that the vase was not imported. The design also included snakes with drill holes which were once filled with coloured inlays of paste or stone which recur not only in Khafaje but also in some Indus pectorals and the stone sculpture of the so-called "priest-king" of the Indus. "The meaning of the design remains obscure. It seems certain that it is in some way concerned with the great natural forces which the Mesopotamians worshipped. It consists of four groups, forming a continuous frieze of even density, as on the cylinder seals. A long-nosed, long-haired Sumerian figure is seated upon two-humped bulls; above are a snake, the crescent moon, and a six-leaved rosette, the last possibly emblematic of the planet Venus, a manifestation of Inanna-Ishtar. From the hands of this personage flow two streams of water. Plants which appear in front of one bull and at the rim of the vase may be thought to spring from this life-giving stream. In another group the same (or similar) personage appears standing between, or upon, two panthers. The rosette recurs; this time the hands grasp snakes. They possibly symbolize the fertility of the earth, balancing the fertilizing power of water in the other group. But this is a mere hypothesis, as is the suggestion that the rosette in both groups may identify the chief figure with Inanna. When we follow the design of the right we meet the ascription of the Agrab vase, and then a fresh group; a lion and an eagle devouring a bull. The space left between this scene and the first is occupied by a date-plam flanked by small cunning bears who lick their paws after eating the sweet fruits."

Frankfort's analysis of the symbolism which contains vivid proto-Indus parallels provides a number of clues to the proto-Indus alchemical tradition. Frankfort elaborates how the artistic tradition evidenced by the design on the Khafaje vase continued into the Mitanni era (*c.* 1450-1360 BC). On a gold bowl from Ras Shamra, the lion is drawn in a style closely resembling Egyptian styles; dots or hatching accompany the outline of the body (a technique seen on Indus seals depicting panthers). The Ras Shamra bowl also depicts a lion and an eagle pouncing on a bull, beardless small personages battling a lion, symbols of squatting griffins, winged bull (referred to as Asiatic in origin by Frankfort), goats and antelopes (images which are paralleled by motifs on Indus seals and tablets). Another cognate design Frankfort analyses is a gold vessel also from Ras Shamra. This is a flat-bottomed plate with a vertical rim. In the centre four wild goats resembling unicorns are shown. Round this decorate centre-piece a chase whirls. A hunter is shown in his chariot overtaking the game (a herd of wild cattle) and drawing the bow. A bull brings up the rear, followed by a cow accompanied by her calf, then again a bull which is lowering its head for a charge (a motif depicted on Indus seals). "The Ras Shamra plate gives us the earliest version of a theme found throughout the ancient Near East in the second and first millennia BC...(illustrating) the cosmopolitan character of the Mitannian era—cosmopolitan in the sense that intercourse between countries was easy and stimulating, yet national individuality was everywhere reserved," observes Frankfort.

The point to note is that the Khafaje vase and Ras Shamra motifs on gold vessels may be inerpreted as depicting an alchemical process, possibly conveying a message to the owner of the plate on the processes used to part the precious metals—gold and silver and to purify them by "killing" the baser metals such as lead.

In many alchemical traditions, the symbols and motifs that recur are: snake or a pair of snakes, bull, lion or panther, a personage standing upon a panther or between panthers, a panther or lion pouncing upon a bull, an eagle devouring a bull, jackal eating a corpse, water flowing from a vessel or vase, crescent moon, six-petalled rosette. It is remarkable that many of these symbols and motifs occur in proto-Indus seals and also in iconography. The Khafaje vase with the representation of zebu or humped Indian Brāhmaṇī bulls is contemporaneous with the Indus civilization and it is permissible to read the message of this vase in proto-Indus terms. The Mother Goddess cult and the iconographic symbols of the Mother Goddess subduing a panther or lion can be related to the alchemical tradition. *Sindhura* is the female principle; *rasa* or mercury is the male principle: one is a representation of Śakti and the other of Śiva as a *rasa-liṅgam.* The snake is *nāga,* lead. The panther is *vēṅkai* (Sanskrit *vyāghra*); proto-Dravidian *veṇ* is white, silver, the eagle is *paruntu,* may be, cognate with *parada* mercury. The killing of the bull is an alchemical representation of the "killing" of gold by other elements such as silver and mercury. Remove the entanglement of the snakes or lead and obtain the six-petalled rosette, the sun or gold; and the crescent moon, or white-coloured silver. The scorpion is *kaṭaka* or astringency, may be connoting the alkalies or salts used as reducing agents. The flow of water from the vase is comparable to the flow of the fluid gold during the extraction process, parting gold and silver from electrum, a naturally occurring mineral.

The symbol used for mercury in early Greek alchemical texts bears a striking similarity to the proto-Indus "cult object" which almost invariably appears in front of the so-called "unicorn" on Indus seals. If the "unicorn" was *tang* (means "bull" in Gadaba language; *taṅk-am* "gold" in Tamil and Chinese; *ṭaṅkaṇa* means "borax" a calx used in gold-smelting; Tibet was a major source of borax), the "cult object" was sublimation device in the *kampaṭṭam-complex* (Greek *gammadium,* coinage or mint apparatus, possibly producing *accu* moulds or stamps > *akṣa,* gold cowries, units of account in currency media in the days of *Arthaśāstra.*) One possible interpretation is that the "cult object" was used to produce mercury from cinnabar, by a sublimation process; a *rasa* of fundamental importance in metallurgical operations on minerals containing gold. Treating the *rasa* as a water principle or principle of liquidity, the use of the term *amṛtam* as a synonym of gold in the Brāhmaṇa days can be explained. It is an extension of the concept of "perfection" in metals or "the killing" of impurities to the concept of "immortality or non-death" of bodies; cf. *amṛtam āyur hiraṇyam* refrain in the days of *Śatapatha Brāhmaṇa.*

What started as a mercantile proto-Indus legacy of producing gold beads in purely metallurgical, materialistic terms or colouring and glazing faience artifacts made of clay and other earthly substances, degenerates into alchemy with bizarre alchemical connotations. A devastating social impact of the extension of the *suvarṇa* (desirable colour) concept is the *varṇa* hierarchical classification of society, enforced by a royal-priest consortium. The consortium attempts to sustain state power by controlling the production of gold (which is related to an extraordinary lure for possession of gold amongst the royalty as well as the common people) and "transmuted gold" as currency medium, relegating a *śvapāka* (is this relatable to *aśvamedha* or the use of horse-meat and bones as reducing agents in smelting operations?), an artisan with alchemical potential, to an outcast or *a-varṇa* status.

Ornaments and cultural artifacts of proto-Indus[55]

A remarkable feature of the ornaments found in proto-Indus sites (e.g., Amri-Nandara-Nal, Zhob, Kulli-Mehi, Harappa, Mohenjo-daro, Jhukar, Jhangar, dating from *c.* 3000 BC to 15000 BC) is that an entire range of materials is used, equating gold, for instance, with faience or ivory. Pins of bronze and ivory are found at Jhukar. Silver ring made of thin wire is found at Ghazi Shah (Amri-Nal culture). A steatite seal found[56] at Nal is like an ear-top mould, oval in shape. It is decorated with a vulture with a snake in its claws. [Cf. alchemical symbolism.] Ear-ornaments of Harappa are made of faience and burnt steatite with knobs at the back.[57] One ear-ornament threads together a spherical and a tubular carnelian bead.[58] Two gold studs of Mohenjo-daro are 1.5 inches in diameter and with beads soldered around the edges.[59] Four copper coins with perhaps thin foils of gold on them are separated by disc-shaped steatite beads and joined together by a copper wire.[60] Graduated beads are made of carnelian, agate, limestone, unpolished stone and even paste glazed with a greenish-blue colour.[61] A crystal pendant found in the grave of an infant had a variety of bead combinations.[62] Harappan necklaces were made of faience (blue glaze), gold, jade, agate, jasper, and haematite.[63] Pendants on necklaces had beads of copper (cylindrical), gold (short-barrel shaped, hollow-discs soldered, hexagonal barrel-shaped, cylindrical), silver (globular).[64]

Crucibles found at Dabarkot by Aurel Stein[65] were upto five inches high. The crucible face had four holes pierced which met in a small cavity below the centre, to mould ingots of gold, half tubes of pottery were used. A shallow spoon 4.6 inches long, may have been used to handle molten gold.[66]

Silver occurs more commonly than gold in Indus sites; the evidence for this statement is the number of finds of large-sized vessels made of silver. These silver vessels use of shapes used for copper vessels. "Among examples of finer workmanship is a silver buckle from Harappa, with soldered scroll pattern of gold wire and gold-capped beads, and a boss of silver inlaid with conch-shell.... Objects of silver are almost unknown in later prehistoric or proto-historic contexts in the subcontinent. A rare, indeed unique, occurrence is the copper hoard from Gungeria where about a hundred thin silver plates in the form of bulls' heads were discovered. Their age is still a matter for speculation. The Indus cities also provide testimony that lead—often found naturally in association with silver—was imported in ingot form, and occasionally used for manufacturing objects such as vases or plumb-bobs. In spite of the common use of metals, stone was not abandoned.... An alkali was probably applied to the surface (of steatite seals) before firing to assist in the whitening and to glaze it. Their importance was doubtless linked in some way with their role in trading activities.... Steatite was used for a wide variety of other objects: beads, bracelets, buttons, vessels, etc., but its use for making faience is of particular interest.... Minute disc-cylinder beads of this material were apparently extruded in plastic form, fired and then snapped off. Pieces of glazed earthenware and even faience pots, some with coloured decoration, are recorded, and again testify to a remarkable level of technical achievement...deserves Childe's acclaim as 'technically the peer of the rest' (that is, of Egypt and Babylonia)."[67] In the stock of tablets and seals from the Indus civilization, there are also two seals made of silver and many tablets made of copper. Copper, silver, faience: all had equal value as media for communicating some important messages using the Indus script signs and pictorial motifs. What was of 'value' was the message, not the material on which the message was conveyed.

"Value" of gold = "value" of lapidary's faience

Hundreds of examples can be added in the same tenor. The main point to note is that there appears to be no differentiation in the specific materials used in any apparent perception of "relative values" of different materials. The lapidary-artisan seems to have created shapes and forms depending upon the nature of the material and his ability[68] to work with the material. Another crucial point to note is that the ornaments were found almost on many clay figurines and in laymen's households, unlike the hoards found at Ur in the queen's grave. The range of colours of gold beads[69] ranged from coppery red to pale yellow, indicating different proportions of silver-gold alloys used. In the Chanhu-daro bead factory, carnelian beads had two varieties, white design on red background, and black designs on white base, using a popular design of the figure of eight,[70] a symbol often found in later-day punch-marked coins.

Measurement of "value"

Juxtaposed to this plebeian perception of equality in value among material artifacts, is the proto-Indus invention of balances. Two finds of balances at Mohenjo-daro are significant. One consisted of a copper bar in the visible notch at the perfect end.[71] Another find was a set of bronze beam and copper pans kept in a copper canister. The balance was apparently of some importance in the lives of the lapidary or merchant for the latter to have carefully kept the balance in a metal container. The balances and the chert weights fit into a system of measurement of economic value, to facilitate equitable barter trade. At the present stage of understanding of the proto-Indus artifacts, and without a successful decipherment of the Indus script,[72] it is reasonable to infer that the measure of value was based on a quantitative and arithmetical nexus of proportions, and not based on any notion of scarcity value or any qualitative dimension of "desirability of a particular substance" such as gold or silver, for instance. We seem to be dealing with a truly plebeian perception of *māna* as value, *māna* connoting what the artisan has imputed into the material he has worked with.

From proto-Indus to the Brāhmaṇa periods is a big jump, not only of almost a millennium but of ideology. It is a challenge of no mean order for the historian to unravel the socio-economic context within which the massive shift took place across the subcontinent. For, in the Vedic and Brāhmaṇa texts, we find a fiery passion for gold (and silver) which contrasts vividly with the plebeian, proto-

Indus archaeological finds.

In the Ṛgvedic days, the impoverishment of some classes of people subjected to the greed of money-lenders is noted:

> To *vadhyasva*, when he worships her with gifts, she gave fierce Divodāsa, cancellor of debts, consumer of the churlish niggard, one and all, thine, O Saraswatī, are these effectual boons. (*ṚV*, VI. 61.1)

The poet is adoring Divodāsa who fights the Paṇi-s; he is *ṛṇa-cyuta*, the cancellor of debts.

"During the Ptolemaic period the ratio (of silver to gold) was 10 for 1 in Europe, and $12^1/_2$ to 1 in Egypt, whilst it was 6 to $6^1/_4$ for 1 in the Orient. The control of money and trade must have been in very powerful hands to maintain gold in the West at twice its value in the East, or silver in the East at twice its value in the West. Whose hands were these? The answer is, the priesthood; the priests of Brahmā or Buddha in the East, the priests of Cyrus, Darius, Tiglath-pil-Esar, Nebu-Nazaru, Osiris, Alexander, Ptolemy, and the Caesars in the West."[73] This lead by a historian of money can be fruitfully followed to explore also the alchemical tradition, its science potentials and its impact on society.

References

1. Buddha Prakash, *Ṛgveda and the Indus Civilization*, Hoshiarpur, 1966.
2. I. Mahadevan, *The Indus Script: Text, Concordance and Tables, MASI*, no. 77, Delhi, 1977; cf. the plates containing the field symbols.
3. Agni may be linked with Latin *ignis*, fire; Lithuanian *ugnis*; Old Slavic *ogni*; Ugarit in North Syria *agn* (M.H. Pope cited in Jairzabhoy, 1963, p. 17). The Persian *Avesta* denotes fire by a different word *atar* which parallels the Vedic Atharvan, the fire-priest. Vedic *Agni* is the mediator between god and man; he is called *narā-saṁsa*, analogous to Avestan messenger of Ahura, *nairyo-sangha* (Jairzabhoy, 1963, p. 17). The proto-Dravidian morpheme was perhaps *anala* (< *agn-?*), a synonym which also occurs in the Vedic texts.
4. A.K. Coomaraswamy, *History* of *Indian and Indonesian Art*, p. 41 notes: "The wheel which later on becomes the mark of a *cakravartin*, the discus of Viṣṇu and the Buddhist Wheel of Law, originally represented the Sun. The disc of gold placed behind the fire-altar to represent the sun may well be origin of the later *prabhāmaṇḍala* or *śiraścakra*."

   In a text of extraordinary alchemical secrecy, *Taittiriyasaṁhitā* (V.2.6-9) prescribes: a lotus leaf, a gold disc, a golden man (*hiraṇmaya puruṣa*), two wooden ladles, a perforated brick, a brick of *dūrva* grass, a living tortoise, the heads of dead animals including those of a horse and a bull, a mortar, a pan in the middle of which the head of a man is put, and the head of a snake. These can be rationalized as reducing agents in a cupellation-smelting process complex. J.N. Banerjea (1956, reprinted, New Delhi, 1986, p. 61) draws a parallel between *hiraṇmaya puruṣa* and *vāstau puruṣa* or a brick with the painted figure of a man placed on a foundation trench of a building. Banerjea (p. 516) also describes an icon: Brahmā is four-faced, has a staff, the hide of a black antelope and a ritual water-vessel; he holds *śruk* and *śruva*, sacrificial implements and the Veda in his hands; he rides on a swan. The so-called sacrificial implements may indeed be the metallurgist's tools! Cf. *amṛta* and the water-vessel; the sulphur or arsenical or mercury—divine water of alchemical antiquity!

5. Varāhamihira's *Bṛhatsaṁhitā*, ch. XLII, Indra-dhvaja-sampad; A.M. Shastri, 1969, pp. 199ff.
6. *Chāndogya Upaniṣad* identifies Kārttikeya with Sanatkumāra, a mind-born son of Brahmā and adds that people called him Skanda. Proto-Dravidian *kanda* is a stake. Cf. the central clay stele in the so-called fire-altars of Kalibangan and Banawali, Indus sites. *ṚV*, 1.34.8 cites seven mothers (without naming them). *Sapta mātṛ* or *mātṛkā* nurse Kārttikeya. Seven tongues (*sapta jihva*) of *agni* are referred in mythology as: *kālī, karālī, manojavā, sulohitā, sudhūmra-varṇa, ugrā* or *sphuliṅginī*, and *pradiptā*. Cf., the metallurgical overtones in *kālī, lohitā, dhūmra, sphuliṅginī.*
7. Joseph Needham, *SCC*, vol. 3, 1959, p. 404.
8. J.N. Banerjea, op. cit., pp. 177-79.
9. *Bṛhatsaṁhitā*, XLII.46 refers to Tvaṣṭṛ as a creative aspect of the sun. He gave an ornament to Indramaha and presided over the constellation Citrā: *ratha cakrābham daśamam sūryas tvaṣṭas prabhāyuktam.*
10. P.R. Deshmukh, *The Indus Civilization in the Ṛgveda*, p. 41; Buddha Prakash, op. cit.
11. Paṭala XI; P.C. Ray, *HCAMI*, 1956, p. 148.

    "Refiner's fire" (cf. J. Needham, *SCC*, vol. 5, part II, pp. 37-38).

    "Gold or silver, with or without other metal, is heated with lead in a vessel made of bone-ash, a crucible, or shallow hearth, set in an oxidizing furnace with a muffle and reverberatory heat-flow. Lead monoxide (litharge) is formed, as well as the oxides of any base metals, and these separate with any other impurities, soaking into the porous ash and being blown off in the fumes, until a cake or globule of the precious metal remains. This is the 'refiner's fire,' but it will not separate silver from gold (a process for centuries called 'parting'), which is why so much of the early Mesopotamian and Egyptian gold is really 'electrum,' the alloy of the two metals. The ancient method of separation is called 'dry parting' or 'cementation.' Common salt and brick-dust or clay with 'vitriols' (copper and iron sulphates), are packed around; then on strong heating chlorides of the metals are formed, including the silver but not appreciably the gold, and those volatilize ore are absorbed like the oxides by the ash of the cupel, leaving a cake or button of pure gold."

12. Mackay, *Chanhu-daro Excavations 1935-1936*, New Haven, 1943; reprinted, 1967, pp. 175-76.
13. S.R. Rao, "Further Excavations at Lothal," *Lalit Kalā*, 11, 1962, pp. 23-24.
14. Vats, *EH*, 1940; reprinted, New Delhi, 1998, p. 379.
15. H.C. Bharadwaj, *Aspects of Ancient Indian Technology*, Delhi, 1979, pp. 102ff.
16. R. Multhauf, op. cit., pp. 109ff.
17. The Latin *soma* meaning "body" is interesting. If this semantic radical had any nexus with Vedic *soma* is conjectural, since the references in the Vedic texts to *soma* deem it to be a substance or used an an allegory/metaphor with "celestial" attributes and invariably linked with possibilities of wealth and prosperity.
18. Cf., J.C. Ray, *Ancient Indian Life*, Calcutta, 1948; B. Walker, *The Hindu World*, 2 vols., reprinted, New Delhi, 1990, p. 309: "...the knowledge of the Indian art of distillation spread to the West through the Muhammadans." *Kohola* is a *surā*, liquor, made from barley; combined with the Arabic prefix *al*, Ray traces the origin of alcohol to a proto-Indian tradition. Walker cites *yūṣa* highly intoxicating brew made from meat and bone broth mixed with spirits; *sunda*, a heady concoction from grasses, flowers and leaves stored in elongated earthen jars and fermented juice drawn off from a hole in the bottom; *hāḷa*, distilled from tree-bark, roots, raw sugarcane, onion juice and various spices, into which a drop or two of snake venom was mixed and stored in wooden vats to be drunk on special occasions; *āsava* made from date treacle; *pariśrut* from wood-apple mixed with spices.
19. A.J. Hopkins, op. cit., p. 74.
20. W.F. Bynum, E.J. Browne and Roy Porter, eds., *Dictionary of the History of Science*, Princeton, 1981, p. 106.
21. F.R. Allchin, "India: The Ancient Home of Distillaton?" *Man*, vol. 14, 1979, pp. 55-63.
22. S. Mahdihassan, "The Earliest distillation units of potter in Indo-Pakistan," *Pakistan Archaeology*, no. 8, 1972, pp. 159-68.
23. F.S. Taylor, *The Alchemists*, 1951, pp. 2, 17.
24. John Marshall, *Taxila*, 3 vols., Cambridge, 1931, vol. III, p. 420; figs. 129 and 192a.
25. F.R. Allchin, op. cit., pp. 59-63.

26. Suryakanta, *A Practical Vedic Dictionary*, Delhi, 1981.
27. Cf., sublimation apparatus in the Bower Manuscript; the manuscript is dated to *c.* AD 450 and makes no reference to Caraka but quotes Suśruta. It deals with eye diseases, elixirs, aphrodisiacs, hair-dyes and a panegyric on garlic apart from formulae for medicated oils, enemas, tonics, collyriums, hair-washes and other drugs and powders.
28. Joseph Needham, *SCC*, vol. 5, part II, p. 157. The picture K 128 is interpreted as portraying a tree from the trunk of which, like sappan or haematoxylon, a red dye-pigment is obtained. The glyph, however, has the bottom vessel inverted, unlike the pottery stamp. The glyph K 812 c, d has two parts; the top part is comparable to the pottery monogram. The entire glyph is interpreted as an indigo plant, with its juice being collected in a pan. Since all the colour terms have the textile radical, a reasonable conjecture is that they had been derived from dyeing.
29. K. Paddayya, "On the form and function of perforated pottery of the Deccan Neolithic Culture," *Man*, vol. 4, 1969, pp. 450-53.
30. A remarkable Greek alchemical parallel is relevant; cf. A.J. Hopkins, op. cit., pp. 72ff.: "Zosimus registers his belief that Democritus accomplished the whitening of copper by use of arsenic or mercury and not sulphur. This is the occasion for his introduction of the description of the *aludel* and *kerotakis*, instruments used for volatilizing sulphur or arsenic or mercury in a closed vessel so that the elements could be sublimed and purified; and in the case of *kerotakis*, act upon a leaf of copper suspended in the closed space. [The first actual drawings of these pieces of apparatus are found centuries later on the margins of the manuscripts, such as the MS. St. Marc (eleventh century).] They are familiar tools to Zosimus. These reflux condensers have always been considered alchemistic inventions, destined to play a part in confirming alchemistic theory in the minds of the ancient world. One of the descriptions runs as follows:

    Taking some arsenic [he means the sulphide], whiten it in the following manner. Make a clay disc of the thickness of a little mirror and pierce it with little holes, like a sieve. Place above, adjusting it, a recipient into which put one part sulphur; and into the sieve as much of arsenic as you wish; and having covered with another recipient and luted the joints, after two days and nights you will find white lead ['white arsenic']. Cast on a quarter *mīna* of this and heat a whole day, adding a little bitumen and you will have [the result]; and such is the construction of the apparatus. [The underlined terms are comparable to the perforated Indus bowls and *mīna* sign in Indus script.]

    [Harmmer-Jensen claims that this instrument made possible the great alchemistic discovery: that of a substance (sulphur) which as an 'earth,' solid, inactive, could be changed into a 'spirit,' volatile, active; and then changed to a 'water.' *Die alteste Alchemie*, 1921, pp. 40-41.]"

31. John Marshall, *MIC*, p. 313.
32. E.J.H. Mackay, *FEM*, 2 vols., reprinted, New Delhi, 1998, p. 207.
33. A.J. Hopkins, op. cit., pp. 3-74.
34. B.K. Thapar, "Kalibangan: A Harappan Metropolis beyond the Indus Valley," in G.L. Possehl, *ACI*, pp. 198ff.
35. B.B. Lal, "Some reflections on the structural remains at Kalibangan," B.B. Lal and S.P. Gupta, eds., *Frontiers of the Indus Civilization*, pp. 57ff.
36. R.S. Bisht, "Excavations at Banawali: 1974-77," in G.L. Possehl, *Harappan Civilization*, pp. 115ff.
37. Aurel Stein, *An Archaeological Tour in Gedrosia, MASI* 43, Calcutta, 1931, pp. 64, 130, pl. XXV.
38. A. Aiyappan, "Pottery braziers of Mohenjo-daro," *Man*, 39, 1939, pp. 71-72.
39. O.P. Jaggi, *Technology in Ancient India*, vol. I, Delhi, 1981, p. 103.
40. J. Needham, *SCC*, vol. 5, part II, p. 69.
41. A.J. Hopkins, op. cit., p. 75, provides a note, "In a recent article by F. Sherwood Taylor (*Journal of Hellenistic Studies*, 1930, p. 109), there are given two drawings of the aludel with *kerotakis* as given in outline in the ancient manuscripts, faced by two drawings of the same, as they would appear in modern perspective. They give a very clear idea of the possible use of this ancient piece of apparatus...." The ancient distillation apparatus as reconstructed by Mahdihassan and Allchin; and the so-called "cult object" on the Indus seals, described as a filter by I. Mahadevan may as well be perceived as the proto-Indus distillation and sublimation devices used by the lapidary.
42. J.R. Partington, *A Short History of Chemistry*, London, 1951, p. 24; diagrams of *ambix* (for distillation; the lower part called *lopas*; the upper part *phiale*; these are sometimes heated by lamps *phota*, sometimes on a sandbath); of *kerotakis* or sublimation apparatus. Cf. concordant etyma: Tamil *puṭam*, refining; *kampaṭṭam*, coinage, mint; Sanskrit *sampuṭa*, hemispherical bowl.
43. J.R. Partington, op. cit., p. 30; diagram of *valuka yantram* as given in P.C. Ray, *HCAMI*, p. 190, fig. 30d.
44. I. Mahadevan, "The cult object on unicorn sales: A sacred filter?" in N. Karashima, *Indus Valley to Mekong Delta: Explorations in Epigraphy*, Madras, 1985, pp. 219-68.
45. Cf., Tibetan bon legends; potters known as *seastika* or *pon*.
46. In compounds: Tamil *puṭam-iṭudal*, to refine metals, to calcinate, to preserve by burying under their earth, to cremate; *puṭa-pākarm* a particular method of preparing drugs in which various substance are placed in clay cups covered over the clay and heated over the fire,

digestion, cooking; *puṭa-t-tailam* medicinal oil extracted by *puṭam* processes; *puṭa-bhedanam* city. In Sanskrit, interpreted as "break of bulk packages." A cognate etymon: *DEDR*, 1236, Tamil, Malayalam: *kampaṭṭam*, coinage, coin, mint; Kannada: *kammaṭa*, a coiner. Cf., Greek *gammadium* and symbol which also appears on Indus seals as a Greek cross. *CDIAL*, 8253: *puṭā*, cavity, small receptacle; Kashmiri: *purī*, any small thing (esp. powder) wrapped in paper or leaves; Sindhi: *puru*, lid, cover; Assamese: *puriyā*, packet of lead; Bengal: *purā*, straw vessel for grain; Gujarati: *paree*, small packet of drugs; Marathi: *puḍī*, packet. *CDIAL*, 8255: *puṭati*, enfolds, envelops. *CDIAL*, 8254, Prākṛta: *puḍaiṇi*, lotus pond; Hindi: *purain*, lotus, lotus leaf. [Cf. lotus symbolism in *yakṣa* and *brahma* icons, which may be interpreted as alchemical symbolisms and myths.] Hyper-Sanskritisms are in *CDIAL*, 13481: *sphuṭa*, blossomed, opened; Pāli: *phuṭa*, expanded, spread out over, blossoming; Prākṛta: *phuḍa*, open, clear; Old Marathi: real, true. *CDIAL*, 13483: *sphuṭana*, bursting; Prākṛta: *phuṭṭai* is manifest.

47. J. Needham, *SCC*, vol. III, p. 672.
48. Ibid., vol. V, part II, p. 48.
49. *Chamber's Encyclopaedia*, London, 1967, p. 234.
50. P.C. Ray, *HCAMI*, p. 194.
51. Ibid., cf. 40-42, pp. 132, 180, 206.
52. J. Read, *Prelude to Chemistry*, Massachusetts, 1969, p. 63.
53. Ibid., p. 105.
54. Henri Frankfort, *The Art and Architecture of the Ancient Orient*, Harmondsworth, 1958, p. 19.
55. R.G. Chandra, *Studies in the Development of Ornaments and Jewelry in Proto-historic India*, Varanasi, 1964.
56. Hargreaves, *Excavations in Baluchistan*, *MASI*, 35, pl. XV, 7; R.G. Chandra, op. cit.
57. R.G. Chandra, op. cit., pl. IX, b to f.
58. Ibid., pl. XVII, a.
59. Ibid., pl. XXII, i, j.
60. Ibid., pl. XXXVII, g.
61. Ibid., pl. III, c to g.
62. Ibid., pl. III, b.
63. Ibid., pls. VIII, i; X, a, b.
64. Ibid., pl. XII, b, e, g.
65. Aurel Stein, *MASI* 37, p. 60, fig. 20.
66. E.J. Mackay, *Chanhu-daro Excavations*, p. 221, pl. XCII, 25.
67. Bridget Allchin and Raymond Allchin, *The Rise of Civilization in India and Pakistan*, Cambridge, 1982, pp. 195-202.
68. The proto-Indus lapidary's repertoire of skills included: moulding, beating into thin sheets, drawing wire, mixing silver and copper alloys with gold, soldering, box-plaiting the sheet, hammering designs *en*

repousse and in-laying coloured stones of faience or shell in jewellery; cf. *EH*, pls. CXXV, 51; CXXXVI, 8; CXXXIX, 7. The tools used were: harmmer stones (*FEM*, p. 393), copper blowing tubes (*FEM*, pl. CXXXII, 20), copper spatula (*FEM*, pls. CXXI, 33; CXXXII, 13), copper drills (*FEM*, p. 475, pl. CXXXI, 6), small saw, pointed chisel (*FEM*, p. 474), pottery crucibles with convex bellies (*FEM*, pl. LIII, 37).

69. R.G. Chandra, op. cit., pl. XXII, c to g.
70. Ibid., pl. XXXVIII, o.
71. Mackay, *FEM*, p. 477, pl. CXXXII, 7.
72. Cf., S. Kalyanaraman, "Indus Script and Indus Currency," *Journal of the Institute of Asian Studies*, Madras, March 1989, vol. 6, no. 2; the hypothesis is that the script signs and pictorial motifs recorded measurements of value [as deeds of conveyance or bills of lading], in quantitative and qualitative terms. Cf. an elaboration in this essay that the "cult object" may connote a sublimation tower, anticipating the *keratokis* of the Greek alchemist, Mary, the Jewess.
73. A. del Mar, op. cit., pp. 126, 471.

3

Yakṣa: Alchemical Potential and Transmutation

Alchemy and Yakṣas

Yakṣas are primordial alchemical symbols of transmutation. *Artha-śāstra* gives recipes for a variety of wines: *medaka* from rice, *prasannā* from flour of barley, *āsava* from sugarcane juice and *kapittha* fruit, *maireya* from jaggery, etc., *madhu* from grape juice and *ariṣṭa* or medicinal liquors of various kinds (2.25.17-25). Liquors were offered at funeral rites (11.1.24;12.4.4), a practice found even today among the "common" people. During festivals, permission is given for the manufacture and consumption of liquor without control (2.25.36). Wine is to be drunk in state ale-houses, which seem to be intended for providing lodging for strangers (2.25.5, 15; these are the places where the Chinese and Tibetan tantrics might have transacted, with the alchemists of the *yakṣa*-lineage, their exchanges of alchemical knowledge).

Origins of alchemy: the economic hypothesis

Well before the observance or non-observance of "Vedic sacrifices" became the determining factor to declare a group as *caṇḍāla*, it is possible that there was an economic conflict between two groups of people with alchemical potentials, to gain and retain access to mineral resources.

Here is a reconstruction, a hypothesis and an argument: the ruling-priest class consortium was engaged in building up an important economic monopoly which necessitated the exclusion of groups who had the potential to upset or even threaten the monopoly. Almost all the groups categorized as *caṇḍāla* possessed the ability to produce or participate in the production of gold and silver metals which were gaining increasing use as currency in economic transactions. The ruling-priest class endeavoured to treat the production of gold and silver metals as a state monopoly. The craze for gold, particularly among the ruling-priest classes, had reached extraordinary proportions as early as in the Vedic period, considering gold and silver to be important metals for aesthetic reasons and also due to their currency value. In *Arthaśāstra* fines are prescribed for stealing gold possessed by Brāhmaṇas, giving the impression that this class had, in league with the ruling class, monopolized the possession of this metal. This craze intensifies in course of time into alchemy and becomes a pre-occupation with many groups of people for almost two millennia.

Plan for testing the hypothesis

The historical test of the hypothesis has to proceed from *yakṣas,* traverse through the Indus valley civilization, focus on key alchemical techniques and apparatus of antiquity, unravel the Ṛgvedic allegory of *soma*, as aurifaction, decipher the *Śatapatha Brāhmaṇa* as an alchemical text for aurification, and link with the *Arthaśāstra*'s documentation of alchemy as a state enterprise. As the Yakṣa and Soma traditions converge, overlap, conflict in the historical periods, and mingle in the cross-roads of alchemical traditions from contemporary civilizations, the plebeian and "state" alchemical traditions branch into a number of channels: Buddhist tantrism, Jaina tantrism, Śaiva tantrism, Vaiṣṇava tantrism, Indo-tibetan tantrism, yoga, *siddha* and Arabic schools of alchemy. For analytical purposes, the broad streams will be tagged as: "plebeian alchemy" and "alchemy as a state-enterprise."

The trace to the *yakṣas* is crucial because, a thesis will be advanced that the icons of historical periods, sculpted in the Yakṣa tradition, with characteristic action-postures and multiple hands to carry alchemical tools and symbols and convey alchemical processes. The icons are the "silent" alphabets of the plebeian tradition.

Yakṣa: from being to becoming

Yakṣas[1] are of the underworld and as messengers, their Lord is Yama. Understanding the true nature of *yakṣa* is crucial to unravel the antiquity of the alchemical-tantric tradition, foundations of many Lokāyata doctrines and the general perceptions of underground riches, treasures and potential paths to *physical immortality*. The basic philosophical postulate is that *manussa* can become a *yakkha.* A primordial motion is from being to becoming. This movement paralleled in the flow of *rasa* gets elaborated as a generalized concept of transmutation in the alchemical tradition. The *dhātuvāda* is alchemy, based on properties of elements, components of being; the *bhūta* as a *yakṣa* is the personification of becoming, however vaguely defined.

The origins of the alchemical tradition in the Yakṣa doctrine may be inferred from an alchemical treatise attributed to Nāgārjuna: *Rasaratnākara.* Nāgārjuna reportedly acquired the secrets of alchemy after he had adored, for twelve years, goddess Yakṣiṇī, the protectress of the *Ficus religiosa.*[2]

That the priestly attitude towards the Yakṣa tradition represents counter-ideology is another story: *Baudhāyana Dharmaśāstra* (I.5.9) includes *caitya-vṛkṣa* among the list of objects which, when touched defile a person and require purification. *Kauśikasūtra* (93.3) categorizes *yakṣa* as *adbhūtāni,* creatures of ill-omen. The Vedic references are a complex of fear, dislike and respect:

> *ṚV,* IV.3.13: Do not (O Agni) consort with the *yakṣa* (?familiar spirit) of any smooth swindler, intriguing neighbour, etc.
> *ṚV,* V.70.4: Let us not, O ye gods of great power, encounter a *yakṣa.*
> *ṚV,* VII.56.16: *yakṣadṛṣo,* espying the *yakṣa.*
> *ṚV,* VII.6.15: *yakṣa,* the invisible is contrasted with *citra,* visible.
> *AV,* X.7.38: (Reference to Varuṇa, Brahman or Prajāpati as the supreme and ultimate source of Life.) A great *yakṣa* in the midst of the universe, reclining in concentrated-energy (*tapas*) on the back of the waters, therein are set whatever gods there be, like the branches of a tree about a trunk.
> *AV,* VIII.10.28: Kubera and his son are called *puṇyajana,* good folk; they milk form Viraj the power of concealment.

Gopatha Brāhmaṇa (I.1) and *Taittirīya Brāhmaṇa* (3.12.3.1) quote a Brahman: "...by concentrated energy (*tapas*) I became the primal *yakṣa.*" *AV,* X.3.43 refers to the indwelling spirit or self of man as *ātmanvat yakṣa*: "The lotus flower of nine gates, veiled by the three qualities (*guṇas*), what self-like *yakṣa* dwells therein, that (only) the Brahman-knowers know."

Proto-Indian concepts of immortality

The connection of *yakṣa* to water cosmology, Soma and Varuṇa are pointers to a unique alchemical tradition in India. The section 2 of part II of Coomaraswamy's *Yakṣas* is a magnificent analysis of water cosmology:[3]

> ...Kubera's inexhaustible treasuries are a lotus and a conch, innumerable Yakṣīs have a *makara*[4] or other fish-tailed animal as their vehicle, Kāmadeva the *makara* as his cognizance, the greater tutelary Yakshas control . . . 'that germ which the waters held first and in which all the gods exist' rose like a tree 'from the navel of the unborn,' who in the oldest passage is Varuṇa and in the *Atharvaveda* is called a Yakshā...Yakshas, then, are the Lords of Life...they are also deities closely connected with the waters, though their habitat is terrestrial. . . . Yakshas control, not so much the waters as mere waters, but that essence (*rasa*) in the waters which is one with the sap in trees, with the *amṛta* or elixir of the Devas, especially Agni, with the Soma, and with the seed in living beings . . . the importance of the Yakshas in what has often been vaguely referred to as a Life Cult, to suggest that this life cult, with which is also connected the worship of the Great Mother, may have been the primitive religion of India. . . .
>
> ...(Iranian cosmology) Ahura Mazda corresponds to Varuṇa; Anahita and Ashi, his daughters, present a close analogy with Sri-Lakshmi; the Amesha Spentas, especially Hauravatat and Ameretat, 'Health' and 'Immortality, genii of plants and waters, have much in common with the Yakshas . . . Apam Napat = Apam Napat; *haoma = soma; yasna = yajā, Zendavesta* gives us a better picture of Varuṇa than can be found in the Vedas themselves.
>
> ...we should have to go further back, to parallels such as that of Ishtar with Aditi, and of Sumerian *apsu* (the underworld sea of sweet-water) with Sanskrit *apaḥ*. . . . In Semitic and European conceptions of the Water of Life, the draught is conceived of as bestowing immortality forever. In India we meet with the more sober conception of repeated rejuvenation . . . the gods whose life is renewed by repeated draughts of *soma*, or that of human beings magically restored to life or rejuvenated by the good offices of Indra or the Asvins. All the life charms of the *Atharvaveda* are directed to restoration to health, or to longer or fuller life, never to immortality in a literal sense . . . all conceptions of well-being were thus connected with life on earth, and its perpetuation in offspring. . . . (Cf. Debiprâsad Chattopadhyaya, *Lokāyata*, on the materialist doctrines of life on earth.)

Manomohan Ghosh[5] traces the etymon: "(The root) *vṛṣ* 'to rain' and words like *vār* and *vāri* meaning water, appear to be connected with *vṛ* and this seems to give a clue to the etymology of the word Varuṇa which may be analyzed into *var*[6] and *-uṇa*. This suffix *-uṇa* is an adjective-forming one and seems to be allied in meaning with the suffix *-uṇa* found in *aruṇa, karuṇa, taruṇa* and *dāruṇa*. Varuṇa originally meant probably something like 'one who covers with water' and this suits admirably the character of the god."

Rasa and Varuṇa

Bhagavadgītā (VII.8 and XV.13) says: "I am the vital essence (*rasa*) in the waters; it is I that as *soma*, vary self of *rasa*, nourish all plants."

Many early Vedic texts will be cited in other sections to identify *soma* with the essence in the waters. In *Aitareya Upaniṣad* (I.2.3) "the waters became semen, and entered the virile member." In *Chāndogya Upaniṣad* (I.1.2) "the essence (*rasa*) of tall beings is the earth, the essence of the earth is water...."

Varuṇa and Mitra are *asurā āryā*, noble *asuras* (*ṚV*, VII.65.2); Varuṇa is an *asura* who rules and commands the gods (*AV*, I.10). "...Varuṇa's noose or fetters (*pāśa*) are called into play as penalties for sin. These fetters are drought, and the disease *yakṣma*, perhaps dropsy.... In Hillebrandt's view the Agniṣṭoma of the spring festival is offered to Varuṇa for the release of the rivers from their winter fetters."[7]

"... (*soma, amṛta*, etc. are) always conceived as contained in or drunk from a special vessel, e.g., the cup-fashioned for the gods by Tvaṣṭṛ. When the *soma* is represented in art, it is as a full vessel (cf., pl. 45, fig. 1; Varuṇa, Bādāmi), and precisely such a full or brimming vessel (*punnaghaṭa*, etc.) is the commonest of all Indian symbols of plenty...Varuṇa...is called the Lord of Vessels."[8]

A remedy for rheumatism was to induce sweating by using herbs or a steam bath. A pit filled with burning charcoal and covered with a coating of earth and sand was prepared. Specified leaves were spread on it, the patient's limbs were rubbed with oil and the patient was made to lie and to turn on the bed of leaves until the whole body was steamed. An alternative method was to use hempwater and hot baths in water seeped with medicinal herbs.[9]

Rhys Davids and William Stede in the *Pāli-English Dictionary* provide a very extensive etymological excursus, of unparalleled excellence, on *yakkha*. The following extensive quote is an important piece of philological evidence which can be related to later-day iconographic traditions and perhaps, treated as echoes of the proto-Indus beliefs: "... the customary (popular) item of Pāli commentators is *y*, as quasi gerund of *yaj*, to sacrifice, thus; a being to whom a sacrifice (of expiation or propitiation) is given. See e.g., *yajanti tatt'ha balin upaharanti ti yakkhā; pūjanīya-bhavato yakkho ti vuccati*—The term *yakṣa* as attendants of Kubera occurs already in the Upaniṣads...:

1. ... they correspond to our 'genii' or fairies of the fairy-tales and show all their qualities. In many respects they correspond to the Vedic *piśācas,* though different in many others, and of different origin. Historically they are remnants of an ancient demonology and of considerable folkloristic interest, as in them old animistic beliefs are incorporated and they represent creatures of the wilds and forests, some of them based on ethnological features....
2. Their usual capacity is one of kindness to men. They are also interested in the spiritual welfare of those humans with whom they come into contact, and are something like 'tutelary genii' or even 'angels' (i.e., messengers from another world) who will save prospective sinners from doing evil.... A somewhat dangerous 'mentor' is represented at *Dīgha,* I.95, where the Y. Vajrapāṇi threatens to slay Ambattha with an iron hammer, if he does not answer the Bhagavā. He is represented as hovering in the air...*na yo vā so vā yakkho, Sakko devarājā ti veditabbo:* it is to be understood not as this or that *y,* but as Sakka the king of *devas....* Whole cities stand the protection of, or are inhabited by *yakkhas.* . . . The female *yakkhas* seem on the whole more fearful and evil-natured than the male.... They eat flesh and blood....
3. Various classes are enumerated at *Dīgha,* II.256-57; in a progressive order they rank between *manussa* and *gandhabba* at *Aṅguttara,* II.38; they are mentioned with *devas, rakkhasas, dānavas, gandhabbas, kinnaras,* and *mahoragas* at *Jātaka,* V.420.... Some are spirits of trees (*rukkha-devatā*)...are also called *bhumma-devā* (earthly deities).... Their cult seems to originate primarily from the woods...and secondarily from the legends of seafaring merchants....
4. Their names too give us a clue as to their origin and function . . . their bodily appearance...*khara* 'rough-skin' ...*sūci-loma* 'needle-hair...place of inhabitance'...*ajakalāpaka* 'goat-bundle'...*aḷavaka* 'forest-dweller' ...*uppala* 'lotus' ...*kakudha* 'k.tree (*Terminalia arjuna*)'...*kumbhīra* 'crocodile'...*gumbiya* either 'one of a troop' (soldier of Yama) or 'thicket-er' (from

gumba thicket)...*vajira* 'thunderbolt' alias *vajirapāṇi* or *vajirabāhū serisaka* 'acacia-dweller'...*katattha* 'well-wisher' ...*dhamma* 'righteous' ...*punnaka* 'full (-moon?)'...*māra* the 'tempter' ...*sakata* 'waggon-load' (of riches)....

5. They stand in a close relationship to and under the authority of Vessavana (Kubera), one of the four *lokapālas.* They are often the direct servants (messengers) of Yama himself, the Lord of the Underworld (and the Peta-realam especially)... *dve yakkhā Yamassa dutā, Vimānavatthu,* 52...keepers (and liberal spenders) of underground riches, hidden treasures, etc. with which they delight men.... They enjoy every king of splendour and enjoyment, hence their attribute *kāma-kāmin....* Hence they possess supernatural powers, can transfer themselves to any place with their palaces and work miracles.... Their appearance is splendid, as a result of former merit...they are shy, and afraid of palmyra leaf and iron...their eyes are red and do not wink...their abode is their self-created palace (*vimāna*), which is anywhere in the air, or in trees, etc.... Sometimes we find a communion of *yakkhas* grouped in a town....
6. Their essential human character is evident also from their attitude towards the 'Dhamma.' In this respect many of them are 'fallen angels' and take up the word of the Buddha, thus being converted and able to rise to a higher sphere of existence in *saṁsāra....*
7. Exceptionally the term *yakkha* is used as a philosophical term denoting the 'individual soul' ...hence probably the old phrase: *ettāvatā yakkhassa suddhi* (purification of heart)... *yakkha-gaṇa,* 'the multitude of *ys'*... *yakkha-nagara,* 'city of *ys*... *yakkhiṇī,* adj., persecuting, taking vengeance, applied to Varuṇa at *ṚV,* VII.88; a female *yakkha,* a vampire...as a goat...eating a baby . . . singing . . . bad-coloured...*haritā,* 'charming' or from *harita,* 'green.'"

Ananda K. Coomaraswamy's *Yakṣas* provides the principal references to the tradition elaborated in the following paragraphs. A significant concordant etymon is provided in Dravidian languages: *DEDR,* 20; Kannada: *akkaja, aṛkaja,* wonder, surprise; a wonderful thing; Telugu: *akkajamu,* wonder, surprise, astonishment; Kui: *akkaja, āva* to be dumbfounded, confounded, confused through fear and awe.

Hillebrandt[10] interprets the word *yakṣa* to mean: "magician, uncouth being, unseen spiritual enemy, etc. then simply a supernatural being of exalted character." *Jaiminīya Brāhmaṇa* (III.203, 272) uses the word *yakṣa* to connote 'a wondrous thing,' analogous to the Dravidian morpheme *akkaja.* Gṛhyasūtras refer to the *yakṣas* associated with their chief, Kubera, as spirits, called *bhūtas.* Śiva is Bhūteśvara. *Mahāvaṁśa* (ch. X) refers to *yakkha-bhūta,* "those that had become *yakṣa.*" *Mānava Gṛhyasūtra* (II.14) describes them as possessing spirits of disease. *Śatapatha Brāhmaṇa* calls Kubera a *rākṣasa* and a lord of robbers and evil-doers, perhaps treating him as a proto-Aryan or aboriginal deity, alien to Brahman orthodoxy. The Sūtras invoke Kubera together with Īśāna for the bridegroom and his hosts are described as plaguing children. From spirituality to diseases, it is a big leap indeed to find in the *Rāmāyaṇa* (III.2.94) the phrase: *yakṣattva amaratvam ca,* spirithood and immortality, boons bestowed by a god or gods. *Mahābhārata* (6.41.4) categorizes *sāttvika* (pure) worshipping gods, *rājasika* (passionate) worshipping *yakṣas* and *rākṣasas,* and *tāmasika* (dark) worshipping *pretas* and *bhūtas,* thus ranking the *yakṣas* in the hierarchy between *devas* and the *bhūtas* (those who were originally humans and who have become spirits).

Arthaśāstra (II.4) states that statues of Kubera are to be set up in the crypt of a treasury. Kubera or Kuvera (Vaiśrāvaṇa, Vaiśramaṇa); also in Buddhist literature Vessavana, Pacika, Jambhāla, etc., is one of the four *mahārājas,* a *lokapāla,* Regent of the North (sometimes with Indra of the East). His city is Alaka on Mt. Kailāsa, a walled town in which dwell not only *yakṣas,* but also *kinnaras, munis, gandharvas,* and *rākṣasas.* Vaiśrāvaṇa is represented iconographically with shoulder flames. His followers possess the power of assuming any shape. Together with Maṇibhadra, he is the patron of merchants; "this may be the explanation of the status at Pawaya, set up by a guild (*goṣṭha*)."[11] Coomaraswamy also notes that Gaṇeśa with his big belly is also a *yakṣa* type. (Cf., Debiprasad Chattopadhyaya's *Lokāyata* for the Gaṇapati lores.) "Some *yakṣagrahas* (demon possessors, causing disease) are attendants of Skanda, who is sometimes called Guha, a name which may be related to the Guhyas, attendants of Kubera. *Yakṣas* (like *nāgas*) are sometimes regarded as constructive or artistic genii...it is beyond doubt that *yakṣiṇīs* were extensively worshipped, in part as beneficent, in part as malevolent beings...they do not differ essentially from their modern descendants, such as the Bengali Śītalā, goddess of smallpox, or Olabibi, goddess of cholera. The Seven Mothers (who are in part connected with Kubera), the Sixty-four Yoginīs, the Ḍākinīs, and some forms of Devī, in medieval and modern cults, must have been *yakṣiṇīs*.... Hariti is too well-known to need a long discussion.... The *Atanatiya Suttanta* (*Dīghanikāya*, III, 195f.), however, speaks of good and bad *yakkhas*.... Vessavana himself supplies to Buddha the proper invocation, and gives a list of the *yakkha* chiefs; the list includes Ind(r)a, Soma, Varuṇa, Pajāpati (cf., Prajāpati, name of a Yoginī, Patainī Devī temple), Maṇi(-bhadda), Alavaka, etc."[12] Coomaraswamy also observes that the essential element of the haunt of abode (*bhavanam*) of a *yakṣa*, is a stone table or altar (*veyaddi*, *manco*); the holystead is often referred to as a *caitya* [Pāli *cetiya*, Prākṛta *ceiya*, Tamil *ceṭi* or *āyatana* (Prākṛta *āyayana*)].

Manu (XI.96) says that "meat and intoxicating drinks are the food of *yakṣas*, *rākṣasas* and *piśācas*. . . . The prospector, before digging for treasure in northern India, makes offerings of meat, sesamum seeds, and flowers, to Kubera, Maṇibhadra, etc. (*Mahābhārata*, XIV.65.2). . . . Rites for attracting *yakṣīs* are mentioned in the *Kathāsaritsāgara*, chap. XLIX. These rites are performed in cemeteries, and are evidently Tāntrika. . . . Maitreya, the earliest Bodhisattva to be designated as such. . . . His characteristic emblem is the *amṛta* (nectar) flask, held in the left hand . . . there are both bacchanalian *yakṣas*, and bacchanalian *nāgas*, who hold a cup or flask in their hands.... (Cf., *Lalitavistara*, VI.91, 'with the Water of Life (*amṛta*) shalt thou heal the suffering due to the corruption of our moral nature.')"[13] (Cf., Jung's reference to Isis who reputedly possessed a medicine of immortality.)

Within the alchemical framework delineated so far, *yakṣas* are indeed comparable to the Taoist genii. *Yakṣas* are the beneficent powers of wealth (cf., the well-known Besnagar, the *kalpadruma* capital with a banyan tree and three money bags below its branches; a conch, lotus and jar from which square coins well up, connoting Kubera as wealth-giver) and fertility and the *amṛta* they offer is the elixir of immortality, the Water of Life or literally, *am* + *rita*, internalising the Natural Order. (Cf., the analogy of the *an*-prefix in *anvīkṣikī*, knowing of what is already known.)

Plant(?) of "immortality" from India?

Searching for the eschatalogical roots to the tradition of material immortality in China, Needham observes[14]: "...after the beginning of the fourth century the conviction everywhere spread that there were technical means whereby men could enlarge their length of days so much as to be virtually immortal, not somewhere else out of this world, nor in the underworld of the Yellow Springs, but among the mountains and forests here and for ever. Something happened after this time to strengthen greatly this belief, perhaps a message from Babylonia, Persia or India about a drug-plant, herb or medicine of immortality, even perhaps slightly misunderstood so as to interlock with Chinese world-views. The result was a great wave of activity concerned with what is sometimes called the cult of the Hsien, a distinctively material immortality in which the body was still needed, preserved in however etherealized or 'lightened' a form, whether the deathless being remained among the scenic beauties of earth or ascended as a perfected immortal to the ranks of the administration on High—in either case with the natural world suffused by the Tao of all things."

What indeed was the "drug-plant?" Elsewhere, it has been noted that *soma* had attained the notoriety of being such a "plant" in the Brahmin circles. The ritual texts were suffused with references to *soma* and the proximate links with immortality and prosperity here and now, without waiting for a disembodied other-worldly salvation. The extent to which proto-tantrism is traceable to such perceptions of "material immortality" may have to be elaborated in the context of the synthesis that emerged from Buddhism, Jainism, and the post-Vedic cults. We may with the rebel-poet Kutsa ask (*ṚV*, I.105.5 and 15): "...Where, again, the absence of *ṛta*? Where, as of old, are the *yaja* (*āhuti*) of ours?... We ask of Varuṇa, the knower of the path and the maker of food,—I utter this from my heart, let the *ṛta* be born anew (*navyaḥ jāyatam ṛtam*). Know this of me, O Heaven-and-Earth." What is the old *yaja* Kutsa is talking about? Is he lamenting that the *yaja* practised in his days had become a mere mirage, an illusion, couched in metaphysical gambol, verily forgetting what Tao calls the Order of Nature, which is a synonym of *ṛta*? The parallels among Tao, yoga, tantra and *ṛta* are so stunning and vivid, that the Tibetan links between Buddhist and Hindu tantrism may ultimately have to be traced to the links between more ancient Ṛgvedic *ṛta* and Chinese theory of Tao; between *yakṣa* and genii;

between tantric *sādhanā* and Tao *wu wei*, not inaction but "no action contrary to nature." Sivin uses a beautiful phrase to describe elixirs as "time-controlling substances." Tantra uses the term *kāla bhairava*. Could he speed up the growth of minerals and metals?

Elixir of life? Smear of life! Bhasmam, vibhūti!

The tantric Haṭhayoga techniques and mercury-based preparations were perceived as liberating or releasing from "enslavement," the united body and mind of man and physical matter. [Cf., the use of *bhasma* as body-smear by *siddhas*.] The Chinese *wai tan* related to the production of potable gold elixir; that of *nei tan* to the production of an "inner elixir" by an adept (*siddha!*) to prevent ageing. This is an analog of the microbiotic component of Chinese alchemy. While the Chinese alchemist sought to drink gold compounds for physical immortality, the Indian alchemist used the ashes after smelting operations, to smear his body imitating the ability to lend colour and lustre to base metals. One had a potable elixir; the other had a smear, a body talc![15] The woman used the red vermilion, *sindūra* for a mark on her forehead!

Indian traditions of Āyurveda relate not only to the cure of diseases but to the maintenance of health;[16] literally, it meant "the knowledge of longevity."[17] In the process of treating mercury (*rasa*) as the major divinity,[18] it became the basis of most mineral/metal-based elixirs combined with mineral and vegetable juices. A number of chemical processes were perfected, for example: oxidation, reduction, carbonation and sulphuration.[19] A typical phrase used is "tincturing;" a substance was treated with a "higher"[20] substance, containing a "higher" degree of spirit, colour or volatility. The alchemical theory is founded on the premise that it is the quality which becomes gold and it then makes gold. "But our gold which possesses the desired quality can make gold and tint [transmute] into gold. Here is the great mystery...."[21]

In the alchemical texts of the early centuries of the Christian era, the use of terms connoting "killing," "injuring," "putting to sleep" provides a possible psychological explanation on the state of mind of the alchemist. For him, some ontological distinct elements existed encouraging him to use metaphors of war. He was perhaps attempting to explain transmutation of a substance from one form to another; he had personified and deified *yakṣa* in the same manner, as a transformation from the state of being to becoming. The entire Ṛgvedic text dealing with *soma* may be seen as an allegory on the "killing" of Vṛtra.

References

1. Cf., Gananath Obeyesekere, "The impact of Ayurvedic ideas on the culture and the individual in Srilanka," in Charles Leslie, ed., *Asian Medical Systems,* Berkeley, 1976, p. 205. A sorcery ritual, an underworld charm known as the *Rīri Tīnduva* is described. "Rīri means blood and refers to *Rīti Yakka,* the blood demon. *Tīnduva* is a crucial word connoting the consummation of any ritual act. This consummation is generally achieved by cutting some object—e.g., water cutting. According to Āyurveda the five elements (earth, water, fire, air, ether) and converted into the seven *dhātus,* one of which is blood. The charm enlists the aid of the demon to destroy the enemy by casting a *diṣṭi* (look or gaze of a demon) on his blood. Since death may result, this demon is also known as *maru yakka,* death demon.... This rite culminates with the ash melon being placed on the chest of the priest and cut by a sword-wielding assistant. Thus a constellation of ideas from the medical tradition occur today in popular demonology."
2. P.C. Ray, *A History of Hindu Chemistry,* sec. edn., Calcutta, 1904-9, 2 vols.; vol. II, p. 7; *Jaiminīya Brāhmaṇa,* III.203, 272 refers to a *yakṣa* as a wondrous thing; Gṛhyasūtra interprets him as a spirit or genius.
3. A.K. Coomaraswamy, *Yakṣas,* part II, pp. 13ff.
4. Cf., Mahdihassan, "Cinnabar-gold as the best chemical drug of longevity, called Makaradhwaja in India," *American Journal of Chinese Medicine,* 1985, 13 (1-4), pp. 93-108; quote from an abstract: "A drug of longevity, prior to alchemy, was peach, from which the god of longevity has emerged. Alchemy began by synthesizing red colloidal gold with gold to make the body everlasting and redness, as soul, to make life eternal. Its climax was reached in cinnabar-gold, which is blood-red, while red-gold is only brick-red. It was called Makaradhwaja in India. There have been fertility gods. Hermes was one and Alchemy has been named a hermetic art. Makara was a crocodile-cum-fish, god of fertility. Makaradhwaja means Emblem of God of Fertility, signifying a drug conferring vigour of youth."
5. Manomohan Ghosh, "Varuṇa: His Identification," *IHQ,* vol. XXXV, no. 4, December 1895, pp. 281-94.
6. The suffix *-vara* of *urvara* (fertile) is probably connected with this *var,* and our meant "land" and is related to *urvi* (earth), and the word *urvara* originally meant "land with moisture," *DEDR,* 5356, Tamil: *vār,*

to flow, trickle, overflow; Gondi: *var*, irrigation channel.

7. A.K. Coomaraswamy, *Yakṣas*, part II, p. 27.
8. Ibid., p. 40.
9. *Vinaya*, III.205.
10. A. Hillebrandt, *Vedisch Yaksha*, in Festgabe Richard Garbe, Erlangen, 1927, loc. cit. in A.K. Coomaraswamy, *Yakṣas*, part II, p. 1.
11. A.K. Coomaraswamy, *Yakṣas*, p. 7.
12. Ibid., pp. 8-12.
13. Ibid., pp. 25-27, 32.
14. J. Needham, *SCC*, vol. 5, part II, p. 82.
15. The link between ashes and the alchemist's artificial sal ammoniac (made from goat's hair or animal excrement) will be discussed elsewhere.
16. Cf., A.J. Hopkins, op. cit., pp. 125ff.: "...Emperor Shapur (240-73)...founded and made his capital Jundi-Shapur in southern Persia [near the site of Susa, about 300 miles southeast of Baghdad and 120 miles north-northeast from (modern) Basra [*ISIS*, XVI, 1931, p. 480], and established in that city a world-famed school of medicine...[in the sixth century, the Neoplatoonists, protected by the Emperor Khusraw (Chosroes)] ...brought into Jundi-Shapur Indian medicine (and possibly, Indian physicians) to improve medical training. Probably there occurred here the first union, afterward so marked, between alchemy and medicine.... In the pinnacle of its glory, it was destroyed by the Ummayads in AD 639. We hear no more of its medical school nor of its academy."
17. *Suśrutasaṁhitā* (I.1.1): The purpose of the book is "to cure the diseases of the sick, to protect the healthy, to prolong life," cf., *Caraka*, VI.1.4. Caraka is emphatic (III.3.29-30) that life may be lengthened by human effort; and that health and disease are not pre-determined.
18. Cf., Greek tradition; A.J. Hopkins, op. cit., p. 68: "Mercury was considered a spirit. [Later writers, such as Geber and Albertus Magnus, list as spirits mercury, sulphur, arsenic, and sal ammoniac.] A spirit was said to be 'accidental,' because it does not exhibit its properties until it is associated with metals. To associate spirits with metals, it is necessary to make the metals as pure possible by subliming mercury upon them. The apparatus for this purpose was the aludel or *kerotakis*."
19. The alchemical processes are directly relatable to a theoretical framework that there was perhaps an "ultimate substance" from which the cosmos emerged. The substance may be manifested either as a liquid (*rasa*) or a powder (*cūrṇa*). The mortar or the grinding stone did not necessarily yield the *dhātu* or an alchemical element. The key process was "burning" to oxidize accretions and to reduce the *carakku* or substance to its primeval state. *Rasa* seemed to be even more

extraordinary since the "ash" could sometimes be dissolved in it.

20. Cf., A.J. Hopkins, op. cit., pp. 68ff.: "Thus lead or tin is tinctured by molybdocale (the lead-copper alloy); copper by gold; silver by gold; gold by the 'coral of gold.' The degree of excellence seems almost always to be one of colour, acting as a ferment to improve or increase all the natural colour of the metals...." The morphemes closest to the concept of tincturing are: *niṣkarṣa, kaṣāya, vyāpana, prasana.* It is notable that *niṣka* is a gold coin and *karṣa* is an antelope, a pictorial on Indus coins. Cf., also, notes on *kaṭu, kaṣau.*
21. Zosimus, cited in Berthelot, *Collection des anciens alchemists grecs,* III.VI.20: "Nothing is whitened first and yellowed later, but one whitens and yellows in one continuous operation." A.J. Hopkins, op. cit., p. 71.

4

Soma and Alchemy

The argument: Ṛgveda is a metallurgical allegory; soma is electrum ore

According to Louis Renou, the immense Ṛgvedic collection in present is nice in the themes related to *soma*. About 120 hymns out of a total of 1028 hymns or a thousand verses and almost the entire ninth book deal with *soma*. *Soma* is a material and also the only process elaborated in the *Ṛgveda*. The rest of the hymns related to Agni, Indra or other facets of Vedic life will have to be concordant with this process which seems to constitute the very essence of Vedic life, a process integral to the day-to-day living of the Vedic seeker. The *aṁśu* were pressed and processed almost like a religious act.

Soma *yajña* in Ṛgvedic days, in particular, connotes the process of parting/extracting gold and silver from *soma*, electrum ore (gold-silver pyrite ore). This may be called aurifaction in alchemical terms; the *ṛṣis* or sages who composed *ṛks* abounding in philological brilliance, perhaps believed that they were in fact producing gold.

The interpretation of the *Ṛgveda* as a metallurgical allegory, in respect of the processing of *soma*, declares a change of paradigm in Vedic studies.

The oral tradition of transmitting the knowledge of gold-smelting operations was continued over millennia to maintain secrecy. The tradition of secrecy becomes allegorical as the Brāhmaṇas and Śrautasūtras bureaucratize the process with allegorically-coded manuals for smelting operations. A nexus develops between the Brāhmaṇas and the ruling classes and the former are generally in the employ of kings, led by a *ṛtvij* and a *purohita*; and live in the same quarters of the royal palace, where goldsmiths live. The processes indicate that the alchemical tradition sustained by the ruling-priestly class-consortium was *aurifiction*; that is, the priests knew that they were not, in fact, producing gold. The state-power was used to monopolize this operation of accumulating gold and silver metals into the state treasuries.

The analysis is advanced with reference to three historical milestones, and three related facets of alchemy as an enterprise:

1. *Ṛgveda* and aurification;
2. *Śatapatha Brāhamaṇa* and aurification; and
3. *Arthaśāstra* and alchemy as a state enterprise

Soma and the dawn of Indian alchemy

P.C. Ray evaluates the contribution of *soma* to Hindu alchemy: "Even in *Ṛgveda* we find that *soma rasa* (juice of *soma* plant) has been described as an *amṛta* (allied to the Greek ambrosia), which conferred immortality upon the gods, and a medicine for a sick man. In *soma rasa* and its attributes, it may, therefore, be said that we have the dawn of Hindu alchemy. But it was during the Tantric period that the practice of alchemy reached its highest development in India."[1]

Coomaraswamy[2] extends this insight and links *soma, amṛta* and *rasa,* terms of great importance in the Indian alchemical tradition: "For *yakṣas* are primarily vegetation spirits, guardians of the vegetative source of life (*rasa* = sap in trees = *soma* = *amṛta*), and thus closely connected with the waters, cf. *ṚV,* VII.65.2 and 88.6; also *Dīghanikāya,* II.204, where Varuṇa is called a *yakṣa*; *AV,* XI.2.24: 'Thine, O Paśupati, is the *yakṣa* within the waters, for thine increase flow the waters of heaven;...(there is) the connection of the *yakṣa* and *yakṣīs* with *makaras* and other river monsters as 'vehicles.'" According to Varāhamihira,[3] the sun in its course of motion should reach the *rāśi* Makara before retracing its path [referred to as Makara-Saṁkrānti or entrance of the sun into Capricorn]; and similarly the *rāśi* limit on the southern course of motion was *karkaṭaka*; the astrological belief is that a movement without reaching either limit forebodes destruction to the south and west and to the north and east respectively. If the sun returns after crossing the two *rāśis,* welfare and prosperity of crops was promoted.[4]

These insights by indologists reinforce the pursuit of alchemical traditions in the Ṛgvedic processes related to *soma,* dealing with it as a substance.

Ṛgveda, an alchemical allegory

The argument which will be elaborated further, is simple: *soma* is electrum; *Ṛgveda* cannot be interpreted meaningfully without understanding the true meaning of *soma*; *Ṛgveda* is an alchemical, metallurgical allegory. Śulvasūtras are texts concerned with the sciences of mines and extraction of metals. The *vedi* is the metallurgist-alchemist's hearth. The so-called "cult object" seen on hundreds of Indus seals in indeed a sublimation apparatus [possibly yielding mercury from cinnabar], later-day *somanāla yantra.*[5]

Ṛgveda may, therefore, be the earliest alchemical treatise continuing the remembered metallurgical legacy—symbolized by the forge, the crucible and the *kamaṇḍalu*—of a civilization of great antiquity. The Brāhmaṇas documenting an ideology, counter to substratum tantric, Lokāyata views of nature, enshrine the earlier alchemical practices as sacrificial rituals.

"Spiritualized versions of alchemy" emerge, unique in the annals of alchemy. This spirituality, claiming direct descent from the Vedic tradition, gets ramified in two dimensions: Brahmanical tantra and yoga. Buddhism and Jainism attempt to stem the onslaught of counter-ideology by doctrinal build-up of varieties of tantra, from the folk, Yakṣa-Śakti traditions.

Soma, as a metaphorical elixir of immortality

We have drunk the *soma* and become immortal;
We have attained the light the gods discovered.
What can hostility now do against us?
And what, immortal God, the spite of mortals? (*ṚV*, VIII.48.3)

This hymn from the world's oldest recorded oral literature seems to deal with the preparation and use of an "elixir." This hymn sets the framework for tracing the Indian alchemical tradition and its science potentials. The trace will perhaps lead us to the earliest alchemical tradition of the ancient world. It is significant that in a contemporary civilization, Gilgamesh of Babylonian myths too sets out to discover eternal life and finds a miraculous plant of immortality growing at the bottom of the sea. He plucks it, leaves it unguarded. It is stolen by a water snake. Water, plant and snake symbolisms are indeed central to all alchemical traditions.

Soma is not a drink

Chāndogya Upaniṣad (V.10.4) is emphatic: *eṣa somo rājā. tad devānām annaṁ. tam devā bhakṣyanti.* [*Soma* is king. *Soma* is food for the gods. Gods eat *soma*.]

Two Vedic hymns reiterate that *soma* is not a drink of mortals:

> One thinks to have drunk *soma*, when they crush the plant. Of him (*soma*), which the Brāhmaṇas know, no one ever tastes.
>
> (*ṚV*, X.85.3; the same hymn in *AV*, XIV.1.3)
>
> O *soma*, guarded by that which is meant to cover you, guarded by him who lives in the high (heaven?), you stand listening to the pressing stones. No earthly one eats you. (*ṚV*, X.85.4)

Atharvaveda refers to the deficiency in name; this stanza is used, as a primary authority by some scholars, to justify the identification of *soma* as the moon, since *darśa* is interpreted as the slender crescent of the moon:

> O stem of *soma* (*somasyaṁśo*), lord of the combatant (*yudhām*), you are indeed not-deficient by name (*nūno nama*); make me, O first sight (*darśa*) not-deficient (*anūnam*), both by progeny and wealth.
>
> (*AV*, VII.86.3)

Soma, has the radical *su*, to press; pressing is the key process. *Soma* is that which is pressed. In the developing allegory, *soma* is seen to be released from the cover, Vṛtra or the "Aryan dragon motif"[6] or Vṛtra, who possesses the waters, using the *vajra*[7] thunderbolt. Buschardt also observes that the mountains which are Vṛtra's body are also the same on which the *soma* plants grow; Vṛtra-killing and *soma*-pressing are one and the same act; *soma*-pressing is *soma*-killing; killing signifies making him "whole" and this is creation.[8] *Vajra* is a concept related to the reducing agents: Lahiri[9] summarizes Buschardt's perceptions succinctly. "Buschardt traced the origin of the *vajra*, the weapon with which Indra kills Vṛtra, to the cultic implements,[10] the pressing stone used to crush the *soma*-stalks, or pestle. Sometimes, even *ajya* (melted butter), *sphya* (spade of *khadira* wood), *abhri* (spade), *yūpa* (posts in the sacrificial site where the victim used to be bound), the waters, etc. are styled *vajra*[11] (pp. 138ff.) ...the cult instrument which happens to be decisive at that particular moment is referred to as *vajra*. . . . *Vajra* is the cult's demon killing power as such, and Buschardt thought that the origin of *vajra* must be traced to the pressing stones which play a dominant role in the central moment of the cult, the pressing of the *soma* (p. 142). . . . At the *soma* pressing water is poured over the *soma*-stalks and hence they actually take part in the *soma* pressing, that is, *Vṛtra*-killing.... The separation of *soma* and Vṛtra becomes complete with the purified *soma* on the one side, and the crushed lifeless demon on the other. This *soma* 'lear flowing' fills up the gathering vessel.... Thus the conflict is over."

Secrecy and allegory[12]

The allegorical nature of the references to *soma* in the Vedic texts is highlighted by riddles such as *śaraṇyavan* and by references to the nature of the product:[13] One thinks himself to have drunk *soma* when they crush up a herb (*oṣadhim*[14]); what *soma* the priests (*brahmāṇo*) know, of that no earthly man partakes. Griffith induces a metaphorical meaning by equating the second reference to *soma* as the moon or perhaps, to the power of the deified *soma* juice. If *soma* could not be drunk by mortals, why search for a plant? Saṁhitās, afterall, enjoined Brāhmaṇas not to drink. *Soma* was meant for the gods, to Indra,[15] in particular, the perforated proto-Indus pottery[16] with a thousand eyes, which could hold the *kṣāra*, the mixture of curds, butter, etc. which would percolate into the electrum pellets.[17] [Indra may drink the juice; but the riches are for the sacrificer!] The verse will be meaningful if *soma* is interpreted as electrum, the processing of which has to be kept a closely-guarded secret of *madhuvidyā*. *Rasakalpa* or *Rudrayāmala Tantra* explains an analogous process to extract the essence of copper pyrites: "*Mākṣikam* (pyrites), digested hundred times with juice of plantain leaves, and then steeped for three days in oil, clarified butter and honey, and then heated strongly in a crucible yields its essence."[18]

Riddles in the Ṛgveda

There is a well-known riddle in *ṚV*, 1.164.20-22. There are two birds on a tree. One bird eats the sweet fig—*pippalam svādatty*. Some more birds in the tree sing for a portion of the *amṛta: yatrā suparṇā amṛtasya bhgāgam . . . abhisvaranti*. Many birds eat the sweet substance, *madhu*. They rear their young on the tree, where they also rest: *yasmin vṛkṣe madhvadaḥ suparṇā nivisante suvate cādhi viśve*. [Cf., the use of the same metaphor of the father and mother mounting and playing on top of the tree . . . with the little bird on the top of the tree used in the infamous references in the *Śatapatha Brāhmaṇa* to the *mahiṣi* and the "sacrificed" Aśvamedha horse; elaborated elsewhere as a metaphor.]

While attempts have been made to equate *soma* with *aśvattha* and other fig trees, the key term is *pippalam*. The morpheme is concordant with Herodotus' reference to the gold-digging ants of India: *pippalika.* The reference to *amṛta* and *suparṇa* (*suvarṇa*) nails the identification of the riddle: the birds are the metallic veins on the ore-block. *Plakṣa, nyagrodha, udumbara* are figs which find later-day textual references as ingredients in the metallurgical operations. Etymologically, *pippalam* may be related to its Dravidian radical: *paḷa,* shining; *paḷa-paḷa,* dazzling. *Pippala* is a synonym for *aśvattha* or *Ficus religiosa*; the dried leaves of the *bodhi* tree and its twigs are powdered, mixed, with certain juices and drunk as a potion reportedly good against "throbbing eyes, fearful dreams, and designs of enemies. The wood of *aśvattha* was used for *soma* vessels, and for the drill called *pramantha* that ignited the sacrificial fire."[19]

There is a fascinating story in *Rasopaniṣad*[20] the origin of which is traced to Nāgārjuna and indicating a mineralogy-alchemy nexus: "The sage Nāgārjuna had the vision of a magical procedure: in the southern kingdom of Kerala, where there are so many forests, not far from the sea, in a village named Affection (*prīti*), thence they extract rocks in the shape of *pippalis* that have deposits of gold. They are taken and reduced to soft powder. This powder is treated with horse blood; it is liquefied seven times by means of human blood; it is ground again in the water of the basilisk with the five products of the cow; then it is dried in accordance with the rules so that it forms a sort of paste, which is passed through a sieve; into the liquid obtained, a hundredth part (?) of copper is put; each part of this copper thus treated is doubled; the whole is melted together and combined with a portion of gold; it is mixed with honey, milk, etc.; thus one obtains a magnificent gold, as bright as river gold."

Another riddle relates to the story of Atharvan and his son, Ṛṣi Dadhyac who are regarded as the earliest institutors of sacrifices.[21] Aśvins gave the head of a horse to Dadhyac. Indra had warned Dadhyac that his head would be cut off if he revealed to anyone the mystic *madhuvidyā*—the true nature of *soma.* Dadhyac imparted this knowledge to Aśvins. Indra then cut his head off and the bones of the head were converted into a thunderbolt. Indra used the thunderbolt to slay Vṛtra who withheld the waters. Armed with the bones, found at Śaraṇyavana (lake near Kurukṣetra, adds the commentator), Indra found what he sought: "Then verily they recognized the essential form of Tvaṣṭṛs bull here in the mansion of the moon." What was Śaraṇyavana? One possibility is that this refers to a coded phrase combining *kṣāra* and *lavaṇa.*[22]

Vāk (*ṚV,* X.125; synonym: Saraswatī, goddess of learning or speech) says: "I give wealth unto him who gives sacrifice...." What was the sacrifice, the secret science which the Vedic seers were explaining through their mystical chants? If *Ṛgveda* is viewed as a metallurgical allegory, an alchemical tract, the myth unravels vividly Soma *yajña* and *madhuvidyā*! The Vedic texts are suffused with an extraordinary passion for secrecy—*satyasya satyam* ('secret' word). Jitendra Nath Banerjea,[23] approvingly cited Deussen's interpretation of Upaniṣad: "Sitting down at the feet of a teacher to receive secret instruction: hence a secret conversation or doctrine."

The mākṣikā, fly, betrays the secret of soma

While the allegorical texts and riddles almost succeed in guarding the secrets, one vivid clue to the riddle occurs in the following Ṛgvedic hymn:

> *uta syā vām madhuman mākṣikārapan madey somasyausijo huvanyati.*
> [To you, O Aśvins, that fly betrayed the Soma.] (*ṚV,* 119.9)

What links exist between Aśvins, the *mākṣikā,* fly and *soma?* The *mākṣikā,* fly does indeed unravel the Vedic secret. In Egyptian hieroglyphic, the bee connotes a small authority and kingship. In Gondi language, *mas phukī* means a bee.[24] More important, etymological, evidence is that *mākṣikā*[25] are pyrites. They are of two types: *hema mākṣikā* and *tāra mākṣikā* (gold and silver pyrites). *Soma* is a pyrite, gold-silver ore, *asem, asemon, electrum* (cf. *ayas,* metal).

Mākṣikā, the fly, the pyrite ore, is the mineral-ore which yields *soma,* electrum. [A related etymon is notable: *āśātika* means "egg of fly or other insect," *nit* (BHSkt.); fly's egg, *nit* (Pāli); *āsāḍī, asāḍī, āsāḍī, āsḍī, asḍī,* spawn of files settling on a wound, fly-blow, maggots (Marathi) (*CDIAL,* 1489); *admasad,* fly (*ṚV,* I.124.4) (alternative meaning: "guest at a meal"); *aũso* maggot, insect, worm (Nepali); *aṁśāi,* maggot in a wound, grub appearing in a stale cowdung (Oriya) (*CDIAL,* 241). This etymon is homonymous with the *āṣāḍha* brick which is referred to as *svayam-ātṛṇṇa* or self-perforated in the Brāhmaṇa literature. The imagery is vivid: *mākṣikā,* the fly or pyrite ore, impregnated with gold or silver (electrum) nuggets like flies settling on a wound, appearing like a perforated brick! The *āṣāḍha* brick is of fundamental importance in the grand sacrifice, officiated among others, by the queen. Āṣādha, the Malaya mountain; the month, commencing with the sun's entrance into Gemini (June-July); *āsaḍa, āsaḍi, asaḍi, aṣāḍha,* id.; a staff of *palāśa* wood carried by an ascetic (or student) on the day of full moon of the month Aṣāḍha; *āṣāḍhi,* the day of full moon in the month Āṣāḍha; the plant *Asparagus racemosus* (Kannada *lex.*). In the context of the allegorical elucidation of Vedic and Brāhmaṇa texts, semantic link between *mākṣikā* and *āṣāḍha* (the fly and the maggots) is indeed remarkable: one connotes the pyrite ore and the other the protrusions of gold-silver electrum pallets in the mineral ore block which is subjected to a refining process to extract the valuable metal, *soma* electrum!]

Armed with this cracked code, *Atharvaveda* (*AV*, IX.6) can be interpreted as providing the clearest statement on the smelting process of the Soma *yajña* which is echoed in later-day alchemical texts:

> ...the shed for housing the *soma* cars...green sticks that surround the sacrificial altars (as a fence to restrict the range of fire).... The grains of rice and barley that are selected are just filaments of the *soma* plant. The pestle and mortar are really the stones of the *soma* press. The winnowing-basket is the filter, the chaff the *soma* dregs, the water the pressing-gear. Spoon, ladle, fork, stirring prong are the wooden *soma* tubs; the earthen cooking pots are the mortar-shaped *soma* vessels; this earth is just the black-antelope's skin.... The man who supplies food hath always pressing stones adjusted, a wet *soma*, filter, well-prepared religious rites . . . he who hath this knowledge wins the luminous spheres.

Ayas and alloys

Ṛgveda recounts how Tvaṣṭṛ uses the sharp axes made by him to fashion bowls to hold the *amṛta.*[26] *Āyasi vāsi* is a copper celt, a weapon of Tvaṣṭṛ[27] who is also associated with the copper axe, *āyasa paraśu.*[28] Tvaṣṭṛ is a key personage linking alchemical and other crafts to manual operations, as distinct from the tendency of the counter-ideology to deify or state in metaphysical terms.[29] *Chāndogya Upaniṣad* (IV.17) provides evidence of alloying metals: gold in joined by salt, silver by gold, zinc by silver, lead by zinc, iron by lead, wood by iron and leather.[30] The Ṛgvedic term *ayodaṁṣṭra* (*agni*) is interpreted as "with teeth of *ayas.*" The morpheme *ayas* is used to describe the car-seat of Mitra and Varuṇa as *ayosthūṇa* "with pillar of *ayas.*"[31] Chakraborty interprets *ayas* as bronze. In *Vājasaneyisaṁhitā* days, however, three terms are used to specify bronze, iron and copper: *ayas, śyāma* and *loha; Atharvaveda* (IX.5.4; XI.3.7) uses the compound *śyāmāyasa; Chāndogya Upaniṣad* (IV.17.7) refers to *kārṣṇāyasa* and also *ayas*. Citing Schrader, Chakraborty[32] opines that *loha* which originally denoted copper was later used for iron. *Śatapatha Brāhmaṇa* (II.11.5) *lohāyasa* may therefore, connote a copper-alloy. Suryakanta[33] interprets *loha* to mean "reddish" and *loha-mani* as a "lump of gold" and *loha-pacanīya* as a means of testing which reddens a jar on being baked. The morpheme *ayas* parallels Greek *aes*, metal, alloy,[34] and is phonetically proximate to *assem*, *soma*.

Identification of soma

Wasson,[35] proceeding on the premise of Ṛgvedic textual evidence that *soma* is not a plant, identifies it as a mushroom[36] which after processing, yields a spirituous liquor. The most recent survey of the literature which includes efforts at identifying *soma* is contained in Harry Falk.[37] Falk refutes[38] Wasson's thesis and provides new insights to revive an earlier identification of *soma* as the "ephedra plant." Wendy Doniger O'Flaherty includes a survey, "The post-Vedic history of the *soma* plant," in part Two of Wasson's book.[39] In this exhaustive survey, O'Flaherty provides a list of high-sounding[40] names of plants, grasses, creepers, herbs, beverages, drugs which had been tagged to identify *soma*.[41] The list reads like a mini-materia medica! She also notes that epithets used equate *soma* in metaphorical terms with: *śyenhṛta* (brought by a falcon); *śvetākṣa* (white-eyed); *aṁśuman* (smells like ghee); *muñjara* (like garlic leaves).

In this context, it may be apposite to recall a message contained in Leiden papyrous (Papyrus V of the Egyptian civilization: cited in Berthelot, *Collection des Anciens Alchimistes Grecs*, 1924, p. 82): "Interpretation drawn from the sacred names, which the sacred writers employ for the purpose of putting at fault the curiosity of the vulgar. The plants and other things which they make use of for images of the gods have been designated by them in such a way that for lack of understanding they perform a vain labour of following a false path. But we have drawn the interpretation of much of the description and hidden meanings." *Soma* as a metallurgical allegory, see Yāska's interpretation of gods' names in his *Niruktam*.

Soma as a metaphor of the moon or the sun

The allegorical identification of Hillebrandt[42] relates *soma* to the moon. Oldenburg criticizes Hillebrandt and notes that if *soma* has to be connected with a heavenly body, it is the sun to which it should be related.[43]

Proto-Indus and the sun symbol

Treating the *Ṛgveda* as an allegorical tract, which records the faint memories of proto-Indus metallurgy of the lapidary, this allegorical identification of Oldenburg is remarkable, in the context of a hypothesis tracing the *Ṛgvedic* legacy to the Indus civilization; for, the proto-Indus seals do provide vivid evidences of solar symbolism.

Soma is *giriṣṭhā;*[44] it is plucked from the rock by the falcon (*ṚV,* I.93,6; cf. *ṚV,* IV.85.2, *somam adraus*). Hence, the search for plant that grows on mountains! That ores grow on mountains provide the direct semantic content of the allegory. *Śatapatha Brāhmaṇa* equates *soma* to *usāṇā,* a term which has also been interpreted in the context of mineralogy. R.S. Singh[45] links the term to *uṣa,* salty ground and looks for a plant growing on alkaline earth. C.G. Kashikar[46] refutes this and seeks the semantic radical *vas* to shine, since the colours of *soma*—tawny, ruddy and brown—mean shining. *ṚV,* X.30.9 uses the term *ausāna* which may be related to the term *usāṇā* of the Brāhmaṇas.[47]

Soma/Haoma

Both *soma* and *haoma* are linked with the waters. *Soma* is closely linked with the fire or *agni. Haoma* is linked to Zoroastrian fire temples.[48] Both are yellowish; the terms used for *soma* and *haoma* are: *hari/zairi* yellowish; *aruṇa/aruṣa* reddish. The *soma* juice is *babhru,* greyish brown.[49]

Haoma has a good scent (*hu-baoioi;* Yasna, 10.4). Śrautasūtras[50] add a smell to *soma.* For the pressed *soma, ṚV,* IX.107.2 uses the epithet *surabhintara.*

Haoma is believed to be an imperishable plant; in burial rites, the Pārsis "poured a few drops of the consecrated *haoma* juice into the mouth of (a) dying person."[51] Epithets used in the *Ṛgveda*[52] for *soma* are: *amṛtam* imperishable, living, life. *Soma* is called an "ancient" (*pratnāsaḥ; ṚV,* IX.98.11).

Dubs[53] observes that the ancient intoxicating sacred drink (Indian *soma,* Iranian *haoma*) was regarded as in some sense an elixir of immortality. [The Chinese extensions of alchemy into microbiotics, may also be relatable to the *soma/haoma* traditions of contemporary civilizations.] "But in general it must be said that the parallels which can be adduced (between China and Indian myth and religion) remain always vague and uncertain, while the whole atmosphere and intellectual climate of Chinese thought is radically different from either the Indian or the Persian."[54]

A few key morphemes such as *aṁśu*[55] (comparable to *asu* of *haoma*), *virudh,*[56] *oṣadhi*[57] and the link with the watery element leads scholars to search for a substitute "plant"[58] to be used in the rituals.

The morpheme, *oṣadhi* is closely associated with the smiths and with alchemists; and need not, therefore, be interpreted as a "plant" or "herb" in all references. For example, the morpheme used in Patañjali's *Yogasūtra* (IV.1) has been interpreted to mean an elixir of long life, obtained through *rasāyana.* The *Ṛgveda* (X.72.2) sustains the tradition of *oṣadhi* (vegetable juices?[59]) in the possession of smiths in the phrase: *jaratibhiḥ oṣadhibhiḥ.*[60]

Falk brings out the contrasts between *soma* and *haoma*: *haoma* is not needed for a particular god; *soma* is for Indra. *Haoma* is an energizing offering to different gods. "This tendency of *soma/haoma* to look for a suitable place in already existing mythologies proves to my mind that the mythological qualities of *soma/haoma* did not stand at the beginning of its career. If what we have is not mythology which needed a plant, but a plant which was given places in mythologies, then it is legitimate to expect one single plant *soma/haoma.* This plant should have some properties which explain why it was thought fit to join the gods."[61]

That *soma* might have been a hallucinogen[62] is surmised from a later-day hymn of the *Ṛgveda* (X.119.8), called the Labasūkta. This refers to a winged creature[63] which touches the sky and earth with its wings and extends even beyond, after consuming *soma: abhi dyam mahinā bhuvam abhimām pṛthivīm mahīm.* Rejecting this and adverting to the possibility of *soma* being a stimulant (hence *ephedra*),[64] which prevents sleep: *jāgṛvir* alerting drink (*ṚV*, X.34, 1), Harry Falk cites Windfuhr[65] who argues that *soma* is neither hallucinogenic nor intoxicant.

Poetic degrees of freedom

Ṛgvedic hymns are philological tracts *par excellence.* Hillebrandt notes the poetic, lyric potential created by *soma.* It is the procreator of thoughts (*janitā matīnām*; *ṚV*, IX.95.5). The poet *soma* procreates the thought (*janayam matim kaviḥ somo*; *ṚV*, IX.107.18). *Soma* is *ṛṣikṛt* (*ṚV*, VIII.44.29), a maker of seers. Indra kills Vṛtra and places the sun (*soma*) in the sky (*ṚV*, II.11.5). Indra gives light to the *āryas* (*apāvṛṇor jyotir āryāya*; *ṚV*, II.11,18). *Haoma* is never referred to as sweet. *Soma* is referred to as *madhu*, sweet and also as *tīvra*, sharp (*ṚV*, I.23.1). *Soma* is referred to as a young man (*yuvan*; *ṚV*, IX.67.29).

The poetic treatise on Soma *yajña* is an allegorical treatise. Hence, Yāska's explanation of "deities" in his *Niruktam*, a magnificent etymological work of very ancient times. Hillebrandt and Oldenburg expatiate on the metaphorical connotations admirably and their perceptions (treating *soma* as a metaphor for the moon or the sun respectively) are too well-known to require repetition.

The notable reference to the "retinue" *gaṇa* may be recalled from the Śrauta ritual:

> *indav indrapītasya ta indriyāvato gāyatrachandasaḥ sarvagnasya sarvagaṇa upahūta upahūtasya bhakṣayāmi.*
> [Of thee, O *soma*, that are drunk by Indra, of thee that containest vigour, that hast the Gāyatrī for metre, that art accompanied by the whole troop, that art invited, I partake, being accompanied by my whole troop and having invited.] (*PB*, 1.5.4; cf. 1.6.1, 13, 16)

Indra and Bṛhaspati are called *gaṇapati* (*ṚV*, II.3.1; X.112.9); Bṛhaspati is *sarvagaṇa* (*ṚV*, 5.51.12). The verse in the Śrauta ritual relates to the Atirātra; which may be deemed a reference to the smelting process which has to be undertaken, day and night.

That Soma *yajña* was an "industry" of no mean order is apparent even from the Ṛgvedic days. An analysis of the "industrial" processes is crucial to interpret the reality of the Ṛgvedic artisans' lives.

Provenance of soma

Soma comes from the mountains.

> ...plant from the mountain (*giriṣṭhām*)...(*ṚV*, V.43.4); ...born on the mountain top (*girā*)...the *soma* juice is placed for Indra (*ṚV*, IX.62.15); ...(this *soma*)...that grows in the mountain (*parvatāvṛdham*)...(*ṚV*, IX.71.4)...at the navel of the Earth (*nabhā pṛthivyā*), in the mountains (*girīśi*), (*soma*) has placed his residence...(*ṚV*, IX.82.3).... In the firmament of heaven the seers milk...the bull-*soma* seated on the mountain top (*ṚV*, IX.85.10).... Here is the flow of *soma* that is come from within the most distant mountain (*adreḥ*)...(*ṚV*, IX.87.8).... This (*soma*)...(this) stalk (*aṁśu*), (this) bull seated on the mountain top...(*ṚV*, IX.95.4).... This *soma* juice, god (himself), sitting on the mountain (*devo devī giriṣṭhā*)...(*ṚV*, IX.98).

No plant, not even the fly-agaric mushroom grows in the navel of the earth! What is this *soma* that does so? *Adreḥ* also means a stone; is *soma* derived from deep within the stone? *Aṁśu* is the key word which recurs again and again as an epithet of *soma*. It is interpreted as a stalk, assuming that *soma* is a plant. It can also denote the metallic protrusions and veins of an ore-block. The Vedic texts and also the Brāhmaṇa literature make no mention of the process of cultivation or of the gathering of un-purified *soma*. One conjecture is that "the Indo-Aryans, having conquered only the valleys did not control their *soma* supply. The mountains were still held by their enemies, probably the Dasyus, the hated and despised dark-skinned Dasyus. Under the circumstances, there could be no ceremony attending the gathering of the sacred *soma*, such as had perhaps attended it in the homeland.... In the *Śatapatha Brāhmaṇa* (as well as elsewhere) there is an account, absurd by our standards, of the ceremonial purchase, complete to speckled cane to beat the seller with, wherein a cow of a particular hue of skin and eye is exchanged for the Sacred Element. (Eggeling translation, part II, pp. 66ff.)"[66]

Colour of soma

Soma is not black, nor grey, nor green, nor dark, nor blue in colour. [Were it a mushroom, subjected to incessant fire, during the sacrifice performed day and night, it would have been reduced to a charcoal-black colour!] The frequently used epithet is *hari*. *Hari* is *hiraṇya* or golden. The embellishing terms used are: brilliant, dazzling, flaming—to denote the intensity of the colour which might have been within the spectrum from red to light yellow. *Hari* connotes enhancement; *hari* is Viṣṇu; *soma* is also *vṛṣa* the bull, the bull which is red, *vṛṣa sono* (*ṚV*, IX.97.13). Other epithets used are: *aruṇa*, reddish, bright brown, golden-yellow, red of the morning sun; *aruṣa*, red, fire-colour, dawn; *babhru*, reddish brown, tawny. *Soma* is radiant.

By day he appears *hari* (colour of fire), by night, silvery white (*ṚV*, IX.97.9). [A remarkable parallel to electrum, gold-silver ore.]

With unfading vesture (*vāsasā*), brilliant, newly clothed, the immortal (*amartyo*) *hari* wraps (*nirnijānaḥ*) himself all around. By authority he has taken the back (i.e., the vault) of heaven to clothe himself in, a spread-cloth like to a cloud.... (*ṚV*, IX.69.5)

Aggressive as a killer of peoples he advances, bellowing with power.

He sloughs off the Asurian colour (*asuryam varṇam*) that is his. He abandons his envelope, goes to the rendezvous with the Father. With what floats he makes continually his vesture-of-grand-occasion (*nirnijam*) (*ṚV*, IX.71.2). [The artisan is not referring to colour when the term *asuryam varṇam* is used; he is denoting the radiance linked to *asurā* the *yakṣa* divinities. *Nirnij* is *robe d'apparat* according to Renou. That the *yakṣa* tradition may be traced to the Indus civilization in another story; the so-called "priest-king" statuette of the Indus civilization is depicted wearing a tri-foil garment, interpreted by Asko Parpola as a sky garment. The trefoil patterns may have been inlaid with red colour.]

Soma has a costume. This costume is linked to the milk of the cows (possibly a reference to white-coloured silver pyrites on electrum). In another imagery, *soma* is like a serpent who creeps out of his old skin: *ahir na jūrṇam ati sarpati tvacam* (*ṚV*, IX.86.44). *Soma* is golden; the vesture is a vivid poetic imagery that envelops the colour which is the key characteristic. An epithet of *soma* is *sahasrapājas* (*ṚV*, IX.13.3 and 42.3) interpreted as thousand forms or colours or rays or studs. It is an ore with a thousand metallic veins shooting out its rays. "The *soma* rests his well-appointed birth-place. The hide is of bull, the dress of sheep," *a yonim somaḥ sukṛtam ni sīdati gavyayī tvag bhavati nirnig avyayī* (*ṚV*, IX.70.7). What a magnificent costume for *soma*! The bellows are made of red-coloured ox-hide and fluffy tufts of white sheep's wool (or as ingredients to produce artificial sal ammoniac[67]). The remarkable evocation of the smelting apparatus is strengthened by referring to *śṛṅge sisāno hariṇī*, the golden-coloured horns which harden the soft molten metal.

Aṁśu of soma

Aṁśu is the principal attribute of the shape of *soma*. *Aṁśu* means a shoot. When *soma* is interpreted as a plant, *aṁśu* is interpreted as a stalk. Since *soma* is electrum ore, *aṁśu* can as well denote the metallic shoots of the ore, *aṁśu* is not the teat of a cow; but is compared with it, as yielding the liquid, by milking:

tam vām dhenum na vāsarim aṁśum duhanty adribhiḥ somam duhanty adribhiḥ.
(*ṚV*, I.137.3)

[The priests milk this *aṁśu* for you both (Varuṇa and Mitra, two gods), like the auroral milch cow, with the aid of stones they milk the *soma*, with the aid of stones. (The intriguing reference to *adribhiḥ* or "with stones" can be explained since *soma* is electrum ore which has to be crushed down to powder from metallic ore-blocks.)]

Indra is farther than this seat when the milked *aṁśu*, the *soma*, fills him. When the swollen *aṁśu* were milked like cows with (full) udders.... (*ṚV*, VIII.9.19)

They milk the tendering (*stanayantam*; *stan* to roar or to thunder; *stana* also means breast) *aṁśu*.... (*ṚV*, IX.72)

They milk the *aṁśu*, this bull at home on the mountain. (*ṚV*, IX.95.4)

[The link between the bull and milking becomes meaningful since *soma* is electrum ore with "horns," or metallic protrusions.]

Soma as a material-in-process

A number of *ṛks* can be reviewed to evaluate *soma* as a raw material, as a material-in process and as a processed product itself. The majesty is portrayed in its flow: as *soma* flowed through the filter, it is likened to Parjanya, the god of thunder, the father of *soma* (*ṚV*, IX.82.3).

It may be easy to enumerate what *soma* is not: *Soma* is not a plant grown in the valleys; it came from the high mountains; it could not have been *bhaṅga* or marijuana, hemp or *haśīśa* (*Cannabis sativa*) which grow on the plains. It is not a substance for fermented drink; it could not have been *rhubarb.* It is not a substance for fermented drink; it could not have been *rhubarb.* It is not a cultivated plant; there is no mention of its cultivation. If it was a plant that could be grown, there is no mention of any gardens of the priests growing such a plant. The Ṛgvedic hymns of early dates do not refer to the roots of *soma*; there is no reference to the leaves of *soma*; blossoms of *soma* are not mentioned; seeds of *soma* are not recorded.

Soma is not a man-made material; it is a naturally-occurring or a divine product:

nṛcakṣasaḥ pitaro garbham ā dadhuḥ.

[The (gods, whose) fathers with a commanding glance, laid the (Somic)....] (*ṚV*, IX.83.3)

Soma is *ṛtasya jihva* (*ṚV*, IX.75.2), the tongue of the way. Bergaigne[68] interprets this as a picturesque statement, connoting a prayer. The way is *ṛta*, the divine order of things. How is *soma* equated with the tongue? This metaphor is extraordinary and brilliantly connotes the nature of the substance with its metallic protrusions or hanging tongues of ore. It is also a product of nature; the outcrop of the Order of Nature, *ṛta.* Another imagery may be that *soma*'s tongue like *agni*'s tongues of fire roars forth into Indra, within the smelter-filter apparatus.

Soma is not, *surā*, it is not a fermented drink. This epithet is never used to denote *soma. Surā* is used in the context of undesirable phenomena: "Malice has not been of my own free will, O Varuṇa; it was *surā*, anger, dice, a muddled head." (*ṚV*, VII.86.6.) *Soma* is not a drink for the mortals. There is no mention in the *Ṛgveda* that *soma* was drunk by ordinary people.

Ṛgvedic *soma* may antedate Avestan *haoma*. The references to plants in the Brāhmaṇas and the interpretation of *haoma* as ephedra may indeed be to substitutes of the original *soma* after its sources got depleted, for whatever reasons. Darmesteter who has provided a German rendering of *Avesta* believed that Hoam Yast, in *Yasna* 9, 10 and 11 in adoration of *haoma*, was a later-day interpolation (between 140 BC and AD 50). *Yasna* 10.5 refers only to the trunks, branches of stems of *haoma*: "Grow by my word in all thy trunks, in all thy branches, in all thy stems."[69] The Pahlavi terms used by H.W. Bailey to explain the term *varesṣaji* were *bun*, stalk or trunk and *advan*, stalk.

Soma is like a rain of stones:

> While *soma* enters into contact with the fingers of the officiants, he protects his head (*śiras*).
> *ruvati bhīmo vṛṣabhas tavisyaya śṛṅge sisāno.* (*ṚV*, IX.68.4)
> [An apparent reference to the pressing of the ore with stones held in hand and the need to avoid the ore-stone fragments which may hit the artisan's head.]

Soma has horns:

> He (*soma*) bellows, terrifying bull, with might, sharpening his shining horns, gazing afar.... (*ṚV*, IX.70.7)
> *Soma* with sharpened horns (*tigma śṛṅgo*), i.e., *soma* the bull attains his (full) reach. (*ṚV*, IX.97.9)

Soma is not a plant with thorns; it was a lump of ore with pointed metallic protrusions (sharpened horns).

> *sahasra bhṛṣṭir jayati sravo bṛhat.* (*ṚV*, IX.86.40)
> [With his thousand knobs, he conquers mighty renown.]
> This bull, heaven's head (*mūrdhan*), *soma*, when pressed, is escorted by masterly men into the vessels, he the all-knowing. (*ṚV*, IX.27.3)

The company kept by soma

Soma keeps company with Indra and Agni. If *soma* is a plant or even a mushroom, with incessant firing, day-in and day-out for several days, it will be reduced to the state of pure carbon. So, the incessant drinkers of *soma* are only gods, Indra and Vāyu who drink *soma* pure or mixed with milk or curds.

> ...Here is the *soma* (that) pressed in the vat is poured around inside the cup, he dear to Indra, to Vāyu.... I Vāyu, arrive hither for the invitation, accepting it, to share in the oblation! Drink (of the juice) of the pressed stalk, up to (thy full) satisfaction!... Indra and thou, Vāyu, ye have a right to drink of these pressed (stalks). Accept them, immaculate ones, for (your full) satisfaction! . . . Pressed for Indra, for Vāyu, have been the *soma* plants (*somāso*) requiring a mixture of curds. (*ṚV*, V.51.4-7)
>
> Enter into the heart of Indra, *soma*'s receptacle, like the rivers into the ocean, thou, (O *soma*) who pleasest Mitra, Varuṇa, Vāyu, O thou supreme Mainstay of the sky! (*ṚV*, IX.108.16)
>
> [The reference to the receptacle placed within Indra leads to a plausible interpretation of Indra as a pottery vessel, possibly perforated.]
>
> The waves of *soma pavamāna* advance into the *belly of Indra.* (*ṚV*, IX.81.1)
>
> Cleansed like a winning race horse, thou hast spilled thyself in the *belly of Indra,* O *soma*! (*ṚV*, IX.85.5)

When *soma* is interpreted as a substance, the associated Indra and Vāyu lose their personality and the latter can, therefore, be treated as metaphorical references to the apparatus of a smelter-filter and the air-flow from the bellows used to blow the refiner's fire. It may not, therefore, be necessary to deify and use capital letters for a number of morphemes in the Ṛgvedic texts. Deities are allegorical surrogates of a smith-lapidary's devices.

Indra—a component of the lapidary's filter apparatus

> The inebriating drinks (*madāso madirāsa)*, swift, are released ahead, like teams running in divers directions, like the milch cow with her milk towards her calf; so the *soma* juices, waves rich in honey (*madhumanta ūrmayaḥ*), go to Indra, thunderbolt carrier (*vajrinam indram indavo*). (*ṚV*, I.86.2)
>
> O *soma pavamāna* . . . penetrate into the entrails of Indra. (*ṚV*, IX.76.3)
>
> O *soma,* advance into the belly of Indra, having been held in hand by the officiants, pressed by the stones! (*ṚV*, IX.109.18)
>
> O *soma,* thou clarifiest thyself for Indra.... (*ṚV*, IX.80.2)
>
> In the belly of Indra the inebriating *soma* clarifies itself (*indrasya kukṣā pavate madintama*). (*ṚV*, IX.80.3)
>
> ...the (officiants)...draw the *soma* by milking into the belly of Indra (*indrasya somam jathare yad āduhuḥ*). (*ṚV*, IX.72.2)
>
> The Atharvans have mixed milk with thy sweetness, longing for the god,

the god (Soma) for the god (Indra). Cleanse the *soma*, pressed out by the hand-worked stones: dilute the sweet one in the sweetness (milk or water). Approach with reverence; mix him with curds, put the *soma* juice into Indra. (*ṚV*, IX.2.5-6)

The beautiful plant beloved of the gods, (the *soma*) washed in the waters, pressed by the masters, the cows season (it) with milk. Then like drivers (urging) on a horse, they have beautified (the *soma*), the juice of liquor for drinking in common, for the immortal one (Indra). (*ṚV*, IX.62.5-6)

All the gods drink this *soma* when it has been mixed with milk of cows and pressed by the officiants. The prize-winning *soma* has flowed, in a thousand drops cleansed by the waters, mixed with the milk of cows. O *soma*, march ahead toward Indra's bellies, having been held in hand by of officiants, pressed by the stones! (*ṚV*, IX.109.15, 17-18)

The reference to Indra are metaphorical references to belly, and entrails. Indra "drinking" *soma* is relatable to Indra as a bigger container within which a *soma* vessel is inserted. It is plausible to treat Indra as an allegorical reference to a pottery component of the smelting apparatus; his act of "drinking" *soma* is a metaphorical representation of the smelting process, facilitated by a "thousand" holes on the perforated-pottery, a characteristic find in proto-Indus sites.

Other partners of soma: Sūrya and Agni

Soma is dazzling, bright, shining, like the sun and golden fire.
The *soma* envelops himself all around with rays of the sun.... (*ṚV*, IX.86.32)

...by a thousand paths free of dust, *soma*, armed with verses, knowing the word, the sun passes the filter (*ṚV*, IX.91.3). [*Soma* is the sun resplendent.]

(*Soma*) who has for eye the sun (*ṚV*, IX.97.46). [The eye is a metaphorical reference to the metal contained in the ore, which is elsewhere compared to the sun in colour and brightness.]

Light has come to the plant (shoots) (*abhūd u bhā u aṁśave*), a sun equal to gold (*hiraṇyam prati sūryaḥ*).... (*ṚV*, I.46.10)

He (*soma*) wraps himself around with the rays of the sun. (*ṚV*, IX.86.32)

(Once) born, thou (*soma*) doest fill the sun's ray (*ṚV*, IX.97.31)

O *soma* juice...go bellowing to the sun's ray. (*ṚV*, IX.97.33)

Here he is, racing with the sun, *pavamāna* in the sky. (*ṚV*, IX.27.5)

Thou hast made the sun to mount the sky. (*ṚV*, IX.86.22)

He (*soma*) has made the sun to shine. (*ṚV*, IX.28.5)

The juice has engendered light for the sun. (*ṚV*, IX.97.41)
Thine, O *pavamāna*, are the lights, the sun. (*ṚV*, IX.86.29)
He (*soma*) joins forces with the sun's. (*ṚV*, IX.61.8)
Pavamāna has hitched *etasa* (the sun's steed) to the sun.... (*ṚV*, IX.64.7)
(*Soma*) races against the rays (of the sun), vehicle beautiful to see, celestial vehicle beautiful to see. (*ṚV*, IX.111.3)
Purify thyself with this stream by which thou (*soma*) modest the sun to shine. (*ṚV*, IX.63.7)
(The *soma*'s flowing liquor) like the rays of the sun. (*ṚV*, IX.64.7)
He has clothed himself with the fire-bursts of the sun. (*ṚV*, IX.71.9)

The ties between *soma* and *agni*, refiner's fire are so intense that "Bergaigne even went so far as to advance the hypothesis that the two (*soma* and *agni*) had been interchangeable." Soma is called Agni (*ṚV*, IX.66.19-21; 67.23-24). Soma is the child of the thunder-storm, its brilliance is like lightning or the fire caused by lightning and its liquid nature is like the rain. The Vedic artisan prays to Soma, "make me to burn like fire started by friction." (*ṚV*, VIII.48.6)

Allegory of soma: alchemical transmutation?

That the account of *soma* as a process, is an allegory is reinforced by the references to two forms (dual, not plural):

Cleanse thyself, O (thou) to whom all peoples belong, for all wondrous deeds, the praiseworthy god, the friend for the friends, with those two forms (dual, not plural) which stand facing us, O *soma*, thou reignest over all things, *pavamāna*! (*ṚV*, IX.66.2, 3, 5)
The forms (plural, not dual) that are thine, thou pervades them, O *soma*, through and through, O *pavamāna*, at the appointed hours. O wonder-worker! (*ṚV*, IX.66.3)
Thy shining rays spread a filter on the back of heaven, O *soma*, with (thy) forms (plural, not dual). (*ṚV*, IX.66.5)

The dual reference is to (1) an unpurified form of the electrum (silver-gold pyrites) ore and (2) a metallic form achieved after smelting or purification.

Smelting-filtering apparatus: somanāla yantra?

Soma has the filter for his chariot; like the sun in heaven, *soma* rides across or flows through the heavens.[70] There are a thousand studs, *bhṛṣṭi* (or, metallic studs on the ore block) which carry him through. *Soma* is king; he has a filter for his chariot analogous to the sun's chariot riding the heavens.

> *rājā pavitraratho vājam āruhat sahasrabhṛṣṭir jayati sravo bṛhat.*
> [King, having the filter for chariot, he has attained the victory prize; a thousand studs, he conquers puissant renown.] (*ṚV*, IX.86.40)
> The heavenly *somas* (suns,[71] *surā*) spread the stainer of their (sun's) rays for themselves to come down (*ṚV*, IX.10.5). [In this imagery, which is tough to interpret literally, *soma* as a metaphorical reference to electrum clarifies the imagery in the text. *Soma* is bright as the suns of heavens with bright rays of metallic outcrops or shoots (*aṁśu*). As the metal in the ore melts down the filter, the brightness spreads through the earthen smelter structure. Bhāwe[72] interprets this verse as the 'mysterious sieve through which the sun's rays pass.' The filter strains the rays of the suns. The suns are the bright pellets of gold, as the drops collect in the bottom vessel of the apparatus.]
> Thy clear rays spread over the back of heaven, the filter (*pavitram*), O *soma*... (*ṚV*, IX.66.5). [The same hymn continues, referring to *soma* as *agni*.]

Electrum and fire are the material and the process unified. *Soma* cleanses himself:

> Monarch of everything that sees the sunlight, *soma* cleanses himself. Triumphing over the prophets, he made the Word of the Way (*ṛtasya dhitim*) to resound, he who is cleansed by the sun's rays, he the father of poems, master-poet never yet equalled! (*ṚV*, IX.776.4)
> Thy filter has been spread, O Brāhmaṇaspati (*soma*).... (*ṚV*, IX.83.1)
> The filter of the burning (*soma*) has been spread in heaven's home. Its dazzling mesh was spread afar.... They climb the back of heaven in thought. (*ṚV*, IX.83.2)

The burning *soma*; the refining celestial strainer or filter (*pavitram*); the song that accompanies the days and nights of incessant smelting process; and the dazzle of *soma* are recurrent imageries of the Ṛgvedic hymns.

> As for thee, O *soma*-juice, thou art clarified in the filter so as to establish thyself (in) space for the gods. (*ṚV*, IX.86.30)
> The guardian of the *ṛta* (*ṛtasya gopā, soma*); [*soma gopā* is a *yakṣa!*] cannot be deceived, he of the good inspiring force; he carries three filters inside his heart. (*ṚV*, IX.73.8)
> Thou runnest through the three filters stretched out; thou Lowest the length, clarified. Thou art fortune, thou art the giver of the gift (*dātrasya dātā*), liberal for the liberal, O *soma*-juice. (*ṚV*, IX.97.55)

The three filters are:

1. Filter of the powdered electrum ore mixed with water through the lamb's wool into the vessels [the use of lamb's wool may also denote the bellows used to stoke the refiner's fire; or burnt into sal-ammoniac, *navasāra,* to "kill gold"].
2. Electrum melting down from the top vessel flowing through the rows of alkalis.
3. Oxidation with the alkalis kept in an Indra, perforated pottery to oxidize the lead content of the ore. [Indra and Vāyu consume the liquid mixed with milk or curds.]

Like a race horse launched in movement for the victory prize, flow, O *soma,* thou who procurest the light-of-the-sun for heaven's vat, whose mother is the pressing stone; thou, bull-seated in the filter above the calf's wool, clarifying, clarifying thyself, thou *soma,* that Indra may have his pleasure! (*ṚV,* IX.86.3.) [Since *soma* is seated above the calf's wool, the reference may be to sal-ammoniac, made by bring calf's wool.] Purify thyself in Indra's stomach, O juice! As a river with a vessel, enable us to pass to the other side, thou who knowest; thou who battlest as a hero, save us from disgrace! (*RV,* IX.70.10)

pavasva soma devavītaye vṛṣendrasya hārdi somadhānam ā visa
purā no bādhād duritāti pāraya kṣetravid dhi disa dhā vipṛcchate.

[Clarify thou thyself, O *soma,* for the invitation to the gods. Thou who art a bull enter into the heart of Indra, receptacle for *soma*! Enable us to traverse the evil passages saving us from oppression! *For he who knows the country gives the directions to him who informs himself.*] (*ṚV,* IX.70.9)

[The italicized sentence may be a very important statement on the need for interacting with the indigenous population after the Vedic seeker had travelled across the lands containing minerals. Like the Director of Mines of the *Arthaśāstra,* the Ṛgvedic alchemist needed the advice and technical expertise on the lay of the land, *kṣetravid;* he needed the *kṣetravid*'s directions, *dhi disa dhā,* for he knew not fully the legacy of metallurgy exemplified by the proto-Indus lapidary.]

He advances to the rendezvous with Indra, the *soma* juice.... (*ṚV,* IX.86.16)

krānā sindhūnam kalaśān avivasad indrasya hārdy āvisan manīṣibhiḥ.

[By the action of the streams he has made the utensils resound while penetrating into the heart of Indra.] (*ṚV,* IX.86.19)

pavasva soma divyeṣu dhāmasu sṛjāna indo kalaśe pavitra ā sidann indrasya jathare kanikradan nṛbhhir yataḥ sūryam ārohayo devi.

Clarify thyself, O *soma,* in the celestial structures of thine essence, thou who has been released roaring into the vessel, in the filter. Lodged in

the belly of Indra, roaring with vigour, held in hand by the officiants, thou has made the sun to amount the sky. (*ṚV*, IX.86.22)
indrāya soma pātave nṛbhir yataḥ svāyudho madintamaḥ pavasva madhu mattamaḥ.
[For Indra, that he may drink, clarify thou thyself, O *soma*, held in hand by the lords, well armed, inebriating....] (*ṚV*, IX.108.15)
adribhiḥ sutaḥ pavase pavitra ān indav indrasya jatharesv āvihan.
Pressed by the pressing stones, thou clarifiest thyself in the filter, O *soma*-juice, when penetrating into the entrails of Indra!
(*ṚV*, IX.86.23)

Running through this allegorical outpouring of magnificent poetry, incessant chantings accompanying the relentless smelting process, for days and nights, on the refiner's fire, is the picture of a smelting apparatus, the centre-piece of which is the *soma* receptacle placed within the heart, belly or entrails of Indra. These imageries will come alive as the later-day alchemists describe the *yantras* used by them in pursuit of *rasa vidyā.*

pavamānaḥ so adya naḥ pavitrena vicarṣaniḥ yaḥ potā sa punātu naḥ; yat te pavitram arciṣy agne vitatam antar ā Brahma tena punīhi naḥ; yat te pavitram arcivad agne tena punīhi naḥ brahmasavaiḥ punīhi naḥ; ubhābhyām deva savitaḥ pavitrena savena ca mām punīhi viśvataḥ.
[This *soma*, which today circulates in the distance, which is a cleanser, may it cleanse us in the filter! The filter that has been spread in thy flame, O Agni, with it, cleanse our song. Thy filter, O Agni, equipped with flames, may it cleanse us, cleanse us with the fruits of sacred songs! With these both, the filter and the fruits (of song), O god Savitṛ, cleanse me through and through.] (*ṚV*, IX.67.22-25)

This hymn is the most eloquent testimony to the smelter-filter apparatus and the entire metallurgical process and a homage to Agni and Savitṛ, integral to the refining process. Fire spreads through the entire apparatus. The sacred songs and the hymns are the accompaniments to an ordeal of an extraordinary order of intensity, unrelenting day after day until the refining is completed in intense heat...the refiner's fire. Cleansed *soma* is brought into being because of *agni. Soma* is *agni.* A hymn from *Atharvaveda* may be cited as the veritable preface to the alchemical tradition of India, linking the fire across a whole gamut of phenomena:

ye agnayo apsvantar ye vṛtre pursuṣe ye asmasu; ya āvivesoṣadhir yo vanaspatīs tebhyo agnibhyo hutamastvetat.

[Those fires which are within the waters, which are in Vṛtra, which are in man, which are in the stones; and that (fire) which has entered the herbs, which (has entered) the forest trees, to these fires be this oblation presented.] (*AV*, III.21.1)

Soma artisans

dasam kṣipo yuñjate bāhū adrim somasya samitāra suhastā madhvū; rasam sugabhastir giriṣṭhām caniscadad duduhe śukram aṁśuḥ.

[The ten fingers, the two arms, harness the pressing stone; they are the preparers of the *soma*, with active hands. The one with good hands (the priest) has milked the mountain-grown sap of the sweep honey (*soma*); the *aṁśu* has yielded the dazzling (sap).] (*ṚV*, V.43.4)

nṛbāhubhyām codito dhārāya suto nuṣvadham pavate soma indra te....

[Spurred on by the two arms of the efficient, in jets, the pressed *soma* is clarified according to its nature, suitable for thee, O Indra!] (*ṚV*, IX.72.5)

[The apparent reference is to the working on the bellows to provide the jets or blast of air to stoke the refiner's fire.]

Lahiri summarizes the theory of Ronnow on the two waves of integration of peoples of antiquity. Ronnow here postulated a "vorvedischen" reconstruction of the Soma sacrifice and from this he deduced two conclusions:

> (1) The Indra-deva worshippers took over an *asuric soma* offering which they re-worked in a Vedic direction and (2) originally this was concerned with the snake gods. Varuṇa took over the function of these snake gods because, as Ronnow contended, the *asuric* religion was of a peaceful missionary type, amalgamating with the local cults. These snake gods were the original possessors of *soma* which is not only an intoxicating cult drink, but also the essence of the waters, ensuring fertility, the cure of illness, etc.[73] [Cf., snake as an alchemical symbol for lead, *nāga*.]

Varuṇa and Indra are gods of considerable eminence, perhaps even before the separation of the Indians and the Iranians. Mitra, Varuṇa, Indra, and Nasatyas are the names of four gods which appear in the Bogazkoy treaty concluded between the Hittite king Shubbiluliema and the Mitanni king Mattiuaza about 1400 BC.[74] Ronnow's theory may be highly speculative since there is no evidence that the Varuṇa worshippers "entered" India first, to be followed by other streams. In the Ṛgvedic hymns, Vṛtra appears as a resisting force, an enveloping cloud from which the "waters" of *soma* have to be extricated. The artisan, therefore, makes friends of Indra and Varuṇa: "The mortal who has made Indra and Varuṇa his ally (and) won both the gods for friendship, feeding (them); he kills the Vṛtras and enemies in battle (and) becomes famous by (their great help)." (*Ṛ*V, IV.41.2)

Smelting process

There are references to the placement of *soma*, electrum ore, on the top of the smelter structure, in allegorical terms:

Soma is the pillar, the fulcrum, the mainstay on the *skambha* of the smelter-filter structure. The key terms are: *vistambho, dhāruṇo* or *dhartāsi*.... *Soma* or electrum ore is kept on the top structure of the filter constituting as it were, the dome of the sky. It is above the earth, denoted by the lower vessel of the filter apparatus and above Indra, the receptacle, pottery vessel.

> Thou *soma* art the mainstay of the sky (*vidharman*).... (*Ṛ*V, IX.109.6)
> The ocean (of *soma*) has been cleansed in the waters; mainstay of the sky (*vistambho*), the *soma* in the filter, he who is favourable to us. (*Ṛ*V, IX.2.5)
> In the navel of the earth (is situated the *soma*), which is also the mainstay of the sky (*dhāruṇo*)....(*Ṛ*V, IX.72.7) [The earth is a reference to the pottery vessel.]
> Mainstay of the sky (*skambho*), well laid, the full *aṁśu* runs throughout everything.... (*Ṛ*V, IX.74.2)
> ...thou sittest in the vessels, having been pressed for Indra, inebriating drink (*madyo madeḥ*), which inebriates, supreme mainstay of the heaven (*divo vistambha*), (*soma*) who gazes in the far distance. (*Ṛ*V, IX.86.35)
> He has spilled forth, mainstay of the sky (*asarji skambho*), the offered drink; he flows throughout the world.... (*Ṛ*V, IX.86.46)
> ...father of the gods, progenitor of the moving force, mainstay of the sky (*sudakṣo vistambho*), foundation of the earth (*divo dhāruṇaḥ pṛthivyaḥ*). (*Ṛ*V, IX.87.2)
> Mainstay of the sky (*vistambho divo dhāruṇaḥ*), foundation of the earth, all establishments are in the hand of this (*soma*).... (*Ṛ*V, IX.89.6)
> ...he has placed the *soma* on the mountain top (*divi sūryam adadhāt somam adrau*). (*Ṛ*V, V.85.2)
> ...the *soma* seated on the mountain top. (*Ṛ*V, IX.18.1)
> ...the *soma* stalk...seated on the mountain top. (*Ṛ*V, IX.62.4)

The navel of the earth is a remarkable idiom of the Vedic texts. It is not the umbilicus; in this meaning, it reportedly occurs only once in the *ṛk*, *Ṛ*V, X.90.14. "As the 'hub' of a wheel it occurs three times.... What we call 'blood kin' for the Vedic poets was 'umbilical kin;' in this sense we find it nine times. By far the most interesting citations of the word are the ones where it is used transcendentally, to express a mythological idea, in a reverential and sacred context. *Soma* is the navel of the way (= *ṛta*), says the poet. By *ṛta* he means the divine order of things, a word that seems to convey somewhat the same idea as the *tao* of Lao Tze."[75] Navel denotes the metallic core of the ore block. To use another metaphor, it is the eye of the sun. It is *soma.*

> *divi te nabhā paramo ya ādade pṛthivyas te ruruhuḥ sānavi kṣipaḥ.*
> [Your highest navel is attached in heaven; your fingers grow on the back of the earth.] (*ṚV*, IX.79.4)

Liquefying process

Soma is not the udder but is compared to the under (protruding studs!) in terms of its appearance and its liquid-yielding potential.

> Approaching his mother, he (Indra) cries for food; he looks toward the sharp *soma* as toward the udder. (*ṚV*, III.48.3)
> What priest's sacrifice has (Indra) enjoyed, (approaching) *soma* as it were an udder? (*ṚV*, IV.23.1)
> When the swollen stalks were milked like cows with (full) udders.... (*ṚV*, VIII.9.19)
>
> The sweet juices have hurried to the god-like milch cows (to a calf). Resting upon the barhis, noisy, with full udder, they have made the red ones flow their flowing garment. (*ṚV*, IX.68.1)
> Enter into the heart of Indra, receptacle of *soma,* like rivers into the ocean, thou (O *soma*) who pleaseth Mitra, Varuṇa, Vāyu, supreme mainstay of heaven! (*ṚV*, IX.108.16)

Soma and parting of gold

Atharvaveda[76] explains the production of god (*hiraṇyam*) in three metaphorical stages: Triply born by birth (is) this gold: one was Agni's dearest; one fell away from *soma* when *soma* was injured; one they call the seed of devour waters; let that triple gold be thine in order to lifetime. Griffith embellishes the interpretation adding that it originally came partly from the moon (*soma*) when eclipsed. Whitney's translation is literal and appears more appropriate. The significant point is that *soma* when "injured" produced gold in one of three stages. This reinforces the interpretation of *soma* as electrum (silver-gold ore). [Terms such as "injured" or "killed" are typical alchemical technical terms used to describe the chemical transformations.]

Continuing the saga of alchemy, Needham quotes Levey who places the invention of cupellation for purifying silver about the—third millennium in the neighbourhood of Asia Minor. "That was the region, probably, which gave rise to the later technical terms (Greek *obryza*), forming (Latin *obrussa*) and post-classical *obryza*," test of gold or tested gold, which were taken to mean cupellation and cementation. Hittite-Hurrian *hubrushi* meant a clay or earthen vessel or container. *Hiaruhhe* is Hittite-Hurrian term for gold, paralleling Hebrew *haaroos*. Comparable Dravidian etyma: *DEDR*, 2353, Tamil: *carakku*, gold; Kuwii: *harku*, jewellery; *DEDR*, 661, Tamil: *urukku*, fuse, dissolve; *DEDR*, 1408: *kaṇukku*, mellow by heat; *DEDR*, 1292, Telugu: *karugu*, crucible, what is melted. *Atharvaveda* uses a term *barhis*:[77] In three vessels, the heavenly cow took that *soma*, where Atharvan, consecrated, sat on golden *barhis*. Griffith interprets *barhis* as sacred grass of gold. A technical term used by goldsmiths in the Tamil tradition and also the south Indian Siddha tradition to connote gold is: *pari*.

Berthelot observes that pure metals with specific characteristics were not distinguished from their alloys; all carried names such as aes, electrum, etc. *Ayas* meant metal. *Asem* denoted the natural alloy of silver and gold; it also meant any bright metal made with copper, tin, lead, zinc, arsenic and mercury. Twelve or thirteen different alloys were called *asem*.[78] "At Gungeria, in district Balaghat, 102 pieces of silver plates were discovered along with 424 copper implements. The silver was found to be admixed with 3.7% gold[79] (...1100-800 BC). The presence of 3.7% gold in these silver pieces indicates the extraction of silver from electrum...."

Asem was *soma*; this hypothesis will be the running-thread of this review of the alchemical tradition of ancient India, dating back to *Ṛgveda*. Hopkins[80] states: "The existence of this alloy (*assem*) may have been the original cause for the suggestion of transmutation since by adding silver to it, one would get a metal nearly identical with the crude silver from the mine; and by adding gold, something indistinguishable from gold. [The paucity of the Egyptain language may perhaps have been responsible for a confusion. Gold was the 'yellow metal,' and the alloy produced was also a 'yellow metal.'] The parallels with the Indian alchemical tradition are apparent: *ṭaṅkam* gold in Dravidian-Chinese becomes *ṭaṅkaṇa* borax (a reagent!) in Indo-Aryan, *ṭaṅka*,[81] gold coin; the terms *hiraṇyam*, *hema-bījam*, connote the yellow metal. "The use of borax (*pheng sha*) as a preparatory agent for soldering and brazing (in the molten state it cleans metal surfaces by dissolving metallic oxides) goes back in China to the +eleventh century, for it is mentioned by Su Sung (*kno han chin yin*)...Li shi-Chen says that borax 'kills' the five metals, as saltpetre does; presumably this refers to the preparation of metallic salts. The mild and non-irritant antiseptic quality which has given it such wide use in Western and even modern, medicine, was appreciated by the Chinese pharmacists, who prescribed it for all kinds of external, including phthalic, affections."[82]

In the Babylonian Talmud (+second century), asemon is a commonly used word referring to bullion (gold, silver or mixed.) Leiden X papyrus (*c.* +third century) says: "no. 8. It will be *asem* (i.e., electrum, an alloy of gold and silver) which will deceive even the artisans (a tin-copper-gold-silver alloy); no. 12. Falsification of gold (a zinc-copper-lead-gold alloy)...."[83] Soma *yajña* as a ritual, can be interpreted as an elaborate justification for the memories of processing *asemon, asem, electrum.* A Tamil lexicon of Winslow (1862) provides a philological trace: *soma maṇal,* is interpreted as meaning *veḷḷi maṇal,* sand containing silver ore! *Soma, soma maṇal, asemon, asem, electrum* may perhaps denote the same substance that dazzled and drew travellers of antiquity in search of Indus gold. It may perhaps be the same substance [which required the purificatory "mineral waters"] contained in the *kamaṇḍalu* symbols in the icons of the *yakṣa* legacy. It may perhaps be the same substance said to be *amṛtam* which was considered to be the elixir of life, of immortality. It may perhaps be the same substance referred to, in sheer poetry, as *amṛtam āyur hiraṇyaṃ,* Gold is immortality.

Soma! The very justification for the Vedic hymns; the quintessence of the only technological process elaborated in magnificent poetry and philological excursus in the grand allegory, the *Ṛgveda.*

References

1. P.C. Ray, *HCAMI,* pp. 114-15.
2. A.K. Coomaraswamy, *Yakṣas,* part II, p. 2, n. 2.
3. *Bṛhatsaṁhitā,* III.4.
4. Ibid., III.5. The semantic connotation of *makara* may ultimately have to be traced to the Dravidian numeration/economic roots: Tamil, *makara* a treasure of Kubera, a great number; decorative designs about

the dais built for seating the bride and bridegroom at the time of marriage. [Cf. *makaradhvaja* of *kāma* symbol of love.] *Vājasaneyi Saṁhitā* uses *nakra* to connote a kind of aquatic animal; if *n-* was the proto-Indic phoneme, it is plausible to hypothesise that the morpheme may be related, in alchemical terms, to *nāga*, lead; Dardic: *nan*, lead; Kashmiri: *nāga*, lead. Pursuing this trace, the astrological myth may relate to the processes of oxidation of lead while smelting gold ore containing lead, a process attested in the Indus civilization. [Cf., the pictorial motif on Indus seals of a *makara*, or *ghaḍiyāl*, alligator; sometimes, the alligator found in the Indus river is seen to with a fish caught in its snout.]

5. It is significant that the morpheme *mūṣa* which connotes a crucible is of Austro-Asiatic origin. Cf., F.B.J. Kuiper, "An Austro-Asiatic myth in the *Ṛgveda,*" *Mededelingen der koninklijke Nederlandse Academie van Wetenschappen*, XIII.7, 1950, pp. 163-82. The myth refers to the killing by Indra of a boar, which guards a treasure, a dish of rice, using an arrow shot through the mountain. The words in *Ṛgveda* for the bow (*drumbhūli*), the arrow (*bunda*), the dish of rice (*odana*) and the boar (*ēmūṣa*): these are proto-Muṇḍa or Austro-Asiatic morphemes. A synonym for boar, *varāha*, becomes an important symbol in later-day numismatics and of course, the *daśāvatāra* myths. It is conjectured that the pottery item incorporated in the smelter-filter structure might have been called *ēmūṣa*, a homonym for a boar. The allegory proceeds to depict how Indra succeeds in extracting the juice, *soma*. The *odana* may indeed be the perforated pottery, connoting the dish which contains the barley gruel, mixed with curds, as reducing agents in the smelting/sublimation/cupellation/parting processes; a practice attested in later-day alchemical texts. It is further conjectured that the proto-Indic *yakṣa* traditions may echo proto-Muṇḍa folk traditions.
6. L. Buschardt, *Vritra: Det Rituelle Daemondrab iden Vediske Soma-kult*, Kobenhavn, 1945, p. 48; A.K. Lahiri, *Vedic Vṛtra*, Delhi, 1984, p. 21.
7. Crysocole, or copper carbonate, was used by goldworkers as a solder. Two oxides of copper, red and black, were known. Mary, the Jewess-alchemist, often refers to the "little leaf of copper," the copper foil hung on the *kerotakis* to be subjected to the attack of mercury vapours or of sulphur vapours which was sublimed in the aludel fitted with *kerotakis*. Cf., A.J. Hopkins, op. cit., p. 108. The "leaf" motif has a remarkable parallel in Indus script signs and in an exquisitely executed pictorial motif which depicts two "unicorn" heads surrounding a stylized "sublimation device," may be *kampaṭṭam*, topped by nine leaves [Fig. 14]. In the jeweller's art, a process called "royal cement" is used, which may perhaps be traced to Tvaṣṭṛ gilding techniques. "To a large quantity of fused base metal a little gold was added and the whole cooled to form one metal, and this solid solution

was then shaped into some form such as a ring. This was then etched on the surface by alum or other mordant salt. The surface of the base metal, such as lead, by this process would be dissolved away, leaving granules of pure gold in relief, thus making the ring appear to be made wholly of gold. This process had been known from very early times." A.J. Hopkins, op. cit., p. 49. Some etyma: *ṚV*, IV.20.6, *vajra* mark; in *ṚV*, X.108.7, *vajrabhir-nṛyuṣṭaḥ* qualifying *nidhi*; in VI.22.5, *vajra-hastam* holding *vajra* in hand. Pāli: *vajira*, Indra or Sakka's thunderbolt; diamond. Tamil (lex.): *vaccira-kantam*, yellow orpiment; *vaccirakam*, pericarp of the lotus; *vaccirappacai*, a king of glue; *vacciram*, a treatise on architecture; *vaccira-yāppu*, glueing, in woodwork; *vacciraraśam*, purified mercury. *DEDR*, 5214, Tamil: *vaci*, rain, water; Kannada: *basi, bose*, to drip, drop, trickle. *DEDR*, 5217, Tamil: *vaciram*, a sea-fish, bluish.

8. Buschardt, op. cit., pp. 112, 114ff.
9. A.K. Lahiri, op. cit., p. 23.
10. The cultic implements on icons are remarkable records of alchemical legacy. Since the artist wanted to symbolize the representation with great fidelity, he used enormous degrees of freedom in adding to the icons four, six or eight hands; so that on each hand, he could represent the symbolism related to a cult implement such as a *kamaṇḍalu*, an *akṣa-māla*, a ladle, a *vajra*, etc. Many of these implements are alchemists' tools and relate to his apparatus. If this iconographic tradition can be extrapolated to the proto-Indus seals, the so-called "cult object" in front of the unicorn comes alive as a smelter-filter of the lapidary, the centre-piece of his very craft and life-mission.
11. Linking *vajra* with the waters finds significant support from Dravidian etyma: *DEDR*, 761: Kannada *vajjara, ojjara*, a spring, foundation; *orale*, oozing, *oravu*, spring; Tamil *ūru*, to spring, flow (as water in a well); *ural*, small spring, spring-water, oozing, percolation; Kui *urpa*, to ooze, spring up; Maltese *orbe*, to fall in showers. The imagery sought to be evoked by the Vedic poet-artisan is relatable to the intense desire to use a weapon that will enforce the flow of the metallic essence, *rasa*. *Vajra*, therefore, connotes the resin that flows from the male trees!
12. Cf., Allison Coudert, "Renaissance Alchemy," in *ER*, p. 200. "Alchemists were masters of metaphor. They dressed up their instructions in parables and allegories, veiled them in symbols, delighted in enigmas, and preferred to call a substance by any name other than its common one. Even the great genius Sir Isaac Newton found himself baffled by the obscurity of alchemical literature and symbolism.... The opacity of alchemical writings was partly a response to opposition from the church, which was suspicious of the religious implications of alchemical symbolism."

13. *AV*, XIV.1.3; W.D. Whitney, op. cit.
14. The interpretation of *oṣadhi* as a herb is questionable. Cf., the commentaries of Vyāsa and Vācaspatimiśra on a Patañjali *sūtra (Yoga-sūtra*, IV.1) which refers to *auṣadhi* as a means of gaining perfection; the interpretation by the commentators is that *auṣadhi* is an elixir of long life, obtained by *rasāyana*. The link between *soma* and *rasāyana*! *Soma* and immortality! *Soma* and gold!
15. *AV*, VII.77: Boldly drink *soma* from the beaker, Indra! hero in war of treasure! Vṛtra slayer, fill thyself full at the mid-day libation; thyself possessing riches grant us riches.
16. In the *abhiplava* ceremony, the mixture of curds, clarified butter, milk, barley and honey mixed with *soma* is tied in a piece of cloth (*pari-srayana; somapanahana*) and kept in three *kadruka* or *vṛtra* vessels. Cf., Mackay's view that the perforated pottery might have been used to press the curds.
17. *Soma* was mixed with *dadhyāśir* (curds), *ghṛtam vasānaḥ* (clarified butter), *gavāsir* (milk), *yavāśir* (barley), and *saumyam madhu* (honey): *ṚV*, I.19.9; IX.23.3; 61.13; 82.2. It was pounded with stones or in a mortar. (*ṚV*, I.83.6)
18. P.C. Ray, *HCAMI*, p. 157. M.K. Sharan (*Tribal Coins—A Study*, New Delhi, 1972, p. 59) explains that *kandalī* (mushroom), barley ashes, black beans, *palāśa (Butea fondosa)*, *pīlū (Carnea asboria)*, milk of cow and sheep, cow's teeth, and horn were added at different stages to extract gold from ores.
19. B. Walker, *The Hindu World*, p. 358. *Uḍumbara (Ficus glomerata)* was categorized as masculine; the rod of the tree was used in the rites of marriage.
20. Mircea Eliade, *Yoga*, p. 415; K.S. Sastri, ed., *Rasopaniṣad*, Trivandrum Sanskrit Series, XCII, 1928; tr. by Eliade, after Lévi, "Kaniṣka Sātavāhana, deux figures symboliques de l'Inde au I-er siecle," *Journal Asiatique*, CCXXVIII, 1936, pp. 61-104 ff., 121. This text is also significant in the context of an observation by Eliade about incorporation of mineralogical ideas into alchemical tradition.
21. R. Griffith, tr., *Atharvaveda*, p. 362.
22. Cf., *Chāndogya Upaniṣad*, VIII.5.3 which refers to *soma*-yielding *aśvattha: tad aśvatthaḥ somasavanaḥ*.
23. J.N. Banerjea, *Development of Hindu Iconography*, p. 67.
24. *DEDR*, 4843.
25. *Rasaratna Samuccaya*, 77, 81, 89-90; P.C. Ray, *HCAMI*, p. 168: "*mākṣikam* is born of mountains yielding gold...and is produced in the bed of the river Tapi and in the lands of the Kirātas, the Chinese and the Yavanas. Pyrites is of two kinds—golden and silver; the former is a native of Kanoj and is of golden yellow colour." [Cf. the interpretation of the bronze status of the "Dancing girl" from "Mohenjo-daro as a woman of

the Kirātas in Indus Images and Meanings" by S. Kalyanaraman in the context of the reading of the category of Indus inscriptions as related to traders and caravans.] The silvery pyrites is associated with stones and is of inferior quality. *Mākṣikā*, repeatedly steeped in honey, oil of the seeds of *ricinus communis*, urine of the cow, clarified butter and the extract of the bulbous root of *Musa sapientum* and gently roasted in a crucible, yields and essence of copper. [The vv. 89-90 also occur in *Rasārṇava*, VII.12-13 and Nāgārjuna's *Rasaratnākara*, 25-30.] The reference to cow's urine may explain the enigma of *ṚV*, IX.63.7: clarify thou thyself by that stream by which thou madest the sun to shine, putting into movement the human waters (*mānuṣir āpaḥ*)! Piss on it!

26. *ṚV*, X.53.9-10.
27. *ṚV*, VIII.29.3: *vaṣīmeyko bibharti hasta āyasoamantardeyveṣu* (divine architect).
28. *ṚV*, X.53.9.
29. Cf., D.C. Sircar, 1967, p. 11: Tvaṣṭṛ is the divine carpenter and Ṛbhus are the skilled artisans. *AV*, VI.25: "Tvaṣṭṛ, celestial artist, lay within the body of this dame, a male germ with the noblest form for her in the tenth month to bear." He is the great artificer, creator of all forms. Tvaṣṭṛ is the artisan who assembles the smelting apparatus: *AV*, XIV.1: "Bhaga hath formed the four legs of the litter, wrought the four pieces that compose the framework. Tvaṣṭṛ hath decked the straps that go across it. May it be blest, and bring us happy fortune. Mount this, all-hued, gold-tinted, strong-wheeled fashioned of *kiṁśuka*, this chariot lightly rolling, bound for the world of life immortal, Sūrya."
30. H. Chakraborty, op. cit., p. 224.
31. *ṚV*, V.62.8; H. Chakraborty, op. cit., p. 224.
32. H. Chakraborty, op. cit., p. 224.
33. Suryakanta, *Practical Vedic Dictionary*, 1981.
34. The concordant Greek morpheme *ios* has remarkable alchemical connotations: It connotes the highest colouring, purple or violet that artificial gold can attain. "By operating on gold you will have the Coral of gold." "...this great marvel, this indescribable marvel, has been named Coral of gold." "It is the tincture forming in the interior [of the gold] which is the true tincture in violet, which has also been called the *ios* of gold." [Cf., A.J. Hopkins, op. cit., p. 98; Berthelot, *Collection des anciens alchimistes grecs*, II.1.7; 2.5; III.29.3.]
35. R.G. Wasson, *Soma—Divine Mushroom of Immortality*, The Hague, 1968.
36. Latin: *Amanita muscaria*; English: *fly-agaric*; German: *fliegenpilz*; Russian: *mukhomor*; French: *crapaudin*; a brilliant red mushroom of northern Eurasia.
37. Harry Falk, "Soma I and II," in *BSOAS*, vol. LII, part I, 1988; incorporating a revised version of an article read at the World Sanskrit

Conference in Leiden, August 1987.

38. Falk provides a very useful bibliography on the *soma*-controversy which has continued unabated since 1968: thesis: R.G. Wasson, "The *soma* of the Rig Veda: what is it?" *JSOAS*, 91, 1971, 169-87; John Brough, "Soma and amanita muscaria," *BSOAS*, XXXIV, 2, 1971, pp. 331-61; "Problems of the *soma*-mushroom' theory," *Indologica Taurinensia*, 1, 1973, 21-32; R.E. Emmerick, "Ein Mannlein steht in Walde," *Acta Iranica*, 24, 1985, 179-84; F.B.J. Kuiper, review of Wasson's book in *IIJ*, 12, 1969-70, pp. 279-85; Ilya Gershevitch, "An Iranist's View of the *soma* Controversy," in Ph. Gignoux et A. Taffazzoli, ed., *Memorial Jean de Menasce*, Louvain, 1974, pp. 45-75; T.I. Elizarenkova et V.N. Toporov, "Les representations mythologiques touchant aux champignons dans leurs rapports avec l'hypothese de l'origine du Soma," in Y.M. Lotman and B.A. Ouspenski, ed., *Traveaux sur les systemes de signes. Ecole de Tartu* (Brussels, 1976), 62-68; Stella Kramrisch, "The Mahavira vessel and the plant Putika," *JAOS*, 95, 1975, 222-35, refuted by F.B.J. Kuiper, "Was the Putika a mushroom?" in S.D. Joshi, ed., *Amṛtadhārā: Professor R.N. Dandekar Felicitation Volume*, Delhi, 1984, pp. 219-27. Also cited in David Stophlet Flattery, "Haoma," Ph.D. dissertation, Berkeley, 1978; updated and extended in D.St. Flattery and Martin Schwartz, *Haoma and Harmaline*, Berkeley, 1989. The authors show that the rue, *Peganum harmala*, was used as a hallucinogenic drug in Zoroastrian circles some time before AD 900. I. Steblin-Kamenskij, *BSOAS*, L, 2, 1987, 377a, *harmālā* is burnt for fumigation, not pounded.
39. pp. 95-147.
40. O'Flaherty notes the tendency to use high-sounding Latin names. Vedic scholars have often resorted to special pleading and converting undefinable terms into divinities, resulting in polytheistic overtones. The use of a Latin name for *soma* does not make the identification any more exotic than the morpheme itself!
41. Plant (*virudh* to grow): *phālguna, ādāra, putīka* (plant which grew from a lead, *parṇa*), *somarājī (Veronia anthelmintica); Conyza anthelmintica* (moon plant—a species of mountain-rue or *Ruta graveolens*), *soma-latā (Sarcostemma brevistigma*; used by farmers to rid the fields of white ants; = *Asclepias acida, Sarcostemma acidum=Sarcostemma viminale, Cynanchium viminale), Crinium latifolium* (emetic/purgative *soma-vela*), *Sarcostemma brunonianum* (acidic milky juice), *Periploca aphylla* (fragrant flower, tastes like raisins), *nyagrodha* (*Ficus religiosa*), *Vitex negundo* (bitter leaves, used against fever=*indra hasta* or *indra surā*), *rānsera* (a Deccan plant), *Cocculus hirsutus* (cure for venereal diseases); mushroom, *Amanita muscaria;* grass, *dūrva, kuśa, arjunāni, muñja, kattṛṇa, Setaria glauca* (spiked grass of Marwar); creeper, *putīka, somavalli (Cocculus cordifolius, latā kṣīriṇī=Menispermum glabrum), Ipo moea muricata* (a purgative), *Sarcostemma intermedium, Tinosporo cordifolia* (aphrodisiac,

used to treat urinary diseases), *Poederia foetica* (to treat rheumatism); herb *somavalli (Serratula anthelmintica), rhubarb* (purgative with drug *emodin*), *Ephedra vulgaris* (containing ephedrine which causes dilation of the pupil), *Ephedra intermedia* (red fruit, stem used to treat fever); beverage, *soma* beer (*Sarcostemma brevistigma*), *Eleusine coracana* (*rāgī*, the common millet, used to make *marua*, intoxicant); drug *Cannabis sativa* (hemp), *Cannabis indica (bhaṅga, gañja, hašīša*, marijuana, pot).

42. Alfred Hillebrandt, *Vedische Mythologie*, 2 vols., reprint, Hildesheim, 1965, vol. I, pp. 193ff.
43. Hermann Oldenberg, *Die Religion des Veda*, third and fourth edn., Stuttgart and Berlin, 1923, p. 176.
44. *Śatapatha Brāhmaṇa*, 3.4.3,13 and 4.2.5,15 refers to the dictum of Śvetaketu Auddālaki that rocks are the habitat of *soma*. The verses elaborate: Vṛtra was *soma*; its body is of (the same nature as) the mountains, as the stones. In this way is born the plant named *usānā*...this they bring hither and press.
45. R.S. Singh, "Contribution of Unani Materia Medicas to the identification of Vedic plants with special reference to Ushana," *Studies in History of Medicine*, 3, 1979, 42-48.
46. C.G. Kashikar, "Identification of the Vedic plant Ushana," *Studies in History of Medicine*, 4, 1980, 190-93.
47. Cf., also *BSS*, 21.12 (90.1): *usānā nāmeyam oṣadhir bhavati.*
48. James W. Boyd and Firoze M. Kotwal, "Worship in a Zoroastrian fire temple," *IIJ*, 26, 29, 83, 306f.; Harry Falk, *BSOAS*, vol. LII, part I, 1988, p. 77.
49. B.H. Kapadia, *A Critical Interpretation and Investigation of Epithets of Soma*, 1959, p. 4.
50. *PB*, 1.3, 9, *somo gandhāya*; *MB*, 2.4, 11, *soma iva gandhena.*
51. Jivanji Jamshedji Modi, *The Religious Ceremonies and Customs of the Parsees*, Bombay, 1922; reprint, New York/London, 1979, p. 54.
52. Cf., *Ai. Gr.*, II, 2, p. 578. The *aṁśu* of *soma* are also described as containing nodes, *parvan, parus* (cf. Hillebrandt, *Vedische Mythology*, I, 217ff.; *ṚV*, I.9, 1; *VS*, 20, 27; *TB*, 3.7, 13; *VS*, 24,1). As an ore-block, the nodes are easily explained.
53. H.H. Dubs, "The beginnings of alchemy," *ISIS*, 1947, 38, 62.
54. J. Needham, *SCC*, vol. I, p. 153.
55. Comparable to Pāli *aṁśu* thread; or *śulba* veins of mines, referred to in *Arthaśāstra.*
56. While the etymon *vṛdh* to grow is apt to describe a plant, Dravidian etyma provide a more picturesque connotation in *viṛutu: DEDR*, 5431, Tamil: *viṛutu*, aerial root as of the banyan; Malayalam: *uṛi*, falling roots of a fig tree; Kannada: *biṛal* root that grows downwards from the branches of a banyan and other trees, pendent root; Telugu: *ūḍ*, aerial root of banyan. The parallel with the electrum ore and metallic veins

is apparent.

57. Cf., Patañjali's *Yogasūtra*, IV.1; an interpretation by Vyāsa and Vācaspatimiśra linking *oṣadhi* (an elixir of long life) obtained by *rasāyana* and means of gaining the "perfections."
58. B. Mukhopadhyay, "On the Significance of *Soma*," *Vishveshvarananda Indological Journal*, 16, 1978, p. 7.
59. Cf., S. Mahdihassan, "The Tradition of Alchemy in India," *American Journal of Chinese Medicine*, Spring, 1981, 9(1), pp. 23-33; extract from abstract: "...the ascetic (Aryan) begins searching for a strength-giving drug so that he could collect edible plants from the forest. He discovered ephedra or the *soma* plant as an energizer-cum-euphoriant.... He then took *soma* juice thrice daily to prevent exhaustion. With such benefits *soma* became a popular drink in the Aryan community as a whole. When the Aryans entered India, *soma* became unavailable. Its needs persisting, the ascetic substituted ephedra with a mixture of other drugs. If *soma* was *rasa*, or the juice, the substituted medicament was called *rasāyana*, signifying 'juice-incorporate.' *Rasāyana* was a geriatric medicine which promised rejuvenation. Later came contact with the Chinese and their use of mercurials. These proved to be efficient energizers and were accepted as *rasāyana*. Then Aryan medicine first extolled ephedra, next some herbal drugs, and finally mercurials. As energizers-cum-euphoriants, both ephedra and mercurials are anti-somnolents, a feature absent in intoxicants and narcotics."
60. Cf., Manindra Nath Banerjee, "Iron and Steel in the Ṛgvedic Age," *IHQ*, V.3, 1929, pp. 432-40; and "On Metals and Metallurgy in Ancient India," *IHQ*, III.1, 1927, pp. 121-33; III.4, 1927, pp. 793-802.
61. Harry Falk, "Soma I and II," *BSOAS*, vol. LII, part I, 1988, p. 78.
62. Sadashiv A. Dange, "Three stages in the advent of soma," *Journal of the Oriental Institute*, Baroda, 14, 1964-65, 63. Harry Falk adds that there is nothing shamanistic in Vedic or Iranian references to *soma/haoma*; shamanists use hallucinogenic drugs to visit the realms of ancestors and to be led to visions.
63. Cf., the parallel with *syena cit* of the *Śulvasūtra*. The creature is identified with the lapwing in Rainer Stuhrmann, "*Ṛgveda*, X.119: Der Rausch des Kiebitz," *Studien zur Indologie und Iranistik*, 11.12, 1986, 299-309. The comparable allegorical references are: *ṚV*, I. 81.5; VIII.88.5; Indra who grows and extends beyond heaven and earth. If the heaven and earth are equated with the two crucibles of the smelter-filter apparatus, the poetic imagination may be explained reasonably. The morpheme *vṛdh* to grow may be meaningful in the context of an expanding mineral during cupellation/cementing processes mixed with reducing agents and flux.

64. S. Mahdihassan, "Soma, in the light of comparative pharmacology, etymology and archaeology," *Janus*, 60, 1973, 91-102; idem, "A Persian painting illustrating Ephedra, leading to its identity as Soma," *Journal of Central Asia*, 8, 1985, 171-75. The painting of the sixteenth century shows a plant growing on the top of hills. The archaeological evidence is based on a terracotta from Gandhāra (cf., J. Marshall, *The Buddhist Art of Gandhāra*, Cambridge, 1960, fig.61; Harald Ingholt, *Gandhāran Art in Pakistan*, New Haven, 1957, fig. 59). In this picture, Buddha and Vajrapāṇi face a person who has cut grass; Buddha holds a bunch of the plant in his left hand, tips downwards; a heap of similar plants is shown beside him. Mahdihassan interprets these as ephedra cut bush. Harry Falk interprets, using textual evidence, that the man is a grass-cutter, Pāli *sotthiya, Svastika* who gives a bundle of grass as seat for Buddha. [Could the frequently occurring sign of *svastika* in Indus seal inscriptions denote this "grass=cutter" or, in general, a person wielding a scythe.]
65. Gernot L. Windfuhr, "Haoma/soma: the plant," in *Acta Iranica* 25, Papers in Honour of Professor Mary Boyce, Hommages et Opera Minora, 11, Leiden, 1985, pp. 703, 707. He goes on to equate it with the stimulant, ginseng. Falks notes that this does not grow in the areas of the texts and that it has no parts to represent *aṁśu/aśu*.
66. R.G. Wasson, op. cit., pp. 23-24.
67. Cf. *Rasārṇava*, "Killing of gold. Saltpetre (*sauvarccala*), green vitriol (*kāsīsam*), sea-salt (*sāmudram*), rock-salt (*saindhavam*), mustard (*āsurī*), borax (*ṭaṅkaṇa*), sal-ammoniac (*navasāra*), camphor (*karpūra*), the pyrites (*mākṣikam*)—all these are taken in equal parts. This crucible (*mūṣā*) is to be smeared with the milky juice of *Euphorbia nerifolia* and *Asclepias gigantea*; then having added the power of the aforesaid *vida*, the gold (*kanakam*) is to be killed (*jārayet*), my beloved." (XI.83-86). That sal-ammoniac can be artificially produced from goat's hair or ashes of animal excrement [cf. *bhasma, bhūti* of Śaiva tradition = *vibhūti* (Skt.)] is recorded in Arabic alchemical texts.
68. Abel Bergaigne, *La Religion Vedique d'apres les hymnes du Ṛgveda*, Paris, 1963, vol. III, p. 241; Wasson, op. cit., p. 58.
69. R.G. Wasson, op. cit., p. 20.
70. The imagery of two vessels, one connoting the heaven and the other the earth finds a remarkable parallel in Greek alchemic mysticism. Cf., A.J. Hopkins, op. cit., p. 114: "Surrounding the use of the aludel fitted with the *kerotakis* of Mary, in which the vapours constantly rose to the top to be condensed and fell again to the bottom, only to repeat the cycle, the ancient alchemists wove a sort of spiritual reverence, a mysticism expressed by the words: 'Above are the things celestial and below the things terrestrial.' It was this continuous process which was typified by the Ouroboros Serpent."

71. Cf., A.J. Hopkins, op. cit., pp. 115-16: "Gold was the only element which could resist fire. It was yellow like fire and was dedicated to the sun whose symbol stood in all the literature for gold. Again, the yellow spirit of gold is constantly referred to sulphur, the yellow 'spirit' of the sublimation process...which was used to bring out upon gold the unique violet or purple bronze ... sulphur was the 'spirit of fire'... gold contained the 'spirit of liquidity' or water...could the alchemist succeed in joining these two opposing elements, he would have, not gold only, but the highest spirit of gold, the spirit of metallicity, higher even than the famed 'is of gold!'...and at last the alchemist, by aid of the *kerotakis* of Mary and the mysterious sublimation process, did succeed in causing the union of sublimed sulphur with mercury in the *kerotakis* cup; and the product was a colour more brilliant than any heretofore obtained, the red or scarlet of artificial sulphide of mercury." It is tempting to extrapolate this brilliant statement to the Indian tradition of *sindūra,* red lead/vermilion [*sinduvāra, Vitex negundo,* tree] or *kuṁkuma* saffron [Pliny: *cancanum*; Gujarati: *kākū*?>Greek] that adorns the parting of the hair of Mother Goddess. In Tamil, *kuṁkuma-varṇi* connotes yellow sulphuret of arsenic, saffron stone.
72. S.S. Bhawe, *The Soma-hymns of the Rigveda: A Fresh Interpretation, ṚV,* 9.1-70, in 3 parts, M.S. University, Baroda, 1957, 1960, 1962, part I, p. 53.
73. A.K. Lahiri, *Vedic Vṛtra,* p. 130; Kasten Ronnow, *Trita Aptya: Eine Vedische Gottheit.* Uppasala Universitets Arsskrift, 1927. Filosofi, Skprakvetenskap och Historiska Vétenskaper, pp.13, 15.
74. P.E. Giles, "The Aryans," in E.J. Rapson, ed., *Cambridge History of India,* vol. I, pp. 64ff.
75. R.G. Wosson, op. cit., pp. 48-49.
76. *AV,* V.28.6, Whitney, tr.
77. *AV,* X.10.12.
78. Needham, *SCC,* vol. 5, part II, p. 45.
79. V.A. Smith, *Indian Antiquary,* V, 1905, pp. 233 ff.; H.C. Bharadwaj, *Aspects of Ancient Indian Technology,* p. 138.
80. A.J. Hopkins, op. cit., pp. 103-4.
81. A semantic transfer occurs: tang bull in Gadaba language becomes *ṭaṅkana* a kind of horse in Sanskrit; *ṭagun* a species of hill pony in Kashmiri. [Cf. the importance of *vṛṣan,* bull in *soma* hymns in the *Ṛgveda,* This morpheme *tang* may perhaps denote the so-called "unicorn" pictorial on Indus seals (as a pictorial metaphor connoting gold) which appears in front of the so-called "cult object" which has elsewhere been deciphered as *kampaṭṭam,* the proto-Indus sublimation apparatus comparable to the Greek alchemist's *kerotakis.*]
82. J. Needham, *SCC,* vol. 3, p. 663.
83. Cited in Joseph Needham, *SCC,* vol. 5, part II, pp. 18-21.

5

Brāhmaṇas: Aurifiction

Immortality

In a precise article, Julien Ries[1] provides a perspective on the concept of immortality across civilizations, across time:

> (About India) In all three of the great directions of Indian religious thought—Vedic, Brahmanic, and *bhakti*—the belief in immortality is clear and constant. Vedic India. The Sanskrit word *amṛta* (Pāli *amata*) is formed from privative a plus *mṛta* (death) and means 'non-death.' Related are the Greek *am(b)rootos* (immortal) and *ambrosia* (elixir of immortality); the Avestan *ameretaat,* the name of an abstract divine entity meaning 'deathlessness, immortality;' and Latin *immortaalitaas.* Thus our word immortality is of Indo-European origin and means literally 'nondeath'.... In the Vedic texts, particularly in sacrificial contexts, *amṛta* appears together with *soma. Amṛta* is the heavenly elixir of immortality, as *soma* is a sacrificial oblation offered to the gods by the priests. *Amṛta* is the drink of immortality of gods and men; *soma* is the elixir of life that has come from heaven to bestow immortality (*amṛtam*). Both words contain the idea of the winning of immortality, conceived as a perpetual renewal of youth and life.... The immortality symbolized by *agni,* the divine fire, and *soma,* the drink of life, is perpetual rebirth. *Agni,* the golden embryo, the sun, *soma,* and the celestial tree (the *Ficus religiosa*) are all symbols of immortality....
>
> Brahmanic India. By laying stress on perpetual renewal, the Brāhmaṇas deepen and systematize this idea of the infinite extension of the cosmic order. Their foundation is threefold: fire, the sacrificial altar, and Prajāpati...the ritual becomes a transcendence of death.... The sacrifice confers long life and immortality.... *Bhakti*...takes the place of the elixir of life, conferring eternal life with Kṛṣṇa. A number of texts emphasize the destiny of the *bhakta,* who is a *siddha* (perfect), *amṛta* (immortal), and *tṛpta* (happy)....
>
> Summary...Gold pieces,[2] symbols of deathlessness, are placed on the facial openings (of the corpse)... *Bṛhadāraṇyaka Upaniṣad:* 'Lead me from death to non-death.... ' (1.3.28)

Conclusion (spanning the wide cultural and religious range of humanity from prehistory up to the great monotheistic systems....) *Homo religiosus* believes that his life does not end, for death is a birth into a new life and an initiation into the after-life.

Jīvanmukti (Salvation)

If the early Brāhmaṇas are dated to *c.* sixth century BC, the phrase, *amṛtam āyur hiraṇyam,* may perhaps be the earliest written reference to the magisteries of gold and alchemical paths to immortality. Immortality is a concept which, in the Indian context of multiple philosophical paths (Sāṁkhya, Yoga and Lokāyata) gets a variety of expressions: *mokṣa* (heaven), *yoga* (union), *siddhi* (merit), *bhūti* (prosperity; the smear of immortality) and of course, *amṛtam* (connoting both elixir and immortality).

The mingling of concepts spanning from alchemy to mysticism seems to be in vogue across millennia. *Ṛgveda* (10.136) refers to *muni* (ascetics) who possess the power to fly on the wind. *Chāndogya Upaniṣad* (8.6.6) lists the features of a mystical anatomy which is elaborated as "veins" or *nāḍī,* a psychic structure in Haṭhayoga. *Śvetāśvatara Upaniṣad* (2.8-15, 12); proposes a road to immortality through yogic practices, including breath control.

Rasārṇava beings with a query from the goddess to Śiva about the secret of *jīvanmukti* or liberation in life; the answer is not encouraging: even among gods, the secret is rarely known.

What indeed, does the term, *jīva* mean? The vaguely defined search for the "quintessence" or some sort of radical change, is evident.

Pammena

Who are the *pammena* referred to in the Egypto-Greek traditions? They are also the *polomen* referred to in the Chinese tradition! Vedic Brāhmaṇa![3] Basham[4] summarizes the Greek references succinctly: "We are toid that the highest of the seven classes of India, that of the philosophers is divided into two sections, the *brachmanes* and the *garmanes.* The identity of the first is obvious. The letter is clearly an error for *sarmanes,* equivalent to Sanskrit *śramaṇa,* and implying ascetics, especially unorthodox ascetics. The *garmanes* are divided into several subgroups, the most honoured of which are the *hylobii,* who are forest hermits. Next in repute after these are physicians. . . . They subsist by alms and begging. They are skilled in rites to produce offspring and they cure diseases, mostly by dietary methods. They have effective ointments and poultices, but their other remedies have much in them that is bad. They practice forms of penance, such as remaining in the same posture for long periods. The passage has been taken as applying to medical men generally.... *Pramnae,* also different from the *brachmanes.* This word seems also be another corruption of the Sanskrit *śramaṇa,*[5] since one group of *pramnae* habitually go naked. As well as these Naked *pramnae,* there are also Mountain *pramnae* and City *pramnae.* The last wear linen garments and live in the towns. The Mountain *pramnae* wear deerskins and carry about with them bags of roots and drugs, with which they pretend to cure the sick, also making use of sorcery, spells, and amulets for the same purpose."

In Pāli texts, *samaṇas* are often held as a foil to or contrasted with the Brāhmaṇas; in a compound, *samaṇa-brāhmaṇā* are generally "leads in religious life." In Tamil tradition, *samaṇ* refers to Jainism and to nudity. A typical categorization refers to: *camaṇarum cākkiyarum.* It may, therefore, be appropriate to interpret the Greek texts as referring to Hindu and Jaina ascetics as *brachmanes* and *garmanes.*

In such a classification, *hylobii* (*bairāgī?*) may perhaps connote *haṭhayogī.* The use of the morpheme-*maṇa* in both the terms: *brāhmaṇa* and *śramaṇa* is significant. The morpheme by itself can be related to the Muṇḍa concept of *mana,* the *ṛta* or the natural order inherent in man; or the concept of *māna,* measurement, which can be broadly interpreted as grouping or ordering concepts in numeration and mensuration. These concepts find their parallels in the ordering of the zodiac in twelve groups with symbols and morphemes with vivid links to mensuration; the morpheme *rāśi* itself connotes a heap or mathematics. [Cf., Śaṅkara's interpretation of the morpheme in *Chāndogya Upaniṣad,* VII.2, as mathematics.[6]] That Old Sinhala treats *maṇa* as a synonym of *Śramaṇa,* ascetic lends added significance to this interpretation of the *-maṇa* in the compounded terms used to denote two groups of religious leaders. Ancient civilizations do attest to the role of religious leaders as focal points for measurement and storage of produce in treasuries or granaries.

A Brāhmaṇa in India of *c.* 300 BC, after a grand Soma sacrifice called Aśvamedha, could make the *mahiṣi*, the queen mate with the sacrificed horse. Is this an allegorical reference too? If interpreted literally, what justfying philosophy and what control over the ruling classes could have resulted in such irrationality? What nexus with the ruling classes did have that the priest could dictate to the queen after a major Soma *yajña*? [These absurdities recorded in *Śatapatha Brāhmaṇa* can be explained in an analysis of the allegorical terms used in this complex text; this allegory will be unfolded in this essay.]

Similarly, the Śrauta versions related to technical aspects of the Soma ritual appear to degenerate into mere gestures of a feeble memory of the Ṛgvedic artisan's efforts to smelt electrum, without the assistance of the artisans who had carried with them the legacy of the proto-Indus lapidary crafts including gold-silver-copper smelting. The Brāhmaṇa literature ritualises the proto-historic incident of chasing away the *yakṣa* or *gandharva* from Mt. Muñjavat who brings the *soma* raw material (ore, *mākṣikā*; electrum, *asem, asemon*). In fact, Soma ritual gets organized as and when the source material becomes available. Why is the Brāhmaṇa so keen that the *yakṣa* should not witness the ritutal? Is he afraid that the *yakṣa* would have called the bluff of the artificial gold using the technique of *puṭam*[7] or Sanskritized *sphuṭa*, cupellation and cementation? He can "rationalise" it by the hierarchical classification; *yakṣa*'s touch may pollute the sacrifice.

There is a fascinating Chinese historical chronicle which Needham cites: The official history of the Sui dynasty, completed in+636 by Wei Cheng, contains, in the usual bibliographical catalogue, the titles of a large number of books, now lost, beginning with the words "po-lo-men" or Brahman. Thus we have *Polomen Thien Wen Ching* (Brahman Astronomy), *Polomen Suan Fa* (Brahman Mathematics), *Polomen Yin-Yang Suan Li* (Brahman Calendrical Methods), *Polomen Yao Fang* (Brahman Drugs and Prescriptions), etc.... But in spite of these facts, evidence of a lasting influence either Indian or Western on Chinese science and medicine is hard to adduce. It would need a careful comparison of the traditional pharmacopoeias of China and India to trace out the pharmacological borrowings involved. It is usually supposed that drugs such as *caulmūgra* oil for leprosy, which have been for many centuries in the Chinese pharmacopoeia, were of Indian origin ... one of the earliest passages on mineral acids ... Tuan Chheng-Shih, writing in his *Yu-*

Yang Tsa Tsu of +863 about events which took place between +647 and +649.

> Yuan-Tshe captured an Indian prince named A-Lo-Na-Shun. He had with him a scholar versed in curious art named Na-Lo-Mi-So-Pho, who said he could make people live for two hundred years. The Emperor (Thai Tshung) was very astonished, and invited him to live in the Chin Yen Men Palace, to make the drugs for prolonging life.... The Indian said that in India there is a substance called Pan-chha-cho Water, which is produced from minerals in the mountains, has seven varieties of different colours, is sometimes hot, sometimes cold, can dissolve herbs, wood, metals, and iron; indeed if it is put into a person's hand, it will melt and destroy it.[8]

If the *pan-chha-cho water* perhaps referred to the alchemist-metallurgist's *pañca kṣāra,* five salts, the reference to Na-Lo-Mi-So-Pho may be related to the historical account related to the emperor Thai Tshung of the seventh century, to whose court was brought a scholar named Nārāyaṇaswāmin.[9] While this alchemist reportedly specialized in *amṛtam āyur* techniques or the art of prolonging life, Kao Tshung, in +664-665 sent to Kashmir, the Buddhist monk, Hsuan-chao. The mission was to bring back an Indian magician called Lokāditya, who reportedly had the *amṛtam,* the elixir of life.[10] [Are the *yakṣa* icons carrying in their *kamaṇḍalu,* the *pan-chha-cho water*? Cf., notes on iconography provided in another section of this essay, with particular reference to alchemical symbols carried on the multiple hands of icons in the Yakṣa tradition.]

"The *Rasārṇavatantra* (dated by Renou and Filliozat as of the +twelfth century) speaks of the 'killing' of iron and other metals by a *vida* (solvent?) which is prepared from green vitriol (*kasīsa*), pyrites, etc. From the *Rasaratnasamuccaya,* which according to Renou and Filliozat may go back to about +1300, the process of 'killing' certainly seems to be the formation of salts from metals...the present passage...clearly suggests a knowledge of mineral acids in India in the +seventh century."[11] It is reasonable to propose a hypothesis that the *pan-chha-cho water* was some type of mineral water used by the alchemist.

Did the Chinese succeed indeed no obtaining from India, the techniques related to *amṛtam* the elixir of life? At least one alchemist of the thirteenth century frankly answered, "No." He was the Taoist alchemist Ch'ang Ch'un who was brought to Genghis Khan's court in 1222. He reportedly told Genghis Khan: "I have a means of protecting life: talismans against evil influences, but no elixir of immortality."[12]

Marco Polo[13] describes the yogins (*chugchi*) who live "150 or 200 years:" "These people make use of a very strange beverage, for they make a potion of sulphur and quicksilver next together and this they drink twice every month. This, they say, gives them long life; and it is a potion that they are used to take from their childhood."

The grand deception[14]

Reverting to the great question of how the *pamena, polomen, brāhmaṇa* could get away with aurifiction, the great pioneer Berthelot[15] may be quoted, in reference to the close parallels between the Papyri[16] and the Corpus and amazed at the fact that "aurifaction" had arisen despite the knowledge of cupellation to call the bluff which had existed for over one millennium: "...the chimerical claim of aurifaction, evokes fresh astonishment in our minds. How can we comprehend the mental and intellectual state of men who practised these fraudulent techniques, intending to deceive others by the appearances of the products, and who yet ended by deceiving themselves, and believing that with the aid of some mysterious rite they could bring about a transformation of these gold- and silver-like alloys into real gold and silver?...he added magical formulae and prayers to his art, becoming thus the dupe of his own industry."

Needham provides a remarkable insight: "...the whole environment of both the artisans and the philosophers was saturated by magic, gnosticism and theurgy.... This disdain for the work of the artisan gives us, perhaps, the key to the whole problem...(which) can be understood if we give up the *idee fixe* of the pioneer historians of chemistry that the artisans and the 'alchemists' were the same people...there was a radical difference of social class between the artisan metal-worker and the dilettante philosophers."[17] The *yakṣa* who belonged to the artisan class, and who symbolized the Lokāyata philosophy of materialism, was deemed a danger to the metaphysical integrity of the Soma *yajña*; he had to be chased away! To use the powerful phrases of Berthelot, how can we comprehend the mental and intellectual state of the *aśvamedha mahiṣi* who followed the instructions of the priest? One easy solution is to treat the particular text as a mischievous interpolation [such a solution is not, however, necessary; since, the bizarre episode in the Aśvamedha can be explained as an allegory]; but then, the whole structure of the *yajña* remains unexplained if the *yajña* itself is not interpreted as a well-orchestrated exercise in aurifiction, to produce a *rasa* that is not drunk.[18] Is *mahiṣi* (buffalo) a synonym of *soma* bison (*DEDR*)? If so, the mating of *mahiṣi* and *aśva* may mean the reduction of the electrum ore (*soma*) using horse meat and bones.

The stage is set for a bureaucratic process involving some technical manuals for constructing the "place of sacrifice" and the *agni*, interpreted as the "fire-altar." The technical manuals are the Śulbasūtras.

Śulba and minerals

The link between the proto-Indus baked-brick industry and the Śulbasūtra has been convincingly established.[19] In the introduction (1984) to Thibaut's *Mathematics in the Making in Ancient India* (being reprints of the Śulbasūtras and *Baudhāyana Śulbasūtra*, Debiprasad Chattopadhyaya observes (p. x): "The very word *śulva* of rope or cord is so elitist-esoteric that it is difficult to come across it outside the titles of the texts. Within the texts, however, the word is never used; cord or rope being referred to as *rajju*—a word so plebeian that it is the same also in Pāli." What does the morpheme in the title of the Sūtra texts, *śulva*, mean?

Śulba is a "geometry" metaphor; it connotes a mine, copper

Geometry of antiquity is earth measurement; this semantic structure finds a parallel in Monier-Williams' Sanskrit lexicon: *kṣetram, rekhā gaṇitam* (*rekhā* may be interpreted as a streak or vein?). Brown's Telugu lexicon: *kṣetra gaṇitam, mahā gaṇitam.* If *śulva* is a *sūtra, rajju* string, cord, rope, why use both the morphemes: *śulva* + *sūtra*? A very unsatisfactory construction can be that the phrase denotes: Rules of the Cord. The term *khāṇi* occurs in the *Ṛgveda*, connoting affinity of *soma* with the mines and minerals (interpreted as channels) in the following hymns: *vajrena khāṇy atṛṇam nadīnām* (*ṚV*, II.15.3): He (Indra) pierced the channels of the rivers with the thunderbolt. *Apāvṛṇod apihiteva khāṇi* (*ṚV*, IV.28.1): He (Indra) opened the channels (of the waters), obstructed as they were.

According to Monier-Williams' lexicon, *śulvam* means copper![20] Some etyma from the so-called Aryan and Dravidian linguistic streams may be reviewed to fix the semantic structure underlying the morpheme *śulva*:

CDIAL, 12544 *śulva*, string, cord; Prakṛtsuvva cord; Lāhṇḍa, *sub* band on a sheaf of corn; Punjab, *subb, chubb* id. twist of tobacco, swab to clean utensils; *subbā, chubbā,* band of twisted straw, bandage; marathi, *sub, subh* fibrous integuments of coconut.

The transformation from *k-* to *c-*; and *-p-* to *-v-* across the *DEDR* and *CDIAL*, linguistic streams is well-known. The morphemes closest to *suvva* are found in the following:

> *DEDR* 1909: Tamil, *kūval* a well, hollow, hole, pit; Koraga *kuyyeli,* well; Tulu *guvelu,* a well; Koḍagu *ku-va,* shallow well (where water can be dipped by hand) < Prākṛta *kūva* < Sanskrit *kūpa.*[21]

The linguistic transition may therefore be hypothesized: *kola, kulya* [colliding with *kūpa*], *śulva,* ditch.

The main argument is that proto-Indic or proto-South Asian morpheme: *suvva,* does not connote merely a cord. It connotes a pit or mine, and the science is "mineralogy," closely allied with *dhātuśastra* which is a science of minerals and metals! This is reinforced in later-day traditions of *Arthaśāstra.*

Arthaśāstra interprets "śulba" as mineralogy

Kauṭilīya Arthaśāstra (2.12.1) makes a dramatic announcement no the bureaucratic requirements for the key function: *ākara karmānta pravartanam* [starting of mines and factories]:

> *ākarādhyakṣaḥ śulba dhātuśāstra rasa-pāka*
> *maṇirāgajastajjha sakho vā....*

Since the reference is of fundamental importance in relating the *vedi* to metallurgy, the translation of Kangle and commentaries will be reproduced:

> The Director of Mines, being conversant with the science of (metal) veins in the earth and metallurgy, the art of smelting and the art of colouring gems, or having assistance of experts in these, and fully equipped with workmen skilled in the work and with implements, should inspect an old mine by the marks of dross, crucibles, coal and ashes, or a new mine, where there are ores in the earth, in rocks or in liquid form, with excessive colour and heaviness and with a strong smell and taste.
>
> [*Notes*: *Śulbaśāstra,* 'the science of metallic veins in the ground, or that of transmutation of copper into silver or gold;' alternatively, *bhūmiparīkṣāśāstra.* Broeler (another commentator of *Arthaśāstra*) understands 'geometry;' *rasapāka,-* alchemy and smelting; it seems, however, that we have a single idea 'smelting of liquid ores....']

Arthaśāstra, 2.12.2 (Those liquids) that flow into a hole, a cave, a table-land at the foot, a rock-cut-cave, or a secret dug-out in mountains whose regions are known (to contain gold-ore)....

Reading both 2.12.1 and 2.12.2 in the context of mineral extraction, it would appear that the morpheme *śulba* refers to the science of metallic veins (lit. *kulya,* pits) in the ground.

A hypothesis may, therefore, be formulated: Śulbasūtra relates to the science of metallic veins, mineralogy or proto-geology. Kātyāyana and Baudhāyana were dealing with one segment; the mathematics of construction of hearths to smelt the ores or minerals in. Śulbasūtra needed the assistance and expertise of workmen with the skills and tools to discover metallic veins and to work the pits. It is also a proto-Indus legacy of workmen with which the Vedic priests/Brāhmaṇas were, perhaps, not fully conversant. Theory of *śulva* was of no avail without the knowledge of the technology baking bricks and without the expertise of a *yakṣa* to bring *soma* or other mineral products/plant substances from Mt. Muñjavat [Cf. the so-called "fire-altars" (*kūpa, kulya!*) in Kalibangan and Banawali, Indus sites. That *soma* itself is electrum (*suvarṇa/ rajata mākṣikā*) is an alchemical hypothesis argued elsewhere based on the evidence of the Vedic texts and archaeological finds.]

This reconstruction of the scope of Śulbasūtra is confirmed by Monier-Williams, lexicon entry: *kulya,* mine.[22] Śulbasūtra should therefore, have had parts which went beyond, "geometry" and bricks, to the real juice, *rasa* and not a mere mirage of a sacrifice. In the proto-Indus and possibly, in the Ṛgvedic period, the *śulva* technology was perhaps only aurifaction (not aurifiction, not microbiotics), to use Needham's classification to depict advances in metallurgical technologies and their end-uses.

Kātyāyana explains that this "sūtras" have their meaning concealed

Kātyāyana concludes his *Śulbasūtra* with the following statement: "Ācārya Kātyāyana the talented has finished this Śulba (*śaulbee*), the rules therein are faultless and their meaning is concealed (*gūḍha mantra*)."

What secret[23] was Kātyāyana trying to conceal by not using the morpheme *śulba* in the text and using it only in the concluding verse? What, indeed, did *śulba* mean?

Arthaśāstra use of the compound *śulba-dhātuśāstra* holds the key; the science relates to mines and minerals. The Vedic artisan, *adhvaryu* is engaged in a simulation of the mine; the process involves extraction of the metal *par excellence* from unrefined *soma*; he is giving shape to proto-Indus archaeological evidence of aurifaction crafts of the Indus lapidary-goldsmith.[24] Both the Director of Mines and the *adhvaryu* of the Brāhmaṇa days, need the assistance of skilled artisans and workmen in performing their trades; the Indus lapidary was dealing with aurifaction; the *adhvaryu* is engaged in either aurifaction, concealing the process in allegories or in later historical periods, simply, with aurifiction. The Director of Mines with knowledge of *śulva* science were dealing with real gold. *Ṛtvij* and *adhvaryu* with knowledge of *śulva* science was dealing with "fake gold" or "copper transmuted to gold" and *saṁnidhātṛ* was the builder of the "secret treasury" to store the products of this state enterprise, yielding 3/4th fee to the king and 1/4th to the priests.

Kātyāyana in his "secretly" coded *Śulbasūtras* in indeed describing the procedures for the extraction of gold from the artificial (allegorical) mine, the so-called "fire-altar." Hopefully, the Soma sacrifice *dakṣiṇāgni* would yield the *indu, pṛḍa, mṛḍa* or *pruḍ*[25] or simply, *hiraṇya piṇḍa* (a lump of gold; *ṚV*, VI.47.23; *daso hiraṇya piṇḍān*, ten gold-lumps). The *adhvaryu* is the priest-artisan-alchemist who worked on the goat-skin bellows, *adhvara* (which in Lāhṇḍa-Punjabi means half-a-goat skin) to stoke the refiner's fire. Suśruta, the surgeon can certainly draw a comparison between the physician and the *adhvaryu*. In the absence of the *adhvaryu* (comparable to the role of a qualified physician bringing medicinal herbs to a patient), religious services of an *udgātṛ, hotṛ* and Brāhmaṇa will prove abortive.[26]

What are the technical terms used in the Śulbasūtras?

Terms such as *aratni, puruṣa, īṣā, akṣa, yugam, śamyā* are used in the Śulba texts to connote linear measures. For example, *aratni* = 24 *aṅgula* (or 24 finger-breadths); *puruṣa* = 120 *aṅgula*;[27] *īṣā* = 188 *aṅgula*;[28] *akṣa* (axis) = 108 *aṅgula; yugam* (yoke) = 86 *aṅgula; śamyā* (yoke pin; called also *jānu*[29]) = 32 *aṅgula*.[30] While defining these technical terms related to the construction of the *vedī*, some metaphorical references are made:

> *aṅgulai rathassammitāyāḥ pramāṇam* "the (unit) measure of the *vedī*, which is measured according to the dimensions of a chariot is the finger-breadth (*aṅgula*)."[31]
> *hiraṇyasakalārthe tu hiraṇyam yasya nocyate; kṛṣṇalenaiva tadyākhyā yaje*

sidhyati yājikī "red peas are offered at the time of sacrificial work. These though not of gold serve its purpose."[32] [*kṛṣṇala* in later tradition, is equated to a *raktika* or *guja* seed as a basic unit of measure for weighing gold, silver and gemstones.]

The *sūtras* go on to explain that one red pea or *kṛṣṇala* = 3 *yava* and that the next weight is of copper. "In the case of *bahusuvarṇika* distribute 3073 gold pieces and half the gold in *māṣas.* One anxious to know about bigger measurements than these should approach the goldsmith[33] (*svarṇakāro*) or an engineer (*sthapati*)." The reference to *bahusuvarṇika* and its weighment in *māṣas* and the reference to the goldsmith are an indication that the Śulbasūtra may not, in fact, be dealing with "real bricks." What is at stake here, is something allied with that dazzling metal, gold.[34]

These statements are followed by another technical term: *iṣṭaka,* brick:

> *hrasate śoṣa pākābhyām dvātri, śad bhāgam iṣṭakā,*
> *tasmādārdra pramāṇam tu kuryān mānādhikam budhyaḥ.*
> [Bricks decrease (in length, breadth and thickness) by 1/32 while drying and burning. Therefore, a wise man should always keep these measurements slightly in excess.][35]

Kātyāyana has hidden the "weight" measures in "linear" terms

The point to be noted is that the term 3 *yava* = one *kṛṣṇala* red pea. In linear measures, 6 *yava* are equal to one *aṅgula.* The use of the same term *yava* in both linear and weight measurements provides a possible clue to the metaphors of geometry of the Śulbasūtras. The so-called linear measures are, in fact, convertible to weights of gold or other precious metals using the common unit *yava.*

In this perspective, the term *iṣṭaka* interpreted as a brick subjected to *pāka* can also denote a lump or button of gold or other precious mineral ore-blocks or copper ore readied for transmutation, which are piled up in layers to construct the *vedī,* the smelting furnace. This may offer a plausible explanation to the sudden interpolations in Kātyāyana, referring the builder of the *vedī,* to a goldsmith or an engineer for gaining knowledge on bigger measurements. For that matter, how is a goldsmith or reference to gold relevant, if the subject matter relates only to clay, burnt or sun-dried bricks or if the subject is concerned only with geometry or measures for the fire-altar?

That there is some metaphorical symbolism is also apparent from a phrase used in Baudhāyana: "There is liberty regarding, the length of *pada, yuga, prakrama, aratni,* and *śamyā,* if these words denote measures."[36] why does Baudhāyana use this disconcerting italicized phrase? These technical terms are used in describing a cart or *ratha.* The term *ratha* is used frequently in the context of the *soma filter,* as if the apparatus may be conceived as a cart with two wheels, a pole, a yoke-pin and the axis *akṣa.* [Cf., the parallels with the proto-Indus so-called "cult object," sublimation apparatus or portable furnace.] The term *akṣa* gains fundamental importance in the gold-workshop and record-keeping for the treasury: *akṣa-śālā, akṣa-paṭala,* etc. It would appear, therefore, that the Śulbasūtras are dealing with an allegorical representation of a process closely connected with *akṣa,* and resulting in gold or financial transaction handling. That allegory is involved in the text is categorically stated by Kātyāyana, in his concluding statement. [*Akṣa*: gold cowrie, standard unit of account for the state treasury.]

Kātyāyana says he has concealed the meaning in the Śaulbee

"Ācārya Kātyāyana the talented has finished this Śulba, the rules therein are faultless and their meaning is concealed (*śaulbee... gūḍha-mantrasya*)."[37] Baudhāyana implies a secret code by his phrase, "if these words denote measures."

Śulbasūtras denote "area" by the term *bhūmi* while in later days, the meaning is expressed by *kṣetra.* The morpheme, *karaṇi* meant originally not the side of a square but the *rajjuḥ karaṇi* the cord used for the measuring of a square.[38]

That the term *śulba* also denotes "copper" according to Monier-Williams' lexicon and Shamasastry, another commentator of *Arthaśāstra,* should provide a pause for thought. The term, *śulba,* is not used in the texts to man "a cord;" the technical term used for a "cord" is *rajju.* [Was the process an alchemical secret to colour or "tint" or transmute copper ore into gold?] It may also be surmised that the term *rajju* may relate to *rajata* silver or "lock of braided hair" (Tamil lexicon, *iraccu, rajju*[39]). *Arthaśāstra* states that the *ākara-adhyakṣa,* the director of mines should be versed in the sciences of *śulba, dhātu, rasa-pāka*; in this sequence of scientific-technological expertise, *śulba* has been interpreted as a science related to the veins of mines containing ores (< *kulya,* mine, pit; colliding with *kūpa,* ditch = *śulba*). This may provide a clue to the "enigma" that the important term *śulba* which is used in the titles of the *sūtras*, is not used in the body of the *sūtras*. The science of *śulba* allegorically elaborated as geometry of the *vedī* may indeed have referred to the science of extraction/processing of metals from mineral ores. The *iṣṭakas* are desirable blocks: *iṣṭi*, *Ṛgveda*: seeking after, wish; Prākṛta: *iṭṭhi*, wish. A homonym is: *Ṛgveda: iṣṭi*, impulse; Hindi: *īṭhī*, lance, spear; Tamil: *īṭṭi*, lance; etyma which may explain a synonym for lance: *śūla*, *tri-śūla*. An allegorical complex, therefore, unravels yielding a number of "pictorial" metaphors; the brick is a desirable (substance), *iṭṭhi*. The process uses the science, *śulba*, mineralogy. The apparatus is a smelting (*pāka*) device. Lance the ore, kill it; take out the juice, *rasa*, that is gold. [Cf., the section dealing with *iṣṭakas* in *Śatapatha Brāhmaṇa*; and the metaphor of the "bricks."]

The technical term *rasa* is used in the medical texts to connote six types of taste or the dominant property of a substance; it is also used to connote the chemical property of a substance derived from an amalgam of elements or *dhātu*:

pṛthvī + *āp* = *madhura* (sweet)
tejas + *pṛthvī* = *āmla* (sour)
āp + *tejas* = *lavaṇa* (salt)
ākāśa + *vāyu* = *tikta* (bitter)
tejas + *vāyu* = *kaṭu* (acidic)
pṛthvī + *vāyu* = *kaṣāya* (astringent)[40]

The five elements or *dhātu* are also treated as manifested five dominant attributes: *rasa*, *guṇa*, *vīrya*, *vipāka*, and *prabhāva*, resulting in the formation of different substances.[41] The proto-scientist had to coin technical terms to achieve precision in communication; in this process, he had tended to use terms from cognate technologies or sciences. Alchemy can be viewed as the integrating domain of the proto-sciences, relating chemical, medical, mensuration, metallurgical technologies and related devices or substances and processes. For example, in Indian alchemy, as in alchemical traditions of other civilizations, *rasa* or *parada* relates to the use and treatment of mercury in transmutation processes; the substance is so central in a variety of colour- and *rasa* taste-transformations, a science-complex grows around it, yielding *rasa-viddha* or *rasa-ayana* driven, principally, by the dominant search for ways of "making" gold.

Since Śulbaśāstra related not only to geometry of the fore-altars but also to mines and mineralogy (e.g., metallic veins in rocks), according to *Arthaśāstra*, and since the baked-brick technology of the Śulbasūtra is traceable to the proto-Indus evidence of practical production of baked-bricks, it is reasonable to extrapolate the Ṛgvedic Soma *yajña* as a metallurgical legacy which continued to be practised by the proto-Indus lapidary. The archaeological evidences are the chert weights used for weighing precious metals, smelting furnaces, the fire-altars with central clay stele (Kalibangan and Banawali), pits containing animal bones and significant quantities of bronze, copper, gold and silver artifacts with clear indications that some metals were deliberately alloyed. The proto-Indus "cult object" may indeed be a smelter-filter or a proto-*kerotakis*, sublimation apparatus, paralleling the *soma pavamāna* and close affinities between *soma* and gold in Vedic, Brāhmaṇa texts. Soma *yajña* in the *Ṛgveda* maybe explained as the earliest recorded alchemical allegory, interpreting *soma* as electrum, gold-silver pyrite ore and the *yajña* as a smelting process, yielding *rasa* or *amṛtam hiraṇyam*. In the *dakṣiṇāgni* portion of the fire-altar, what is produced is *hiraṇyapiṇḍam* (from out of *hiraṇyagarbha*, the golden womb), the gift for the alchemist-priests—*amṛta*, which according to Manu, is something that is given unasked. [As to why it is given "unasked" is related to the state enterprise which is, in effect, a royalty-priest consortium with predetermined shares of the partnership: three-fourths of the produce goes to the king; and one-fourth to the priests.]

Gold and soma: continuing the saga in Śatapatha Brāhmaṇa

The religious act of *soma* pressing, nay, an industry or the veritable life activity of priesthood, almost becomes an obsession in the days of the Brāhmaṇas:

> As the substance of the sacrifice became diluted and finally vanished, as the Divine inebriant was reduced to a fading sacerdotal memory, inevitably more and more emphasis was placed by the priests on the efficacy of pure liturgy, and sacerdotalism proliferated to a point that the world has never seen equalled.... With the passing of the generations, Soma, the Divine Plant, no longer a part of Hindu experience, became sublimated in later Hindu mythology and took its place in the heavenly firmament as the Moon God.[42]

Use of soma in counter-ideology

A remarkable development occurs as Lokāyata is countered through the force of the rituals and the priest-ruling class consortium.

Soma which was a drink for the gods, Indra in particular, gets appropriated by the Brāhmaṇas. In the *Aitareya Brāhmaṇa* (7.29.2) *soma* is the food for the Brāhmaṇas. For the Kṣatriyas, *Aitareya Brāhmaṇa* (7.32.2) allocates the downward-growing parts of the *nyagrodha*, fruits of the *aśvattha, uḍumbara* and *plakṣa* trees which are regarded as equivalents of *soma*:

athāsyaiṣa svo bhakṣo nyagrodhasyāvarodhās ca phalāni cauḍumbarāṇi āśvatthāni plākṣāny abhiṣunīyāt.

The ritual text justifies this proposition: *parokṣam iva ha vā eṣa somo rājā yan nyagrodhaḥ*; the *nyagrodha* is a hidden form of king Soma.

If a Vaiśya desires partake of *soma* drink, being a sacrificer, he is given *nyagrodha*-buds pounded and mixed with curds, declares Kātyāyana.[43] These references are underscored by Kashikar.[44] The real juice, *rasa,* will perhaps be retained by the priests? The *yakṣa* from Mt. Muñjavat from whom the unpressed *soma* was purchased has of course-been beaten and driven away and hence, is not relevant for the *aṁśa* distribution reckoning.

Needham[45] provides an insight into the possible links between alchemy and *soma,* pointing out the intimate association between gold and the Soma sacrifice:

What is much more important for us is the remarkable fact that in ancient India gold was intimately bound up with the soma sacrifice itself. This is clear from many passages of the *Śatapatha Brāhmaṇa,* datable like all the Brāhmaṇas between the eighth and the fourth centuries, but probably mostly of the seventh. This work is a veritable treasure-house of liturgiology, and gold (*hiraṇyam*) is continually mentioned in it. Let us study a few examples. Gold is the semen of the fire-god Agni, the purest of earthly things, a sacramental symbol of light, fire and immortality....

He (the priest) then brings (an object of gold). Now Agni at one time cast his eyes on the Waters. 'May I pair with them,' he thought. He came together with them, and his seed became gold. For this reason the latter shines like fire, it being Agni's semen. Hence too it is found in water, for he poured it in (Needham adds: surely a reference to placer gold). Hence also one does not cleanse oneself with it, nor does one do anything else with it. Now there is splendour (to honour the fire), for he (the priest) thereby makes it to be possessed of divine seed....[46]

Already we have a passage of strangely alchemical significance, in view of the *conjunctio oppositorum* and the 'marriage of fire and water,' though written and recited perhaps half a millennium before the birth of alchemy. Another version says that after Indra slew Viśvaroopa, son of Tvashtri, the latter burst him into fragments, and 'from his seed his form flowed and became gold.'[47] Afterwards the gods re-integrated him, so the priests 'purify by means of gold, that metal doubtless a form of the gods.'[48] And, 'by means of gold they cleanse themselves, for gold is immortal life, and in this they thus establish themselves.'[49]

For gold is light and fire is light, gold is immortality and fire is immortality.[50] During the liturgy a piece of gold is laid on the altar,[51] in the footprint of the sacrificial cow,[52] and in the wheel-track of the *soma chariot.*[53]

> ...The Buying of *Soma*...why he (the priest) washes his hands. Clarified butter being a thunderbolt and the *soma* being a seed he washes his hands lest he should injure the seed, *soma,* with, the thunderbolt, the ghee. Thereupon he ties the piece of gold to the (ring) finger. Now twofold indeed in this (universe), there is no third, truth there is an untruth; the gods are the truth and men are the untruth. Gold having sprung from Agni's seed, he ties the gold to this (finger) in order that he may touch the stalks (of the *soma*) with the truth, and handle it by means of the truth....[54]

He then makes (the sacrificer) touch the gold and say:

> 'Thee, the pure, I buy with the pure.' For he indeed buys the pure with the pure, when (he exchanges) gold for *soma,* 'the brilliant with the brilliant'...'the immortal with the immortal....'[55]
>
> ...gold threads were woven into the strainers for the *soma* juice.[56] At certain points in the service the priest had to stand on a piece of gold,[57] and it was in gold that his fee was to be paid.[58]
>
> ...if an Agnihotra priest should die, 'the celebrant inserts seven pieces of gold in the seven seats of his vital breaths (*prāṇa*), for gold is light and immortality; thus bestows he light and immortality upon him.'[59] ...a gold plate and the gold image of a man, were essential cult objects in the Agnicayana sacrifice in which the fire-god was exalted.[60] The gold plate, with its 120 knobs representing the rays of the sun, was identified with Indra, or Sūrya the sun; the image with Agni himself, or Prajāpati the creator.[61]
>
> ...in the greatest Indo-Aryan liturgy, the Aśvamedha or horse-sacrifice, gold is inevitably prominent. The slaughtering knife is made of gold, for shining light, and 'by means of the golden light the priest goes to the heavenly world.'[62]

The highlight of the Aśvamedha sacrifice is the investing of the priest-king with a gold ornament (*niṣka*) by the Adhvaryu priest:

Versicle. Fire thou art, light and immortality.
Response. Gold indeed is fire, light and immortality.
[Fiery mettle, brilliance and everlasting life thus he bestows upon him.[63]]

The *Atharvaveda* (XIX. 26; tr. Griffith) extols the giving of a gold ring for long life: The gold that, born out of the fire, immortal, maintains itself over mortals—who so knows it, he verily merits (*arh*) it; one that dies of old age becomes he who bears (*bhṛ*) it.

Plant of longevity

Elaboration of the *soma* aurifaction into alchemical microbiotics occurs in *Suśruta Saṁhitā*[64]: the ritual includes the pricking of the bulb of the *soma* plant by a golden needle and collection of the milky exudation in a golden vessel. Then the medicine was given to "prevent death and decay of the body." When the supply of electrum was no longer available, and when the Indo-Aryan settlers had not fully comprehended the nature of *soma*, the ritual alone remained and a plant was perhaps substituted to attune the process to the *pada-pāṭha* of the texts.[65] This is clearly a reference to one of many substitute "plants which are mentioned in *Śatapatha Brāhmaṇa* to conceal the technologies of the smelting processes described."

"Iṣṭaka" in Śatapatha Brāhmaṇa

Just as the morpheme *śulva* is not used in the text proper of the Śulbasūtras, the morpheme *iṣṭaka* is not used in the *Ṛgveda* or the *Atharvaveda.*

The term used in the *Śatapatha Brāhmaṇa* which may perhaps be linked to the morpheme *śulva-* is: *śulavabhṛta*[66] which is explained as the "spit-bath." The spit is used to substitute for the "purificatory bath;" the "heart of the animal" is roasted not the spit before it is offered; the spit is buried at the point "where the dry and the moist meet."[67] The next Brāhmaṇa adds that some perform the animal sacrifice without *soma,* and others do so with *soma.* The morpheme *śulva* also means copper. The reference is apparently to the process of extracting metal using roasting, smelting processes, in the context of the fire-altar, called *agni,* constructed with *iṣṭaka.* What do *iṣṭaka* mean?

The morpheme is found, possibly as the earliest occurrence in any literary text, in the *Yajurveda: iṣṭaka* (Ṛṣi Medhātithi), *iṣṭakānām* (Gotama), *iṣṭakam* (Viśvadevāḥ), *iṣṭake.*[68] "The words as they occur in the *Yajurveda* may also not mean brick primarily. Only in the Brāhmaṇic age, they have come to mean brick as the construction unit for the sacrificial altars."[69]

A thesis will be advanced that in the *Śatapatha Brāhmaṇa*, the use of the morpheme *iṣṭaka* is metaphorical, shrouding a key alchemical process in mysticism. It can also be hypothesized that the process elaborated in this Brāhmaṇa text is aurifiction, a deceptive attempt to create "gold," knowing that what is produced is not indeed gold.

Alchemical laboratory: pots, pans, substances and the artisans

A precise account of the preparation for the *pravargya* implements and the cauldron (*ukhā*) according to the Baudhāyana (Taittirīya recension) is provided by Kashikar.[70] The substances used include:

skin of black antelope,
earth grubbed by a boar,
earth from an ant-hill,
potsherds from a deserted place,
hair from the skin of a black antelope,
hair of a goat,
a clump of *ūtīka* or *ādāra* plant,
milk of goat,
lumps of the dung of a stallion.[71]

[*Note:* Imagine explaining *soma* as a mushroom-drink consisting of these ingredients; what kind of a medicine is that! How could anyone but the gods drink such a potion? This bill of materials alone may be the most convincing argument the 'decipherment' of *soma* as a plant or a mushroom.]

A skilled artisan is required to prepare the bowl of *mahāvīra pot* (*gharma*) plus the entire apparatus with a broad bottom and contracted in the middle; he is also required to bore it through two parts of the entire height by means of the bamboo-piece. The cavity is meant to hold the liquid libation. According to *Kātyāyana Śrauta-sūtra* (XVI.2-4), the preparation of the cauldron requires some additional substances or preparations: *palāśa-kaṣāya* (*Butea frondosa*), powdered rust of iron and powder of stone (*sarkara-ayorasa-aśma-cūrṇa*). The need for a potter (*kulāla*) is mentioned in the *Maitrāyaṇī-saṁhitā* (I.8.3).

From this bill of materials, devices, and list of talented artisans required, two facts emerge: the help of a potter and other artisans is essential, since the priest lacks the skill to prepare the utensils or the apparatus; some alchemical substances are used in the process. The earth grubbed by a boar are relatable to the later-day numismatic evidence of Varāha connoting a gold coin; the ant-hill evokes the imagery of the "ant-gold." The hairs of goat and antelope are relatable to the method for preparing sal ammoniac as a reducing agent. Powdered rust of iron and powder of stone evoke memories of the *pāṣaṇḍa*; so do potsherds from a deserted place recall the proto-Indus sites and traditions of lapidary crafts and artifacts. The link with the *caṇḍāla* images is extraordinary indeed, though the context is the *soma* liquefying process called a *yajña*.

Agni-rahasya: the "secrecy" of the fire-altar and the "divine brick"

The entire tenth book of *Śatapatha Brāhmaṇa* is called *agni-rahasya*, continuing the topic dealt with in the preceding four *kāṇḍas*. The chief authority for this secret process is Śāṇḍilya whose lineage in fire rituals is traced to a teacher called Tura Kāvaṣeya,[72] stated to be discoverer of the fire-altar. Tura Kāvaṣeya reportedly built a fire-altar for the gods at Kārotti.[73] In *Aitareya Brāhmaṇa*, he is stated to have officiated at the inaugural of the king Janamejaya Parīkṣita.[74] Thus the Brāhmaṇas trace a dual tradition, one from Yājñavalkya and the other from Śāṇḍilya.

Yajurveda invokes the celestial brick, using imagery which the *Ṛgveda* has used for *soma*:

> Thou spreading with a hundred, thou that branchest with a thousand shoots,—Thee such with our oblation will we worship, O celestial brick (*devīṣṭake*).[75]
>
> Indra and Agni, in its place securely set the unshaking brick.[76]

While the *Śatapatha Brāhmaṇa* echoes the layers of fire-altars as depicted in the *Yajurveda* [for example, the lotus-leaf, burial of the tortoise, *dūrva* brick, *dviyajus* brick, two *retaḥsic* or seed-pouring bricks, *ṛtavya* or seasonal bricks, all-light brick, *aṣāḍha* or the invincible brick] an imposing array of specialized bricks is organized in the ritual, including for instance, *aśvini* bricks, *vaiśvadevi* bricks, *prāṇabhṛta* or breath-supporting bricks, *disyās* or directional bricks, *spṛta* or deliverer bricks and even *sṛṣṭis* or creation bricks. Out of this imposing ritual edifice, how to unravel the key alchemical ideas weaving through a geometrical, architectural (altar) allegory?

"Geometry" of the fire-altar as in alchemical treatise

There is an apparent link between the Śulvasūtras and the

Śatapatha Brāhmaṇa. For, the first Brāhmaṇa of the third *adhyāya* in Book (*kāṇḍa*) VII begins with a refrain: "Built is the *garhapatya,* unbuilt the *āhavanīya;* he then buys the king (*soma*)..." followed by explanatory statements on why he buys the king when *garhapatya* is built and the *āhavanīya* unbuilt. In the course of this explanatory excursus, the Brāhmaṇa includes some impressive statements:

> ...he interlinks the performance of the (*soma*) sacrifice and the performance of the fire (altar) for the purpose of unity of performance, thinking 'Uniform shall be this performance.' And, again, why he interlinks them,—Agni (the fire-altar) is the body, and the (*soma*) sacrifice is the vital air; he thus places the vital air in the midst of the body, and hence that vital air is in the middle of the body.[77]

The import of these statements is that *soma* is an integral part of the fire-altar itself. *Soma* is embedded in *agni.* [Cf., the interpretation of *soma* as gold-silver-pyrite or electrum ore; in this perspective, the process of assembling the fire-altar may be seen as the process of organizing the materials in layers, to transmute "some specific" (called *āṣāḍha*) base mineral ore- or metal-block, called an *iṣṭaka.*]

The *āṣāḍha* is the "invincible" brick formed by the *mahiṣī,* queen (cf. *soma* = buffalo: *DEDR*). The material used is the "earth...created first of the three worlds. She forms it of that same clay, for this earth is (one) of these worlds."[78]

There is a reference to a difference of opinion among the Brāhmaṇa schools on who has the competence to build the fire-altar. Aktakṣya is of the view that "only he who knows abundant bricks possessed of prayers, should build up the fire (altar); abundantly indeed he then heals Father Prajāpati." A contrary view is expressed by the elitist group represented by Tāṇḍya, "Surely the bricks possessed of prayers are the nobility (*yajuṣmati*) and the space-fillers (*lokam-pṛṇa*) are the peasants; and the noble is the feeder, and the peasantry the food; and where there is abundant food for the feeder, the realm is indeed prosperous and thrives; let him therefore pile-up abundant space-fillers!" Such then was the speech of those two, but the settled practice is different therefrom.[79] In technical terms, the Brāhmaṇa refrain is: *lokam-pṛṇa chidrem pṛṇa,* "fill the space, fill the gap." The architecture of the altar is therefore at two levels: one with special bricks and the other with space-fillers. [Cf., the analysis of Debiprasad Chattopadhyaya, in *Lokāyata* on the ideological import of the distinction between the nobility and the peasants.] "He lays down this (*lokam-pṛṇa*) in all the (five) layers, for those layers are these (three) worlds: he thus places the sun in (all) these worlds, whence he shines for all these worlds. And, again, as to why he lays down a *lokam-pṛṇa,*—the *lokam-pṛṇa,* doubtless, is the nobility (or chieftaincy), and these other bricks are the peasants (or clansmen)...he thus places the nobility, as the eater, among the whole peasantry (or in every clan)."[80] The clash in views between Tāṇḍya and the author of the Brāhmaṇa is apparent. *Lokam-pṛṇa* was the food and an integral component of the fire-altar structure, filling all its spaces and making it a whole. The author was, perhaps, trying to draw analogies from the hierarchical order of society with clans and chieftains, an order with which he was familiar.

A reference to a mixing process which is tough to interpret relates to *sūdadohas.* "Those his well-like milking ones—a well (*sūda*) means water, and milking means food;—'the speckled ones mix with *soma,*'—the speckled (cow) means food;—'at the birth of the gods,'—the tribes (*vis*), doubtless, are the sacrifice, for all beings are ranged (*viṣṭa*) under the sacrifice;—'in the three spheres of the heavens,'—the three spheres of the heavens, doubtless are the (three) pressing (of *soma*): he thus means the pressings.... This same *sūdadohas,* whilst being a single (verse), extends over all the bricks, whence—*sūdadohas* being the vital air—this vital air, whilst being one only, extends over all the limbs, over the whole body."[81]

The *sūdadohas* verse from *Ṛgveda,* VIII.69.3 (also in *Yajurveda,* XII.55) is interpreted as follows: "At his birth, the well-like milking, speckled ones mix the *soma* (drought), the clans of the gods in the three spheres of the heavens." This difficult verse has received a variety of translations. The *Śatapatha Brāhmaṇa* gives its own fanciful interpretation, as explained above. The morpheme *dohas* means "milking," "a milk pail." The morpheme *sudā* means "giving willingly." The radical *sūd-* ="to enjoy, eat." [It is not clear if *sūda-dohas* may be interpreted as a reconstruction of two morphemes: *suddha* + *dohas* or purified body.] The morpheme *sūda* is traceable to proto-Dravidian origin[82]: *cun-ai,* mountain pool or spring; tank, reservoir, pasture-ground with tanks and shady trees. The etyma point to its key characteristics: it is water from the rocks; it is speckled. Maybe, placer gold is referred to. In this etymological perspective, it may be appropriate to interpret the compound, *sūdadohas* to mean "well-milking or well-yielding."

Alchemical idiom of the plebeians: "āṣāḍha-bhūti, swindler"

An idiom is popular in Tamil tradition: *āṣāḍha-bhūti.* The phrase connotes a swindler, a semantic expansion of a term which originally perhaps referred to an alchemist who believed that gold had been created. The plebeian tradition is so vibrant that the term *āṣāḍha* rings true as the alchemical symbol *par excellence.* The meaning of this symbol has to be unravelled to gain insights into the reality of the *rasa-pāka* operations of the *ṛtvij, purohita, adhvaryu* and their *sakhās* (artisan-associates or associates with technological, metallurgical, alchemical skills.)

A succinct explanation is provided on the provenance of the clay use for *āṣāḍha,* the special, invincible brick: "...when that deity (Prajāpati) became relaxed, he flowed along this (earth) in the shape of this life-sap (*rasa*); and when the gods restored him (put him together), they gathered him up from this earth, this earth then is that one brick (*āṣāḍha*), for Agni is this earth, since it is thereof (viz., by means of the clay bricks, and the loose soil put between the layers) that the whole Agni is built up...."[83]

The key explanation lies in the five-layered architecture [involving the solid-geometry computations of the Śulbasūtras] of the *agni* or the fire-altar:

"...But if he (*agni*) thus consists of one brick, how then (comes to be) a five-bricked[84] one? Now surely the first brick of clay is this earth (*āṣāḍhā brick*),—whatever made of clay he places on that (altar) that is that one brick. And when he puts thereon the heads of the animal victims,[85] that is the animal brick (so-called *iṣṭaka-paśu*). And when he puts on the gold plate and man,[86] when he scatters gold shavings thereon, that is the *golden brick.* And when he puts on two spoonfuls (of ghee),[87] when he puts on the mortar and pestle,[88] and fire-sticks,[89] that is the *wood brick.* And when he puts on a lotus-leaf (petal), a tortoise,[90] some curds, honey, ghee, and whatever other food he puts on, that is the fifth brick, the *food* (brick). Thus, then, it is a five-bricked (*agni*)."[91] The central portion of the fifth layer with a ring of 29 *stoma bhāga* bricks, symbolises the firmament.

The *agni* or the fire-altar is thus, composed of five layers (*citayaḥ*):

1. *āṣāḍha* (some kind of porous stone),
2. animal omenta with embedded gold buttons,
3. gold plate and shavings,
4. fire-sticks, and

5. other calx/reducing agents (food) [including a tortoise—*kūrma, kaśyapa*—, the yonder sun]

The libation of ghee is the incessant process. This is required to be made[92] using the verse containing (the name) *hiraṇyagarbha* (cf., *ṚV*, X.121.1, *hiraṇyagarbhaḥ samavartatāgre*): *"hiraṇyagarbha* (the golden child) came first into existence; he was born as the only lord of all being; he sustained this earth and sky: what god (or the god *Ka*) shall we serve with offering." The intent is clear: the *rasa* has to be extracted from the womb to transmute the "naturally-perforated bricks" in the centre, the *svayam-ātṛṇṇa* bricks laid down with the formula: "May Prajāpati settle thee!"[93] The settlement of this *svayam-ātṛṇṇa* bricks is the key technological process involved in the entire Soma *yajña*. "May the Most High settle thee!"[94]

The *svayam-ātṛṇṇa* gets equated with the resplendent sun as the *yajña* proceeds; sun, the primordial symbol of gold. The allegory gains added dimensions by references to the bird bringing in the *amṛta* from the ocean [the ocean is the gold plate, the bird is the (gold) man[95]]. The alchemical process is vivid: he gold man and the gold plate are expected to yield the *rasa* to tint and transmute the invincible *āṣāḍha* brick, the *svayam-ātṛṇṇa*, the naturally-perforated one.[96]

A possible semantic structure of the two phrases: *lokam-pṛṇa* and *svayam-ātṛṇṇa* may be proposed: *loha-* is metal; *ayas-* is metal. *Lohāyas* is a Vedic term generally connoting a red metal, either a copper ingot or copper alloyed with some other metal. The explanation of *lokam-pṛṇa* as the food in metaphorical terms may link it to *loha-* as the red-coloured copper. The morpheme, *svayam-* may be a metathesis of *ayasam* and since the *svayam-ātṛṇṇa* is a pebbled, perforated block, specially prepared by the queen (cf. the king is entitled to three-fourth share of the produce from the Soma *yajña*), the block may indeed be the unrefined electrum or *soma* ore block, given the general connotation of metal, *ayasa*, with the impurities of lead and other metallic oxides, not excluding iron or ferric oxides. That *kārṣṇāyasa* or black metal means iron in *Chāndogya Upaniṣad* lends credence to the interpretation of *ayasam* or its metathesis (*svayam-*) in *svayam-ātṛṇṇa* as connoting a natural alloy of metals, which will be subjected to the *yajña* process in great secrecy, under the supervision of the *ṛtvij* and *adhvaryu*, the specialists in the metallic veins, bellows and well-versed in Śulvasūtras [*śulva* connoting copper, in particular (according to the

Sanskrit lexicon of Monier-Williams), or metallic veins in general, as distinct from *dhātuśāstra* which relates to metals]. *Ṛgveda* refers to smelting by the blacksmith: *brahmaṇaspati-r-etāḥ sam karmāra ivādhamat* (*ṚV*, X.72.2). The *pravargya* vessel, cauldron of metal is received by the *ṛk* singers: *gharma-ś-cit tapaḥ pravṛje ya ādīd ayas-mayas-tam vādāma viprāḥ* (*ṚV*, I.31.15). The morpheme *tṛṇṇa* is interpreted as "pierced, cracked" and used in compounds with prefixes: *ati-*, *aa-*, *vi-*, *sam-*. In Kashmiri *tronu* means a dark hole, chasm; in Hindi, *tiṅkanā* means "to prick, break into a passion." No wonder, the queen, *mahiṣi* breaks into a passion with the horse in Aśvamedha, even if only in allegorical terms. The connotation of the dark hole in the cognate Kashmiri morpheme *tronu* lends added weight to the interpretation of *svayam-ātṛṇṇa* as a naturally-occurring alloy of metals, electrum.

The nature of the *āṣāḍha*[97] brick is likely to yield some clues to the alchemical objectives involved. It is "eight-fold appointed . . . which had been created aforetime."[98] It is made of clay. The clay is prepared by very special procedures: The water (used for working the clay) is boiled by means of resin of the *palāśa* tree (*Butea frondosa*), just for the sake of firmness . . . "the *palāśa* tree doubtless is *soma*, and *soma* is the moon and that (moon) indeed is one of Agni's forms: it is for the obtainment of that form of Agni (that *palāśa* resin is used)."[99] What is allegorical and what is real in such a statement? Is it not plausible to perceive in this statement a reference to the preliminary treatment of *soma* ore by first mixing it with water and treat the metaphorical reference to the moon as a reference to the colour of the ore, possibly, *rajata-mākṣikā* or silver-copper pyrite ore? The reference to the "waters" is important since it is a triplet almost deifying the "waters:" "Refreshing ye are, O waters; lead us to strength, to see great joy!—whatever is your most benign sap (*rasa*), therein let us share, like loving mothers!— For you will readily go to him, to whose abode ye urge us, O waters, and quicken us."[100]

An *āṣāḍha* brick is also *svayam-ātṛṇṇa*. The latter compound may be interpreted as *śalkarā* or *śarkarā* "having the shape of pieces" or *mṛṇmiśra sūkṣma pāṣāṇ*, "grit, pebbles, gravel."[101] *Śarkarā* in Pāli refers also to a potsherd; a significant phrase is: *loṇa-śarkarā*, "salt crystal, a solid piece of natural salt."[102] Other comparable Pāli compounds: *loṇa-sakkharikā*, a piece of salt crystal used as a caustic for healing wounds; *loṇāni bhesajjāni*, alkaline medicine among which *sāmuddan kākla-loṇan sindhavan; loṇa-kāra,* salt-maker; *loṇa-phala,* crystal of natural salt. The compound is therefore interpreted as the *śarkarā* having natural holes. A brick made of clay with grit, pebbles and gravel; a brick with *śalka* or chips, shavings, pieces; a phrase exemplifies this: *hiraṇya*[103] *śalkān pratyaśyanti.*[104]

In specific terms, therefore, the *āṣāḍhā* brick may be interpreted as a lump of unrefined silver-gold, electrum ore or *hema/rajata mākṣikā* (gold/silver pyrite ore).

In the Tamil and Siddha traditions, *hema* connotes "alchemical gold" and *taṅkam* connotes "pure gold." The task of the Soma *yajña* is to refine this *āṣāḍhā* block and lend lustre through an alchemical, transmutation process. The morpheme-*ātṛṇṇa* "pierced, split, injured or with holes" is descriptive of its physical shape, clearly distinguishing this brick as not made of smooth or soft caly.[105]

The term *āṣāḍha* may also be related to the later-day compounds: *aṣṭa-dhātu* or *aṣṭa-maṅgaḷa* having eight auspicious signs. In Prākṛta, *āṣāḍhī* means "full-moon day."[106] The association of *soma* with the moon is perhaps echoed in the use of the synonym, *āṣāḍha* to denote the *soma* brick (perhaps white-coloured like the moon which will become golden after the *yajña!*). The term *āṣāḍham* means in Tamil "fourth lunar month, roughly corresponding to *āṭi,*" a month of the ripening of crops, mainly pulses; in Punjabi, *hāḍhi* refers to crops sown in winter; Sindhi: *hāḍu,* summer, hot weather (June-July).

Tamil tradition provides the semantic expansion, in folklore, of the remarkable phrase: *āṣāḍha-bhūti,* "hypocrite, swindler, as resembling a character of the name in the *Pañcatantra.*" The alchemical tradition of working with *āṣāḍha* mineral ore and ashes, *bhūti* seems to encapsulate the nature of the secretive operations of the Brāhmaṇa *svayam-ātṛṇṇa* brick carefully laid by the Mahiṣī, the queen who also participates in the final, bizarre act of mating with the sacrificed horse in Aśvamedha, before the transmutation process is brought to a successful conclusion.

In the eleventh book of *Śatapatha Brāhmaṇa* the full- and new-moon sacrifices are explained. [Cf., the concordance with *āṣāḍha* full-moon.] The recurrent use of "alchemical" technical terms is significant, for example: "Now when they spread (and perform) the sacrifice, they kill it; and when they press out king *soma,* they kill him; and when they 'quiet' and cut up the victim, they kill it. By using the mortar and pestle, and by using the two mill-stones, they *kill havir-yajña* (grain-offering). And having killed the sacrifice, the sacrificer pours it, as seed, into the fire as its womb, for indeed, the fire is the womb, for indeed, the fire is the womb of the sacrifice, from out of it, it is produced: let him therefore perform those ten oblations for which the *vaṣaṭ* is uttered."[107] In an extraordinary text of mixed metaphors, mythology, mysticism and allegory, it becomes incredibly difficult to extract the technological processes and substances involved. A statement such as: "...for indeed, the Aśvamedha is the same as the moon"[108] can be related to the white colour of the horse and the white colour of the electrum ore allegorized as the moon in Brāhmaṇa texts. For another refrain is: "...for the moon, doubtless, is the same as king *soma*, the food of the gods."[109] The repeated desires relate to the attainment of brilliance, glory, holy lustre, prosperity,[110] evoking the lustre and effulgence of gold, symbolizing the sun.

Threefold science: bhūḥ, bhuvaḥ, svar

"He (the priest) heated these three Vedas, and from them, thus heated, three luminous essence were produced—*bhūḥ* from the *Ṛgveda*, *bhuvaḥ* from the *Yajurveda*, and *svar* from the *Sāmaveda* ...and what luminous essence there was in the threefold science, therewith the work of the Brāhmaṇa priest then proceeded."[111] Sāyaṇa interprets the morpheme *śukra* in this Brāhmaṇa in the sense of "flame, light" while the *St. Petersburg* dictionary interprets it as "sap, juice." In the latter part of the verse, the morpheme is interpreted by Sāyaṇa as "pure, essential part." In another context, the triple science is explained as: *stoma, vedas* and *bṛhat (rathāntara)*.[112] The point to note is that the science of the Vedas guarded as a secret with extraordinary fidelity by enforcing only oral transmission is related to the economic- or life-activity of the priestly-royal classes, which is controlling and manipulating the production of *śukra*, the luminous essence, also referred to as *rasa* in other contexts. "...wherewith then is the work of the Brāhmaṇa (performed)? Let him reply, 'With that threefold science.'"[113]

The death of an *angihotri* calls for the use of symbol of immortality: "He then inserts seven chips of gold in the seven seats of his vital airs (orifices of the corpse); for gold is light and immortality: he thus bestows light and immortality on him."[114] If the ritual related to death are allegorical references to the death of the *hiraṇya puruṣa*, some texts and symbolisms are significantly alchemical: "...from that intestine of his, filled with foul matter, when it is burnt, a jackal[115] is produced...having washed him out inside, he anoints him with ghee, and thus makes it (the body) sacrificially pure."[116] The phrase *somena yakṣye* means, "I will sacrifice by means of *soma*."[117] The remarkable etymological concordance between *yakṣa* and *yajña* is perhaps not accidental. [Cf., notes on the *purve yājñikāḥ*, the sacrificers of antiquity].

In the *sautrāmaṇi* one of the seven divisions of the *havir-yajña* involving *iṣṭi*, the use of spirituous liquor or *surā* is linked with "*soma* juice suitable for witchery" and withheld from Indra. (Withholding from Indra means that this liquor is not used in the *yajña* process.) The use of the term *surā* is relatable to the newly-acquired knowledge of distillation from the "peasantry."[118] An extraordinary allegory of substances and symbols in presented relating Indra's slaying of Tvaṣṭṛ's son, Viśvarūpa: "From his mouth his strength flowed, it became that animal, the bull; and what foam there was became barely, and what moisture there was became the *karkandhu*-fruit. From his ear his glory flowed, and became the one-hoofed animals, the horse, mule and ass.... From the breasts his bright (vital) sap (*rasa*) flowed and became milk, the light of cattle (wealth)...and became the talon-slaying eagle,[119] the king of birds. From his navel his life-breath flowed, and became lead,[120]—not iron, nor silver;[121] from his seed his form flowed, and became gold; from his generative organ his essence flowed, and became *parisṛt* (raw fiery liquor); from his hips his fire flowed, and became *surā* (matured liquor), the essence of food. From his urine his vigour flowed, and became the wolf, the impetuous rush of wild beasts; from the contents of his intestines his fury flowed, and became the tiger, the king of wild beasts; and from his blood his might flowed, and became the lion, the ruler of wild beasts...from his skin his honour flowed and became the *aśvattha* tree (*Ficus religiosa*); from his flesh his force flowed, and became the *uḍumbara* tree (*Ficus glomerata*); from his bones his sweet drink flowed, and became the *nyagrodha* tree (*Ficus indica*); from his marrow his drink, the *soma*-juice, flowed, and became rice: in this way his energies, or vital powers went from him."[122]

This is a precis of the Brāhmaṇa language of alchemy, an extraordinary evocation of the ingredients integral to the *yajña* process and of the imageries which recur in distinct steps elaborated in Brāhmaṇa texts.

Perforated pottery and integration of two alchemical traditions

The *sautrāmaṇi* sacrifice is a representation of the mingling of two alchemical traditions. A notable reference to the perforated pot with a hundred holes evokes the images of the proto-Indus archaeological finds[123] of perforated pottery (*kumbhi*)[124] perforated with a hundred holes, for in many ways did that (*soma*) flow out of (Indra):[125] "...for the *sautrāmaṇi* is a means of purification." The following explanatory note by Eggeling is quoted in full because of its archaeological-historical relevance: "...according to *Kātyāyana Śrautasūtra*, XIX.3.20, and Mahidhara on *Vājasaneyisaṁhitā*, XIX.37, use is made of this pot at this juncture in much the same way as is described in V.5.4.27ff.; viz., two poles are driven into the ground north and south of the southern fire, and a bamboo stick laid thereon: on a string fastened to this stick the pot, containing a tail-whisk (for straining) and the piece of gold,[126] is then made to hang over the fire, and the remains of the *surā*-liquor poured into it; and whilst it trickles through into the fire, the priests make the sacrificer pronounce the verses *Vājasaneyisaṁhitā*, XIX.37-44, 52-60, addressed to the different kinds of departed ancestors."[127] A recollection, perhaps, of the legacy of the proto-Indus techniques of distillation and aurifaction!

The *śatarudrīya* lustration[128] to Rudra, after completing the construction of *agni*, fire-altar, is a prayer in reverence, almost out of fear, to the alchemists (and artisans who might have assisted in the construction process) who do not subscribe to the ideology of the Brāhmaṇas: "III.22. Reverence be to the turbaned mountaineer, and to the lord of spoilers be reverence! Reverence be to shooters of arrows, and to ye bowmen, be reverence!... IV.27. Reverence be to the carpenters, and to ye, wheelwrights, be reverence! Reverence be to the potters, and to ye, blacksmiths, be reverence! Reverence be to the jungle tribes, and to ye, fishermen, be reverence! Reverence be to the dog-keepers, and to ye huntsmen be reverence! Reverence be to dogs, and to ye masters of dogs be reverence! Reverence be to Bhava and to Rudra! Reverence be to Sarva and to Paśupati (Lord of Beasts)!... [the golden-armed leader of hosts (*gaṇa*)]."[129]

The naturally-perforated brick, *aṣāḍha* is from the *uttara-vedī*, a preparatory process before leading it to the fire of the *agni*, fire-altar; and everytime, the ghee libation is made, chips of gold are thrown down, with the *svāhā* calls.[130] There is a conscious attempt to hide the nature of the sacrifice from the *asuras*: They had become aware of the offerings; they should be made to go away thinking "It is something else they are doing."[131]

The Aśvamedha process may be explained as an alchemical allegory: the horse symbolizes the seeding of the *āṣāḍha* brick formed (hence, personified) by the *mahiṣi. Soma* juice is the seed of the vigorous steed. In the *agni* or the fire-altar, the *stomabhāga* bricks refer to the *soma* ore blocks; the *āṣāḍha* bricks the base-metal block to be transmuted. The sacrificed horse, the brick-layer among the five layers of the sacrifice, impregnates the base metal and transmutes it. The *mahiṣi, āṣāḍha,* unites with the *aśva*'s seed, *soma.* The sacrificial essence of the horse has been gained. The *mahiṣi* lies down near the horse; in heaven she envelops herself; "may the vigorous male, the layer of seed, lay seed," she says for the completeness of union: *niryāyatyāśvasya śiśnam mahiṣi upasthe nidhatte; "vṛṣa vāji retodhā reto dadhātv" iti mithunasyaiva sarvatvāya.* Brahman and *mahiṣi,* their father and mother (ancestral forms of the lustrous metal) mount and play on the top of the tree..., with that little bird (*rasa,* essence).[132] The divine service or transmutation is accomplished. The *āṣāḍha-bhūti* has completed his grand process of aurification, and explained the process in erotic, orgasmic allegory. *Mahiṣi* = *soma* = buffalo; the *mithuna* (mating) of *mahiṣi* and *aśva* is the process of using horse meat and bones as reducing / oxidizing agents in purifying *soma,* electrum (silver-gold ore), i.e., oxidizing other metallic components of the ore (such as lead and silver) and extracting the lustrous metal, gold.

Gnawing conscience: alienated labour

The *śatarudrīya* lustration which is a clear concession made by the bureaucratic priests (royalty-priest combine) to the terrifying *sva-pākas* and their kind (who were fiercely free and functioned independently of the royal patronage); the lustration made out of fear also involves some admiration because these *śva-pākas* can perform the *pāka* daily, *śvaḥśvas,* each morning, everyday; as opposed to the royalty-priests' predicament of starting the *rasa-pāka* only after the *gandharva* delivers the *soma* raw-material.

The *śatarudrīya* lustration as well as the dialogues between Śāṇḍilya and Tura Kavaṣeya are examples of a gnawing conscience of the Brāhmaṇa priest who is unclear if he has alienated himself by performing sacrifices for others (the royalty in particular), for a fee; and tries to find justification for his mode of living, which yields only a *dakṣiṇā* for all his *sava* or labour:

> ...having performed them for another person, they either perform them (sacrifices) for themselves or cause them to be performed again: this is the atonement.... And Śāṇḍilya once up a time said—Tura Kavaṣeya once built a fire-altar for the gods at Kārotti. The gods asked him, 'Sage, seeing that they declare the building of the fire-altar not to be conducive to heaven, why then hast thou built one?' He said, 'What is conducive to heaven, and what is not conducive thereto? The Scarifier is the body of the sacrifice, and the officiating priests are the limbs.... And, verily, if the priests have no place in heaven, then the Scarificer has none, for both are of the same world. But let there be no bargaining as to sacrificial fees, for by bargaining the priests are deprived of their place in heaven.'[133]

The priest who has gained a nexus with the royalty and privileged classes is indeed trying to find an extraordinary justification for a situation he has landed himself in; unlike the *caṇḍāḷa* or *pāṣaṇḍa* or *śvapāka*, the Brāhmaṇa priest has lost the freedom to perform the sacrifice [using the *ṛk* (hymn verses) to put the vital fluid into the *soma-cup*][134] for himself. as a free person, as a person who owes allegiance, if at all, only to Rudra and to the Mother Goddess, for instance. *Agnicit* (he who has built an altar) is borne in yonder world as one made of gold[135] (Sāyaṇa assigns to *hiraṇmaya* the meaning of "colour resembling gold").

The priest has realized that he has lost his individuality; he has become the mere limb of the body (of the sacrificer); he is locked into a consortium with the royalty, elite, ruling class. His alienation is complete. A *śvapāka* can perform the *pāka* daily; but the priest cannot. A *śvapāka* is free; the priest is not. A *śvapāka* does not work for a *dakṣiṇā*; the priest does. A *śvapāka* is free; the priest is "employed for a wage." He has become "the limbs of the body" of a sacrificer—the royalty. Catechism of labour! Seeds of isolation and eventual decline of both the *caṇḍāḷa (śvapāka)* and the Brāhmaṇa or sacerdotal classes had been sown. The *caṇḍāḷa* is relegated to the background by the ruling classes because he is free; the Brāhmaṇa gets reduced to abject dependence on "gifts" from the ruling classes because he works for a "fee" or *dakṣiṇā.*

Brāhmaṇas: the texts are bureaucratic "procedure manuals" for the priests

"They represent the intellectual activity of a sacerdotal caste which, by turning to account the religious instincts of a gifted and naturally devout race, had succeeded in transforming a primitive worship of the powers of nature into a highly artificial system of sacrificial ceremonies, and was ever intent on deepening and extending its hold on the minds of the people, by surrounding its own vocation with the halo of sanctity and divine inspiration.... Though the *dānastutis*, or verses extolling often in highly exaggerated terms, the munificence of princely patrons, and generally occurring at the end of hymns, are doubtless, as a rule, later additions, they at least show that the sacerdotal office must have been, or must gradually have become during this period, a very lucrative one...the religious service would seem to have been already of a sufficiently advanced nature to require some kind of training for the priestly office . . . priesthood in the community was that of a *regular profession*, and even to some extent, a *hereditary* one. A post of peculiar importance, which seems to go back to a very early time, was that of the *purohita*[136] (literally 'propositus'), or family priest to chiefs and kings . . . a minister of public worship and confidential adviser of the king . . . (with) exceptional opportunities for promoting the hierarchical aspirations of the priesthoood . . . the more complicated the ceremonial, the greater the dependence of the lay worshipper on the professional skill of the priests...."[137]

The *āṣāḍha* brick refers to the gold brick resulting from the accumulations by *akṣapaṭalādhyakṣa* from all departments of the State who are required to submit the "revenues" to the treasury on *āṣāḍha* or full-moon day. This is corroborated by the procedure documented in the *Arthaśāstra*. *Arthaśāstra*[138] stipulates the procedure for submitting the accounts (by each department) on the *āṣāḍha*[139] full-moon day: "When the (officers) have come with sealed account books and balances in sealed containers, he (*akṣa-paṭalādhyakṣa*) should impose restriction in one place, not allowing conversation (among them)." The *āṣāḍha* day is, obviously, a big event in the affairs of the State. The actions which follow the accumulation of the treasure (in the form of *akṣas* of gold pellets in standard units of measure) is fundamental in the processes of the big sacrifice in which even the queen participates.

The *purohita* is a dignitary in the king's court. His role is crucial in a state enterprise organized for *alchemy*. To trace this extraordinary evolution of capitalism, *Arthaśāstra* provides some leads which will be pursued.

References

1. Julien Ries, translated from French by David M. Weeks, "Immortality," in *ER*, pp. 122ff.
2. Cf., A striking Dravidian parallel: *Dravidian Etymological Dictionary (DEDR)*, 5457: *Kota, vi-ra-ṇy vaṇm*, small gold coin put in mouth of dead man and burned with body (*paṇm* coin); Toda: *pi-r boṇm* small, old coins in bag, used at funeral; Kodagu: *bira-ni*, pagoda = 4 rupees. Tamil (lex.): *vīra-k-kal*, memorial stone.
3. Strabo (XV.70; R.C. Majumdar, *The Classical Accounts of India*, Calcutta, 1960, p. 281) uses the term, *pramnae*, based on Megasthenes (*c.* 300 BC).
4. A.L. Basham, "Practice of Medicine in Ancient India," in Charles Leslie, ed., *Asian Medical System: A Comparative Study*, p. 24; R.C. Majumdar, pp. 273-75.
5. Cf., *CDIAL*, 12683: *śramaṇa*, ascetic, religious mendicant, *Śatapatha Brāhmaṇa*; Pāli, Prākṛta: *samaṇa*, ascetic; Dardic: *shamana*; Old Sinhala: *mahaṇā, māṇa*, id.; *CDIAL*, 8723: *pramāṇa*, measure, standard, authority; Pāli, Prākṛta: *pamāṇa*, measure; Old Sinhala: *pamaṇin* according to scale. In Pāli: *pamāṇika* is one who measures (lex.). The Tamil tradition distinguishes between *camaṇarum cākkiyarum*, an apparent reference to Jainas and Buddhists, perhaps to the two broad schools of Lokāyata and Sāṅkhya.
6. Cf., Debiprasad Chattopadhyaya, *HSTAI*, p. 116, n. 6.
7. Cf., cognate Tamil *kampaṭṭam*, coinage, coin; Greek *gammadium*, cross; Sanskrit *sampuṭa*, a fold, casket hollow inside; cf. also Ṛgvedic *tvaṣṭṛ* and *Arthaśāstra*, 2.13.44, *tvaṣṭṛkāru*, gilder plater!
8. Joseph Needham, "The Unity of Science in the Old World," *Clerks and Craftsmen*, pp. 19-21.
9. Arthur Waley, "Notes on Chinese Alchemy," *BSOS*, 1930, VI, 1, pp. 1-24.
10. Edouard Chavannes, ed. and tr., *Memoire sur les religieux eminents qui allerent chercher la loi dans le pays d' Occident, par Yi-tsing*, Paris, 1894, p. 21.
11. Needham, "The Unity of Science in the Old World," *Clerks and Craftsmen*, pp. 19-21.
12. Arthur Waley, "Notes on Chinese Alchemy," *BSOS*, 1930, VI, 1, pp. 1-24.
13. Henry Yule, *The Book of Ser Marco Polo*, ed., Henri Cordier, 2 vols., third edn., London, 1903; reprinted, New Delhi, 1993, vol. 2, pp. 365ff.
14. Hopkins, op. cit., pp. 44-45, "Just as the magician became the astrologer and later the astronomer, in the same way the maker of imitation—the counterfeiter if you will—became the alchemist and later the chemist.

It has been said that the whole object of alchemy was deception.... But this characterization of the alchemist should be accepted, even if granted, not as a disgrace; for the artisans were supplying the people with metals which were frankly baubles like our jewelry. Their only fault was that they succeeded too well." *Śatapatha Brāhmaṇa* of the White *Yajurveda* stipulates a certain *yoṣā* (female) shape for the fire-altar, and a *vṛṣaṇa* (testicle) shape for the fire. *Aitareya Brāhmaṇa* links the *vājapeya* verses and coitus: "He separates the two syllables, the woman separates her thighs, he utters the first two syllables, the man activates his hips. This is pairing." The term "deception," is not used lightly; apart from metaphor, a metaphysical justification is offered by *Bṛhadāraṇyaka Upaniṣad*: "The gods love the obscure and hate the obvious." [A vivid reference to allegorical nature of the gods names used in the Veda.] Of course, *mantras* cannot be disclosed to the *paśu,* the herd, the proletariat. Tantrics too evolve a *sandhyā bhāṣā,* twilight speech. *Guhyād guhyam* or secret of secrets cannot be committed to writing but dealt with as *karṇa-tantra,* doctrines whispered in the ears of the adept-disciple. In *Bṛhadāraṇyaka Upaniṣad,* Yājñavalkya tells Ārtabhāga (of Jaratkaru lineage) that the destiny of the dead is not to be discussed in public; he says, "we two alone shall talk of this" and leads Ārtabhāga to a hidden place for the teaching. Some truths are so secret that they cannot even be uttered but conveyed only through *mudrās.*

15. Needham, *SCC,* vol. 5, part II, p. 44.
16. Cf., Hopkins, op. cit., p. 61 on the Layden Papyrus X (with which may be joined the Papyrus Holmiensis). The papyrus has separate books, one for each letter of the alphabet, mostly concerned with law, cases, contracts, magic and dreams. Book X is concerned with metal industry. It presents 101 recipes including at the end, 10 recipes for preparing a false "royal purple." The remaining recipes relate to preparation of alloys of the colour of silver or gold, the bronzing of metals, etc.
17. Needham, *SCC,* vol. 5, part II, pp. 44-46.
18. Needham also refers to the growth of Buddhism in China after the second century with an emphasis on personal cleanliness originally Indian but gave powerful reinforcement to the indigenous medical prescriptions in China.... "The Taoists also had bathing customs which figured prominently in connection with their fasts and purification ceremonies before important festivals.... Bath-houses and bathing-pools were also attached to colleges, as we know from a number of stories concerning (for example) poems written on their walls.... By the time (*c.* +1200) when the Sung capital had been transferred to Hangchow the common name for such public baths was hsiang shi hang, 'perfumed water establishments.' They advertised their presence by hanging up a water-pot or a kettle as their shop sign, These were the

baths so much admired by Marco Polo." The passage evokes images of the famous bath in the Indus civilization at Mohenjo-daro.

19. Debiprasad Chattopadhyaya, *History of Science and Technology in Ancient India—The Beginnings,* Calcutta, 1986, pp. 172 ff.

20. Shamasastry translates v. 84 of his text of Kauṭilya's *Arthaśāstra* (cf., Kangle's text: 2.12.1) dealing with the duties of the Director of Mines as follows:

"...should possess knowledge of the science dealing with copper (*śulva*) and other minerals (*dhātu*); he should have experience in the art of distillation and condensation of mercury (*rasa-pāka*) and testing gems. Aided by experts in meneralogy and provided with mining labourers and necessary instruments he shall examine mines which, on account of their containing mineral excrement, crucibles, charcoal and ashes, may appear to have been exploited, or which may be newly discovered on plains or mountain slopes possessing mineral ores, the richness of which can be ascertained by weight, depth of colour, piercing smell and taste."

21. Suryakanta, *Practical Vedic Dictionary, ṚV,* I.105.17, *kūpa* [*ku-āp*] well, hole, hollow cave; *Taittirīya Saṁhitā, kūpya* being in a hole or well.

CDIAL, 3400: Pāli: *kūpa,* pit, well; Dardic: *kūe,* valley; Bihari: *kūā,* well without masonry < Pashto *kūhai=guhā.*

In metrology, *kulyā-vāpa* is an important compound. In Manu, *kulya, kula* is as much land as can be cultivated by two ploughs. According to *CDIAL,* 3350, it is also a winnowing basket (a measure of seeds as equivalent measure of land). In the Tamil tradition, *kuṛi* is a measure of land and also a synonym for a pit.

But the most dramatic concordance occurs in *CDIAL,* 3352: *kulya,* small river, ditch [echoing the Vedic meaning.] Prākṛta: *kulla,* stream, channel; Dardic: *kull,* natural or artificial stream; Nepali: *kulo,* channel, drain, ditch. [*DED,* 1828, Tamil: *kuḷam,* tank; *glūnju,* a small pond, puddle; Telugu: *kolanu,* tank, pond; *DEDR,* 1827(b): Telugu: *kola* measurement; *kālādi,* limit, extent, measure, count.]

22. A synonym in Sanskrit for a mineral is *khanija,* lit. "pit-born," alluding to the source of minerals—from the bowels of the earth. The Vedic philologist, to maintain the secret, may be conjectured to have coined a compounded morpheme: *śulba* to connote a comparable process; *soma,* created or pit-born, from the *agni* pit. In *Silpaśāstra, dhātu* (metal) is considered the best of materials followed by *pāṣāṇa* (marble) and *prastara* (stone), providing added significance to the possible origins of *dhātuvāda* or alchemy from metallurgy, or to use the picturesque phrase of Mircea Eliade, from the forge and the crucible.

23. Cf., Homer H. Dubs, "The Beginnings of Alchemy," *ISIS,* 1947, XXXVIII, pp. 62-86. Secrecy is noted in the Chinese alchemical tradition also.

Pao P'u Tzu (Ko Hung, AD 254-334) explains that books are inadequate to achieve transmutation; information in books suffice only for beginners; all the rest is taught only by word of mouth and is secret.

24. Cf., the glazed steatite and clay, faience artifacts and glazed seals, and beads of various colours prodcued by the proto-Indus lapidary.
25. D.C. Sircar, *Studies in Indian Coins*, Delhi, 1968, p. 62: "...many words used in the Vedic literature, including a few indicating particular weights, have not yet been properly understood. Take, for example, the word *mṛḍa, pṛḍa*, or *pruḍ* (cf., *Kāṭhakasaṁhitā*, XI.1; XIII.10; *Taittirīya-saṁhitā*, III.4.1.4 et seq.; Pāṇini's *Aṣṭādhyāyī*, III.1.123). Passages like *aṣṭāmṛḍam hiraṇyam* and *aṣṭā prudh-hiraṇyam* no doubt show that this was a small metallic weight or currency. Who can say that *mṛḍa, pṛḍa* or *pruḍ* was not the ancient name of the modern *majāḍi*?"
26. *Suśrutasaṁhitā*, I.34.15 and 17, KSS ed.
27. *Baudhāyana Śulbasūtra*, I.16, 19; according to *Kātyāyana Śulbasūtra*, *aratni* = 24 *aṅgulas; vitasti* ==12 *aṅgulas; puruṣa*=120 *aṅgulas* (7.26-27).
28. *Baudhāyana Śulbasūtra*, I.10 equates it to only 88 *aṅgulas.*
29. Ibid., I.13. *Samyā* and *bāhu* are treated as distinct units of measure = 36 *aṅgulas.*
30. *Kātyāyana Śulbasūtra*, 2.2-5.
31. Ibid., 2.1.
32. Ibid., 7.27.
33. The sudden and abrupt reference to a goldsmith in the context of "linear or soild geometry" is extraordinary. One explanation may be that the linear measures used in the Śulbasūtra are surrogates for equivalent "weight" measures; using the *yava* as the common link between the allegorical "linear" measures and the real "weight" measures, a concordance may be proposed:

	Linear: *aṅgula* (6 *yavas*)	Weight: *kṛṣṇla* (3 *yavas*)
aratni	24	12
samya	32	16
yugam	86	43
akṣa	108	54
puruṣa	120	60
iṣā	188	94

34. *Kātyāyana Śulbasūtra*, 7.28-30.
35. Ibid., 7.30.
36. *Baudhāyana Śulbasūtra*, I.18.
37. *Kātyāyana Śulbasūtra*, 7.39.
38. G. Thibaut, *Mathematics in the Making in Ancient India*, Calcutta, 1984, pp. 10 and 66.
39. In a Tamil compound-term, *rajju-p-poruttam* means: a felicitous correspondence between the horoscopes of the bride and the

bridegroom; analogous to *rāśi* matching; the term *rajju* may therefore, also be a metaphorical representation of *rāśi* mathematics or heap, or measurement, in general.

40. *Suśrutasaṁhitā*, XLII.3; B.V. Subbarayappa, "The Indian doctrine of five elements," *IJHS*, vol. I, no. 1, p. 64.
41. *Suśrutasaṁhitā*, XL.1-2.
42. R.G. Wasson, *Soma-Divine Mushroom of Immortality*, 1968, p. 69.
43. *Kātyāyana Śulbasūtra*, 10.9, 30ff.
44. C.G. Kashikar, "Soma-drink vis-à-vis the ruling class," *ABORI*, 67, 1986, 247-50. Cf., *Chāndogya Upaniṣad* , 8.5.3 which refers to *soma*-yielding *aśvattha: tad aśvatthaḥ somasavanaḥ*.
45. Needham, *SCC*, vol. 5, part II, pp. 118ff.
46. *Śatapatha Brāhmaṇa*, II (1), i, 5 (Eggeling trans., vol. I, p. 227).
47. Ibid., XII (77), i, 7 (Eggeling trans., vol. 5, p. 215).
48. Ibid., XII (8), i, I, 15 (Eggeling trans., vol. 5, p. 236).
49. Ibid., XII (8), i, 22 (Eggeling trans., vol. 5, p. 239).
50. Ibid., VII (4), i, 15 (Eggeling trans., vol. 3, p. 366).
51. Ibid., III (2), iv, 8, 9 (Eggeling trans., vol. 2, p. 54).
52. Ibid., III (3), i, 3 (Eggeling trans., vol. 2, p. 59).
53. Ibid., III (5), iii, 13, 14 (Eggeling trans., vol. 2, p. 130).
54. Ibid., III (3), ii, I, 2 (Eggeling trans., vol. 2, p. 63). This same formula of the dawn *soma*-pressing (*prātaḥ-savana*) is repeated at the Great *soma*-pressing (*mahābhisava*), the mid-day pressing (*madhyandina-savana*) and the evening one (*tṛtīya-savana*); cf., Eggeling tr., vol. 2, pp. 238, 256, 390.
55. Ibid., III (3), iii, 6 (Eggeling trans., vol. 2, p. 70). The procession and entry of the kingly *soma* follows.
56. Ibid., V (3), v, 15 (Eggeling trans., vol. 3, p. 84.).
57. Ibid., V (2), i, 20 (Eggeling trans., vol. 3, p. 35).
58. Ibid., IV (5), i, 15 and XIV (3), i, 32 (Eggeling tr., vol. 2, p. 390; vol. 5, p. 503).
59. Ibid., XII (5), ii, 6 (Eggeling trans., vol. 5, p. 203).
60. Ibid., VI (7), i, i and VII (4), i, 10, 15, 43; ii, 117, 18 and VIII (1), iv, 1; (7), iv, 7ff. (Eggeling trans., vol. 3, pp. 265, 364 ff., 375, 382; vol. 4, pp. 18, 146).
61. Ibid., X (4), i, 6 (Eggeling trans., vol. 4, p. 342).
62. Ibid., XIII (2), ii, 16 (Eggeling trans., vol. 5, pp. 303-4).
63. Ibid., XIII (4), i, 7 (Eggeling trans., vol. 5, p. 348).
64. II, p. 53.
65. Cf., Wendy Doniger O' Flaherty, "The post-Vedic history of the soma plant" in part 2 of R.G. Wasson, *Soma-Divine Mushroom of Immortality*, pp. 95-147; "By 800 BC, the days of the Brāhmaṇas, a search was on for *soma* substitutes." The substitutes mentioned are: Phālguṇa (reddish-brown

or *aruṇa*) plant, called *somasya nyaṅga; śyenahṛta* plant; *ādāra* plant; *dūrva* grass; *kuśa* (yellow) grass; *muñja* grass; *kattṛṇa* grass; *putīka* creeper (*latā*); *nyagrodha* (a sacred tree). It is notable that the search was focused on golden-coloured vegetable substances, to be consistent with the incessant references to gold whenever *soma* is mentioned!

66. *Śatapatha Brāhmaṇa*, XI.6.2.5-7, "...when the *ida* of the cake-offering has been invoked, he should bring up the *dakṣiṇās*...let them (*gaṇaḥ* explains Sāyaṇa) sustain him (*soma*) till the purificatory bath,—to wit, the *adhvaryu*, the *partiprasthatṛ*, the *hotṛ*, the Maitrạvaruṇa, the Brahman and the Agnidhra, for it is through these that this (formula) is called *ṣaddhotṛ* (for the animal sacrifice). . . . Adhvaryu, when didst thou take him (*soma*) down to the purificatory bath? Well, when they perform with the *hearth-spit* (spit-bath, *śulvabhṛtha*), that is his purificatory bath."
67. Ibid., III.8.5, 8-10.
68. *Yajurveda*, XIII.2; 31; XIV.11; XVII.2; XXXV.8.
69. Svami Satya Prakash Sarasvati, *Founders of Sciences in Ancient India*, Delhi, 1989, p. 40.
70. C.G. Kashikar, "Pottery in the Vedic literature," *IJHS*, vol. 4, nos. 1 and 2, pp. 15-26.
71. Alphonso, king of Portugal has written a treatise on the Philosopher's stone; he refers to a moist fire, called the *hot ventter equines* which may be translated into English as the "horse belly" or "horse dung;" the theory was that where there was moisture, there remained heat. J. Read, *Prelude to Chemistry*, pp. 144-45.
72. *Śatapatha Brāhmaṇa*, X.6.5.9.
73. Ibid., IX.5.2.15. Cf., *Rasārṇavakalpa* (*c.* eleventh century AD), pp. 73, 158-60 reference to the use of *karkoti*, a bulbous root (*Luffa cylindrica*?) to "swoon" mercury, finally "kill" it. "Killed" mercury is kept in a parrot's beak and roasted in *puṭa*. Imbibing this mercuric preparation is supposed to impart *deha siddha*, rejuvenate and prolong life. This is an example of "microbiotics" in Indian alchemical tradition.
74. Svami Satya Prakash Saraswati, op. cit., vol. 1, p. 38.
75. *Yajurveda (Vājasaneyisaṁhitā)*, XIII.21.
76. Ibid., XIV.11.
77. *Śatapatha Brāhmaṇa*, VII.3.1.4-5.
78. Ibid., VI.5.3.1.
79. Ibid., VI.1.2.24-25.
80. Ibid., VIII.7.2.1. Eggeling adds: "At VI.1.2.25, Tāṇḍya was made to maintain that the Yajuṣmatis or bricks laid down with special formulas, were the nobility, and that the *lokaṁpṛṇas*, laid down with one and the same formula, were the peasants, and as the noble (or chieftain) required a numerous clan for his subsistence, there should be fewer of the former kind of bricks, than the established practice was. This

view was however rejected by the author of the Brāhmaṇa, and hence, in opposition to that view, the *lokampṛṇa* is identified with the nobility, and the *yajuṣmatis* with the clan." Cf., part IV, p. 132, n. 2.

81. Ibid., VIII.7.3.21. In VII.1.1.31, *sudadohas* is pronounced while settling the two arms of Agni.
82. *DEDR*, 2716, Tamil: *cuṉai*, mountain pool or spring; *cuṉaivu*, rock water; Kannada: *doṇe*, a small natural pond in rocks, a hole; Telugu: *dona*, a pool on a hill; Sanskrit: *cuṇḍhi*, small pond; Prākṛta: natural pool; Pāli: *soṇḍi*, a natural tank in a rock; Sanskrit: *cuṇṭi*, well.
83. *Śatapatha Brāhmaṇa*, VI.I.2.29.
84. Eggeling adds a footnote: Sāyaṇa refers only to the fact the *yajña* or sacrifice is called *paṅkta*, the fivefold.
85. *Śatapatha Brāhmaṇa*, VII.5.2.1ff. In VII.5.2.8 and 15, after placing the parts of the animal victims, he "thrusts gold chips into each of them,—gold is vital air, and the vital airs go out of these animals when slaughtered...the horse and ram on the left side...the bull and he-goat on the right side...." Some blood is also mixed with the clay of which the bricks are made. The key determinant in the processes is the colour of the substances used: red. The apparent intent is to colour the central brick and transmute it to a golden, yellow and may be, purple red. [Cf. the Greek alchemical tradition.]
86. Ibid., VII.4.1.15ff. ". . . (gold man) is made of gold, for gold is light, and fire is light; gold is immortality, and fire is immortality. It is man (*puruṣa*) for Prajāpati is the Man...."
87. Ibid., VII.4.1.32ff.
88. Ibid., VII.5.1.12ff., "The mortar and pestle bricks are to be placed at the distance of the two *retaḥsic*, as far north of the central (naturally-perforated) brick, as the two *retaḥsic* lie in front (towards the east) of it. This distance is ascertained by means of a cord (*rajju*) stretched across the bricks hitherto laid down (from the *svayam-ātṛṇṇa* to the *aṣāḍha*), and knots made in the cord over the centre of the respective bricks." (Eggeling, p. 393, n. 1.)
89. Ibid., VII.5.1.15 and 22: *uḍumbara* (*Ficus glomerata*), "mystically called *ulūkhala*, mortar."
90. Ibid., VII.5.1.ff., "He then puts down a (living) tortoise (*kūrma, kaśyapa*)—the tortoise means life-sap: it is life-sap (blood), he thus bestows on (*agni*). This tortoise is that life-sap of these worlds which flowed away from them when plunged into the waters (cf. VI.1.1.12).... He anoints it with sour curds, honey, and ghee,—sour curds doubtless are a form of this (earth-)world.... Now this tortoise is the same as the yonder sun...."
91. Ibid., VI.1.2.30.
92. Ibid., VI.2.2.5.
93. Ibid., VII.4.2.6; *Vājasaneyisaṁhitā*, XIII.17.

94. Ibid., VIII.7.3.13ff., "I seat thee (*svayamātṛṇṇa*) in the seat of the vital power,—the vital power, doubtless, in yonder (sun), and his seat this is:—'the animating,'—for he (the sun) animates all this universe...; 'the radiant, the luminous,'—for radiant and luminous is the sky;—thou that illumines the sky, the earth and the wide air;—for thus, indeed, does he (the sun) illumine these worlds. May Parameṣṭhin settle thee,—for Parameṣṭhin saw this fifth layer...."
95. *Śatapatha Brāhmaṇa*, VII.4.2.5.
96. Ibid., VII.4.2.14ff., "Growing up joint by joint, knot by knot. . . . Thou that spreadest by a hundred, and branchest out by a thousand (shoots)...to thee, O divine brick, we will do homage by offering; as the text, so the meaning...." An apparent attempt to de-link the message from the allegorical setting of the entire Brāhmaṇa text.
97. Suryakanta, *Practical Vedic Dictionary: aṣāḍha*, invincible (*ṚV*, III.15.4); *aṣāḷho vṛṣabhaḥ* (*śatrubhir aparājitaḥ*); *sodhum aśakyaḥ aṣāḍham yutsu* (*Vājasaneyisaṁhitā*, XXXIV.20); *aṣāḍhā*, cf. a sacrificial brick (*Taittirīyasaṁhitā*, IV.2.9.2); a particular constellation (*TS*, IV.4.10.2).
98. *Śatapatha Brāhmaṇa*, VI.3.1.1.
99. Ibid., VI.5.1.1.
100. Ibid., VI.5.1.2; *ṚV*, X.9.1-3. That this occurs in the tenth *maṇḍala* (which is supposed to be a later-day interpolation) is notable in the context of an alchemical hypothesis that during the Ṛgvedic days, Soma *yajña* might refer to aurifaction; and in the Brāhmaṇa days, the Soma *yajña* refers to aurifiction.
101. *AV*, XI.7.21; cf., Suryakanta's Vedic lexicon. A homonym is *śarkota* (*AV*, VII.56.5), scorpion, a zodiacal sign.
102. Cf., *CDIAL*, 12337 and 12338; J. Przyulski postulates that the Pāli morpheme *sakkharā* is of Mon-Khmer origin; applied especially to gritty or pounded sugar; from this may be derived the Dardic and Persian forms: "the aspirate of the word for 'sugar' to have affected the Aryan word for 'gravel' in Pāli." Pāli: *sakkharā*, granulated sugar; Punjabi: *sakkar*, coarse sugar; Konkani: *sākara*; Sinhala: *hakuru*. *CDIAL*, also refers to a concordant Greek morpheme cited in *Periplus*.
103. Cf., *hiraṇyavatī-āhuti* or offering with gold; *Śatapatha Brāhmaṇa*, III.2.4.8-9: "...having tied a piece of gold with a blade of the altar-grass...he offers the butter...O shining (*agni*)! this (gold) is thy light,—for gold is indeed light...." Obtain splendour,—splendour meaning *soma*—he means to say, "Obtain *soma*." *Soma* thus gets equated to gold. In III.3.3.9: "...he indeed buys the pure with the pure, when (he buys) *soma* with gold...he indeed buys the immortal with the immortal, when (he buys) *soma* with gold." Further, in III.8.3.2: "...gold means immortal life: hence it (the animal victim) rests in immortal life...." The same refrain is repeated in III.8.3.26:

"...gold means immortal life...this is why there is a piece of gold on each side."

104. *Satyāṣāḍhā Śrautasūtra*, XXVIII.2.
105. A concordant Pāli term may be *ātabbaṇika* which is the *Atharvaveda* as a code of magic working fomulas, witchcraft, sorcery; used in a phrase: *ātabbaṇika-manta-ppayoga*. The *ātabbaṇika* is one conversant with magic, wonder-work, medicine-man; cf. T.W. Rhys Davids, *Pāli-English Dictionary*, New Delhi, 1975.
106. *CDIAL*, 1473.
107. *Śatapatha Brāhmaṇa*, XI.1.2.1-2.
108. Ibid., XI.2.5.1.
109. Ibid., XI.2.5.3.
110. Ibid., XI.2.7.11.
111. Ibid., XI.5.8.4.
112. Ibid., IX.3.3.14. *Rathantara* may be interpreted as, "transmutation of essence."
113. Ibid., XI.5.8.7.
114. Ibid., XII.5.2.6.
115. Cf., the "jackal" symbol in some Caṇḍī icons; a re-inforcement of the hypothesis that alchemical symbols occur in icons in the Yakṣa tradition.
116. *Śatapatha Brāhmaṇa*, XII.5.2.5.
117. Ibid., XII.6.1.4.
118. Ibid., XII.7.1.1.
119. Both *Ṛgveda* and *Avesta* distinguish between a celestial and an earthly *soma* and refer to the descent of the celestial *soma* to the earth. Eagle or falcon carries off *soma* (*ṚV*, IV.27); Gāyatrī fetches *soma* from heaven. *ṚV*, I.93.6: "Mātariśvan has brought down the one (*agni*) from the sky, and the Śyena has churned the other (*soma*) from the (celestial) rock." In other passages (*ṚV*, I.80.2; IV.18.13), Śyena is seen to bring the *soma* to Indra himself. *Śyena-cit* becomes a geometric form of *agni* or the *vedī*, in the Śulbasūtras.
120. *Śatapatha Brāhmaṇa*, V.1.2.14, "Now when he buys the king (*soma*), he at the same time buys for a piece of lead the *pariśrut* (immature spirituous liquor) from a long-haired man bear by towards the south.... And that lead is neither iron nor gold; and the *pariśrut*-liquor is neither *soma* nor *surā*: this is why he buys the *pariśrut* for a piece of lead from a long-haired man." The long-haired man imagery evokes the images of the *caraka* itinerant medicine-man or a *muni* with occult powers. *Pariśrut* may perhaps connote a distillation apparatus consisting of specially designed pottery.
121. A comparable identification of another metal occurs in *Śatapatha Brāhmaṇa*, V.4.1.1-2, "He puts a piece of copper (*lohāyasa*, literally 'red metal' apparently either copper, or an alloy of copper and some other metal.—The eunuch is sitting on the Sadas) into the

mouth of the long-haired man. [The imagery may relate to the placement of goat-hair—sal ammoniac—as a reducing agent.] . . . and copper is neither iron nor gold; and those miraculous ones (snakes) are neither worms nor non-worms. And as to its being copper,—reddish to be sure are mordacious ones: therefore (he throws it in the face) of a long-haired man." The apparent reference is to some *caustic* substance; maybe, it was some kind of vitriol. It is notable that *nāga,* snake also connotes "lead." The process involved may be some solvent for lead.

122. *Śatapatha Brāhmaṇa,* XII.7.1.4-7.
123. Cf., also the characteristic "knobbed ware" of the proto-Indus era; these may be comparable to the *pañcacūḍa* (five-knobbed) bricks referred to in *Śatapatha Brāhmaṇa,* VIII.6.1.11. The morpheme *-cūḍa* may refer to protuberances or bulges, resembling a top-knot.
124. *Kumbhira* means a crocodile; cf. Indus pictorial motif.
125. *Śatapatha Brāhmaṇa,* XII.7.2.13.
126. Ibid., XII.8.1.15-16: "They purify by means of gold,—that (metal), to wit, gold, doubtless is a form of the gods: by means of a form of the gods they thus purify him. They purify him by means of *surā*-liquor, for the *surā* is purified... (?*balkasa,* clear of impure matter)." Cf., two paths indeed there are, "those of the gods and of the Fathers," XII.8.1.21. Cf., *sva* world linked to Aśvins, Sarasvatī and Indra, XII.8.2.8.
127. *Śatapatha Brāhmaṇa,* trans., Eggeling, pp. 234-35, n. 2; cf., XII.8.1.8.
128. Ibid., IX.1.1; cf., Eggeling prefatory note on the solemn and awful ceremony consisting of 425 oblation to Rudra, I.1–IX.66.
129. *Śatapatha Brāhmaṇa,* IX.1.1.18.
130. Ibid., IX.2.1.5-7.
131. Ibid., IX.5.1.18-26; the refrain in a series of verses.
132. Ibid., XIII.5.2.2-5.
133. Ibid., IX.5.2.14-16.
134. Ibid., X.1.1.5, cf., *Mahāvrata,* the great rite.
135. Ibid., X.1.4.9.
136. Lāṭyāyana defined the object of the Vājapeya (VIII.11.1) a qualification to promote a Brāhmaṇa to the position of a *purohita:* "Whomsoever the Brāhmaṇas and kings (or nobles) may place at their head, let him perform the Vājapeya."
137. Eggeling, *Śatapatha Brāhmaṇa,* Introduction, part I, pp. ix ff.
138. *Arthaśāstra,* 2.7.17.
139. Cf., the importance of the *āṣāḍhā* brick prepared by the Mahiṣī, the first queen for the Aśvamedha Soma sacrifice, described in the *Śatapatha Brāhmaṇa.*

6

Alchemy as a State Enterprise

The birth of a state enterprise

While the reference to the buying of *soma* recounted in the *Śatapatha Brāhmaṇa* is well-known, it is relevant to pursue the investigation of the economic transactions connected with the *yajña* by recalling a (later-day, historical period) reference in *Arthaśāstra* (3.14.28-32):

> Sacrificial priests shall divide the fees as agreed upon or in equal shares, excepting objects received for each one's special duties. And in the Agniṣṭoma and other sacrifices,
> A priest falling ill after the consecration ceremony shall receive one-fifth (of his share),
> After the sale of *soma* one-fourth.
> After the heating of the *pravargya*-vessel on the middle *upasad* day one-third.
> After the morning pressing on the day of *soma*-pressing three-quarters of the share.
> After mid-day pressing, he shall receive the full share. For (at that time) the fees are carried.
> Except in the case of the Bṛhaspatisava, fees are indeed given at each pressing.

These references occur in section 66. Undertakings in partnership linked with: duties of servants. Even assuming that these instructions are later-day interpolations, the nature of the wage-earner relationship of the priest with the sacrificer is vivid.

The receipt of the fees is contingent upon work performance for the capitalist *yajamāna* (lit., joiner-measurer). Each pressing or *savana* is a stage in the industry (*pra-sava*), work-process. Pressing what? *Hiraṇyagarbha*. The *garbha*[1] imagery yields a clue to the semantic radical *sava*. In a compound *pra-sava*, *CDIAL*, 8827 explains the use in *Vājasaneyisaṁhitā* as "procreation;" Pāli, Prākṛta: *pasava*, brinaing forth, offspring; Sinhala: *pasava*, the giving birth.

Suryakanta's Vedic lexicon explains *pra-sava* (*ṚV*, IV. 50.2): pressing out *soma* juice; *ṚV*, III.33.4: onrush of waters; *ṚV*, VI.71.2: impelling activity; *ṚV*, I.102.9: enterprise, industry; *ṚV*, I.102.1: order, word of command, begetting.

An alchemical industry is born. It is *soma* industry. It is a state enterprise, run by the royalty-priest consortium.

The rise of Brāhmaṇas; ṛtvij in state service and śvapāka in śva-vṛtti

According to the *Arthaśāstra*, the king has an *agnyagāra* (1.19.31) and employs *ṛtvij* in his service (1.19.23; 5.3.3), implying that the latter has to perform the Vedic sacrifices. Referring to the special payment to be made to the *adhvaryu* priest, Rājasūya and other *kratus* are referred to.

"He, who receives a stipend for preparing the holy fire, for conducting the *pāka*[2] and Agniṣṭoma, and for performing other sacrifices, is called in this code the *ṛtvij* of his employer." (*Manu*, ch. II, 143). [The morpheme, *pāka*,[3] is a technical term which denotes a basic alchemical operation.]

Six modes of livelihood are categorized in *Mānava Dharmaśāstra*: "(A Brahman) may live by *ṛta* and *amṛta* or, if necessary by *mṛta*, or *pramṛta*, or even by *satyānṛta*; but never let him subsist by *śvavṛtti*. By *ṛta* must be understood lawful gleaning and "gathering;" by *amṛta*, what is given unasked;[4] by *mṛta*, what is asked as alms; tillage is called *pramṛta*; traffic and money-leading are *satyānṛta*; even by them, when he is deeply distressed, may he support life; but service for hire is named *śvavṛtti* or dog-living, and of course he must by all means avoid it." (*Manu*, ch. IV, 4-6).

The philological import of these "legal" postulates is not clear. But it is possible to delineate the functions of a *ṛtvij* [*ṛt-*, *ṚV*, VI.57.4 "flowing;"-*vij* "one who knows;" *ṛtvij* one who knows the science of "flowing," smelter-specialist] who receives a "stipend," a specialist artisan who knows the art of smelting. In fact, in the *Arthaśāstra*,[5] he is the first of many key functionaries mentioned as employees of the king: *ṛtvij-ācāryā* the rank order or dignitaries is: *mantrin*, *purohita*, *senāpati*, and *yuvarāja*. The *ṛtvij* receives a salary, the topmost salary paid to any dignitary employed in state service. In the context of alchemical history, one point is clear. The morpheme *amṛta* can be understood in the context of livelihood and "salary" earned. The morpheme is a synonym of *dakṣiṇā*, something given unasked.

This may help us answer two questions: "What did the Vedic artisans do for a living? Why did Manu equate *śvavṛtti* with dog-living?"

The latter question is of particular interest in the Lokāyata tradition; why did Manu, representing the counter-ideology degrade self-employed persons, and contrast them with those (like the *ṛtvij*) employed for wages paid by the king? Why was free-lancing considered a "dog-living" in this counter-ideology? And, as a corollary, what was special about "living" for wages under the king? One possible answer is that there was a close nexus between the *ṛtvij* and the king; the Soma *yajña* priests received one-fourth of the proceeds by sale of products of the alchemical industry, organized as a state enterprise; three-fourth of the produce was taken by the king. The consortium was engaged in transmuting *śulva*, copper to gold, *hiraṇyam*. The *hiraṇyapiṇḍa* share of the priests had exchange value, a value enforced by law in fiscal transactions backed by the state-power. In the *Arthaśāstra* days, it is clearly noted that the Brāhmaṇas and the goldsmiths lived in the same northern quarters within the royal palace, re-inforcing the link between the gold-buttons possessed by the priests and the possible conduit provided by he goldsmiths to convert the gold metal or the "fake" gold into ornaments or coins.

The bureaucratization, over time, of the liturgical function is interesting. Ṛgvedic *hotṛ*[6] is a primary pourer of oblations; he invokes gods through *mantras*. In *Sāmaveda* tradition, the *udgātṛ* priest takes command, with his specialization in sound articulation of the *mantras*. The *adhvaryu* in *Yajurveda* with emphasis on *yajus* (cementing or union), is in-charge of all manual operations and supplants the *hotṛ* even as a pourer of oblations. Only *Atharvaveda* provides an affiliation for the Brāhmaṇa to become an auditor of the "sacrificial" process and overseer of any flaws or mistakes. As in any bureaucracy, specialists get their assistants.

The *ṛtvij* is an expert in one part of the process. He, like all others employed, is a wage-earner earning his salary from the king, engaged in a very important affair of the state: acquiring *dhātu* into the *koṣṭhāgāra*, the granary-treasury complex.

As the Brāhmaṇas get codified, the priests become *evamvids*, "those who know thus," at times claiming to surpass even what the gods know and certainly claiming that all that needs to be known is contained in the Vedas, the access to which is their exclusive prerogative and privilege.

Purohita in state service

Arthaśāstra (5.3.1-4), within the Book related to Secret Conduct, stipulates the salaries of state servants:

> In accordance with the capacity of the fortified city and the countryside, he should fix (wages for) the work of servants at one quarter of the revenue, or by payment to servants that enables the carrying out of work. He should pay regard to the body (of income), not cause harm to spiritual good and material advantage. The sacrificial priest (*ṛtvij*), the preceptor (*ācārya*), the minister, the chaplain, the commander-in-chief, the crown prince, the king's mother and the crowned queen should receive forty-eight thousand (48,000 *paṇas*). With this much remuneration, they become insusceptible to instigations and disinclined to revolt.

To view the magnitude of the salary (48,000) paid to the sacrificial priest and the preceptor in perspective, it may be compared with salaries paid to other servants:

24,000	Chief palace usher, etc. (with this much they become efficient (*Arthaśāstra*, 5.3.6)
12,000	City judge, Director of factories, etc. (with this much they help in strengthening the entourage of the master (*paribandha*) (*Arthaśāstra*, 5.3.7)
2,000	Physician, carpenter, breeder of animals, etc.
120	Artisans and artists
60	Servants, valets, attendants and guards of quadrupeds and bipeds and foremen of labourers, riders, bandits and mountain-diggers supervised by *āryas*, and all attendants 60 (*Arthaśāstra*, 5.3.17)
	Teachers and learned men should receive an honorarium as deserved, a minimum of 500 and a maximum of 1,000 (5.3.18)

Abhṛta, those not in regular service, namely, casual servants are given food and wages according to their skill and work (5.3.33). By implication, the rest are in regular service, *bhṛtas* of are slaves.

Royal-priestly consortium engaged in "sacrifice," yoga-vṛtta, secret conduct

Enumerating salaries, *Arthaśāstra* makes a remarkable statement about the king getting a share, computed in terms of "fee" paid for some produce in important Soma *yajñas* (*ṛtus*) such as the Rājasūya:

> *samāna vidyebhyastriguṇa vetano rājā rājasūyādiṣu ṛtuṣu.*

[The 'king' should receive three times the 'fee' of those equal in learning at the Rājasūya and other sacrifices.] (*Arthaśāstra*, 5.3.20)

This last statement is astonishing and connotes a definitive state-enterprise related to the Soma *yajña* which will be elaborated in other chapters as an alchemical process of aurifiction.

The commentator, Kangle elucidates that *rājā* is the *adhvaryu* who deputizes for the ruler during a long sacrificial session, as shown by *Āpastamba Śrautasūtra*, 20.2.12.3 and *Baudhāyana Śrautasūtra*, 15.4. Cf., Kane, *History of Dharmaśāstra*, III.28. It is impermissible to introduce the concept of a surrogate representative when the morpheme is emphatically, the king himself, *rājā* who is the "sacrificer" for important ceremonies such as the Rājasūya or Aśvamedha. King and *adhvaryu* are in 3:1 joint-partnership: king gets 3/4 share and *adhvaryu* 1/4 of the manufactured, finished product of *yajña*!

In fact, in the Aśvamedha, the chief queen (who is also a paid servant of the state receiving 48,000 *paṇas*) is present and has an important role to play with the dead horse. It is reasonable to read the text literally that the "king" does in fact receive his share of the "produce" of the "sacrifice." It has been postulated elsewhere, that *soma* was electrum and the *yajña* was a process of smelting the ore to produce gold and silver metals. The "produce" is the "fee." Dividing the total produce into four parts, the king gets three parts and the fourth part is shared among the "learned" or "those equal in learning," the priests. Even assuming that the argument of Kangle that *adhvaryu* represents the "king" is valid, it should be noted that the share of the "fee" is being received on behalf of the king. The *adhvaryu* as a "carrier" may have been the intermediary between the unrefined *soma* seller and also the intermediary between the "king" and the "learned priests" refining or purifying *soma*.

In any case, the text is the clearest statement of the existence of a royal-priestly consortium (or joint-partnership) engaged in a process secretly called the "sacrifice." It is notable that these series of texts on sharing the "revenue" or "the body of income" (*śarīram* or *āya-śarīram*—cf., 2.6.1-9) are included in the Book titled "Secret Conduct" (*yoga-vṛtta*). For obvious reasons of secrecy, the details of the "sacrifice" operations within *yoga-vṛtta* could not be enlarged in the context of the duties of *ākarādhyakṣa*, the director of mines. A point to note is that the mine-workers are required to be supervised by the Aryans; a requirement which is not emphasized in the case of other artisans and other working classes. This jibes with the crucial role of the *ākarādhyakṣa* and his *sakhās* in filling the coffers of the treasury with gold and silver metals.

Brāhmaṇas and goldsmiths

Arthaśāstra[7] states that the residence of the preceptor and the chaplain, the places for sacrifices and for water as well as councillors should occupy its (*antaḥ-pura*, the royal palace) north-by-east part, the kitchen, the elephant stables and the magazine the south-by-east part. Beyond that, dealers in perfumes, flowers and liquids, makers of articles of toilet and Kṣatriyas should live in the eastern quarter. The storehouse for goods, the records and audit office, and workmen's quarters (*karma niṣadyā* should occupy) the east-by-south part, the storehouse for forest produce and the armoury the west-by-south part. Beyond that, grain-dealers of the city (*nagara dhānya vyavahārikā*), factory and officers and army officers, dealers in cooked food, wine and meat, courtesans, dancers and Vaiśyas should live in the southern quarter. Stables for donkeys and camels and the workshop (*karmagṛha* should occupy) the south-by-west part, stables for carriages and chariots the north-by-west part. Beyond that, workers in wool, yarn, bamboo, leather, armours, weapons and shields, and Śūdras should live in the western quarter. The rooms for wares and medicines (should occupy) the west-by-north part the treasury and cattle and horses the east-by-north part. Beyond that, the tutelary deities of the city and the king, and workers in metals and jewels and Brāhmaṇas should live in the northern quarter. In enclosures in non-residential areas, quarters for guilds and foreign merchants should be situated.

Brāhmaṇa, gold, accountancy and the proto-Indus legacies

A question has been repeatedly posed: what did the Vedic artisans do for a living?

The text related to the residences of Brāhmaṇas in the royal palace, seems to provide a vital clue in answering this question: Brāhmaṇas and goldsmiths lived in the same locality, in the days of the *Arthaśāstra*. It has been noted that the term *ācārya* which connotes a teacher in Vedas is concordant with the Dravidian *ācāri* = gold-silversmith. That the Brāhmaṇas and gold-silversmiths and jewellers lived in the same northern quarter is perhaps a crucial piece of evidence which provides an explanation for the Brāhmaṇas earning *dakṣiṇā* in the form of *hiraṇyapiṇḍa* and during "sacrifices" and transferring the gold lumps or biscuits or *pṛḍa* (> *peḍa*) to the "workers in metals and jewels." The *dakṣiṇā* was one-fourth of the total produce retained by the "sacrificial priest;" the other three-fourth went to the *king*. Extrapolating the evidence of *Arthaśāstra* to the Brāhmaṇa times, it may be reasonable to hypothesize that the morpheme *ācārya* indeed connoted a metallurgist specializing in processing or working with gold and silver metals and gem stones. Two categories of Brāhmaṇas are clearly perceived: the artisan classes (including Brāhmaṇas and gold-silversmiths) living in the same northern quarters, in the royal palace and the key functionaries with authority in state service: the preceptor and the *chaplain, ācārya,* and *purohita.* These north-eastern quarters also contain places for sacrifices and for water (obviously essential to quench the refiner's fire.) One was the metallurgist-alchemist of the *amṛtam āyur suvarṇam* doctrine with links to the smiths possibly to make ornaments and in later-days to mint coins; the other was an adept in Atharvan alchemical expertise and occult sciences.

Elsewhere, it has been underlined that the *ṛtvij ācārya* (interpreted as the sacrificial priest and the preceptor) are in state service and ranked with the ministers and paid the highest salary of 48,000 *paṇas.* These dignitaries, *ṛtvij* and *ācārya* each receiving the highest salary of 48,000 *paṇas* live in the north-east quarters of the royal palace. The gold standard or gold-based economy unravels: The *ṛtvij* supervises (an inference, though not specifically mentioned in the *Arthaśāstra*) the *ākarādhyakṣa,* director of mines and (smelting) factories who in turn supervises the superintendent of the *akṣa-śālā* (gold in the workshop); the *sauvarṇika* in the marketplace; and the *lakṣaṇādhyakṣa* mint master and another functionary, the examiner of coins. The important workshop is the *akṣa-śālā.* What does *akṣa-śālā* connote?

What does "akṣa" mean? an economic measurement standard!

"The significance of the name *akṣa-śālā* for the workshop where gold is purified, assayed, etc. is not clear," says the commentator.[8]

Chapter seven, 2.7.1-41 describes the "topic of accounts in the records and audit office" that the compound *akṣa-paṭala* connoted a records-cum-audit office. The compounds containing the morpheme *akṣa-* may be juxtaposed, to gain an etymological trace on the key morpheme: *akṣa-śālā,* the workshop of *akṣa; akṣa-paṭala,* the records office of *akṣa*. According to one commentator of *Artha-śāstra*, "*Akṣa* is what is used for counting, such as a pair of scales, etc., and *paṭala* is a house (*akṣāṇi gaṇakopakaraṇāni pariccheda sādhanatayā indiryāṇīva tulādīni, teṣām paṭalam gṛham*). *Akṣa* primarily seems to refer to 'beads' used as counter or tally."[9] Definitive intimations of the proto-Indus metrology, dice (the role of dice, *akṣa,* is intriguing!), chert weights and lapidary-goldsmith's pairs of scales!

Is it possible that the term, *lakṣa* > *lākh* connoting one-hundred thousand, or a large number, was somehow relatable to the morpheme *-akṣa*? Ultimately, the semantic redical may be traceable to *-ā-k* common to both hyper-Sanskritized *akṣa* and *ākara-* (in *ākara-adhyakṣa*) the proto-Dravidian morphemes such as *āyam* income or revenue or *p-āka,* molten liquid.

Yoga and alchemy

Let us explore the processes involved in the record-offices or the accountancy function of the *akṣa-paṭala-adhyakṣa* in the *Arthaśāstra* days. In connection with jewels, articles of high value, of value and forest produce, the accountant has to enter in the record books, the price, the quality, the weight, the measure, the height, the depth and the container.... In connection with factory produce (perhaps, gold- and silver metals are included in this category), he should also record the *mixing,* the technical word used being, yoga or the mixing of materials in the process of manufacture. One commentator gives an example of yoga: the mixing of colouring matter with gold as in 2.14.9 (about the *sauvarṇika,* goldsmith in the marketplace): "One *kākaṇi* of iron—twice that in the case of silver—is the insertion for colour; one-sixth part of that is the loss (allowed)." Commentators Cb and Cs explain the term, *rūpya dviguṇā* "one *kākaṇi* of iron with two *kākaṇi* of silver forms the colouring for gold."[10]

Roots of alchemical expertise!

One more link to the proto-Indus legacy of lapidary-mercantile activity relates to the procedure for "sealing." *Arthaśāstra*[11] stipulates the procedure for submitting the accounts (by each department) on the *āṣāḍha*[12] full-moon day: "When the (officers) have come with sealed account books and balances in sealed containers, he (*akṣapaṭalādhyakṣa*) should impose restriction in one place, not allowing conversation (among them)." The key phrase is: *samudra pustaka bhāṇḍanīvīkānām* interpreted by Kangle to mean that "accounts officers bring accounts in sealed books and works officers bring actual balances in sealed containers—*ekatra asambhāṣāva-rodham*, i.e., the two sets of officers are not to be allowed to converse among themselves."[13] *Arthaśāstra* (2.7.22) makes a distinction between *kārmika* and *kāraṇika*, possibly between the works officer and the account-keeper. One commentator interprets the latter as *akṣa-paṭalika*.

The use of morphemes related to "sacrifice" in accounting is significant; for example, *Arthaśāstra* (2.8.21) explaining the auditing function to detect forty types of embezzlement, uses terms such as *piṇḍa* and *piṇḍa-viṣamaḥ* interpreted, respectively, as "total amount of the commodity or income" and "discrepancy in the sum-total." Another morpheme used is: *-varṇa* "quality" in the phrase denoting, "discrepancy in quality" as a method of embezzlement. A more restrictive interpretation, in the context of *akṣa* (meaning gold-unit based accounts?), is that *-varṇa* refers to "fineness or touch of gold." The compound *adhyakṣa* itself is suggestive; the *-akṣa* should have denoted something of fundamental importance in the affairs of the state. It connoted the accretion to the treasury of the king, possibly using gold as a unit of account.[14]

If an *akṣamālā* is depicted on a multi-handed icon, the reasonable surmise is that the icon is somehow relatable to the alchemical process of producing or transmuting gold. In this etymological perspective, the *rudra-akṣa* becomes only a specific connoting of the colour of the *akṣa*, a pictorial metaphor used by the *śilpī* to depict an alchemist-preceptor in the Yakṣa tradition. The water-pot, *kamaṇḍalu* carried on one of the hands of an icon, may, therefore, be related to the Yakṣa alchemical tools-of-trade and should have contained some "divine waters," a synonym of "sulphur water" or "mercury" or "sal ammoniac" which are the solvents of antiquity used for transmuting metals to gold.

Akṣā-vāpa

The Rājasūya sacrifice includes a process of getting together the *gavedhuka* (seeds) from the houses of the keeper of the dice (*akṣā-vāpa*) and the Huntsman (*govikartana*). The *gavedhuka* pap is prepared for Rudra.[15] Sāyaṇa explains that *akṣā-vāpa* is "the thrower or keeper, of the dice." Eggeling notes that the verb *ā-vāp* is used

(V.4.4.6) to denote the throwing of the dice into the hand of the player and hence, may denote the function of the keeper of the dice. While throwing the five dice into his hand (*Vājasaneyisaṁhitā*, X.28) he says: "Dominant thou art: may these five regions of thine prosper!"—now that one, the Kali, is indeed dominant over the (other dice, for that one dominates over all the dice...)."

The archaeological finds of dice in Indus sites gains added significance in this context. It should, however, be noted that the dice found, at Indus sites are cubes with six sides and marked with one to six dots. That the Saṁhitās should be referring to cowries or *vibhītaka* nuts is an indication that the proto-Indus art of making dies from chert stones is a variant source material. Sāyaṇa remarks on the passage of the Brāhmaṇa (cf., *Taittirīyasaṁhitā*, I.8.16) "that the dice used here consisted of gold cowries (shells) or of gold (dice shaped like) *vibhītaka* nuts. That the (brown) fruit of the *vibhītaka* tree (*Terminalia bellerica*)—being of about the size of a nutmeg, nearly round, with five slightly flattened sides—was commonly used for this purpose in early times, we know from the *Ṛgveda*; but we do not know in what manner the dice were marked those days. According to the commentators, the game is played with five dice, four of which are called Kṛta, whilst the fifth is called Kṛta; and if all the dice fall uniformly (*ekarūpa*)—i.e., with the marked sides either upwards or downwards—then the player wins, and in that case the Kali is said to overrule the other dice. In this case the Kali would seem to represent the king....

"*Kātyāyana Śrautasūtra*,[16] however, admits of another mode of playing, by which the Kali represents *sajāta*[17] (tribesman), whilst the king and those that come after him (in the enumeration in paragraphs 15-20) play the Kṛta, etc. To understand this mode, we have probably to turn to *Chāndogya Upaniṣad*, IV.1.4, where it is said of the saint Raikva, that everything good fell to him, just as the lower dice submit to the conquering Kṛta. Here the commentators assign the names Kṛta, Tretā, Dvāpara, and Kali to different sides of the die, marked respectively with 4, 3, 2, and 1 marks (*aṅka*).—In *Taittirīya Brāhmaṇa*, I.7.10 the game at dice, at Rājasūya, is referred to as follows—With, 'This king has overcome the regions,' he hands (to the king) five dice; for these are all the dice: he thereby renders him invincible [emphasis has been provided to focus on the term 'invincible' which is also used to describe the *āṣāḍha* brick in the building of the *agni*, fire-altar]. They engage (to play) for a dish of rice (*odana*), for that is (a symbol of) the chief: he thus makes him obtain every prosperity.... The keeper of the dice (*akṣā-vāpa*), having (marked off and) raised the gambling-ground (by means of the wooden sword), and sprinkled it, throws down more than a hundred—or more than a thousand—gold dice...."[18]

This elaborate quote, the use of terms such as *akṣa-śālā* (gold workshop), *akṣa-paṭala* (records and accounts of the treasury) used in the *Arthaśāstra*, the archaeological finds of proto-Indus dice, and the legend of the game of dice which is central to the epic *Mahābhārata*, provide a possible clue to (and a conjecture as to the reasons for) the movements of people across the subcontinent during the rise and fall of the Indus valley civilization. It is for the archaeologist's spade to validate the historical veracity of the key episodes of the epic and the role of "dice" in India's social history.

Sāyaṇa's explanation of the *akṣa-* as a reference to gold cowries finds concordant archaeological evidence of early dynasties from Egypt, where a beautiful necklace made of gold cowries was found [Fig. 2]. An etymological concordance is provided in a proto-Dravidian morpheme[19]: *accu* mould, type, sign, stamp, impression. [Echoes of the proto-Indus seals! Is it not significant that *Śatapatha Brāhmaṇa*, VI.2.1.9 refers to the *iṣṭaka* as *amṛta iṣṭaka*, bricks of immortality: *tasmādagnineṣṭakāḥ pacantyamṛtā evāināstat kurvanti.* Immortality is gold; the *iṣṭaka* is gold (cf., *ṭaṅka*, coin). Some proto-Indus seals/tablets may be *accu*, seals recording the measures of value.]

The terms, *akṣa-paṭala* and *akṣa-śālā* used in *Arthaśāstra* can therefore, be related to *akṣa* as a "gold cowrie," a standard unit of measure of value.

Rasa-pāka, the process of "sacrifice" and śulva, mineralogy

Arthaśāstra has a chapter (2.12) explaining the duties of the Director of Mines and Factories, called *ākarādhyakṣa*. He is required to possess knowledge of *śulba* and *dhātuśāstra*. His functions include the survey of mineral deposits and working of mines. Processes of refining gold and silver are mentioned (2.12.8-11).

In view of the crucial role played by this functionary in the capital accumulation process of the ruling classes, let us trace the etyma: *CDIAL*, 1000, *Ṛgveda: ākara,* one who scatters (Tamil: *āyiram,* a thousand; Skt.: *sahasrā,* id.); Pāli: *ākara,* mine; Prākṛta: *āgara, āyagara* collection, mine; Lāhṇḍa: *era,* foundation; Punjabi: *āira,* embankment made to hold up rain; Sinhala: *āraya*, mine. *Rāmāyaṇa*: *ākara*, accumulation, plenty, mine. In compounds: cf. *CDIAL*, 13643: *skambhākara*, heap of sheaves; Bengali: *khāmār*, barn; Oriya: *khamāra* barn, granary; Marathi: *bhusāre*, rick or pile of staff; Sanskrit: *bhusākara*, heap of chaff.

The semantic radical *-ākara* thus connotes a heap or collection. In Tamil (lex.): *ākaram*, mine[20] of precious stones; source, seat, abode, storehouse; a mineral poison. This etymological stream brings out one point in bold relief: *ākarādhyakṣa* is the principal accumulator for the state treasury, particularly at a period of ancient history when gold and silver were commodities of great value, the veritable financial standards or currency of media of economic exchange for state, fiscal transactions.

It needs to be explored further how the principal accumulator for the state treasury and his associates contended with an autonomous alchemical tradition which operated freely, outside the control of the state. In this exploration may lie a clue to at least some of the unanswered questions; for example; the rise of the *Mānava Dharmaśāstra* which documents an extraordinary social hierarchy and stratifications governed by birth.

Functionaries under the Director of Mines

Lohādhyakṣa is responsible for making and marketing articles from metals other than gold and silver (2.12.23). *Khanyādhyakṣa* manufactures and markets articles from precious stones (2.12.27). *Lavaṇādhyakṣa* supervises the salt-mines (2.12.28; cf., the importance of salts in metallurgy and alchemy). Mining is such an important activity that twelve types of income are derived by the state from mines (2.12.35-36): *mūlya*, price; *bhāga*, share; *vyāji*, a sales-tax; *parigha*, some kind of protective duty; *atyaya*, penalty for violation of state monopoly; *śulka*, customs or excise duty; *vaidharaṇa*, compensation for transfer of state rights of sale to private individuals; *daṇḍa*, fine; *rūpa*, inspection fee of 1/8 per cent; *rūpika*, charge for manufacture at 8 per cent of the price; *dhātu*, metals; and *paṇya*, commodities manufactured from them.[21]

One chapter (2.13) is devoted to the functions of *suvarṇādhyakṣa*, who supervises the refining of metals, of quality-testing and manufacture of ornaments.

Another chapter (2.14) is devoted to the functions of *sauvarṇika*, the royal goldsmith who makes gold and silver jewellery articles for the people in a special workshop in the market-place. [The distinction between *suvarṇādhyakṣa* (chap. 2.13) and *sauvarṇika* (chap. 2.14) should be noted: the latter is concerned with "colouring"—an apparent reference to the *yajña* process which transforms *āṣāḍha* (white) brick into golden colour *soma*!] Coins are manufactured by the *lakṣaṇādhyakṣa; lakṣaṇa* may refer to the mark similar to those found on the punch-marked coins. Silver and copper coins are mentioned (2.12.24). Two types of currency are mentioned: (i) *paṇayātrā*—for trade, *vyāvahārikī* and (ii) for entry into treasury, *kośapraveśya* (2.12.25). Apparently a golden or silver coin could have served as the medium of exchange for trade across rivers and seas. Grains or a nominal unit such as cowries and related units might have served the needs of exchange transactions inland or within the boundaries of a "state." A *rūpadarśaka* inspected the coins.

Arthaśāstra does not elaborate on the processes in the *royal mint;* merchant guilds may have minted coins. A fine of twenty-five *paṇa* for minting coins in another place is mentioned (2.12.26).

A state enterprise for producing gold and silver

The key points to note are that:

1. extraction of metals from mineral ores, particularly gold and silver[22] had been deemed to be a state monopoly;
2. *dhātu,* extracted silver and gold minerals had been deemed state property;[23]
3. the state was manufacturing[24] commodities from gold and silver metals, in particular.

An extraordinary omission, in this context, in the *Arthaśāstra* may be noted; there is no elaboration of the functions of the *ṛtvij.* Was he, the principal state servant supervising the Director of Mines? Or, was he engaged in a special operation, the "sacrifice," an euphemism for "aurifiction?"

The secret treasury

The mystery surrounding the functions of the *ṛtvij* who lives in the north-eastern quarters of the royal palace, near the "place of sacrifice," has a parallel in another mysterious functionary, *saṁnidhātṛ* who has the same status as a *samāhartṛ,* the person in-charge of the state fiscal revenue. The *saṁnidhātṛ* gets the following storehouses built: *koṣagṛha* (state/revenue) treasury; *paṇyagṛha*, general (manufactured/marketable commodities) granary; *koṣṭhāgāra*, where grains, sugar, salt, oils and other edibles are stored; *kūpyagṛha*, store for timber and other forest produce; *āyudhāgāra*, armoury; *bandhanāgāra*, prison-house.

The equality of *saṁnidhātṛs* status with the *samāhartṛ* is explained by the fact that the *saṁnidhātṛ* is responsible for building up a secret treasury, on the borders of the country, for use in times of emergency. The special feature of the building operation of this secret treasury is that only men condemned to death are used as labourers (*Arthaśāstra*, 2.5.4; cf., the parallel in other contemporary civilizations of using slave-labour for mining of gold and silver). The commentator adds: "The idea is that after the building is finished, the convicts would be executed, so that no one alive would know anything about the existence of such a treasure-house. Since it is the *saṁnidhātṛ* who is to get this secret treasury built, he must be ragarded as one of the most trusted officers of the king."[25]

What was stored in this "secret treasury?"

Who indeed was in-charge of the operation of smelting? Since *ākarādhyakṣa* is only a Director, he has to be at a professional level, an expert in the *śulba-dhātu-śāstra*, and *rasa-pāka* (i.e., sciences of copper/minerals, metals and technology of smelting), it may be reasonable to hypothesize that he was indeed the key functionary supervising the royal gold/ silver smelting operations, but working under the over-all policy guidance of the *ṛtvij* of ministerial rank.

The processes elaborated in the Śulbaśāstra perhaps had to be kept secret. What did the morpheme *śulba* mean? *Śulba*! A term used to denote the "geometry" of the *agni* or "fire-altar" for the "sacrifice." A term which also means "copper." If it denotes "copper," the operations may relate to "aurifiction" alchemy—the transmutation of copper into gold. The term may simply be an allegorical reference to "extraction of minerals" by "smelting, parting, cementing operations" on a "refiner's fire-altar." This can be substantiated not only by the qualifications prescribed in the *Arthaśāstra* for a Director of Mines [knowledge of (i) *śulba*, (ii) *dhātu* sciences and also (iii) *rasa-pāka* technology—which have been interpreted as: (i) science of mineral-veins (?geology), (ii) science of metals and (iii) smelting technology respectively] but also by the secrecy shrouding the *śulba-sūtra* texts, exemplified by Kātyāyana's concluding statement about *śaulbī*. The qualifications of the

Director of Mines will have to start with *śulba* because, he should know how to prospect for mineral-bearing strata or mine-pits.

Since the Brāhmaṇas had elaborated on these processes, *Arthaśāstra* is silent on the duties specifically assigned to the *rasa-pāka* technologist or specialist, the *ṛtvij*. Since the Śulbasūtras had elaborated on the construction of the "refiner's fireplace," *Arthaśāstra* is silent on the functions of the *adhvaryu*,[26] the overseer of the kiln and bellows, and possibly the trader who by and carts *soma*.

Suśrutasaṁhitā underscores the importance of the *adhvaryu* using the crucial role played by *adhvaryu* as an analogy to underscore the importance of a physician: "The physician, the patient, the medicine and the attendants (nurses) are the four essential factors of a course of medical treatment.... In the absence of a qualified physician, the three remaining factors of treatment will prove abortive, like a religious service performed with the help of an *udgātṛ* a *hotṛ* and a *brāhmaṇa* in the absence of an *adhvaryu*."[27] *Adhvaryu* apparently organizes for and carts in the source of the juice, the unrefined *soma* (electrum or silver-gold ore), just as a physician prescribes and provides the medicine to cure the patient's ailments.

Kangle[28] provides explanations for the terms: *rasa-pāka, rasa-viddha* and *rasa-dhātu* occurring in the *Arthaśāstra*. The context, however, is his refutation of the suggestion of Jolly[29] that *rasa* means mercury. The suggestion and the refutation are important in the context of alchemical tradition of Kauṭilya's days; Kangle will, therefore, be quoted extensively:

"[Citing J.W. McCrindle's *Ancient India as Described by Megasthenes and Arrian*, pp. 30, 94-95.] We read in Diodorus: 'It (the soil) has also under ground numerous veins of all sorts of metals, for it contains much gold and silver, and copper and iron in no small quantity and even tin and other metals, which are employed in making articles of use and ornament, as well as implements and accountrements of war.' Concerning the alleged ignorance of mining and smelting.... Megasthenes speaks of this ignorance not in connection with Indians in general, but in connection with those people who lived in the neighbourhood of the gold-digging ants and who are called Derdai (i.e., Daradas). After referring to the plateau where Derdai live, Megasthenes describes the activity of the gold-digging ants 'not inferior in size to wild foxes' and goes on to add, 'The people of the neighbourhood, coming secretly with beasts of burden, carry this (gold) off.... This they sell to any trader they meet with while it is still in the state of ore, for the art of fusing metals in unknown to them.' ...it is assumed that in the expressions *rasa-pāka* and *rasa-viddha*, the word *rasa* means mercury or quick silver. But nowhere in the text is that meaning for the word acceptable. In 2.12.1 the text refers to three kinds of ores, *bhūmi dhātu, prastara-dhātu,* and *rasa-dhātu,* the last of which means "liquid ore." In the next *sūtra*, the text then describes the *rasāḥ kāñcanikāḥ*, i.e., liquid ores containing gold. When, therefore, the earlier *sūtra*, contains a reference to *rasa-pāka*, the expression must be understood to refer to the smelting of this liquid ore for extracting gold from it, just as *suvarṇa-pāka* in 1.18.8 means the smelting of gold ore. The *rasāḥ kāñcanikāḥ*, it is stated, can transmute copper or silver when smelted along with them (*tāmra rūpapyayoḥ śatād upari veddhāraḥ*). But the detailed description of the *kāñcanikāḥ rasāḥ* given in 2.12.2 can by no stretch of imagination be regarded as a description of mercury. It is this process of smelting liquid gold ore with copper or silver which produces the *rasa-viddha* type of gold mentioned in 2.13.3. That is shown by the use of the same root *vyadh* as in 2.12.3 and 5. In fact *sūtra* 2.12.5 refers to gold ores from soil or rock (*bhūmi-dhātu* and *prastara-dhātu*) as being also capable of transmuting copper or silver. The same root *vyadh* is used, but there can be no question of mercury being thought of in this case. It is, therefore, not true that *rasa* in the *Arthaśāstra* means mercury and that it is acquainted with alchemy which involved the use of mercury. The attempt (cf., Jolly, pp. 42-43) to find an Arabian or Graeco-Syrian origin for the supposed knowledge of alchemy in this text must be regarded as misdirected.

We feel constrained to disagree with some parts of this exposition, while the attempt to trace Indian alchemical traditions to Graeco-Syrian or Arabian alchemy is debatable. The reference by Megasthenes to Derdai (i.e., *darada*) and "gold digging ants" cannot be dismissed easily. The morpheme *darada* is a synonym of *parada*, indicating the provenance of mercury or cinnabar. If the metaphor, "gold-digging ants" or the *pippala* can be adequately deciphered, the secrecy associated with the bringing in of the gold ores (cf. the analogy of buying *soma* brought in by the *yakṣa* from Mt. Muñjavat) can also be explained in the context of the *pāka* operations being a state monopoly. The *bhūmi-dhātu* and *prastara dhātu* certainly connote ores from soil or rock (underground or spread out); but *rasa-dhātu*, liquid ore does not occur naturally. The *rasa-pāka* is a smelting operation performed on the ores containing *kāñcana.*

There are no liquid ores containing gold which may be connoted by the phrase: *rasāḥ kāñcanikāḥ.* It is possible that this is a reference to placer gold, gold ore from the river beds.

Why should not the morpheme *rasa-viddha* alchemical science be interpreted literally instead of taking recourse to an extraordinary reconstruction of the morpheme *vyadh* in 2.12.3 and 5? Indeed, *vyadh* is a technical term even in the *Ṛgveda* connoting "piercing or wounding."[30] In later-day *rasa*-alchemical texts, synonyms for "killing"[31] are used to describe chemical reactions which occur during smelting processes.

Kauṭilya may, therefore, be interpreted as denoting the three-fold functions of the *ākarādhyakṣa:* extracting gold/silver ore from soil or rock (*bhūmi-* or *prastara-dhātu*) and alchemical extraction from *rasa-dhātu.* The factories in his charge are therefore: soil mines or pits, rock mines and the alchemical workshop, *agni,* for *rasa-pāka* or smelting, exemplified by the Ṛgvedic Soma *yajña* or electrum cementing.[32]

It is in this context that the provenance of cinnabar in Mohenjo-daro and the decipherment of the so-called "cult object" on Indus seals as a portable furnace or sublimation apparatus, perhaps, producing mercury from cinnabar[33] gains considerable importance. And so does the symbolism of the *kamaṇḍalu* associated with the *yakṣa* type icons; what are the "secret waters or *rasa* or *amṛta* contained" in these pots?

We seem to be dealing with two distinct alchemical traditions: *rasa-pāka* of the king-priest consortium, occurring in the royal workshops; and *śvapāka* of the *yakṣa* plebeian tradition, occurring in the junkets of *yakṣa* and in independent kilns. The term *śvapāka* finds an astonishing social classification which will be discussed elsewhere; this is of great importance in unravelling the key questions: what did the Vedic artisan do for a living? what did the *śramaṇa* artisans do in the junkets of *yakṣa*?

Lotamanaḥ sund ṭhap

That an Indus seal/tablet may be used in keeping accounts, just as the *akṣa-paṭala* is an accounts-tablet, may be seen from the use of a seal described in a very pithy Kashmiri proverb: *Lotamanaḥ sund ṭhap;* the seal of Lotaman = a man careless with his accounts. "Lotaman was a Kashmiri banker of great fame and respectability, but most careless concerning his books. He would put his seal to any paper presented to him. The consequence was that he suddenly found himself bankrupt, and ended his days most sorrowfully."

In the context of political economy, let us explore the alchemical practices by freelancers (e.g., those not affiliated with the king), like Lotaman, beyond the pale of the state enterprise.

References

1. *Garbha* < ? Babylonian: *kubu*, embryo, abortion; Telugu (lex.): *kaḍupu*, stomach; cf., Mircea Eliade, *Yoga*, p. 419: "...there is a secret correspondence between metallurgy and obstetrics: the sacrifice that was sometimes performed in proximity to the furnaces in which minerals were prepared resembles obstetric sacrifices; the furnace was assimilated to a womb; within it, the 'embryo-minerals' were to complete their growth, and in a period very much shorter than would have been required had they remained hidden in the ground. In his turn, the alchemist takes up and completes the work of nature, at the same time working to 'make' himself: he dreams of 'completing' the growth of metals, of transmuting them into gold."
2. A definitive alchemical term; possibly of Dravidian origin. *CDIAL*, 8022, "cooking;" Śrautasūtra, Pāli: "baking of bricks;" Manu, *CDIAL*, 8033: *pāka-dhāna*, kiln; Bengali: *poyān*, potter's kiln; *DEDR*, 4047, Tamil: *pākkam*, seaside village; Malayalam: *pākkanār*, of a famous low-caste sage; Kannada: *pāka-nāḍu jogi*, a kind of Śūdra beggars; Telugu: *pāka*, hut, hovel; Konda: *pāka*, hut. *CDIAL*, 7620, Sanskrit: *pakkaṇa*, hut of a Caṇḍāḷa, village inhabited by barbarians; Oriya: *pakāṇa*, woodman's hut, hamlet of woodmen's huts.
3. Cf., *DEDR*, 4260, Kui: *puṭpa*, to roast; Pengo: *put*, to set fire, to kindle; Pushto: *put*, hidden: Sanskrit: *puṭa-pākaḥ*, sublimation, cf., Sanskrit: *rasa karpūraḥ*, sublimate (or mercury); Manu: *pāka*, baking (of bricks); Bengali: *poyān*, potter's kiln; Tamil: *pāka-puṭi*, potter's kiln; Caraka: *pācana*, borax; Bihari: *pāen*, brazier's flux or borax.
4. Almost a synonym of *dakṣiṇā*!
5. *Arthaśāstra*, 1.12.6; 5.3.3; 9.3.12. The high dignitaries are referred to as *mahāmātras* (1.13.1).
6. Pāli: *hotta* (function of) offering; *aggi-hotta*, the sacrificial fire; *CDIAL*, 14176, *Śatapatha Brāhmaṇa, hotṛka*, assistant of the *hotṛ* priest; Prākṛta: *hottiya*, member of a sect of *vāṇaprastha* ascetics; Dardic: *wuto, uto*, high priest, The morpheme *hotṛ* may ultimately be traceable to Dravidian origins. *DEDR*, 957, Tamil: *oṭṭiyam*, kind of witchcraft; Malayalam: *oṭi*, sorcery; Kota: *oṛc*, kills by witchcraft. *DEDR*, 959, Kannada: *oṭṭu*, a vow,

a solemn promise; Kui: *oḍa*, to swear on oath > Prākṛta: *huḍḍā*, a wager. [Cf., Indus pictorial metaphor; *ram*, Prākṛta: *huḍa*, ram; Lahnda: *huṇḍu*, fighting ram > *CDIAL*, 14138. Kashmiri: *hondu*, bill of exchange; Lahnda: *huṇḍi*, id., Semantic radical *hu-* offers libation.]

7. *Arthaśāstra*, 2.4.8-16.
8. R.P. Kangle, op. cit., part 2, chap. 13, p. 11.
9. Notes by R.P. Kangle, ibid., p. 86; cf. 2.7.1.
10. *Arthaśāstra*, 2.7.2.
11. Ibid., 2.7.17.
12. Cf., the importance of the *āṣāḍhā* brick prepared by the Mahiṣī, the first queen for the Aśvamedha Soma sacrifice, described in the *Śatapatha Brāhmaṇa*.
13. R.P. Kangle, op. cit., part 2, pp. 82-83. The conjectures on the possible use of proto-Indus seals may perhaps be expanded to include two types: one for seeing account books, by department; and another for sealing the "currency" in containers.
14. In later-day traditions, a phoneme and related script symbol is used in account-keeping: *gu-an* abbreviation syllable for *gulige*, lit., a pill or a small unit of gold-pellet in the currency system, almost a synonym for Vedic morphemes: *mṛḍa* and *pṛḍa* used in contexts connoting some currency value.
15. *Śatapatha Brāhmaṇa*, V.3.1.10.
16. *Kātyāyana Śulbasūtra*, XV.7.18-19; Eggeling, op. cit., p. 107, n. 1; *Śatapatha Brāhmaṇa*, V.4.4.4.6.
17. Cf., *Śatapatha Brāhmaṇa*, V.4.4.19; the term *sajāta* is explained by Eggeling in n. 2 as one of the peasant proprietors or "sharers" constituting in village "brotherhood" ruled over by the headman, and often actually belonging to the same family as the latter.
18. Eggeling, op. cit., p. 107, n. 1; *Śatapatha Brāhmaṇa*, part III, V.4.4.6.
19. *DED*, 47, Kota: *ac*, mould for casting iron; Koḍagu: *acci*, cake of jaggery sugar with hollow in middle (formed in a mould); Tu: *acci*, form, model; Telugu: *accu*, stamp, impression, print, mould; *CDIAL*, 13096, Sanskrit: *sacaka*, mould. In *Dravidian Borrowings from Indo-Aryan*, p. 10. Emeneau and Burrow trace the semantics of Tamil: *accu*, axle, axle-bolt to Sanskrit: *akṣa*, axle; Prākṛta: *akkha*; Marathi: *ās* and Bihari: *āk*, main beam in the rear of the cart. Turner extends this radical to explain Hindi: *akhār*, a small lump of clay placed in the centre of a potter's wheel (<Skt.: *akṣākāra*). *CDIAL*, 32, Sanskrit: *akṣapaṭṭa*, notched board; Marathi: *akhoṭā*, grooved or notched channel; Nepali: *akhaṭa*, notch, step cup in a tree for climbing. The most characteristic feature of the *gold cowrie* is the notched channel and its grooves!
20. The synonymous radical *āya-* of Prākṛta takes a variety of meanings in Tamil: secret; pit 34″ deep, a standard of measurement; income, revenue, profit, dice; customs, toll; duty, obligation, herd of cows.

21. R.P. Kangle, op. cit., part I, p. 183.
22. Cf., the chap. 2.12 is almost entirely devoted to these two metals (with only a single *sūtra* for iron ore (2.12.15).
23. Chaps. 2.13 and 2.14 do not mention articles made from any other metals.
24. Only a reference is made that factories should be started for manufacturing articles of copper, tin, lead, brass, bronze, etc., along with steel and iron; no details of manufacture are recorded; this indicates that these metals were in the *śvavṛtti* domain.
25. R.P. Kangle, op. cit., part III, p. 200.
26. *Comparative Dictionary of Indo-Aryan Languages* (*CDIAL*), 282, Gujarati: *adhvāyo,* carrier who carts traders' goods, cattle-dealer; Sanskrit: *adhva-vāha,* carrier. *CDIAL,* 281, *ṚV: adhvan,* road; Pāli: *addhan,* road; Old Gujarati: *adhavici* in the middle of the road. *CDIAL,* 660, Lahnda: *adhvār,* half a sheep's skin; Punjabi: *adhvār, adhuār,* half of anything, one side of a leather or piece of cloth; Hindi: *adhwār,* half of anything, half a roll of cloth; Sanskrit: *ardha pāṭa,* half expanse. *DEDR,* 5363, Malayalam: *vāruka,* to cut meat into script; Kota: *vav,* id.; Kannada: *bār,* cut leather lengthwise or in strips; Tulu: *bārane,* stripping the bark of a tree or cutting it lengthwise; Kannada: *bār;* Malayalam: *vār;* Telugu: *vāru,* leather strap.
27. *Suśrutasaṁhitā,* I.34.15 and 17; KSS ed.
28. R.P. Kangle, op. cit., part I, pp. 70-71.
29. J. Jolly and R. Schmidt, *Arthaśāstra of Kauṭilya,* 2 vols., Lahore, 1923-24; Introduction, pp. 40ff.
30. *ṚV,* IV.18.9.
31. *Rasaratnasamuccaya,* V.11: *mṛtam suvarṇam,* "killed gold;" V.13: *lohānām māraṇam,* "killing all the metals" using *rasa bhasma,* "ashes of mercury." Cf., P.C. Ray, *HCAMI,* pp. 180ff.
32. Cf., section dealing with the decipherment of *soma* as electrum. In *ṚV,* III.22.2, *soma* itself becomes the key constituent of "sacrifice;" *yajño jigāti cetanaḥ: "yajñasādhana bhūtaḥ somaḥ;"* cf. Suryakanta's *Practical Vedic Dictionary,* p. 537. The radical *yaj* is repeatedly interpreted as "to create anything of anyone."
33. Cf., Nathan Sivin, *Chinese Alchemy: Preliminary Studies,* Cambridge, Mass., 1968, p. 25, claims: "...the transformation of cinnabar into gold is not spoken of as possible, according to extant sources, before 133 BC.... As an alchemist about a thousand years ago phrased it: 'That cinnabar should emerge from mercury and again be killed by mercury; this is the mystery within the mystery' (*Pi yu chu sha han lin yu shu kuei* of Ch'en Ta-shih, *in Cheng-t'ung tao tsang,* vol. 587). . . . The alchemical vessel is often referred to as an egg. Persistently in China the alchemical ingredients were actually sealed inside an egg-shell."

7

Political Economy of Alchemy

The argument: two alchemical traditions

In the context of the well-known problems of chronology in India's proto-history and the so-called gaps between proto-history and history, i.e., between *c.* 1700 BC and *c.* 600 BC, the tracing of alchemical traditions poses enormous challenges in addition to the "briars and bracken" in the literature of Brāhmaṇa periods and the terms shrouded in mysticism and eroticism in the yogic or tantric traditions of antiquity.

The achievements of and science potentials of alchemical traditions in India cannot be separated from the basic historical fact that the traditions evolved in "mercantile, maritime, city state democracies or *saṅghas, gaṇas* or *rāṣṭras*" of the subcontinent, a tradition that can be traced back to the proto-historic Indus valley civilization.

The evolution of such proto-scientific traditions "can only be explained (that is to say, causally accounted for) in the context of the various possibilities opened and closed by the totality of ideas, values and social attitudes of their time."[1]

For example, just as some of the theoretically-minded Chinese alchemists were concerned with the design and construction of elaborate chemical models of the cyclic *tao* of the cosmos which governs all natural change, the Ṛgvedic artisans who smelted and refined *soma,* electrum and the later-day *siddha* or tantric medical adepts were governed by the concept of *ṛta* guarded by Varuṇa,[2] and the concepts of individual social merit in the *yakṣa* and tantric lore.[3] "The decline of Varuṇa along with his *ṛta* also marked the beginnings of the distinctly class-divided society and the moral codes that followed were invariably tainted by the outlook and interests of the ruling class. As Varuṇa was superseded by Indra, the ancient law of *ṛta* had to give place to the law of *karma....*"[4]

An under-world (or more precisely, a world outside the control of the royalty-priestly consortium) operated which tried to revive the ancient law of *ṛta* in the Tantric and Siddha systems of medicine and yoga; systems which had scientific potentials; systems which perceived the possibility of "perfect freedom in perfect fusion with the cosmos," to use the eloquent phrase of Needham in the Tao context, had to face the onslaughts of the post-Ṛgvedic ideology[5] counter to Lokāyata, an ideology which evolved into rituals and mythologies militating against science and the possibility of knowing by observation.[6] Just as Chinese alchemy ended up as a quintessentially temporal science promising material immortality, Indian alchemy which started with the Indus valley artisan working on gold, silver, lapidary crafts[7] leads to aurifiction (—to cite definitions of Needham, "conscious imitation of gold often with specific intent to deceive and distinct from aurifaction which is the belief, not of artisans but of the philosophers that 'it is possible to make gold indistinguishable from, and as good as natural gold, from other quite different substances, notably the ignoble metals'[8]), attracting Chinese and Tibetan adepts to come to India to learn the magic of making gold and becoming immortal.

There was an ideological underworld[9] where some autonomous actions were possible, outside the control of the royal-priestly consortium. There were those who said that "if professionally paid for we can cure maladies caused by spirits (*yakṣa*), ogres (*rākṣasa*), ghosts (*bhūta*), goblins (*gaṇa-piśācāḥ*), etc." and there were others who loved "to be a stumbling-block among the believers in Vedas by the tricks of futile reasoning and observation of facts." Of course, from the point of view of the Upaniṣad which identifies these people, one should not associate with these people, even though there may be learned people even among the Śūdras (*śūdrāḥ ca śāstra vidvāṁsaḥ*). A reconstruction of this underworld which had also pursued an alchemical tradition is a *sine qua non* to unravel the reality of Indian alchemy which operated in an environment of the passionate search for gold, by the ruler-priestly class consortium; and an environment of social responsibility felt by plebeian medicine-men who endeavoured to extend the alchemical techniques to treat the diseases of people, keep them in good health and to prolong their lives. The *brāhmaṇic soma yajña*[10] and *śramaṇa tantra*[11] *vidyā* may be perceived as two streams of Indian alchemists' search for "liberation," *mokṣa*[12] or "union," *yoga* or "salvation," *siddhi.*[13]

Historical mining and metallurgical perspectives

Metaphorically, the treatment of ores is viewed in antiquity, as an obstetric action which shortens the period of gestation of the metals.[14] The Taoist rationale, for instance, included the "archaic belief in the maturation of minerals within the earth, the complex role of time, and the subtle interplay of quantity and numerology in ensuring that the elaboratory would be a microcosmos."[15] The parallel with the archaeological evidence of the chert-weights of the Indus valley civilization and the later-day zodiacal symbols is vivid; the weights[16] in binary sequence around the standard 27.2 grams were apparently used to weigh precious metals; zodiacal symbols included mensuration terms: *tulā,* a balance, *rāśi,* heap, *mīna,* mediterranean standard weight, a measure of capacity, *dhanuṣ,* a linear measure.

Multhauf[17] notes that the awareness of the transformation of matter as a particular art resulted from the inventions in the field of metallurgy. In this field, it was possible to produce artificial metals through a chemical transformation, by heating certain minerals with reducing agents, usually obtained in contact with the fuel. He cites the conclusions drawn by Aitchison (1960) about the historical sequence of the production of metals: gold, before 5000 BC; electrum 3800 BC; native copper, before 5000 BC (which may contain an impurity of tin of upto 2 per cent); smelted copper, 4300 BC; bronze, 4300 BC; lead, 3500 BC; silver (gold free), 2500 BC; tin, 1800-1600 BC; iron, 1400 BC; brass, or copper-zinc alloy, *c.* beginning of Christian era.

Silver, the first[18] *smelted metal*

Galena was the principal ore for silver. It was a rare mineral until well after 3000 BC. After about 2500 BC very pure silver appears; this indicates the discovery of the cupellation process. In this process, oxidized lead is absorbed by a material such as bone ash and silver content of galena is concentrated. This explains the archaeological finds of bones and antlers in Kalibangan and Banawali in pits next to the so-called "fire-altars" which were clearly smelters for precious metals of silver and gold.

Multhauf notes that large-scale working of galena deposits does not appear in Egypt much before 2000 BC, about two millennia later than the corresponding evidences for copper ores. A few artifacts of lead found in the Mesopotamian excavations lead Multhauf to observe that "galena could have been smelted in the proverbial neolithic cooking fire,[19] through simple heating at a low temperature, and without a reducing agent, for partially roasted galena acts in such a way that portion reacts on the remainder to yield a metal without further addition." Add to this the lexical evidence provided by Winslow for Tamil: *soma maṇal, veḷḷi maṇal* in Tamil or sand containing silver ore! *soma* and silver! Cf., Ṛgvedic nexus between *soma* and gold! *Soma is electrum*!

Leyden Papyrus X which was clearly meant as notes for a practical worker in metals, especially the metals used by jewellers is of great interest in alchemical history. Berthelot translates:[20] "5. Manufacture of asem (electrum). Tin, 12 drachmas, quicksilver, 4 drachmas, earth of chios, 2 drachmas. To the melted tin add the powdered earth, then add the mercury, stir with an iron, and put it into use. [This is the tin amalgam intended to appear like asem or silver. The earth of chios may be a white clay, used by women as a cosmetic, according to Pliny.] ...8. Manufacture of asem. Take soft tin in small pieces, four times purified. Take of it four parts and three parts of pure white copper (or bronze, 'chalchos'), and one part of asem, melt and after casting, clean several times and make what you will with it. This will be asem of the first quality which will deceive even the artisans."

> Another Leiden papyrus (Papyrus V) contemporaneous with this papyrus, there is a clear message[21]: 'Interpretation drawn from the sacred names, which the sacred writers employ for the purpose of putting at fault the curiosity of the vulgar. The plants and other things which they make use of for images of the gods have been designated by them in such a way that for lack of understanding they perform a vain labor in following a false path.' But we have drawn the interpretation of much of the description and hidden meanings.

This reads like a parallel to the allegorical representations of *soma* in the *Ṛgveda*. This reads like an echo of Yāska's observation in *Niruktam* regarding the names of gods in the Veda.

Faience is a moulded product made by heating powdered quartz and held together by soda or lime water. Glazed pottery involves a complex process of applying a glass-like surface to a porous fired clay appeared *c.* 1500 BC, a thousand years after glass. Minerals such as carbonates of copper (azurite and malachite), iron oxides and oxides of tin (ochre [haematite] and cassiterite) and the sulphides of silver and lead (galena, which contains both), seem to have been used as pigments prior to their exploitation as metallic ores.[22]

Tanning, dyes, mining and alchemy

The use of the plant products for making dyes results in an extension of the "tinting" process to metals; particularly, in transmuting base metals to gold; the concept of colour is inherent in the synonym for gold: *su-varṇa.* In an experimental search for substances that "tint," the artisan-alchemist of antiquity equates *oṣadhi* with *soma; oṣadhi* a plant-mineral preparation which is also used by the metallurgist.

A hypothesis can be sustained that the concept of colour as the dominant distinguishing feature of substances may have originated from the use of plants for creating dyes. Anthropologically, leather-working is perhaps a technological process of great antiquity. That two plants *aśvattha* (*Ficus religiosa*) and *khadira* (*Acacia catechu*) should have gained religio-symbolic relevance in the lives of people may relate to their use for tanning leather, apart from their use in medicinal preparations:

> (*Aśvattha*) the bark is astringent and is used in gonorrhoea . . . fruits are laxative and seeds are cooling. The leaves and young shoots are used as purgative; . . . infusion of bark is given internally in scabies... the bark contains some tannin and is used for preparing leather and for *dyeing.*[23]
>
> (*khadira*) the bark contains tannin, which is used for tanning and *dyeing.*[24] 'O! Black or blue (*asita*) medicine, your place of growth is black and you turn those substances black, with which you are associated. As is your colour so is your property. Hence your application may cure such diseases which produce spots, e.g., leprosy.'[25] So does *palāśa* (*Butea monosperma*) tree contain tannic and gallic acid and yield dyes. It is a substitute for *soma* in Brāhmaṇa days.[26]

Mahdihassan interprets *rasāyana* as "gold-making lant juice;" this is however, countered by Ray with the observation that though the term is used in *Caraka* and *Suśruta* Saṁhitās, no reference to gold-making or transmutation process occurs in these texts.[27] *Rasāyana* is also used by tantric texts to refer to mercurial preparations and in the context of the quest for long life. In the context of alchemy, exemplified by the Soma *yajña,* it is indeed permissible to postulate a later-day modification of the process in *rasāyana*, treating the *soma* as the primordial manifestation of *rasa*, fluid, *indu*, yielding or "transforming" to potable gold or gold-buttons.

Historical social perspectives

Evaluating the ultimate origins of the Egyptian traditions, Stillman[28] argues: "To what extent these chemical arts originated in Egypt or to what extent they were dependent upon Asia Minor, Persia or perhaps India, it is difficult to determine.... It is quite certain that both in China and India the chemistry of the metals and alloys, methods of dyeing and the use of certain chemicals in medicine were practised at ancient periods, but their chronology is difficult to determine with certainty...it is generally admitted that the Greeks and Romans received their chemical arts mainly from Egypt ... (in the Leyden Papyrus in treating of the making of gold, silver or electrum)... there is no illusion as to any transmutation of the baser metals into precious metals. Their purpose is to produce an imitation that for practical purposes of the jeweller's trade will pass for the more expensive materials and yet will cost less." The Egyptian *pammena* left no traces of the mystery and secrecy of the Brāhmaṇa! There is only one magical invocation in a loose leaf papyrus: "Sun, Berbeloch, Chthotho, Miach, Sandum, Echnin, Zaguel, accept me who come before thee. Trust thyself [to the God], anoint thyself and thou shalt see him with thine eyes." Were they the names of metallurgical *yakṣas*? Or, were they the astral genii governing the weekdays and the seven basic metals?

Sometime between the Ṛgvedic times and the Brāhmaṇa era, the exclusion of *caṇḍālas* from the *varṇa* classes seems to have occurred; fitting him into the *jāti* framework or complex of occupations and "birth" and even "geographical region" seems to be a later development, but before the Brāhmaṇas were codified. In a Ṛgvedic society, it would seem to be impossible to recognize a class called a Caṇḍāḷa and distinguish him from a Brāhmaṇa.

A hypothesis is advanced that the break between Brāhmaṇa and *caṇḍāḷa* occurred as a result of the class-nexus which developed because of one contingent of the metallurgist-artisan class, namely, the Brāhmaṇa who, in league with the royalty sought to control the resources of producing gold or to control the use of alchemical techniques to transmute base metals to gold. The metallurgist-artisan class or the lapidaries who did not so align[29] themselves with the emerging ruling class might have been considered a threat to the Brāhmaṇa-royalty's monopolistic control on the primary accumulation into the treasury of gold and silver metals. This is a hypothesis based on a retrospective reconstruction of the ways adopted by the Brahman to make a living and to engage himself in a "productive endeavour." It is in this historical perspective that it is remarkable that the Brāhmaṇa and the goldsmith lived together in the royal palace even during the days of the *Arthaśāstra.*

The heritage of the *caṇḍāla* in ancient Indian history is of fundamental importance in unravelling the alchemical traditions of ancient India. His traditions originate with the magnificence of the potter's paste (*cāntu*) and his skills in adding lustre to lapidary and metallurgical artifacts. He personifies the traditions of manual operations, governed by the Lokāyata philosophic tradition of materialism. As ancient India evolved into an industrial culture [i.e. organized working on minerals], he perhaps, poses a threat to the state power in league with the priestly class, a consortium which attempts to build up a surplus of wealth in the form of gold and silver and to control the manufacture of other metallurgical products. He poses a threat because, he could work with ease with the forge and the crucible and he has the freedom to pursue his skills of *pāka*, smelting operations, apart from sublimation and distillation techniques—*pāka* which is a process fundamental to the origins of alchemy.

Classes with alchemical potentials: brāhmaṇa and caṇḍāla

Sometime, somewhere in the mists of proto-history, the *caṇḍāla* is declared to be outside the pale of the so-called Aryan society, the pernicious hierarchy of *varṇa*. The "legal" text, *Mānava Dharmaśāstra,* is perhaps recording this social reality, governed by a bizarre reconstruction of ancient history, justified by myths. The working hypothesis is, therefore, that both the Brāhmaṇa and the *caṇḍāla* had alchemical potentials; hence, the evolution of two streams of alchemical traditions evolved in ancient India: one linkable to royalty and the Soma *yajña* and the other to the Lokāyata *yakṣa-śakti-siddha-tantric* substratum. The extension of the working hypothesis, is that the devastating declaration of the *Mānava Dharmaśāstra* followed by enforcement, occurs since the *caṇḍāla* poses a direct threat to the ruling-priestly class consortium whose economic power is directly related to the accumulation of a currency medium, *dhātu,* replacing, cow as a currency and to a limited extent, barter systems.

Why the extraordinary wrath against *śvapāka* (autonomous, daily smelting) while *rasapāka* (state-enterprise-smelting; viz., smelting/ extraction operations particularly on gold-silver ore; a technical qualification required for a Superintendent of Mines according to *Arthaśāstra*) receives the patronage of the royal-priestly consortium? It would appear to be an impossible task to write alchemical history without understanding socio-political-economic history.

Varṇa in textual sources

Pāṇini and Patañjali categorize *caṇḍāḷas* and *mṛtapas* among the *niravasita* Śūdras; Kane adds that "gradually a distinction was made between Śūdras and castes like *caṇḍāḷas*."[30] *Āpastambasūtra* (III.7) declares that all *pratilomas* (lit. "contrasting *hairs*") except *caṇḍāḷa* are Śūdras; *Yājñavalkyasmṛti* distinguishes between Śūdra and untouchables including *caṇḍāḷa*.

> For a *śvapāka* (synonym for *caṇḍāḷa* or *antyāvasāyin*, one who is declared to be outside the pale of Aryan society) having relations with an Aryan woman there shall be death, for the woman the cutting off the ears and nose. For having relations with a *śvapāka* woman, the man shall go to another land, with the mark of the headless trunk branded (on his forehead), or shall become a *śvapāka* himself if he is a Śūdra (*śvapāka-tvam vā śūdraḥ*). (*Arthaśāstra*, 4.13.35 and 34)
>
> ...the well of the *caṇḍāḷas* is of use only to the *caṇḍāḷas*, not to others.... (*Arthaśāstra*, 1.14.10)
>
> ...*caṇḍāḷa*... (impure persons, *Arthaśāstra*, 3.19.10).
>
> (highest fine of 12, 9, 6, 3 *paṇa*) if an *antyāvasāyin* vilifies a *brāhmaṇa*, a *kṣatriya*, a *vaiśya* and a *śūdra*... (*Arthaśāstra*, 3.18.7)
>
> ...a *caṇḍāḷa* is not to follow the professions of a *śūdra* (*Arthaśāstra*, 3.7.37; cf., *Mānava Dharmaśāstra*, 10.51-56: *caṇḍāḷa* is the lowest of men, lives outside the village, has dogs and donkeys for his wealth, clothes himself with dresses of the dead, eats food from broken dishes, has iron ornaments and wanders from place to place; *caṇḍāḷa* and *śvapāka* have identical occupations; cf., *Amarakośa*, II.10.19-20.
>
> The quarters for heretics and *caṇḍāḷas* (*pāṣaṇḍa caṇḍāḷānam* should be) on the outskirts (*śmaśānānte*) of the cremation ground. (*Arthaśāstra*, 2.4.23)
>
> ...*antyavṛtti* (*Bṛhajjātaka*, Varāhamihira, XII.5; people earning their livelihood by servile work or craft).

Arthaśāstra refers to *śvapāka* (cf., the morpheme *-pāka*) as a community outside the pale of the Aryan society in connection with adultery and other sex offences (4.13.34-35). Kangle (part I, p. 147) suggests that these and other "outcast" communities referred to by the general name of *antyāvasāyin* "living at the end," beyond the pale of Aryan society. *Antyāvasāyin* are mentioned beside the four *varṇa* in connection with the offence of defamation (3.18.7). "If Brāhmaṇas are at one end of the social scale, the *antyāvasāyins* are at the other end, and that term would clearly include *caṇḍāḷa, śvapāka* and other 'outcaste' or *a-varṇa* communities. In the description of the layout of the city, the *caṇḍāḷas* are allotted accommodation 'at the end of or near the cremation ground' along with the *pāsaṇḍas* or heretical monks (*pāṣaṇḍa caṇḍāḷānām śmaśānānte vāsaḥ, Arthaśāstra*, 2.4.23). "The *sūtra*, however, does not appear to be authentic, for though such residential accommodation is quite conceivable so far as *caṇḍāḷas* are concerned, it could not have been meant for the *pāṣaṇḍa* monks. For, the text elsewhere refers to *pāṣaṇḍa vāsa* 'residence of heretical monks' inside the city (*abhyantare*, 2.36.14)."[31]

Arthaśāstra states that in the centre of the city, shrines are to be built for deities, Aparājita, Apratihata, Jayanta, and Vaijayanta (different forms of the God of victory) as well as temples of the gods, Śiva, Vaiśravaṇa, Aśvins, Śrī (Lakṣmī), and Madirā (the "intoxicating one," Durgā or Kālī), 2.4.17; *Śivavaiśravaṇa* also occurs in Patañjali as a *devatādvandva* (dual compound). Temples of Brahman, Indra, Yama and Senāpati (Skanda) are built on the four main 720 gates of the city on four directions (2.4.19). Varuṇa and Nāgarāja are referred to in a context indicating possible images of these divinities (13.2.6).

Followers of heretical and non-Vedic sects are called *vṛṣala* or *pāṣaṇḍa* heavy fines are prescribed for inviting monks of heretical sects (*vṛṣala pravrājitān*) like the Sākhya (followers of Buddha?), the Ājīvaka (sect founded by Gosāla Makkhaliputta, a contemporary, possibly followers for a time, of Mahāvīra; existence of the sect is attested in Aśoka Maurya's and his son Daśaratha's inscriptions) and other to dinner in honour of the deities and the *pitṛ* (3.20.16).[32]

Caraka categorizes three sources of knowledge of medicine: *āptopadeśa*, an authoritative teacher's instruction; *pratyakṣa*, direct observation; and *anumāna*, inference. Based on authoritative instruction, the *vaidya* is enjoined to improve his knowledge by studying his patients.[33] The remarkable secular approach to acquisition of knowledge is highlighted by advise that the *vaidya* may gain from herbal and unusual remedies of hillmen, forest-dwelling hermits and herdsmen.[34]

The use of magicians and experts in *Atharvaveda* for exorcising malevolent spirits causing calamities of "divine" origin and various offerings including that of a goat at Caitya shrines are mentioned in *Arthaśāstra* (4.3.40-41). The lore associated with such practices is called *jambaka vidyā* and the rites evidently involved the use of *mantras* and the roots of herbs (4.4.14). *Māṇava* made use of magic for achieving their object, according to *Arthaśāstra* (4.5.1-7). "Meyer contends that *māṇava* originally meant a Brāhmaṇa boy, a young Brāhmaṇa fellow, and that, therefore, the *māṇava* is the Brāhmaṇa in his original condition when he took to thieving, housebreaking and adultery with the help of magic; according to him, *vrātyas* and *māṇavas* are cousins of the great Brāhmaṇa family who had not raised themselves to a higher position, but had remained true to their natural condition. There does not appear to be much ground for such wild speculation."[35] *Māṇava-vidyā* is supposed to involve the use of *mantras* to get doors of houses of city-gates automatically opened (*dvārāpoha mantra*), to put other persons to sleep (*prasvāpana mantra*), to make oneself invisible (*antardhāna mantra*), also *saṁvadana mantra* for winning a woman's love (4.5.1-6). *Kṛtya* or *abhicāra* or black magic is included as a criminal offence in *gūḍhā jīvas,* secret ways of earning a livelihood (4.4.16). There are indications that occult lores such as *nimitta,* omens, *vāyasa,* interpretation of signs of birds, *svapna,* interpretation of dreams, *lakṣaṇa* or *aṅga-vidyā,* interpretation of the marks or movements of the body and so on (1.12.1; 13.19 et seq.) are used in state service.

Varṇa in historical accounts

Fa-hien, well-known Chinese traveller-social historian, who visited India and Sri Lanka between AD 399-414, reports: "(*caṇḍāḷa*) live away from other people; and when they approach a city or market, they beat a piece of wood, in order to distinguish themselves. Then people know who they are and avoid coming into contact with them." Fa-hien notices fishermen and hunters selling fish and meat, living apart from other castes.[36]

Varāhamihira[37] (*c.* AD 500) explains that *caṇḍāḷa* is one of the six primary *pratiloma* castes deriving its origin from the union of a Śūdra male and a Brāhmaṇa female. Many Brahmanic texts distinguish a *śvapāka* and treat him as an offspring of an *ugra* man and a Kṣattṛ woman, a Kṣattṛ man and an *ugra* woman, a *caṇḍāḷa* male and a Brāhmaṇa female and of a *caṇḍāḷa* male and a Vaiśya female. *śvapāka* are classed among the *antya-jātya* (lit. lowest-ranked caste, by birth) and relegated to the corners of a city, village or building.[38]

Hiuen-Tsiang observes: "...there are four orders of hereditary clan distinctions. The first is that of the Brāhmaṇas or 'purely living;' these keep their principles and live continently, strictly observing ceremonial purity... the fourth class is that of the Śūdras or agriculturists; these toil at cultivating the soil and are industrious at sowing and reaping."[39] He also notes the Brāhmaṇas learnt all the four Vedas, while a teacher was required to "have a wide, thorough, and minute knowledge of these, with an exhaustive comprehension of all that is abstruse in them."[40]

Hiuen-Tsiang adds that *caṇḍāḷas* are "butchers, fishermen, public performers, executioners and scavengers . . . (their jobs include) carry unclaimed corpses and executing criminals."[41] Al-Biruni elaborates that *antyajas* (may be, a synonym of *antya-jāti* or lowest-ranked) are of eight classes: *rajaka, carmakāra, naṭa* (or *śailuṣika*), *buruḍa, nāvika, kaivarta, bhilla,* and *kurvindaka* (fuller, shoemaker, juggler, basket shield maker, sailor, fisherman, hunter of wild animals and birds and weaver). More significantly, Al-Biruni refers to those categorised as lower than *antyajas: hāḍi, ḍoma (ḍomba), caṇḍāḷa,* and *badhatau* not reckoned in any caste or guild, "occupied with dirty work, like cleaning of the villages and other services."[42] It is unclear if the *hāḍi* referred to by Al-Biruni may be linked to Dhāḍis of Rajasthan, singers who are referred to as *śvapāka* by Kalhaṇa. (Cf., *hāḍi* = *āṣāḍha* (white brick) used in Soma *yajña*).

Śvapāka, karmakāra and ācārya

Yet another stream of alchemical tradition may be traced which included the element of the skills of an artisan; to quote Needham on Taoism: "...both the wizards and the philosophers, the diviners and the cosmological thinkers, were convinced that important and useful results could be achieved by using one's hands.... The two ideas of microbiotics and aurifaction came together first in the minds of the Chinese alchemists from the time of Tsou Yen in the fourth century onwards, for the first time, it seems, in any civilization.... (The connection between immortality of some kind or other and the metal gold as such is a good deal older, and seems primarily Indian.) There was aurifiction in China too, sufficiently widespread to evoke an imperial edict in—144 forbidding unauthorized private minting and the making of 'false yellow gold;' and if these metallurgical proto-chemists had no other interests they were certainly not alchemists in our sense."[43] A remarkable parallel is found in *Arthaśāstra* (4.1.30-31): For one securing an (artificial) enhancement of colour or practising removal or mixture (with base metals), the fine shall be five hundred *paṇas*. In case of fraud in connection with these two (metals, gold or silver), he shall treat it as (a case of) removal o colour. The commentator, R.P. Kangle adds: "*varṇotkarṣam* refers to an artificial glitter given to gold and silver ornaments . . . *asāra* in the sense of an inferior alloy; this is given a polish (*varṇotkarṣa*) to make it appear as gold or silver; or it is mixed with gold or silver (*yoga*)... *rāgasya apahāram*: as 4.4.22 shows, this is a vary serious offence. It would seem then that *apakaraṇa* implies a complete substitution of gold or silver by a base metal."

Arthaśāstra refers to *kāru-śāsitṛ* master artisans employing a number of artisans for wages, the master artisan keeping the profits. *Svavittakāru* are independent artisans working with their own capital in their own workshops. For them, the *śreṇi* or guild stands guarantee for the loss, damage, etc. caused by the artisan (4.1.2-3). It is possible that the Brāhmaṇa classes worked in the services of the king to produce gold during the so-called special Soma sacrifices. *Karmakāra* is a free workman with a *saṅgha* or union which deals with the employer and supplies workmen to him from amongst its members (3.14.12-17). Manu's use of the term *śvavṛtti* in the context of *caṇḍāḷas* is significant; the key distinction between a Brāhmaṇa and a *caṇḍāḷa* seems to be the nature of *alienation of labour*, one was a wage-earner under the king or involved in joint-partnership with royalty (a limb of the body) and the other was independent.

The instructor of the whole Veda is called an *ācārya* (*Manu*, ch. II, 141). It is remarkable that the term *ācāri* in Dravidian languages, Malayalam and Tamil, connotes a title of the five artisan classes.

A synonym is: Tamil: ***kammāḷa*** <Prākṛta: ***kammāra*** (whence > ***kammi*** labourer, workman) smith, mechanic, artisan, of five types. The five types are:

taṭṭān—(> Ṛgvedic *tvaṣṭr*) gold-silversmith
kan-n-ān—bell-metal worker
cirpan—stone-cutter/mechanic
taccan—carpenter
kollan—blacksmith (whence, by metathesis > *loha* metal)

The term, *cammaṭṭi*, hammer is relatable to *kammāla*, artisan, and *kampaṭṭam*, coinage, mint.

But, adds the "legal" tract, *Mānava Dharmaśāstra*, the most pernicious of all deceivers is a goldsmith,[44] who comments frauds: the king shall order him to be cut piecemeal with razors (*Manu*, ch. IX, 292). Why this extraordinary wrath against the goldsmiths? Is it because, he has the potential to experiment with aurifiction and hence, a potential rival to the *soma*-pressing alchemist-priest, working for the ruling classes?

Junkets of yakṣas

A perspective of alchemic traditions seems to indicate that two alchemical traditions operated in ancient India: one had royal patronage and the other survived in the "junkets of *yakṣa*," to quote the picturesque phrase of this "legal" tract.

> Inebriating liquor may be considered as of 'three principal sorts;' that extracted from dregs of sugar, that extracted from bruised rice, and that extracted from the flowers of the *madhuka*: as one, so are all; they shall not be tasted by the chief of the twice-born. Those liquors, and eight other sorts, with the flesh of animals, and *āsava*, the most pernicious beverage, prepared with narcotic drugs, are swallowed at the junkets of *yakṣas, rākṣasas* and *piśācas*, they shall not, therefore, be tasted by a Brāhmaṇa, who feeds on clarified butter offered to gods. (*Manu*, ch. XI, 95-96.) *Ambasthas* live by curing disorders. (Ibid., ch. X, 47.)

Reading the statements from the "legal" text together, we may state that the alchemical tradition traceable to *yakṣa* and *ambasthas* may be found in the transactions of beer-houses where the underworld of later-day India gathered. One was feeding on clarified butter offered to gods, an euphemism for smelting *soma*; the others were at the junkets of *yakṣas, rākṣasas*, and *piśācas*. From a reconstruction of the happenings at these junkets, which have left no literary documents analogous to the Brāhmaṇas, it may be possible to reconstruct the core of Indian alchemical history which had the potential to evolve into iatro-chemistry and ancient Indian medicine.

Taboos, spirituous liquors and medicine-men

Caraka makes no mention of surgery. Suśruta has a full treatment of surgery and seems to have links with the Bower Manuscript discovered in Chinese Turkestan in 1890 and dated *c.* fourth century AD. Suśruta fights against the taboo on contact with corpses by specific "cleaning" procedures.[45] *Arthaśāstra*[46] details the preservation of a corpse in oil for post-mortem examination and to examine the contents of the stomach for traces of poison; the need to ascertain the cause of death by this means is described in the section on the detection and punishment of serious crime. The point to note is that the taboo was relentless and could be condoned only in exceptional cases.

The *vaidya* had to function under a very hostile environment of counter-ideology and is relegated to a lower position in the pernicious hierarchy of castes. He did prescribe a meat diet in certain cases and also alcoholic drinks, though he disapproved of intoxication.[47] It is also notable that *Arthaśāstra* and Suśruta[48] refer to an army doctor, marked with a special flag on his quarters and equipped with surgical instruments, medicines, ointments and bandages. A *vaidya* was *rājanujāta* (sanctioned by the king) perhaps indicating a system of licensing a practitioner; an incompetent doctor was put to death by the king.[49]

Abastanoi or Sabastanoi, who lived on the lower Acesines (Chenab) is an ancient Indian tribe mentioned during Alexander's campaign.[50] Nakula is stated to have conquered the western Ambastha tribes in the *Mahābhārata*.[51] (Law-givers') main purpose is plain myth.... The main point of (fanciful) genealogies is to show how they are but base-born offsprings of Aryans born in violation of mating laws, or more simply, as bastards or *varṇa-saṁkaras* in caste nomenclature. In accordance with this general tendency, Manu[52] wants us to believe that the Ambasthas are born of the mating of Brāhmaṇa males with Vaiśya females—a quaint story evidently taken up from the ancient law-codes of Baudhāyana, though according to the law-codes of Gautama, as interpreted by Haradatta, an Ambastha is supposed to be "the offspring of a Kṣatriya from a Vaiśya woman."[53] ...Manu's claim that "medical practice must remain restricted to these base-born persons..." Haradatta says that Ambastha and *śalyakṛta* (surgeon) are synonymous. The Vaidyas of Bengal come to be the Ambasthas of Manu (vide Risley's *The People of India*, p. 114). "...in the law-giver's understanding, medicine and logic are very closely related...(law-givers) detest logic...an excessive indulgence in logic encourage heresy or the tendency to question the scriptures."[54]

Mahābhārata[55] refers to a Vaidya as a caste distinct from Ambastha; a Vaidya is born of hypogamous union of Śūdra man and Vaiśya woman. In Tamil Nadu, *ambaṭṭan* practises medicine and uses the title *vaidya.* A *kucavan* potter sets fractures in south India.[56] Manu refers to Ambastha as descended from Brāhmaṇa fathers and Vaiśya mothers and equipped in the art of healing.[57] A later text of Parāśara limits the patients of Ambastha to Brāhmaṇas only.[58] Manu seems to distinguish Ambastha and Vaidya; the latter must be avoided at meal times, for his very presence defiles the food.[59] He is as impure as a hunter, an *ugra* (fearsome) or a menstruating woman; a Brāhmaṇa should, therefore, never accept food from a *vaidya.*[60] Baudhāyana equates a Brāhmaṇa who practises medicine to a professional actor or a dance-teacher and prescribes that he be treated as an outcaste for two years.[61]

The social framework of the Brāhmaṇa period seems to indicate a state of social tension between the *yakṣa* folk and the ruler-priestly class nexus—a nexus which could enforce the tenets of a document such as the *Mānava Dharmaśāstra.* From the viewpoint of alchemical history, the results have been devastating: bizarre turns in Brahmanical sacrifices [reaching the nadir in Aśvamedha], on the one hand; and tantric excesses, on the other. Both were revolts, in psychological terms: one was a revolt caused by the despair of not having technological skills similar to those of the proto-Indus artificer; and the other was a revolt against the iniquitous social-order, exemplified by the rise and fall of Buddhism and Jainism.

Arthaśāstra, section 35 (2.17.1-17) lists the functions of the Director of Forest Produce and includes principal medicinal plant products, poisons, animal products, metals (other than gold, silver and precious stones; namely, iron, copper, steel, bronze, lead, tin, *vaikrāntaka,* and brass), charcoal, husks, ashes. [Section 42 (2.25.1-40)] describes the functions of the controller of spirituous liquors, both wines and ferments, used as medicines or on festive occasions. The ingredients of *surā, medaka, prasannā, āsava, ariṣṭas, maireya,* and *madhu* and in some cases, the processing techniques (ferment, decoction, formation of essence) are briefly presented. The interesting point is that *soma* is not mentioned even as a comparator or metaphor in this section, lending credence to the hypothesis that *soma* was indeed a very special mineral product, not a liquor to be measured in a *kuḍuba,* pot. *Soma* is associated with specially-named containers and as *indu,* drops; but with no measures of capacity. There are elaborate sections on the activities of Superintendent of mines, of gold workshop, and of the goldsmith in the market highway.

Vedic and non-Vedic professionals with magical, alchemical skills: Purohita is versed in Atharvan remedies

Dharmaśāstras tell us that "the Atharvan performs, especially for the king, inestimable services in the injury and overthrow of enemies. The king's chaplain (*purohita*) was in all probability as a rule an Atharvan priest."[62] An entire book titled *Concerning Secret Practices,* is included in the *Arthaśāstra* (Book 14) to destroy enemy troops, deceiving by means of occult practices (working of miracles and use of medicines and spells) and counter-measures against injuries to own troops. The book is a veritable materia medica of herbal medicines and poisons and occult devices. The chaplain is apparently in-charge of these operations; since his qualifications match the practices prescribed: "He (the king) should appoint a chaplain, who is very exalted in family and character, thoroughly trained in the Veda with its auxiliary sciences, in divine signs, in omens and in the science of politics and capable of counteracting divine and human calamities by means of *atharvan* remedies.... Kṣatriya power, made to prosper by the Brāhmaṇa (chaplain), sanctified by spells in the form of the counsel of ministers,[63] (and) possessed of arms in the form of compliance with the science (of politics), triumphs, remaining ever unconquered." (*Arthaśāstra,* 1.9.9-11)

The Atharvan priest had the potentials to advance alchemical techniques since he was certainly dealing with smelting, distillation and sublimation processes, though principally based on herbal and exotic substances such as urine and excreta of a variety of animals.

Purohita has contacts with the caṇḍāḷa/śvapāka

For example, in a text (14.1.35-37), "bringing fire from a blacksmith,[64] he should offer honey in it separately, wine in the fire from the vintner, and ghee in the fire from the roads.... Meat in the fire from a *caṇḍāḷa,* human flesh in the fire from a funeral pyre, the fat of a goat and human *dhruva* in all these together."

The most remarkable text equating a Brāhmaṇa and a *śvapāka* occurs in *Arthaśāstra* (14.3.77), an indication of the possible equality in skills possessed by these two classes, one in the *varṇa* complex and the other outside the complex, treated as an outcaste, a synonym for *śvapāka* being *caṇḍāḷa*: "One should procure the hairs of a goat and a monkey, of a cat and an ichneumon, of Brāhmaṇas and *śvapākas,* and of a crow and an owl; the ordure (of an enemy) pounded with this causes immediate destruction." The veritable final weapon in the armoury of Adharman's secret practices! What made the *śvapāka* so potent [equal in potency with a Brāhmaṇa] though the *śvapāka* did not subscribe to the former's ideology? May be, he knew the key process, *-pāka*, though he did not work in state service for the "king;" so did the Brāhmaṇa know the process, *rasapāka*, smelting for the "king."

Differing ideologies: yukti- and daiva-

According to *Carakasaṁhitā*, "the physicians may be asked to answer the question, 'Of the four Vedas—the *Ṛgveda, Sāmaveda, Yajurveda,* and *Atharvaveda*—to which Veda the followers of Ayurveda declare affiliation?' ...thus pressed for an answer, the physician should declare his allegiance to the *Atharvaveda* from among the four Vedas...."[65] This, however, is based on *daiva-vyāpārasya bheṣaja* and not on *yukti-vyāpārasya bheṣaja*; therapy dependent on the supernatural and not therapy dependent on reasoning or "rational application," as brilliantly elaborated by Debiprasad Chattopadhyaya in *Science and Society in Ancient India.* One was a therapeutic system based on incantations, charms, etc.; the other was a system based on natural substances as diets and drugs.

Rebels and heretics; and the wrath of priest-ruler consortium

The most remarkable feature of *varṇa* is that it was rigidly observed for millennia; in almost all other civilizations where some social gradations existed, mobility was remarkable and the strata had slowly merged as opportunities existed for every person to decide for himself without any outside interference on developing his skills and choosing his life-activity. [It should, however, be noted that Manu[66] envisages that the seventh generation of an offspring of a Brāhmaṇa father and a Śūdra mother may ascend to the Brāhmaṇa rank.] The doctrine of *a-varṇa* or *caṇḍāḷa* was the most devastating since a person of this "category" was virtually excluded from "civilized" social-living. An explanation of this phenomenon and its origins alone may explain what the so-called high-*varṇa* artisan of the Vedic- and Brāhmaṇa days did for a living.

At some points in time, the following functionaries were treated as "outcasts" or "those that polluted:" cobblers and leather workers, potters, blacksmiths, barbers, washermen, scavengers, toddy-drawers, distillers, boatmen, fishermen, singers and acrobats, salt-and earth-workers, hunters, fowlers. The functional castes which were absorbed into the fourth-ranked *varṇa*, namely, Śūdra included: cultivators, oil-pressers, betel-growers, flower or tobacco growers, artisans such as weavers, carpenters, goldsmiths, brass and bell-metal workers, toilers, cloth-printers and dyers, cowherds, musicians, actors, pedlars, rice-huskers.

What distinguished the Śūdra and the "untouchables?" A Śūdra was servile: "A Śūdra, whether bought or unbought, a Brāhmaṇa may compel to do servile work; for he was created by the Self-existent (*svayambhū*) to be the slave of a Brāhmaṇa. A Śūdra, though emancipated by his master, is not released from servitude; since that is innate in him, who can set him free from it?"[67] The *caṇḍāḷa* was perhaps not prepared to accept a status of servitude.

The "secrets" of the Brāhmaṇa texts had to be safeguarded at all costs: "If a Śūdra intentionally listens to a recitation of the Veda, his ears shall be filled with molten tin or lac; if he recited Vedic texts, his tongue shall be cut out; if he remembers them, his body shall be split in twain."[68] Since a *caṇḍāḷa*, by definition as *śvapāka*, knows the *pākaśāstra*, he has to be an outcaste, a potential rival to the *rasa-pāka* expertise of the royalty-priest partnership, with an *ākarādhyakṣa*. [cf., *Arthaśāstra*]

The most disdainful scholastic speculation

Brāhmaṇas (superior even to the king since they have no king but *soma*[69]), Kṣatriyas and Vaiśyas can receive the initiation to become a *dvija*, "twice born" and perform "sacrifices" but the Śūdra do not participate in these cult practices, though they are a part of the *varṇa* classification. They can perform only the lesser sacrifices: *pāka-yajña*, very simple domestic rituals such as funeral oblations without involving recitation of *mantras*.[70] Śūdra has no course open but to maintain himself by servile occupations and manual tasks, because these tasks are despised by the *āryas*.[71] *Varṇa* is hereditary; it is a social classification and not an occupational grouping. *Jāti* refers to occupations and often used indiscriminately as a synonym for *varṇa* in later-day texts.[72] *Varṇa* are four; *jāti* numerous.[73] Megasthenes distinguished castes (*genea* or *mere*) in the parts of India visited by him.[74] But this social situation cannot be extrapolated into antiquity; even to the days of the Dharmaśāstras, while it is plausible that *varṇas* did give rise to castes. According to Renart, *varṇa* could not have been the origin of the *jāti*. The Ṛgvedic

Puruṣasūkta, which mentions *varṇa* by name is an interpolation and proves nothing about the Vedic period itself. In the Vedas, *varṇa* seems to connote "classification or organization" (for example, *varṇa-mālā,* alphabets) or just, classes; for example, *ārya* and *dasyu,* later Śūdra, possibly aboriginals, called *kṛṣṇa-varṇa* in Āpastamba (I.9.27.11) and Vaśiṣṭha (XVIII.18). (Ārya may be a "classification" consisting of priests, Brāhmaṇa; chiefs, *rājan*; clans, *viś,* Vaiśya (< *viś*) may mean head of a house in Buddhist literature (Greek: *oikos;* Latin: *vicus,* head of a family). The term *viś* may thus have connoted the entire free population.

The consolidation of the privileges of the Brāhmaṇa and *rājan* consortium may perhaps be the basis for the later-day elaboration of rules of caste formation, caste under the alleged authority and tradition of the sacred scriptures. The so-called Vedic authority of the Puruṣasūkta, is clearly a deceptive interpolation; or perhaps, it was a poetic license, an allegorical extension of the Soma *yajña* tracts which were metallurgical allegories. "The castes were superimposed on a regime to which they were originally strangers, less by any organic development than by an intellectual construction . . . a scholastic speculation more disdainful than any other of facts and of history."[75]

The Dharmasūtras clearly indicate that *jātis* existed and clever myths were created to explain to complex social reality, to justify the hierarchical system of *jātis* and assign them to the four *varṇas* and combinations of *varṇa* and attributing their origin to failures to adhere to the prescribed duties of each *varṇa.* Hence, *ambaṣṭha* (Brāhmaṇa father-Vaiśya mother); *niṣāda* or *pārāśava* (Brāhmaṇa father-Śūdra woman); *ugra* (Kṣatriya father-Śūdra woman), etc.[76] (Manu's classification) is obviously theoretical, invented to furnish an explanation for what was already a complex reality and at the same time to justify the existing hierarchy between the castes. Its artificial character will deceive no one. It is in keeping that Gautama (IV.21) derives the Yavanas, i.e., the Indo-Greeks, from an irregular union between Śūdra males and Kṣatriya females. Manu is his turn (X.43-44), depicts "as Kṣatriyas whom various misdeeds,... have reduced to the status of Śūdras, the tribes of Pauṇḍrakas, Coḍas, Drāviḍas, Kāmbojas, Yavanas, Śakas, Pāradas, Pahlavas, Cīnas, Kirāṭas, Daradas, that is to say all the non-Hindu warrior peoples of India or abroad, Dravidian and Chinese, Persians and Greeks, Scythians and aboriginals." This evidently amounts to a system thought up rather late in the day to attach these nations to the Brahmanical organization.[77]

The grouping of *ambasthas* and *niṣādas* in the mating sequences by Manu is of some interest in pinning down the ideology of these groups of people categorized as "untouchables." Yāska[78] distinguishes the *niṣādas* from the other four *varṇas* (*catvāro varṇāḥ*). "The word *niṣada* (= *niṣada*) of the *Vājasaneyisaṁhitā* (XVI.27) is explained by the commentator Mahīdhara to mean a Bhīla or Bhilla, a tribe that exists in the hills of central India and the Vindhyan tracts . . . a *niṣāda-stapathi*, a leader of some kind of craft, is referred to in the *Kātyāyana Śrautasūtra* (I.1.12; Weber's *Indische Studien*, 10.13).... The social duty enjoined on the *niṣādas* was to kill and provide fish for consumption by the people (Manu, X.48).... During the period represented by Epic and Paurāṇic traditions the *niṣādas* seen to have their habitat among the mountains that form the boundary of Jhalwa and Khandesh in the Vindhya and Satpura ranges...."[79] The points to note are that Manu is inventing a myth, using names of people who had lived in specific tracts of the subcontinent; and that Manu is denoting by these names of people, those who led an independent life, independent of the patronage of the royalty.

Each *jāti* was tagged to an occupation. The unions in the reverse order result in degradation in caste hierarchy; e.g., *sūta, māgadha, caṇḍāḷa* (Śūdra father and Brāhmaṇa woman).[80] The *caṇḍāḷa* referred to in this context has to be distinguished from the one declared as an *a-varṇa* in *Manu.* So is the *pāraśava* to be distinguished from the *śvapāka*, a synonym for *caṇḍāḷa* a category of non-*varṇa* which extends back to Brāhmaṇa days.

The key determinant: alienation of labour; "working for another"

Karmakāra by definition was a person "working in favour of another person" and hence, entitled to a salary.[81] The persons obliged to serve were of five types and were called *śuśrūṣaka* (?> Śūdra). One argument advanced to justify the outcaste status of a *caṇḍāḷa* is that the latter was "impure." This argument may not be valid. According to *Nāradabhāṣya* the *śuśrūṣaka* were categorized as "pure" and "impure" but they were in service as "paid workers." The "impure" work included: sweeping the gateway, the privy, the road and the place for rubbish, shampooing the private parts of the body, gathering and putting away food scraps, ordure, and urine, rubbing the master's limbs, when desired. All other kinds of work were considered "pure."[82] Another distinguished categorization of "workers" was based on whether they were "slaves" or not. "Impure" work was done by slaves; slaves were not considered as employees; cf., *Arthaśāstra,* Section 65, Book 3, "Law concerning slaves and labourers." One text states: "It is not an offence for Mlecchas to sell an offspring or keep it as a pledge."[83]

Thus, a *caṇḍāla* is not a Śūdra, not a *meleccha*; not a slave. That he is not a slave seems to be his key attribute. May be, he was a rebel against and did not subscribe to the state ideology. Hence, the equation with *pāṣaṇḍa.* Combined with his *pāka* skills, he might have even been an economic threat to the state (imparing—by his capacity for independent production—the value of state-produced gold as standard of exchange); hence, the wrath against him, leading to an enforcement of a law which treats him as an outcaste.

"The sages have declared that the state of dependence is common to all these (i.e., labourers); but that their respective position and income depends on their particular caste and occupation."[84] This law is apparently related to the *varṇa* classes. The *caṇḍāla* was outside the *varṇa,* not in a state of dependence.

That *caṇḍāla* is "impure" is certainly an argument advanced. This finds dramatic expression in *Arthaśāstra* (4.1.26; suppression of criminals; keeping a watch over artisans) in a remarkable context: buying gold "illegally" from an "impure" person (*aśuci*)! "For goldsmiths purchasing silver (or) gold in the same form from the hands of a disreputable person (*aśuci*) without informing (state officers) the fine is twelve *paṇas,* if in a changed form twenty-four *paṇas,* if from the hands of a thief forty-eight *paṇas.*" An *aśuci* is not a slave, labourer, etc.; he is a suspicious character, hence interpreted as a disreputable person. The morpheme, *śuci* is normally used in the context of "purity." That a *caṇḍāla,* an *aśuci* could sell gold in mineral form or in a refined form is a remarkable evidence of his ability to transmute metals to perfection, a proto-alchemist! A rival to the *yājika*! Hence, the wrath against the *caṇḍāla.*

Varṇa and metals in a social context

Arabs define alchemy as lending colours to the metals;[85] ancient Indians called gold *su-varṇa* (metal) endowed with the best colour. "The alchemists expressed their insight in theoretical discourses, and also in allegorical stories, myths, visions and poems (pseudo-Khālid...). In order to protect themselves against prosecution by orthodoxy or against competitors, they use pseudonyms and availed themselves of obscure, encoded expressions. All this renders the writing apparently abstruse.... The alchemistic texts were rightly veiled by pseudonyms and symbols, because, otherwise, anybody might be able to find out the secret of making gold, and gold would become useless as means of payment. This economic argument was repeated again and again by later authors.[86]

The legend is that gold had a purifying power; a Brāhmaṇa is permitted, subject to a light purification by gold or the fire, to accept food "even from a Śūdra who lives under his protection [and who makes this offering of food to him] for the sake of obtaining spiritual merit."[87] For re-admitting an ex-communicated person to a caste, a new or golden vessel is brought, filled with spring water or water from a sacred stream. The contents of the vessel are poured by the relatives over the person and they bathe along with him in a sacred pool. The vessel is offered to him.[88] The sacrament is analogous to the sacrament for the new-born.[89]

Some groups did not owe their categorization to function; these are typically called "tribes:" for example, *ahīras* or generally referred to as cowherds of upper India [also identified with a tribe near the lower Indus and with *śūdrakas*][90] and pastoral tribes in the Deccan. These may be Abhīras mentioned in the epics located in the tract between Tapti and Devagarh and also dominant in Gujarat (Kutch and Kathiawar) and Nepal. Perhaps, they trace their origins to a Scythian tribe or to a proto-Dravidian group driven south by Scythian invasion. Similarly, *ḍom* scattered all over north India cannot be identified with one occupation: they are scavengers, basket-makers, cultivators in Kashmir and stone-masons in Kumaon, fishermen in Assam and hewers-and-splitters of wood in Assam, scavengers and basket-makers elsewhere.[91]

Muṇḍas, tribes and caṇḍālas

The aboriginal *lohāras* of Chhota Nagpur, for example, are merely Muṇḍas working as blacksmiths and do not belong to a Lohāra caste. Similarly the aboriginal *kalus* are oil-pressers and not of Telī caste (not from *tel*, oil, but from *tula*, balance used by traders!) Iron-working and hunting were the chief occupations of the Muṇḍas.[92] "In Manipur, the iron-ore deposits are under the protection of an *ūmaṅg lai* (forest god) who is propitiated before the iron is worked.... The god's servants or priestesses are two old woman, termed *maibis*, who are often inspired by him and babble incoherently."[93]

Their totems include *soe kili*, fish exogamous sect; *nāga*, serpent; and *horo*, tortoise, denoting water animals. It is notable that *caṇḍāḷa* were described in "legal" texts as hunters and fishermen. It is not unlikely that Muṇḍas were included in the *caṇḍāḷa* de-classification or outside *varṇa*. Their exogamous section names (names—of clans, sects—based on some taboo an association with some animal or vegetable as totem) had been adopted for *gotras*; for example, *śāndi* (or bull) has been transformed into Śāṇḍilya *gotra*, from Ṛṣi Śāṇḍila; *kacchapa* (tortoise) adopted as a Vedic saint and *gotra*, Kāśyapa.[94] A *muṇḍa* was a secular headman; the neighbours who called them *muṇḍa* called themselves *horo-ko*, "men;" the *ko-* radical meant "a man" in Kol and Oraon languages. The passion for "purity" of the Muṇḍas is well-known; hence, "purity" could not have been the justification for declaring the "beyond the pale of *varṇa* or *a-varṇa*" status of people who lived near the cremation grounds.

Ideologies justifying the a-varṇa status

By combining *pāṣaṇḍa* and *caṇḍāḷa*, the focus and wrath of Manu is on people who have no faith in the Vedas and those who have the expertise in *-pāka*, working on substances using fire or, *pāka* may refer to fluids (e.g., in digestive systems of the body). The term *pāka* in a medical context is interpreted as "digestion;" *vipāka* being interpreted as "post-digestive change of a substance within the body."[95] [In Tamil, *pāku* = semi-liquid form, for example, molten molasses.] "Generally speaking, substances with pungent, bitter and astringent tastes are, on post-digestion, changed into substances having ordinarily no pungent taste. Substances with sour taste, remain after digestion substances with sour taste, and so also the *vipāka* of sweet is sweet. By *vipāka*, however, substances with salt taste are transformed into substances with sweet taste."[96]

Cf., the term *pāṣaṇḍa āyataneṣu* in *Carakasaṁhitā*, VI.23.160: "in the house of people who have no faith in the Vedas," if a person is bitten by a venomous creature, the poison becomes incurable.

For the so-called "outcastes," outside the pale of the so-called Aryan society, the classifying morpheme is *varṇa* and is not, *jāti*. The latter morpheme, literally counting "birth" was a complex of sub-classifications based on bizarre combinations of the four *varṇas* and permutations involving two *sexes* and the number of "marriages" permitted. [Cf., Manu's statement that gold and silver arose from the union of water and fire.[97] From the divided body of Indra, metals arose, as well as all kinds of substances and living creatures; e.g. from his navel came lead.[98] The slaughtering knife for the horse should be of gold, that for the *paryaṅgyas* of copper, and that of other sacrifices to Prajāpati of iron; gold is a symbol of the nobility, copper of heralds, messengers and the like, iron of the peasantry.[99]] The "legal" text of Manu assigns a separate origin to each *jāti* based on varieties of cross-breeding in an extraordinary exercise in myth-making combined with some geo-physical and social reality. For example, a *niṣāda* is a fisherman (elsewhere, a *caṇḍāla*) born of Brāhmaṇa and Śūdra woman;[100] and a *caṇḍāla* can be born to Śūdra man and a Brāhmaṇa woman.[101]

The very act of "tracing the origins" of groups of people in a society leads to bizarre conjectures in the hands of a priest-ruling class consortium. The ruling class is apparently appeased by a "legal" sanction that the right to rule belongs to that class alone and becomes a party to the "legal" document by enforcing it, through the force of law or brute force.

We propose to add one more explanation: viz., economic conflict, well before "ideology" or the observance or non-observance of "Vedic or Brāhmaṇa sacrifices" became the determining factor to declare a group as *caṇḍāla*. The ruling-priest class consortium was engaged in building up an important economic monopoly which necessitated the exclusion of groups who had the potential to upset or even threaten the monopoly. Almost all the groups categorized as *caṇḍāla* possessed the ability to produce or participate in the production of gold and silver metals which were gaining increasing use as currency in economic transactions. The ruling-priest class endeavoured to treat the production of gold and silver metals as a state monopoly. The craze for gold, particularly among the ruling-priest classes, had reached extraordinary proportions as early as in the Vedic period, considering gold and silver to be important metals for aesthetic reasons and also due to their currency value. In *Arthaśāstra* fines are prescribed for stealing gold possessed by Brāhmaṇas, giving the impression that this class had access to this metal, obviously paid as wages in *hiranyapiṇḍa* by the "sacrificer-masters" (*yajamāna*). This craze intensifies in course of time into alchemy and becomes a pre-occupations with many groups of people for almost two millennia.

Grāma yājaka; pūga yajiyāḥ vis-à-vis ṛtvij and rāja-yojakāḥ

The law-codes of Gautama, Viṣṇu and Manu: "He who practices for the multitude (*grāma yājaka*) is pronounced impure; we may presume that this kind of activity was largely, if not entirely in the hands of the Atharvan priest."[102] "Let him not feed a thief, a eunuch an outcast, an atheist, a person who lives like an atheist,... a person who sacrifices for women or for a multitude of men," says Gautama[103] in the context of funeral rites. Manu[104] states, "Let him not entertain at a *śrāddha* . . . those who sacrifice for a multitude (*pūga*[105] *yajiyāḥ* = *ye pūgān yajanti*)." Manu adds: "A Brāhmaṇa must never eat at a sacrifice that is offered by ... one who sacrifices for a multitude of men (*grāma yojikṛte*)."[106] Viṣṇu endorses that one must not invite to a *śrāddha* "those who sacrifice for a multitude of persons."[107]

The corollary is simple and direct: those who sacrifice for the multitude are "impure;" those who sacrifice for the king are "pure." The key determinant of this strange ideology is "partnership with or servility to the state-power, represented by the royalty." Clearly, there are two types of alchemists: those alchemists who work in the state enterprise; those alchemists who are freelancers: *grāma-* or *pūga-yajikāḥ*.

The morphemes *grāma-* and *pūga-* have to be juxtaposed to *rāja-yajñikāḥ*. The social context is clear and vivid: the Brāhmaṇa "sacrifice" for the kings which is a synonym for "Brāhmaṇas are in partnership with or in the employ of the kings." This may explain the premier position assigned to *ṛtvij* in *Arthaśāstra* together with other functionaries in state service such as the ministers and entitled to the highest salaries. The *ṛtvij* was the "knower of the flow," perhaps a reference to gold-smelting. Like the *ākarādhyakṣa*, who perhaps reported to the *ṛtvij*, the latter certainly knew Śulba-śāstra. *Śulba* meant a mine, it was also a synonym for copper! If he knew *śulva* and *dhātuśāstra*, i.e., science of minerals (mines) and metals, and of course, *rasapāka* (three primary educational qualifications prescribed by Kauṭilya) the *ṛtvij* could certainly conduct the state-controlled operations to transmute copper into gold and fill the treasury with this precious metal! These operations had to contend with some autonomous "sacrifices," the *ayojya yojakāḥ*, the practitioners of the underworld.

The ayojya yojakāḥ: "sacrifices for the unworthy"

Chattopadhyaya[108] cites the evidence from *Maitrāyaṇī Upaniṣad* on the heretics of the "ideological underworld." These are "continually roving about (*nitya pravasitāḥ*), continually living upon handicrafts (*nitya śilpa upajīnaḥ*), performers of rituals for the unworthy (*ayojya yojakāḥ*), disciples of the Śūdras, inspite of being Śūdras, are learned (*śūdrāḥ ca śāstra vidvāṁsaḥ*), rogues, who wear their hair in a twisted knot, who are dancers, mercenaries, wanderers, actors, renegades in royal service . . . (*cāṭa-jaṭa-naṭa-bhaṭa-pravrajita-raṅgāvatāriṇaḥ rājakarmaṇi patitādayaḥ*). If professionally paid for ...can cure maladies caused by spirits, ogres, ghosts, goblins, snake-harks and the like (*yakṣa-rākṣasa-bhūta-gaṇa-piśācāḥ roga-grahādīnām artham puraskṛtya samayāmaḥ—it evam bruvāṇāḥ*).... And moreover there are those who vainly wear the red robe, ear-rings and skulls (*vṛthā kaṣāya-kuṇḍalinaḥ kāpālinaḥ*).... And moreover there are others who love to be a stumbling block among the believers in Vedas (*vaidikeṣu pariṣātum icchanti*) by the tricks of futile reasoning and observation of facts (*vṛthā tarka-dṛṣṭānta-kuhaka-indrajālaiḥ*)."[109]

Chattopadhyaya finds that the classification was clearly based on the ideologies which governed learning: Vedic or non-Vedic. It would appear that there is a substratum, fundamental economic reason which explains the vehemence and animosity against the so-called "heretics:" that the latter were working for the "multitude" and were not working for the chosen few or were not "in royal partnership or royal service." The Brāhmaṇas thus pitted themselves directly against *caṇḍāḷas.* The former were adept in *rasapāka;* the latter were adept in *śvapāka.* The term *śvapāka* may be explained in the context of an etymological stream related to *śvaḥśvas,* day-after-day, daily and *aśva* (evoking Aśvamedha); a *śvapāka* was engaged in refining activities almost daily, the Brāhmaṇas could start their Soma *yajña* refining activities only when the raw-material was bought from and delivered by the *gandharva* from Mount Muñjavat. The morpheme *-pāka* can certainly be explained as a synonym for the term, "sacrifice" or *yajña.*

Consequences of treating the caṇḍāḷas as "impure"

The "legal" texts are vehemently venomous and equate *caṇḍāḷas* with dogs and the other so-called "impure" manifestations:

Āpastamba summarizes the characteristics of a class, comparable to the *ayojya yojakāḥ,* called the *caṇḍāḷas* (synonyms: *antyāvasāyin; śva-pāka*): "(One must not study the scriptures in a village) in which there is a corpse or in such a one where the *caṇḍāḷa* live. One must not study where corpses are being carried to the boundary of a village."[110]

Gautama: "On touching (i.e., on carrying) a corpse from an interested motive (i.e., with the intention of gaining a fee or the like), the impurity lasts for ten days."[111] "On touching an outcaste, a *caṇḍāḷa*, a woman impure on account of her confinement, a woman in her course, a corpse, and on touching persons who have touched them, he must purify himself by bathing dressed in his clothes. Likewise, if he has followed a corpse that was being carried, and if he has come into contact with a dog."[112]

Manu: "When he has touched a *caṇḍāḷa*, a menstruating woman, an outcaste, a woman in childbed, a corpse, or one who has touched a corpse, he becomes pure by bathing."[113] *Chāndogya Upaniṣad* expands the concept linking it to *karma* and re-birth: "Accordingly, those who are of pleasant conduct here—the prospect is, indeed, that they will enter a pleasant womb: either the womb of a Brāhmaṇa, or the womb of a Kṣatriya, or the womb of a Vaiśya. But those who are of stinking conduct here—the prospect is, indeed, that they will enter a stinking womb: either the womb of a dog, or the womb of a swine, or the womb of an outcaste (*caṇḍāḷa*)."[114]

Source of corpses for the surgeon

Suśrutasaṁhitā prescribes that to gain a knowledge of anatomy, the surgeon should "prepare a dead body and carefully observe by dissecting it, and examine its different parts.... A dead body selected for this purpose should not be wanting in any of its parts, should not be of a person who has lived upto a hundred years (i.e., upto a very old age) or of one who died of any protracted disease or of poison."[115] Chattopadhyaya notes: "It must have been extremely difficult to procure for the purpose of dissection a dead body, specially one with the specifications mentioned by the surgeons. In other words, such a corpse must have been something extremely precious for anatomical studies and hence could not be allowed to be mutilated by the beginners yet to acquire the skill of dissection...." In ancient India of the Brāhmaṇa days, governed by the "legal" texts, there was only one source for corpses: the *caṇḍāḷa* who lived near the cremation or burial grounds.

Somehow, the surgeon should have had an economic nexus with the *caṇḍāḷa* to ensure a supply of corpses for dissection studies and experiments and related observations. This may be one additional reason why the physician was also bracketed as an "impure" category in some Vedic-quarters; not merely because, he was a proponent of an ideology of reasoning or *yukti*; not merely because he had touched a corpse and not merely because he was *aśauca*; indeed, he was enjoined in medical texts to be clean in his habits and appearance.[116]

Dog-living and jackal-symbol

Ramendra Nath Nandi observes that the weapons associated with Caṇḍī to kill the demons are also associated with the Mother Goddesses in the Jaina tantra work, *Jvālinīkalpa*: sprinkling of sacrificial water from the ritual pot of Mother Goddess; trident and wheel of Maheśvarī and Vaiṣṇavī; Kuliśa of Aindrī; Śakti of Kaumārī;[117] sharp tusk of Vārāhī; and sharp nails of Nārasiṁhī. If the killing of the demons depicted in iconography is viewed as an alchemical allegory in icons, it may be possible to relate the symbols of two jackals carrying the bones of human victims in their mouth in temple icons[118] to the parallel tradition of showing a Chinese Tao adept with his dog and his portable brazier. [The bones are used in metallurgical operations to prepare crucibles for smelting gold.] Caṇḍī is included in the *mātṛkā* panel of the Elura sacrificial hall intended for Agniṣṭoma sacrifice. In *ṚV*, II.3.66, *sapta sindhavaḥ* may be interpreted as a reference to *sapta mātṛkā*; the seven are pressing *soma* for the fire-god, Agni.[119] Cāmuṇḍā with six arms holds a skull-mace, a snake, a wine cup; at the base, a jackal gnaws at the left hip of a corpse on the floor. In Bikkavolu Vijayīśvara temple, a similar imagery is presented with a dog and a jackal eating a corpse. The Karālā or Cāmuṇḍā Mother Goddess temple may be located in the cremation ground, a locale close to the residences of the *śvapāka*, *caṇḍāḷa*, the *antyāvasāyin*, the non-*varṇa* group of Manu. The recurrent symbolism of the dog or the jackal, metallic weapons, and the locale of cremation ground related to Mother Goddess, are relatable to the *caṇḍāḷa* who is pictured by Manu as living with the dogs, living a dog-life. The association of Caṇḍī with the Fire-god is also indicative of the tantric tradition running parallel to the Soma *yajña* legacy, apart from her fierce acts depicted for example in Caṇḍī[120] of the goddess drinking the blood flowing from the wounded demon Raktabīja. It would appear that the alchemical metaphors or symbols of the colour red, wounding, *pāka*, dog or jackal are preponderant in the tantric-mother-cult imageries too.

Śakti and Dravidian goddesses

A Dravidian Śakti is generally, a *grāma devatā*, a protectress of a village, a female ancestral spirit of a departed person, who is fierce and has powers. As legends grow, she is said to be an incarnation of Pārvatī. Even an occasional male god, for example, Aiyanār in Tamil Nadu or Venkatasu of the Telugus gets female attributes; in a legend, Bhasmāsura is a Purāṇic demon whose very touch turns everything to ashes. He tries to touch Śiva himself. Viṣṇu tries to overpower him in the guise of a young woman. She tells him to bathe and put oil on his head. He touches his head and turns to ashes. Śiva now asks Viṣṇu to become that young woman again for his benefit. Viṣṇu consents and Aiyanār is their child.[121] The legend is of Brahmanic origin but the Mother Goddess cult seems to be of great antiquity. It is conjectural to state that a connection exists between the Śakti worship of the tantras and the Dravidian Mother Goddess cult. The key point is that *bhasma* is an alchemical symbolism. The association of alchemical symbols with *yakṣa* and Mother Goddess icons and myths are too recurrent to be merely accidental.

Of alchemical significance is a goddess Baṅgāramma, the golden one of the *mādiga* outcastes. Her sister is Mathamma (Mātaṅgī incarnate; cf. the morpheme *-taṅg* meaning gold in the name: *mātaṅgī*) wearing a necklace of cowrie shells, face painted in yellow turmeric offering invectives in the houses of Brāhmaṇas (who in fearful adoration, seek her touch and saliva avidly), though only a few Brāhmaṇa families acknowledge allegiance to her today.[122]

Mātaṅgī or Ellamma incarnate "rushes about spitting on those who under ordinary circumstances would almost choose death than to suffer such pollution from a Mādiga, she breaks into wild, exulting songs, telling of the humiliation to which she is subjecting the proud caste people. She also abuses them all thoroughly, and as in the worship of Baṅgāramma, they appear to expect it and not to be satisfied without a full measure of her invective. After this ceremony she visits the homes of the Brāhmaṇas . . . smears a spot with cow-dung ... a small lamp is placed (by the inmates) on top of this and lighted. This appears to be the nearest approach to worship the Mātaṅgī receives.... [Thurston thinks but few families now acknowledge this allegiance to Mātaṅgī (*Castes and Tribes of Southern India*, IV, p. 297).] So far as I can find, Brāhmaṇas are loth to acknowledge any connection with the Mātaṅgī, but some kind of tribute to her seems very general.]"[123]

Pāṣaṇḍa and caṇḍāḷa/śvapāka

The use of the terms, *pāṣaṇḍa* and *caṇḍāḷa* together in *Arthaśāstra* may provide some possible clues as to the nature of economic activity engaged in by the class of people who seem to have incurred the wrath of the ruling-priestly class consortium. The hypothesis is that this fiercely independent-spirited class posed a threat to the state power which was in the process of monopolizing the production and accumulation of gold and silver into the state treasury; two metals which served as currency media in economic transactions and as units of account for state revenue and expenses.

A term cognate with *pāṣaṇḍa* is *pāṣāṇa*. While a *pāṣaṇḍa* is interpreted as a heretic sect [possibly, not subscribing to the ideology represented by the ruling priestly class consortium], he is comparable to the Tamil Siddhas and Nāṭa Siddhas who roam around in forests, with *bhasma* (ashes) smeared all over their bodies and carrying iron spears, the term *pāṣāṇa* seems to represent a special alchemical category of substances [generally products from animals (maybe bones) or stones or minerals] in the Tamil Siddha tradition, as may be seen from the following technical terms:

īyattin-piḷḷai	=	lit., son of lead; *nīla-pāṣāṇam*
kūral	=	*nāga pāṣāṇam* (?black-lead)
gauri pāṣāṇam	=	*veḷḷai pāṣāṇam* (lit., white p.; ?white-lead); *caṅkaran peṇṭir* (lit., maidens of Śiva)
avuni pāṣāṇam	=	*kutirai pāṣāṇam* (lit., horse p. = ribs?)
nava pāṣāṇam	=	*kendi, liṅgam vīram, pūram, tāḷakam, mano-cilai, veḷḷai, kār-mukil, eli-pāṣāṇam*
ciṅgi pāṣāṇam	=	*kalai mān-kompu* (horns of stag); Skt.: *śṛṅgi*, horned
gandhaka pāṣāṇam	=	*puṇkavan*

A cognate etymon[124] is Nepali: *pāso*, the head of an iron instrument (e.g., axe-head, spade-head); [Pāli-Prākṛta: *pāśa*, spear (if not *prāsaḥ*)]; Hindi: *pāsā*, lump of metal; Marathi: *pās*, silver ingot, iron share of a harrow. It is unclear if the last interpretation is the same as Nepali: *pāso*, a die; pl. *pāsā*, dice; *pāsā khelnu*, to play dice; Sanskrit: *pāśaḥ*, *pāśakaḥ*, a die; Pāli: *pāsako*; Bengali, Hindi, Punjabi: *pāsā*; Gujarati: *pāso*. It is important to note the *pāṣaṇḍa* was said to be carrying iron spears.

The parallel semantic streams for the same morpheme, *pāso* (i.e., dice and silver/iron ingots) is echoed in another morpheme: *akṣa,* a die and also a gold cowrie or unit of account for state treasury. *Akṣa* of gold; *pāso* of silver or iron. It would appear that there are two key metallic substances were in contention as currency media, controlled by two classes: gold and silver sought to be monopolized by the royal-priest consortium and accumulated into the state treasury; silver and iron[125] worked by the *pāṣaṇḍas,* perhaps autonomously. If this etymological nexus is valid, the possible wrath or class-conflict between the *pāṣaṇḍa* and the ruling-consortium can be explained in economic terms.

A synonym for *caṇḍāla* is a *śvapāka.* The morpheme *śva-* in the latter compound may provide some clues as to the nature of the substances dealt with by this class of people. The cognate term is *a-śva,* horse. [The term *a-śva,* may be contrasted with *śvaḥśvas: a-śva,* non-recurrent, occasional; *śva,* daily.] It is notable that the horse *pāṣāṇam* had some specific alchemical use in the Siddha tradition. It is also noteworthy that the special Soma *yajña* organized on a grand scale for the king involves the Aśvamedha or horse sacrifice; in alchemical terms, this may mean the process of adding horse-bones or ribs to the smelting process for refining or "transmuting" gold.

The morpheme *śva-* has a variant in an anatomical term elaborated in the *Śatapatha Brāhmaṇa:*[126] *pariśava* interpreted as ribs on two sides (*pārśva*) of the body formed by 26 *parśus.* [It is notable that the term, *parśu* connotes a spear or spade.] *Jaiminīya Brāhmaṇa*[127] elaborates that the ribs, *pariśavas* are attached to the *aṇḍa-pariśus,* which may cannot globular ends of the ribs or ball-bearings? Another compound *śvāpad* in *Atharvaveda*[128] is interpreted as "wild animals," divided into five classes: jungle animals, winged creatures such as gander, eagle; amphibian such as alligator, crocodile; fish; and insects and worms.[129] It would appear the compound, *śvapāka* may indeed be a technical term to explain the process of smelting using the ribs as reducing agents. It is notable that the cupels for purifying gold are specially made using animal bones, to promote the process of oxidation of lead and other impurities in the ore. In an allegorical representation, the *pariśva* may indeed be treated as the *vajra* to "break into" the ore block to extract the juice or metal out.

It would, therefore, appear that the reference to *pāṣaṇḍa* and *caṇḍāla* in extraordinary wrath, may indeed have an economic basis for a class-conflict; they had alchemical technological competence. [Discovery of the gold-bearing beads is traced to the neolithic period (which in the Deccan is dated between third millennium BC and the first half of the first millennium BC) initially restricted to surface mining, use of stone picks and copper chisels advanced the mining techniques and resulted in human settlements around gold-fields.][130] It is notable that the Superintendent of Mines of the Kauṭilya days is required to evaluate old abandoned workings (Tamil: *pāṛ*, old, decayed structures), attesting to the antiquity of gold-mining. They indeed were dealing with silver and iron ingots and engaged in smelting operations using bones and ribs and certainly corpses, living as they do near the cremation grounds, as *antyāvasāyins* and since they were also hunters with access to *śṛṅgi*, antler horns [with occult/alchemical/medicinal uses], for instance. The ruling-priestly class consortium had reasons to perceive them as a threat to their endeavour to monopolize the gold and silver accumulation process into the state treasury and to use the metals as currency media in economic transactions, to sustain state power. That some deception was involved in producing "false gold" is an alchemical tradition of deception called, aurifiction. In any case, the *pāṣaṇḍa* and *caṇḍāla* had the technical/technological competence to call the "bluff" using the touchstone or a cupellation test; may be, they did and hence, the exclusion from the diabolical *varṇa* hierarchy. May be, they were governed by the Lokāyata ideology which ran counter to the ruling-priest consortium ideology which militated against manual operations. May be, they were a proud people and may be, they refused to be servile, a necessary condition for being included in the lowest rung of the *varṇa*,[131] hierarchy. May be, most of them refused to be in state service to work for the *ṛtvij* and *purohita* engaged in a state-administered aurifiction corporation, supervised by a functionary called *ākarādhyakṣa*.

References

1. J. Needham, *SCC*, vol. 5, pt. II, p. xxvii.
2. *ṚV*, I.105.15: "All these gods, who are in the three spheres, where is the *ṛta* of yours gone?... Where, O gods, is the holding of the *ṛta*, where is the watchfulness of Varuṇa?... We ask of Varuṇa, the knower of the

path and the maker of food,—I utter this from my heart, let the *ṛta* be born anew (*navyaḥ jayatam ṛtam*)...; cf. the brilliant exposition by Debiprasad Chattopadhyaya, *Lokāyata*, pp. 639-44.

3. Cf., Mircea Eliade, *Yoga*, note VI, 1; he cites G. Tucci, "Amimad versionnes Indicae," *JRASB*, NS, XXVI, pp. 125-60 to underscore that some tantric schools several centuries earlier than sixth century AD; for example, the *Suvarṇaprabhāsasūtra* was translated into Chinese in the first half of the fifth century; Kumārajīva had translated *Mahāmāyūrī Vidyārājī* as early as *c.* AD 405.
4. Debiprasad Chattopadhyaya, *Lokāyata*, p. 642.
5. "The Veda-Śāstra could not have been made by human faculties; not can it be measured by human reason unassisted by revealed glosses and comments: this is a sure proposition." (*Manu*, ch. XII.94.) This is the key statement of the ideology which ran counter to alchemical tradition and indeed, all scientific potential inherent in the artifacts which resulted from manual operations and the measurement tools of the tula and binary chert weights, which can be traced to the Indus valley lapidary crafts.
6. Debiprasad Chattopadhyaya, *Science and Society in Ancient India* (hereinafter cited as *SSAI*), pp. 261ff.
7. Cf., Muhammad Sana Ullah, "Notes and Analyses" in J. Marshall, ed., *MIC*, vol. II, pp. 689ff.: "A black coal-like substance found at Mohenjodaro has been indentified by the writer as silaajeet or śilājātu, an ancient Indian medicine. It occurs as an exudation on rocks in the Himalayas, and is popular with the physicians following the old school. Caraka says that 'there is hardly any curable disease which cannot be controlled or cured with the aid of Shilaajaatu....'"
8. J. Needham, *SCC*, vol. 5, part II, p. 10.
9. Cf., Debiprasad Chattopadhyaya, *SSAI*, pp. 286 ff.; *Maitrāyaṇī Upaniṣad*, VII.8.
10. There is an intriguing reference to a Chinese translation of Asaṅga's *Madhyāntānugamaśāstra*, the original of which is reportedly lost. This text mentions the name of a tantric school, *na ya sin mo* (Nyaayasauma, Nayasamya, Nayasauma). G. Tucci, "Animadversiones Indicae," *JRASB*, NS, XXVI, 1930, pp. 125-60 (M. Eliade, *Yoga*, p. 400), studies the history of the school and establishes the antiquity of the school. Chintaharan Chakravarti, "The Soma or Sauma Sect of the Saivas," *IHQ*, VIII, 1, 1932, pp. 221-23 (M. Eliade, ibid.) according to Eliade, also indicates links between saumas and tantrism. It may be reasonably conjectured that the tantric traditions may ultimately find their roots in the *yakṣa* and alchemic legacies of *soma*, electrum smelting traceable to the proto-Indus civilization. Eliade (ibid., p. 415) also notes: "It is quite possible that, besides tantric alchemy, properly speaking, certain

mineralogical observations were incorporated into the alchemical tradition and transmitted under the name of Nāgārjuna: the symbiosis between 'mystical' (or metaphysical) 'truth' and 'observational truth' (rudiments of scientific thought and chemical experiment) is a phenomenon documented throughout the history of alchemy."

11. There are striking parallels with the Vrātya tradition associated with *tapas*, asceticism, disciplines of breath-control (cf. similar Taoist beliefs), *gavām-ayana* sacrifice ending with the *mahāvrata*, a solstitial rite of antiquity, trance or *samādhi*. "They regarded the body as a microcosm, of which the universe was the macrocosm. They experimented with secret recipes for the elixir of life, which earned them the reputation of being 'swallowers of poison.'" (Cf., A.P. Karmarkar, *The Religions of India: The Vratya or Dravidian Systems*, Lonavla, 1950, p. 25; B. Walker, *The Hindu World*, p. 583: "Little more is needed to establish a plausible connection between Chaldean and Elamite magic, the religion of pre-Zoroastrian Persia, the cults of the Indus valley, the magic rites of the Vrātyas of the Middle Gangetic plain, and the arcane teachings of the heterodox Jain and Buddhist cults.") Wearing a *niṣka* ear-ring, accompanied by a *puṁścali* (or *sūlā*) and carrying a magical bowl, the image of a *vrātya* parallels a Kānphaṭa, Aghori or other sadhus. Cf. H.P. Sastri, *Absorption of the Vratyas*, 1926; Debiprasad Chattopadhyaya, *Lokāyata*, pp. 166ff.: "...the *vratyās* were those that lived in the tribal societies...the words *gaṇa* and *vrāta* were used interchangeably...."
12. In Egyptian alchemistic theory, yellowness is a spiritual power which overcomes the earthy, "sublimates it, washes away all its sins" and brings it forth as "higher" in the scale of metals. Cf., A.J. Hopkins, op. cit., pp. 120-21.
13. Cf., an alchemist expression: "To transmute, in these authors, means to give a body to the incorporeal," Berthelot, *Collection des anciens alchimistes graces*, III, XXVIII, 7; also Hopkins, op. cit., p. 18.
14. Cf., A.J. Hopkins, op. cit., pp. 75-76. In addition to the concept of a tincture which adds the golden colours to base metals. Zosimus, the Greek alchemist adds the doctrine of ferment, a catalyst which is added by the alchemist hastens the process of transmutation: "If you wish to tint into silver, add leaves of silver; if into gold, leaves of gold. For Democritus says: Project Water of Sulphur on common gold and you can give it a perfect tint of gold...the Sulphur Water play the part of a yeast, producing the like, whether silver or gold." [Citing Berthelot, *Collection des anciens alchimistes grecs*, III, LII.4. Also, III, XXI.3: "Likewise also the little leaf of gold or of silver produces all the powder of projection and makes everything ferment."]

15. J. Needham, *SCC*, vol. 5, part II, p. xxvii.
16. The concept of "weights" proved to be of fundamental importance in the birth of scientific "chemistry." To quote A.J. Hopkins, op. cit., pp. 231ff.: "Certain branches of the study of nature had been neglected by the alchemists. One of these was the atmosphere and its secrets; another, the significance of weight...Jean Rey (1630) called attention to the *gain in weight* when metals were calcines.... In 1774, Lavoisier was able to show that the gain in weight of tin, or of sulphur,or of phosphorus, when heated in a closed vessel, equals the loss in weight of the air; and is due to a portion of the 'air which becomes fixed during combustion.' ...(alchemical) *tria principia* of Paracelsus, mercury, sulphur and salt (had collapsed).... Matter, in place of being negligible, became the *essentia,* matter which was checked by weight... (leading to astounding statements): (1) No matter is ever created or destroyed; (2) during chemical changes, qualities change but matter (weight) alone is permanent; (3) the total weight before and after a chemical change is the same."
17. Robert P. Multhauf, *The Origins of Chemistry*, New York, 1965, pp. 20ff.
18. Bronze is the copper-tin alloy which seems to have been the second smelted "metal." Unlike galena, tin ore requires the addition of a reducing agent. That bronze was used in the Indus valley civilization is a pointer to the possibility that the proto-Indus lapidary was familiar with the techniques for extracting tin i.e., with the use of reducing agents (mentioned in later-day alchemical texts) and adding it as an alloy to copper.
19. For an experimental demonstration of this, Multhauf cites Tylecote, 1962, p. 76.
20. Berthelot, *Collection des Anciens Alchimistes Grecs*; J.M. Stillman, *The Story of Alchemy and Early Chemistry* (*The Story of Early Chemistry*), first pub. 1924; repr., New York, 1960, p. 82.
21. Berthelot, *Collection des Anciens Alchimistes Grecs*, vol. I, p. 10; Stillman, p. 88.
22. R. Multhauf, op. cit., p. 20.
23. Vaidyaraj Daljit Singh, *Yunani Divyaguṇa Vijñāna*, p. 322; A.L. Sharma, A.B. Seerwani, and V.R. Shastry, "Botany in the Vedas," *IJHS*, vol. 7, no. 1, p. 39.
24. Ibid., p. 160; ibid., p. 40. Cf., K.R. Kirtikar and B.D. Basu, *Indian Medicinal Plants*, vol. II, p. 926.
25. *Atharvaveda*, I.5.23.3.
26. *Śatapatha Brāhmaṇa: somo vai palāśam*, 6.6.3.7.
27. S. Mahdihassan, "Elixir, its Significance and Origin," *Journal of the Asiatic Society, Pakistan*, 1961, p. 41; P.C. Ray, "Origin and Tradition

of Alchemy," *IJHS*, vol. 2, no. 1, p. 14.

28. J.M. Stillman, *The Story of Alchemy and Early Chemistry*, p. 98.
29. It is an important challenge for the historian to determine if the plebeians chose to go it alone or were driven to autonomous actions, resulting from class-conflicts and "marginalisation" of the labouring-classes.
30. Patañjali, *Mahābhāṣya*, II.4.10; ed. by Kielhorn, vol. I, p. 475; cf. Kane, *History of Dharmaśāstra*, 5 vols., Poona, 1930-46; vol. II, pp. 92, 168 and nn. 200, 392.
31. Kangle, *Kauṭilīya Arthaśāstra*, pp. 147-48.
32. Ibid., p. 155.
33. *Caraka*, VI.4.5. Caraka refers also to medical colloquia (*saṁbhāṣā*) as a means of exchanging, debating and widening *vaidya*'s knowledge. Caraka cautions that in the heat of debate, medical secrets learnt orally might be divulged (*Caraka*, II.32.72.85; III.8.15-18).
34. *Suśruta*, I.36.10; V.G. Apte, ed., *Dhanvantarīya Nighaṇṭu*, Poona, 1925, I.6-7.
35. Kangle, op. cit., p. 150.
36. J. Legge, tr., *Fa-hien—A Record of Buddhist Kingdoms*, Oxford, 1886; reprinted, New Delhi, 1991, p. 43.
37. *Bṛhatsaṁhitā*, XV.30; *Yogayātrā*, IX.7.
38. *Bṛhatsaṁhitā*, L.5; LII.82; *Bṛhajjātaka*, II.77 (*antyaja*).
39. T. Watters, *On Yuan Chwang's Travels in India*, Delhi, 1961, vol. I, p. 168.
40. Ibid., pp. 159.
41. Ibid., p. 147.
42. Sachau, vol. I, p. 101.
43. J. Needham, *SCC*, vol. 5, part II, pp. 9, 12-13.
44. *Arthaśāstra* (2.14.20-24) elaborates on the means of pilfering by goldsmithy artisans:

    Two parts of silver and one part of copper constitute *tripuṭaka*. By means of that, mineral gold is removed; that is "removal by *tripuṭaka*." By (substitution of) copper, that is "removal by copper," by (substitution of) *vellaka* (an alloy of equal parts of silver and iron), that is "removal by *vellaka*," by (substitution of) gold containing half copper, that is "removal by gold." A dummy crucible (*mūkamūṣā* which always has a false bottom into which a part of the melting gold drips down), foul dross (*pūtikiṭṭaḥ*), the "crane's beak" (*karaṭukamukham*, a kind of pincers with hollow ends to conceal gold; or a wind-passage at the end of the bellows), the blow-pipe, the pair of tongs, the water-vessel (*joṅgani*; the root *juṅg* means "to set aside, exclude." Can the word mean a sieve, a strainer?), borax (*sauvarcikālavaṇam*), and the same gold, these are the ways of removal. Or, sand made into lumps (*piṇḍavālukāḥ*) and placed (there) beforehand, is taken out of the fire-place on the breaking of the crucible.

45. A new corpse is placed in a basket and immersed in a running river for a week. Suśruta says that the flesh disintegrates and can be removed by scrubbing with a long, stiff brush. Thus intestines may be exposed for study without physical contact. *Suśrutasaṁhitā*, III.5.49.
46. *Arthaśāstra*, IV.7.1.13.
47. *Suśrutasaṁhitā*, I.45.170-216.
48. *Arthaśāstra*, X.3.47; *Suśrutasaṁhitā*, I.34.12-14.
49. *Suśrutasaṁhitā*, I.3.49; 10.03. *Arthaśāstra*, IV.1, however, indicates a lesser fine on a doctor, for permanent injury caused by bad treatment.
50. Sircar, 76n.
51. Sircar, 63 and 65.
52. *Manu*, X.8.
53. Kane, II.71.
54. Debiprasad Chattopadhyaya, *SSAI*, pp. 217ff.; *WLWD*, 185ff.
55. Dutt, 1965, p. 70.
56. E. Thurston, *Castes and Tribes of Southern India*, vol. IV, p. 195.
57. *Manu*, X.8.47.
58. Dutt, 1965, p. 71; A.L. Basham, 1976, p. 37.
59. *Manu*, III.152.
60. Ibid., IV.212.
61. *Baudhāyana Śulbasūtra*, II.1.2; Dutt, 1931, p. 209; 1965, pp. 66-67.
62. Bloomfield, *SBE*, Intro., xlvi.
63. The commentator (Kangle, part II, p. 18) adds: "*edhitam* and *mantri mantrābhi mantritam* contain a punning reference to the kindling of fire and its sanctification by mantras... *śāstrānugama śastritam* 'possessed of weapons in the form of obedience to the *śāstra*,' or 'possessed of weapons on account of obedience to the *śāstra*,' refer to a pun, apparently in the word *śastrita* 'possessed of a weapon' and 'accompanied by a hymn of praise or litany' (*śāstra*)."
64. R.P. Kangle, op. cit., part II, p. 298 suggests: "Cs (another commentary) reads *bhārgyāyagnim*, 'the fire from *ayas*, i.e., *ayaskāra*, with the offering of the *bhārgi* plant and ghee.' But *ayaskāra* could hardly be different from *karmāra* already mantioned...*bhārgavāgnim* 'fire of archers'...is not satisfactory."The interesting point to note is that the *atharvan* is in league with the *caṇḍāḷa* to obtain meat in the latter's fire."
65. *Caraka Saṁbhāṣā*, I.30.20-21; cf. D.P. Chattopadhyaya, *SSAI*, p. 313.
66. *Manu*, X.64.
67. Ibid., VIII.413f.
68. *Gautama*, XII.4-6.

69. *Āpastamba,* II.5.11.5-6; *Gautama,* VI.25; *Manu,* II.139; *Vaśiṣṭha,* I.45.
70. *Gautama,* X.53; XI.65.
71. Ibid., X.60.
72. Even Āpastamba (II.3.61) seems to refer to *jāti* as a synonym for *varṇa.*
73. *Manu,* X.4.
74. Arrian, *Ind.,* xi-xii.
75. E. Senart, op. cit., 152-53; Robert Lingat, *The Classical Law of India,* Berkeley, 1973; reprinted, New Delhi, 1993, p. 36.
76. *Baudhāyana Śulbasūtra,* I.17.3-5; *Vaśiṣṭha,* XVIII.8-9; *Gautama,* IV.16.
77. Robert Lingat, *The Classical Law of India,* pp. 33-34; E. Senart, *Les castes dan l'Inde,* new ed., Paris, 1927, p. 123. In Denison Ross's translation, *Caste in India,* London, 1930, the passage is at p. 102.
78. *Niruktam,* III.8.
79. B.C. Law, *Ancient Indian Tribes,* vol. 2, first published, 1934; rep., Delhi, 1980, pp. 61-62.
80. *Gautama,* IV.17; *Baudhāyana Śulbasūtra,* I.16.8.17.7-8.
81. J. Jolly, ed., *The Institutes of Narada,* Calcutta, 1885, 5.3; L. Sternbach, *Juridical Studies in Ancient Indian Law,* Delhi, 1965, pp. 469-70.
82. L. Sternbach, *Juridical Studies in Ancient Indian Law,* p. 469; J. Jolly, ed., *Institutes of Narada,* 5.6-7.
83. *Arthaśāstra,* 3.13.3. Kangle (op. cit., p. 235) adds: "*mlecchānam* would seem to refer to foreigners as well as tribals not absorbed in Aryan society. Mixed castes would be on a par with a Sudra (3.7.37)...."
84. *Nārada,* 5.6.
85. M. Ullmann, "al-Kimiya," in *The Encyclopaedia of Islam,* Leiden, 1986, pp. 110ff.
86. Ibid., p. 112.
87. *Āpastamba,* I.6.18.14.
88. *Gautama,* XX.10-14.
89. *Vaśiṣṭha,* XV.21.
90. *Vāyupurāṇa*: "Those who were cleansers (?) and ran about on service, and had little vigour or strength, he (Brahmā) called Śūdras...he assigned the practice of the mechanical arts and service to the Śūdras." Muir, I.31; *Harivaṁśa*: the Śūdras were formed "from a modification of smoke...the Śūdras spread over the earth are unserviceable owing to their birth with all its circumstances, to their want of initiatory rites, and the ceremonies ordained by the Vedas." Muir, I.35, *ERE,* p. 915.
91. *Encyclopaedia of Religion and Ethics* (hereinafter cited as *ERE*), p. 231.
92. Ibid., pp. 1-3.
93. Ibid., p. 586.
94. S.C. Roy, *Muṇḍa and Their Country,* pp. 410ff.

95. Cf., P.D. Chattopadhyaya, *SSAI*, p. 167.
96. *Carakasaṁhitā*, I.26.57-8.
97. *Sacred Books of the East* (*SBE*), XXV, p. 189.
98. *Śatapatha Brāhmaṇa*, *SBE*, XLIV, p. 215.
99. Ibid., pp. 303f.
100. *Manu*, X.8.
101. Ibid., X.12.16.
102. Bloomfield, *SBE*, Intro., p. li.
103. *Gautama*, XV.16.
104. *Manu*, III.151.
105. In Muṇḍa, *pāhān* connotes a village-priest; the concordance with *pāka* is notable. Cf. *pahanr* priest in the Santhali tradition.
106. *Manu*, IV.205; cf. D.P. Chattopadhyaya, *SSAI*, p. 246.
107. *Viṣṇu*, LXXXII.12.
108. D.P. Chattopadhyaya, *SSAI*, pp. 286ff.
109. *Maitrāyaṇī Upaniṣad*, VII.8.
110. *Āpastamba*, I.3.9.14-6.
111. *Gautama*, XIV.30-2.
112. Ibid., XIV.23.
113. *Manu*, V.64-5.
114. *Chāndogya Upaniṣad*, V.10.7.
115. *Suśrutasaṁhitā*, III.5.59-61, KSS ed., D.P. Chattopadhyaya, *SSAI*, pp. 94ff.
116. Cf., D.P. Chattopadhyaya, *SSAI*, pp. 212ff.; on "law-givers" contempt for doctors.
117. *Cilappatikāram*, canto 12, II.20ff.; Aiyaikumārī is Goddess Durgā of the hunter class: *maravar*. Cf. Manu's declaration that *caṇḍāḷa* are hunters and fishermen.
118. J.N. Banerjea, *Development of Hindu Iconography*, p. 265.
119. *Indian Culture*, Calcutta, vol. 36, pp. 58ff.
120. *Sri Sri Candi*, ed., Ratneshwar Tantra-jyotishastri, Calcutta (chap. 8, v. 59); R.N. Nandi, op. cit., p. 136.
121. W.T. Elmore, *Dravidian Gods in Modern Hinduism*, 1913; reprint, Delhi, 1984, p. 152, n. 2.
122. Ibid., pp. 97ff.; Thurston, *Castes and Tribes of Southern India*, vol. IV, pp. 295ff.
123. W.T. Elmore, op. cit., pp. 25-26.
124. Cf., R.L. Turner, *Nepali Dictionary*.
125. *IAR*, 1957-58, pp. 34-36: Ujjain excavations revealed used of iron from *c.* 700 BC to 500 BC. In Period III of Ujjain, many pointed crucibles with a vitriolic surface and contractions for blowing air were found. Residue of copper and lead was found on some of these crucibles, indicating the working on these metals. *IAR*, 1964-

65 (unpublished; M.N. Deshpande, "Archaeological Sources for the Reconstruction of the History of Sciences in India," *IJHS*, vol. 6, no. 1, p. 17): At an Asura site (*c.* first-second centuries AD) at Sarakdel, Ranchi district, a large number of iron objects (arrowheads, axe with double or single cutting edges, chisels, nails, longitudinal ploughshare, caltrops, door-hinges, rings, knives, etc.) together with slags were found indicating the existence of an iron-smelting factory.

126. *Śatapatha Brāhmaṇa*, VIII.6.2.8-10; XII.2.4.13.
127. *Jaiminīya Brāhmaṇa*, ed., Raghu Vira and Lokesh Chandra, II.5.3; Mira Roy, "Anatomy in the Vedic Literature," *IJHS*, 1967, vol. 2, no. 1, p. 44, n. 46. Mira Roy notes that the number of ribs accords with modern anatomy; twelve ribs are on each side; the number is increased by the development of a cervical or lumber rib; hence the count of thirteen on either side is acceptable.
128. *Atharvaveda*, VIII.5.11.
129. Ibid., XI.2.24-25.
130. F.R. Allchin, "Gold Mining in Ancient India," *Journal of Economic and Social History of the Orient*, vol. V, part II, 1962, Leiden, pp. 195-210.
131. An example of the extraordinary colour-consciousness created by the *varṇa* concept is seen from Someśvara's *Mānasollāsa* [twelfth century AD (3.1.14-15)]: To select a site for a building, the colour of the soil is considered important; the soil to be selected by the Brāhmaṇas should be white; similarly, the Kṣatriyas should select a soil having red soil; Vaiśyas should select yellow soil and the Śūdras, the black soil. "This opinion of Someśvara has the concurrence of the *Matsya Purāṇa* (252.11) and the *Viśvakarma Prakāśa* (1.24-26)," adds S.S. Misra, *Fine Arts and Technical Sciences in Ancient India*, Varanasi, 1982, p. 82.

8

Siddha and Tantric Alchemy

Holy ascetics or "poets of powers:" Siddhas

Arthaśāstra (4.3.13) describes the remedial measures during the calamity of disease (magicians and others) should counteract with secret means, physicians with medicines or holy ascetics (*siddha-tāpasāḥ*) with pacificatory and expiatory rites. This threefold division exemplifies the alchemical spectrum which in many cultures has ranged from magic through medicine to religious rites. Two whole sections [177: Secret Practices for the Destruction of Enemy Troops and 178: Deceiving (by Means of Occult Practices)] are devoted to the working of miracles and the use of medicines and spells; various secret remedies for political purposes. The recipes kill, maim, or disfigure a person. The objective of the practices directed against the unrighteous is extraordinary: "to protect the four *varnas*" (14.1.1). From an alchemical perspective, the sections provide a list of substances which may perhaps be compared with the pharmacopoeia of other civilizations for their medicinal/poisonous effects. Section 80 (4.5.1 to 18) describes the detection of criminals through secret agents in the disguise of holy men (*siddha*). From the types of tricks suggested, a *siddha* is perceived as a person wielding the power of the charms, possessing the means of charms to induce sleep.

The *siddhas*[1] of Tamil tradition had beliefs comparable to Taoists: "They rebelled against the nauseating caste system, sickening superstitions, foolish fanaticism, repelling rituals and the loathing interpretations of the Vedas, Āgamas and *mantras* by the Brāhmaṇas and the intimidating tales they wove to admonish any free thinker."[2] Vajrabodhi, a native of Kāñcipuram, and his student Amoghavajra are said to have carried the tantric yoga to China in AD 720 and taught the system to a Chinese scholar, Hui-Kuo from whom the Japanese saint Kukai received the learning.[3] Tirumūlar, who is considered to be father of Tamil *siddhas*, is believed to be a saint from north India, a Nāṭa *siddha*. His *Tirumantiram* is a treatise on yoga, has 3000 stanzas divided into nine cantos called *tantirams* or *tantras*. The treatise is an affirmation of life on earth. For him the human body is not evil but the "walking temple of God," a fit medium for self-discipline. The powerful expressions of the *siddhas* are direct and precise:

> Heart is the sanctum sanctorum and the body is the temple. (*Tirumantiram*, stanza 1823)
>
> Why should you garland a stone god and make rounds and rounds around the planted stone all the time murmuring *mantras*? How do you expect the stone to speak when God himself is within you? (Śiva-vākkiyar, *Śivavākkiyarpāṭal*, stanza 481)
>
> A true *siddha* is "...one who wanders like a spirit, renounces everything like corpse, eats whatever is available like a stray dog, roams about like a fox, looks upon women as mothers and is like an innocent child." (Paṭṭinattār, *Tirueikampamālai*, stanza III.9)
>
> Endowed are we with powers to *transform* the three (heaven, earth and the infernal regions) wondrous worlds *into nothing less than pure gold* and transfigure the torried sun himself into a cool moon. So powerful are we to make this gigantic earth vanish. Realize our might and dance. O Snake. (Siddha Pāṁmāṭṭi, *Poems*, in P. Raja, "Tamil Siddhas," *Journal of the Institute of Asian Studies*, vol. VI, no. 2, March 1989, pp. 152ff.)

Tirujñāna Sampantar (AD 650) in his *Tevāram* (II.66.1) views the *tirunīru* or *vibhūti* or sacred ashes as the equivalent of the *mantra* and *tantra*. This echoes the alchemical tradition that the essence of a substance is to be found in its ashes, the end-product of a process of transformation under intense refiner's fire. That the ashes might have constituted artificially made sal ammoniac used in alchemical preparations is indeed remarkable. (Cf., Al-Razi's work)

In Caṅkam literature, there is a category of ethical works of poetry called *padin-en-kīṛ. Kaṇakku* (lit. eighteen lower counts)—eighteen groups of ballads with four or less number of metrical lines. *Tirukkuraḷ* is one such work. *Tirikaṭukam* is another. The author of this work which has 101 *veṇpā*, is Nallātanār (*c.* second century AD). Literally, the term *tirikaṭukam* refers to three pungent medicinal herbs: *cukku, miḷaku, tippili*. This is a work which assumes the medical efficacies of the three herbs. The text resonates with ethical and moral exhortations asking the listeners to perform deeds of merit in this life, listing in each song, three behavioural traits to avoid or foster. The goal to reach is immortality, without losing the awareness of the unity of mind and body in a social context.

The morpheme *kaṭu* helps us to trace an interesting Ayurvedic tradition, analogous to the concept of "tint" or "tincture" in alchemical traditions, in general. *Takatulāyavāgu* or a gruel containing three *kaṭu* or pungents explained to be ginger and two kinds of peppers was found to be useful in *Vinaya*, I.210 and *Vinaya Texts*, II, 68nn. The morpheme seems to be proto-Dravidian pointing to the absorption of the Dāsyu alchemical tradition of preparing *kaṣāya* (lit., yellowish, red, astringent, astringent juice).[4] The build-up of the radical *kas-* connoting *yellowish-red* is apparent: tracing it through a dye, gold-testing, astringency, and medicinal preparation. This morpheme may be deemed to provide the quintessence of the alchemical tradition which integrated—beyond the forge and the crucible—textile, metallurgical, chemical and medicinal technologies of antiquity. *CDIAL*, 2969 reports a Kafiri term: *kashau*, a particular wooden idol formed like a man. This imagery is strikingly reminiscent of the *puruṣa* of the *Ṛgveda*. *Atharvaveda* refers to *kaśyapa*[5] as a semi-divine genii (metath., *yakṣa*?) regulating the course of the sun; did this *puruṣa* image represent the practice of using a human-shaped wooden or metal piece in smelting operations? [Cf., the man-like (bull's head?) silver plate in the Gungeria copper hoard].[6]

The term used by *cittar* to denote medicinal substances is *carakku* (Tamil or *saraku* Telugu) which may also mean, substances, in general and ingredients. The Siddha tradition divides the *carakku* into *āṇ-* and *peṇ-carakku*, male and female ingredients. This grouping may be seen to parallel the *yin-yang* binomial speculation of the Chinese alchemists and medicine-men[7] and also the Tamil tradition of categorizing male plants as those that yield gum-resins after incisions are made in the trunk.

Siddha tradition of transmutation of base metals into gold

The etyma of terms used in Siddha works provide a trace. There are two types of *rasa-vāda* referring to the processes of transmuting base metals into gold: *upa-rasa-vāda* and *rasa-vāda*. The *upa-rasa-vāda* is also referred to as *mantra-vāda*, *dhūḷana-vāda*, *tantra-vāda* (using syllables, urine, dust from the feet, by association with breath). The *rasa-vāda* is of seven types: *sparśa-vāda* (touch or union), *rasa-vāda* (medicine), *dhūma-vāda* (smoke), *dhātu-vāda* (five metals), *vākku-vādam* (words), *akṣa-vāda* (?sight; cf., interpretation of *akṣa* as gold cowries), *aṅkappa-vādam* (meditation).

The morpheme, *vedai* connotes *rasa-vāda*; *daricana vedi* (a root capable of achieving the transmutation); *paricana vedi* (*karkaṭa-pāṣāṇam*, a root for transmutation); *guru-muṭittal* (medicine for removing metals; universal remedy for all diseases); *vakāram* (cf. *vakāram*, *bindu* or *rasa-vādam*; *vakāra vittai=rasa-vāda vittai* or the magic of *rasa-vāda*).

Procedure for "pāka" in the Siddha alchemical tradition

Medicinal preparations are categorized by their ages or shelf-life. The appearance may be determining characteristic: pill (*māttirai*), one year; semi-solid (*lekiyam*), two years; oil (*tailam*), three years; coagulant (*kuṛambu*), five years; foam (*pataṅkam*), ten years; powder (*cintūram*), seventy-five years; ashes (*bhasmam*), hundred years. A technical term used is: *vayatu* (literally, age); this denotes the transmutation of gold (evoking the *amṛtam* refrain of the Brāhmaṇas!) and also the age or shelf-life of a medicine. This interpretation is a remarkable reiteration of the Brāhmaṇa alchemical tradition involving aurifiction.

A *pāka-cālai* is a place where medicines are prepared under the Siddha tradition. The process of *puṭa*-making is called *puṭam-poṭutal* or *puṭam-iṭal*. This process is interpreted as a process of "purification" of substances such as metals and *pāṣāṇa*, minerals or stones. There are six types of *puṭa*: (1) *mahā puṭam*; (2) *gaja puṭam*; (3) *varāha puṭam*; (4) *kukkuṭa puṭam*; (5) *gopura puṭam*; and (6) *bhāṇḍa puṭam*. The first four types are distinguished by the number of cowdung cakes used: 1000, 500, 200, and 8 respectively. The fifth and sixth types use large or small pots within which the pieces of cowdung cakes or paddy chaff are packed for generating the desired heat. Forty holes are pierced on the bottom of a pot.

Each of the five *bhūtas* (*pañca-bhūta*) is assigned a colour: earth, golden; water, whitish-blue (*sphaṭika*); fire, copper (*cembu*): wind, black; and ether, smoke. These categories of colour may explain the rationale for treating the smoke-coloured *bhasmam* or ashes as the representation of ether; and the *sindūra*, vermilion or red-coloured powder symbolizing fire as the representation of Śakti. The *bhūti* or *bhasmam* and *sindūra* become the dominant symbols worn as marks on the bodies of male ascetics and on the parting of the hair of females.

The process of "killing" metals is called *māraka-vedai* an apparent derivation from Sanskrit *vedhana*. The procedure for preparing unguents to docorate the eyes involves the use of a special pot called *yān-ai-k-kan. Caṭṭi* or literally, elephant-eyed pot, a metaphor denoting a pot with small eyes or perhaps, very small perforated pottery evoking the proto-Indus archaeological finds. For preparing the *kumbha-puṭa,* half the pot is filled with charcoal. Medicinal preparation is kept on top of the charcoal. After closing the mouth of the pot with a *maḍakku,* it is hermetically sealed with soft clay, dried in the sun and mounted on fire. On top of the *maḍakku* also embers are laid. The firing continues for a period of three days.

Argument: Tantric alchemy; the extension of alchemical tradition to Tibet

The alchemists of India who were lapidaries, metallurgists, artisans, physicians and surgeons and who could advance the science potentials of practical alchemical technology were driven underground, without the patronage of the ruler-priest ruling class and indeed, subjected to ridicule and social humiliation, treated as outcastes in an extraordinary hierarchical classification of society. [An *ambastha* tagged in Manu on a pernicious caste-profession nexus, for instance, becomes an *ambaṭṭan,* barber in the Dravidian-linguistic stream; and a *vaidya* in the Muṇḍa-linguistic stream; both treated as caste-groups outside of the ruler-priest class consortium.] A reconstruction of the ancient texts related to alchemy, metallurgy and medicine, which vanished from India may perhaps be found only in Tibetan translations and traditions which coalesce Tao, Buddhist and Hindu tantric-alchemic-medicinal activities. References to these ancient sciences of India, may be found in Chinese alchemical texts and alchemical tracts of other ancient civilizations which interacted with the proto-Indus and later civilizations of the subcontinent.

"Indian Buddhist Tantrism appears to have come to China in the +8th century...three Indian monks, Subhākarasiṁha (Shan Wu-Weik) (+636 to +735), who came to China in +716; Vajrabodhi (Chin-Kang-Chih, d. +732); and Amoghavajra (A-Mou-Ka) or Pu-Khung (d. +774). But the Chinese were also active; monks such as Chih-Thung wrote much on tantrism, and the great traveller I-Ching[8] translated a tantric Sūtra, the *Ta Khung Chhueh Chou Wang Ching.* But the most important tantric monk was the monk I-Hsing (+672 to +717), the greatest Chinese astronomer and mathematician of his time, and this fact alone should give us a pause, since it offers a clue to the possible significance of this form of Buddhism for all kinds of observational and experimental science. It would be surprising if there were no alchemical connections, but the subject is difficult to investigate, because, for obvious reasons, tantrists did not advertise their ways. Thus, for example, Shan Wu-Wei approved of the statues showing sexual union, but warned that they were not to be placed in the public halls of temples. So also in India, tantrists employed a 'twilight-language' with allusions not intelligible to the uninitiated (*saṁdhyābhāṣā*), a tantric 'slang.' At first sight, then, tantrism seems to have been an Indian importation to China. But closer inspection of the dates leads to a consideration, at least, of the possibility that the whole thing was really Taoist... a Sanskrit translation of *Tao Te Ching* [Kumārajīva is said to have made a commentary on this] was made for Bhāskara Kumāra, king of Kāmarūpa (Assam), who had asked Wang Hsuan-Tshe for it in +644.... Sages such as Vaśiṣṭha were said to have travelled to China to gain initiation into the cult (of Mahācīnatārā)...."[9]

Tibetan wizard-priests

Waddell equates the Sanskrit *siddha* or *mahāsiddha* with Tibetan grub-t' ob ch'en or 'grub-ch'en, who are credited with supernatural powers, in league with the demons. They are figured usually with untonsured locks and almost naked. The chief of these Indian priests is Padmasambhava and others, names are: Sāvari (sa-pa-ri-pa), Rāhulabhadra or Saraha (sa-ra-ha-pa), Matsyodara (lu-i-pa), Lalita-vajra, Kṛṣṇacārin or Kālācārita (nag-po-spyod-pa). Padmasambhava is almost deified and "sits dressed as a native of Udyāna, holding a thunderbolt in his right hand and a skull of blood in his left, and carrying in his left arm, the trident of the king of death. The top of this trident transfixes a freshly decapitated human head, a wizened head, and a skull."[10]

Dīpaṁkara Śrījñāna, is described as the son of a king of Zahor,[11] a country noted for tantrism. He studied all the schools of Buddhism, including Hīnayāna, but above all the tantras. These works were taught by the famous *siddhas* or yogins such as Dombhi, Nāropa and Avadhūti-pa, all of them teachers revered in Tibet.... (Atisa) arrived in Tibet in 1042 and died there in 1054.... Tantric teachings, with variations, took root everywhere.... Drogmi, "the man of the grazing lands" (992-1074), acquired from yogins in India the teaching known a Lamdre (*lam-bras*, "the path and fruit of action") that made use of sexual practices for mystical realizations... Marpa (1012-96) also went to India...he brought back and handed onto his disciple Milarepa the mystical songs (*dohā*) of the tantric poets of Bengal, and the doctrines called the Mahāmudrā, the "great seal."[12]

Without wealth you don't get religion from India!

Large quantities of gold had to be amassed in Tibet before setting out for India in search of books and oral teachings; Indian masters were paid a considerable sum. "If, for the sake of religious teachings, one goes to India without having much gold, it is like drinking water from an empty bowl," says Marpa, the disciple of Drogmi in a chronicle.... "And Milarepa, telling himself that whichever way he turns 'it is impossible to dispense with offerings; without wealth you don't get religion,' falls into despair and tries to commit suicide."[13]

Indo-Tibetan tantrism: dharma-rasa and physical immortality

The Tibetan tantric, alchemical, medicinal traditions seem to integrate Hindu (typically Śaivite) and Buddhist philosophical and alchemical concepts as also Greek and Chinese alchemy and medicine. Considering the proverbial difficulties involved in breaking into a closed system, governed by oral teachings and "secretive" technical manuals (cf., the secrecy in the Vedic literature and even the Śulbasūtra or the curt, poetic, tantric formulations in for example, *Saundaryalaharī* of Śaṅkara), the Tibetan texts which are translations of Indian originals offer useful source material for a historian of alchemy.[14]

Tantric texts embody an extraordinary social history and social conflict; for the tantrics revolted against a hierarchical classification of the Brāhmaṇas; they are the only ancient philosopher-alchemists known to us who proposed an esoteric process for elevating the status of people classified as *caṇḍāḷa* or other "lower" classes.

A tribute to Michael Lee Walter, on Indo-Tibetan Tantrism

In 1980, Michael Lee Walter presented a doctoral dissertation to the University of Indiana, Bloomington, USA. Helmut Hoffman [cf., his contributions to Tibetan studies] chaired the dissertation committee of the department of Uralic and Altaic Studies which accepted this dissertation. This is the only study of its kind known to us which provides a peep, perhaps for the first time, into the Indo-Tibetan Tantric-alchemical tradition. A number of references appended to this thesis are presented in the bibliography to facilitate further research in this area of alchemical tradition. The following paragraphs will attempt to paraphrase Walter's observations.

Indo-Tibetan tantric, alchemic and medicinal systems provide perhaps the only source material available today in Tibetan translations ["a great gift to the historian of Indian science"] of ancient Indian originals which have been lost or have not been found so far. The discovery of the famous *Bower Manuscript* in Eastern Turkestan in *c.* 1890 as the oldest Sanskrit manuscript extant is indicative of the cross-roads on which Indian medicine traversed in Central Asia in the first centuries of the Christian era. In the realm of Ayurvedic medicine, notes Walter,[15] a number of works not yet recovered may shed light on that tradition and the manner in which it was utilized in Tibet. For example, mention of the *Tsa-ra-ka-sde-brgad*, "The Eight-part (Commentary) on the Caraka," presumably materials on the *Carakasaṁhitā*, mentioned in Rechung Rinpoche's *Tibetan Medicine, Illustrated in Original Texts* (Berkeley, 1973, pp. 8, 11 and 202).

Walter finds that the practice of *rasāyana* as one of those *siddhis* advanced yogins are routinely said to have perfected themselves in. "A precise description of this power has not yet been formulated, in part because it is usually listed only perfunctorily. [Such as when *Sādhanamālā* mentions *rasāyana siddhi* or when a famous yogi's biography speaks of *gser 'gyur gyi rtsi* as separate *siddhis.*]"[16]

"It is obvious that *rasāyana* is interpreted quite differently in these two systems (of Vimalamitra and Padmasambhava). In the literature surrounding Padma the goal is the utilization of individual essence (*bcud* or *rasa*), e.g., of the *mahābhūtas.* This process may be purely meditational—what is internal alchemy only—or it may involve physical (laboratory) labour; most *sādhanas* studied have been rather ambiguous in this respect. And, although other materials certainly point to an actual ingestion of substances in a yogic procedure, there is no certainty that all such texts are susceptible of a literal interpretation...*dharma-rasa* is used less symbolically and takes on metaphysical creative functions.... Padmasambhava, the Alchemist is only a function of Padmasambhava, the Teacher....

"(Vimalamitra's system) is a profound and highly esoteric yogic discipline independent of his personality as a yogin...is centered upon *bodhicitta* as the basis of Reality; its production and perfection are then the results of sexual and alchemical practices. Most of the recipes in these works aim at procuring a particular *siddhi* for the yogin or at fixing his *bodhicitta* (and consequently his body) like a *vajra*. This signifies, at one and the same time, the attainment of the ultimate in a Vajrayāna system, as well as physical immortality.... Fixing the *bodhicitta* is the yogic process of controlling one's flow of semen on the physical level, which develops along with attaining the state of *mahāsukha* (i.e., *nirvāṇa*) as the ultimate spiritual goal. Arresting the flow of semen during a ritual union with a consecreted consort is the heart of the teachings of the Lun Anuyoga vehicle. The texts transmitted by Vimala thus combine this view of *bodhicitta* as *materia prima* with the most sexual aspects of yogic and Tantric teachings; and we see *bodhicitta* as the purely tantric reflex of the more abstract *rasa* in Padma's system. [In fact, we have yet to find Padmaist materials in which *rasa* and *amṛta* carries the real metaphysical importance it has been shown to have in Rdzogschen.]...[17]

"...there is a large element of magic (sometimes black magic) in some of Vimala's recipes; the power to kill is taught, for example, and organs from bodies are used to attain powers. Further, Vimala's texts show clear Hindu influences which, in view of the nature of Padmaism, one could not find in the latter's literature, despite the fact that both concepts of *rasāyana* owe something to Hindu traditions. Finally, there is a large body of Rdzogs-chen terminology embedded in Vimala's texts, which bids us to investigate closely the relationship between this system and esoteric scientific practices in tantrism...[it would be hazardous to date any important *sādhana* cycles or other practices attributed (to Rdzogs-chen) before the twelfth or thirteenth centuries]...these conceptions (of esoteric sciences within Gnosticism and Tantrism) have been developed to a degree not known from Indian materials...."

Alchemy in the "yakṣa" tradition focuses on people: healing

"In the waters exists ambrosia, in the waters exist all medicines (*apsu bheṣajam*). Let the sages be prompt in praise of waters. I am told by Soma that all the remedies exist in the waters (*apsu me somaḥ abravīt antaḥ viśvāni bheṣajam*)."[18] Soma is a physician who treats the ailing ones on earth: *bhiśakti viśvam yat turam.*[19]

The alchemical tradition evolving into proto-medicine operated within the same magico-religious framework, exemplified by the *yakṣa*, that wondrous thing, wondrous being who could perform magical feats and guard the treasures. Causes of disease were relatable not only to the patient himself (*doṣa,* imbalance in the *tri-dhātu*) but many other factors and phenomena external to him such as the *preta, bhūta, yakṣa,* etc. The analogy is with the extraneous matter that surrounded the "gold-principle," the colour of gold, *suvarṇam.* External intrusions had to be "killed."

Ṛta and Tao: the order of nature

The Taoist traditions so admirably analysed by Needham[20] may well serve as a preface to the parallel traditions of the Chinese genii and hsien; Indian *yakṣas,* tantrics, yogis, and *siddhas*! The Ṛgvedic concept of *ṛta* finds a parallel in Tao, exemplified in the Taoist *chhi* and *feng* (comparable to the doctrine of Greek *pneuma* or Indian *prāṇa*); the Taoists believed in a life to be lived in conformity with Nature and early Taoists were "deeply engaged as proto-scientists with their 'natural magic' . . . very practical men...within the framework of a world-view which regarded the Tao as essentially immanent—the Order of Natural itself."[21] Just as a Taoist was a star-clerk, weather-forecaster, man of farm-lore, irrigator, bridge builder, architect, decorator, but above all an alchemist,[22] a village barber (*ambaṭṭan*) in ancient India was a musician who officiated in religious ceremonies, barber-surgeon, medicine-man.[23] *Ambaṭṭan* women are the mid-wives of the village community.

It is indeed a challenging task for the social historian to explore the causes for the pervasive influence of tantric alchemists who had rejected the fine distinctions made by both Caraka and Suśruta (distinctions between curable and incurable diseases, *doṣas,* etc.) The tantric alchemists had, instead, propounded a radical view that the *rasa* formulations could "destory poverty, weakness and death, give kingly attributes to the lowly and power to the powerless...."[24] It would appear that adherents of the Suśruta school had gained the patronage of the ruling classes, since the surgeons were permitted to accompany the army in war. The radicals of the tantric alchemical schools had declared a total revolt with the impassioned, elemental, visceral cry: power to the powerless.

Jaina alchemical tradition

Dhātu-vāda may cannot alchemy in the Jaina tradition. *Vasudevahiṇḍī* (670 f.) refers to a mendicant who smeared a black iron with elixir, put it on the burning charcoal and by blowing it with bellows, turned it into gold (*pāṣāṇa dhātu*; cf., *Arthaśāstra* equating *pāṣaṇḍa* heretic monks and *caṇḍāḷa* as those living near the cremation ground).[25] This is distinguished from *rasa* which refers to gold obtained by moistening copper with mineral fluids (aurifiction). Another instance of aurifiction is: obtaining gold by blowing a piece of clay with certain application or without it, with bellows; the process was known as *dhātu-maṭṭiyā*.[26] "The rich and the kings used golden vessels for eating and drinking purposes.[27] The chair, bed-steads, thrones and royal cars used by kings were inlaid with gold. Golden vases (*bhiṅgāra*) were not unknown."[28]

Salts were: *sochal* (*sovaccala*); rock-salt (*sindhava*); ordinary salt (*lona*); mine-salt (*roma*) [Suśruta: *raumala-lavaṇa* described as a kind of saline earth and the salt extracted from it—some call it salt from Sambhar lake[29] in Ajmer; cf., Monier-Williams]; sea-salt (*samudda*); earth-salt (*paṁsukhāra*, also known as *bila-loṇa*); black-salt (*kāla-loṇa*, also known as *vida*) [*vidam kṛṣṇalavaṇam, Niṣitasūtra*, 8.17; *Cūrṇī*, p. 446; explained as a fractitious salt, procured by boiling earth containing saline particles; or a fetid salt used medicinally as a tonic aperient, commonly called *vitlavaṇ* or *bit-noben*. It is black in colour; it is prepared by fusing fossil salt with a portion of emblic myrobalan—which with soda is boiled down to obtain *sovaccala*. The product is a muriate of soda with small quantities of muriate of lime, sulphur and oxide of iron. *Bida* salt is mentioned in the *Arthaśāstra*, 103. Where salt was not available, saline earth impregnated with saline particles, *osa*, was boiled. This was known as *bila-loṇa*.][30]

Physiological alchemy

Arsenic had been used as an aphrodisiac in India and the tradition was exported to Europe. It was treated as a sexual stimulant; Needham cites Nadkarni who gave in 1954, a classical formula in which arsenic was combined in oil with plant material from Calotropis (= Asclepias) gigantea and the oleander Nerium odorum.[31] Both *Suśrutasaṁhitā* and *Rasārṇavatantra* (+12th century) and *Rasaratna Samuccayatantra* (*c.* =1300) refer to it; Europe had the habit of giving arsenic in fevers. "The wai tan elixirs must therefore have provided a copious supply of the secretion so much desired by the nei tan adepts. A parallel argument is applicable to that other secretion, semen, which was of such vital importance for the physiological alchemists, whether Taoist, tantric, or 'psychologised' as in later syncretic Buddho-Taoism... (the effects of arsenic or plant aphrodisiacs) on libido and potency were doubtless sufficient to assure the adepts that the secretion was not in short supply... (the development of steroid sex-hormones) was itself the result of a synthesis of physiological with chemical alchemy.... From the +fifth century onwards, Ando has been able to record more than fifty cases of self-mummification (defying corruption of dead body at will), nearly all Buddhist, among which are the great founder of the Thien-Thai school, Chih-I (d. +597 or +598), and the Indian Tantrist Śubhākarasiṁha (d. +735)."[32]

Pervasive tantrism for the less-privileged classes

Hevajratantra of the Mahāyāna Buddhism (eighth century AD), *Jvālinīkalpa*, a Jaina tantra treatise of the Deccan (first half of tenth century AD), *Kālikā Purāṇa* and *Rudrayāmala* of the Brāhmaṇa (tenth-eleventh centuries AD) are examples of pervasive adoption of tantrism in the Indian society. According to Ramendra Nath Nandi,[33] "the increasing association of a developing esoteric, tantric ritualism with the mother cults explains the growth of tantrism is early medieval times. The number of goddesses multiplied and with it the tantric sects. By the close of the tenth century, the Buddhists, the Jainas, the Śaivas, and the Vaiṣṇavas developed their tantric systems. Most of the goddesses belonging to these sects were recruits from semi-Brahmanical and aboriginal circles. Women of tribal and untouchable communities also entered the tantric pantheon as Śakti, and received worship.... The economic basis of tantric ritualism was also consistent with the folk character of tantric cults. The tantric worship performed by a rural community involved lesser cost than the earlier costly Vedic or Purāṇic rites. The tantric cults were observed by one or two priests in favour of a congregation, but Vedic and Purāṇic sacrifices were performed by a large group of priests in favour of individual millionaires including kings, vassals, high ministers, rich merchants. The less well off and depressed classes, who supported the tantric system, could neither engage a host of priests nor meet the cost of these sacrifices...providing cheaper remedies for physical and mental ailments. The occultist promised to cure snake-bites, insect-bites, mouse-bites as also lunacy and paralysis caused by evil spirits.[34] He performed rites to placate malevolent planets, fertilise a sterile woman, cause friendship, destroy enemies, hypnotise hostile persons, bestow health, prosperity and peace of the devotee. In short, the tantric ritualism assured the less affluent classes of all those benefits which the Vedic and Purāṇic rites promised to the more affluent communities."

Tracing the origins to yakṣa, Atharvaveda traditions

Goddesses or mothers are guardian spirits; the names of some goddesses are indicative of the possible origins of the associated cults from the *yakṣa* vegetation symbols: Khadiravaṭī, Stambheśvarī, and Parṇaśavarī. Khadiravaṭī is the family goddess of Moḍhā chiefs, who were Brāhmaṇas.[35] The morpheme *khadira-* refers to the tree whose barks may be used for tanning of leather. The tree is venerated in the *Atharvaveda*[36] as a protective amulet shaped like a ploughshare (*phāla*), yielding hundredfold reward of sacrifices, and bestowing faith and might. The amulet is deified, propitiated with clarified butter, wine, honey and food; this process fetches progeny for the householder, cows, goats, sheep, rice, barley, strength, lustre, fortune and fame; it is the abode of gods and fathers.[37] It is indeed a veritable tantric substitute for the Ṛgvedic *soma.* Bṛhaspati ties it on his person for strength, the moon-god uses it for conquering the golden cities of *asuras* and *dānavas.*[38] Aśvins wear it and guard the entire agricultural land.[39] Ramendra Nath Nandi makes a valid comparison between the offering of the fuel of *khadira* wood to Agni in the *Atharvaveda* to devour an enemy and the prescription in *Jvālinīkalpa,* to heat certain magical substances upon a fire of *kandira* wood to torture (*nigraha*) an opponent. Stambheśvarī or Khambeśvarī is the family goddess of the Sulki chiefs in Dhenkanal area of Orissa.[40] The morpheme *stambhu-* is comparable to the *yūpa* or Indramaha pillar as a cult object. Dumals and Kandhas of the south-western border of Sonpur in Orissa continue to worship the deity.[41] Parṇaśavarī is also a deity in the Mahāyāna pantheon. The morpheme *parṇa-* means a leaf; Śavara are a tribe, identified with Juangs, or Kolarians.[42]

Yakṣa, yakṣiṇī and transmutation of iron into gold

An evidence (of the historical periods) that clinches the trace of tantra cults to the *yakṣa* legacy is presented by the Jaina Tīrthaṅkaras who are accompanied by a pair of *yakṣa* and *yakṣiṇī.* Padmāvatī Yakkha is mentioned as a disciple of a Jaina priest in an inscription. A lady was called Jakkisundarī, literally, a beautiful *yakṣiṇī.*[43] In AD 1054 a grant, Padmāvatiyakal is respectfully mentioned on a boundary stone to mark the donation of a field, possibly as its guardian-deity.[44]

"The *yakṣiṇī* cult was the cult of the supernatural, and its origin may be traced back to the magical practices of the occultist. Thus, a *yakṣiṇī* was considered capable of bestowing children upon the childless, transmuting iron into gold,[45] and breaking open locked gates.[46] The *Jvālinīkalpa* and the *Bhairava Padmāvatīkalpa* speak of these supernatural qualities of the deities... the cult was introduced into peninsular India by the Śvetāmbaras of Tamil Nadu and the Digambaras of Mysore. The *Cilappatikāram* refers to the *yakṣiṇī* whose shrine lay outside the city-gates, in the midst of the quarters of the monks, who practised religion (*dharma*)....[47] [It is notable that 'the secret treasury' of *Arthaśāstra* was also located on the borders of a state.] An inscription (*c.* seventh century AD) found at Pañcapāṇṭavamalai in North Arcot district...mentions one Naraṇam, who made an image of Poṇṇiyakkiyar.[48] Poṇṇiyakkiyar means *yakṣiṇīs* of golden hue.... The image...holds a fruit, probably, citron.[49] The *yakṣiṇī* figure is identifiable with Siddhāyikā, the guardian angel of lord Mahāvīra.[50]

"...Jinadatta, the founder of the Sāntara dynasty (AD 920-930), migrated from Mathura, the capital of this father's kingdom, to Pombuccapura, modern Humcha. He reportedly carried a golden image of a *yakṣiṇī*, who blessed him with *the power of transforming iron into gold.* An inscription of the eleventh century refers to a shrine dedicated to the cult of Padmāvatī at Humcha."[51]

Śambala, bhasma and rasa-liṅga

Subbarayappa and Mira Roy provide an account of the alchemical ideas contained in *Mātṛkābhedatantram* (*c.* eleventh or twelfth century AD).[52] A substance called *śambala* is referred to for transmuting copper into silver. [The morpheme is intriguingly concordant with the Tamil term, *cāmpal,* ashes; may be, sal ammoniac made of animal hair.] Two processes are elaborated, to prepare *bhasma* or powder, stating that *bhasma* cannot be achieved without the use of medicinal plants.

1. Mercury is mixed with sulphur and heated; after mixing with paddy water it is heated again to yield *bhasma.*
2. Mercury is heated with *vallī* (a plant) and *ghṛtanārī* (*Aloe indica*); small balls are made and kept, together with black basil (*kṛṣṇatulasī*) and *ghṛtakumārī* (*Aloe indica*) in the cavity of

a thorn-apple; the preparation is heated till it yields *bhasma*.

The *bhasma* can be used to transmute pure and molten copper to gold;[53] as a panacea for all ills; a beautifying agent;[54] and to increase virility. The preparation of *rasa-liṅga* involves the constant stirring (without rubbing) of *pārada* (mercury or seed of Śiva) with extract of *jhinti* (*Barberia cristata*) till the constancy of mud is achieved. Shaping the mixture as a *liṅga* (phallus), sulphur (Devī's principle or menstrual fluid, *svapuṣpa*) is smeared all over the surface and the *liṅga* is heated slightly over the fire of charcoal or cowdung till it hardens. Subbarayappa and Mira Roy note that the text refers to *Cinatantra*,[55] that the focus is on "material immortality" and under-score the significance of the masculine and feminine symbolisms used in comparison with the Chinese alchemical principles of *yin* (female) and *yang* (male).

References

1. Cf., the legendary Bogar (?200 BC-AD 200), reportedly an initiate of the school of the sage Pieng-tsu, associated with the Yellow Emperor. Pieng-tsu tradition refers to Taoist secrets of sex-magic and transcendental alchemy learnt from Five Girls, fairy guardians to enable him to live for eight hundred years. Bogar who returned to India with Pulipani, visited Kāmarūpa, Patna and Gaya founded the Siddha, Nātha and Rasavāda cults and considered also the patriarchs of Chinachara or Chinese way of tantrism. Both Bogar and Pulipani are listed among the 18 Tamil *cittars*.
2. Guna, *Tamil's Philosophy*, Madras, p. 279.
3. Alice Getty, *The Gods of Northern Buddhism*, New Delhi, 1978, p. 31.
4. *CDIAL*, 2974, notes that the variety of suffix in the morphemes in many language streams points to a non-Aryan origin: Pāli, Prākṛta: *kasāya*; Assamese: *kehā*; Bengali, Oriya: *kasā*; Sinhala: *kaha*, turmeric, saffron; (extension with-*ṭṭ*-) Assamese: *kaheṭā*; Sinhala: *kahaṭā*, astringent, bitter, acrid (whence the *Vinaya* reference *kaṭu*); Sinhala: *kahaṭa*, bitter, acrid; Punjabi: *kasailā*, astringent; Sindhi: *kasāro*, astringent. The association with red colour leads to an extension in a compound: *CDIAL*, 2972, *Chāndogya Upaniṣad: kaṣati*, scratches; Pāṇini rubs on a touchstone; Marathi: *kasne*, to test gold; *CDIAL*, 2973, *kaṣapaṭṭikā*, touchstone (a hyper-Sanskritism of *kaṣavartikā* or Bengali: *kasaṭi*; Old Gujarati: *kasauṭau*). The radical *kas* is clearly traceable to the alchemical tradition of the goldsmiths: *CDIAL*, 2970, Prākṛta: *kasa*, striking, rubbing on a touchstone; Kafiri: *ushugu*, comb, scapula;

Kashmiri: *kah*, testing gold on a touchstone; Old Gujarati: *kasi*, touchstone. In Kharoṣṭhī inscriptions (*CDIAL*, 2974) *kaṣara* is a monk's yellow robe.

5. Cf., the tortoise pictorial motif on Indus seals; the use of "tortoise" in a layer of the *agni*, fire-altar in the *Śatapatha Brāhmaṇa*.
6. Allchins, p. 257, fig. 9.20.
7. Jean Filliozat, "Review of *Rasa-jala-nidhi*, by Rasacharya Kaviraj Bhudev Mookerjee," *Journal Asiatique*, CCXXIII, 1933, pp. 110-12. It is also likely that Tamil alchemy had some Chinese influences. Chinese divided the metals into male and female. Cf. M. Granet, *Danses et legendes de la Chine ancienne*, Paris, 1926, 2 vols.; II, p. 496. M. Eliade, *Yoga*, p. 418 adds: "Furnaces became a sort of judge simply by the fact that a highly sacred operation was performed in them; they could recognize virtue, and the greatest penalty inflicted on a criminal was to boil him in this kind of furnace. To construct a furnace was an act of virtue, to be performed by a man who knew the "rites of art" (citing Granet, II, pp. 491 and 496)."
8. I-Ching mentions the eight sections of medical science, eight parts of the Ayurvedic medical system: sores, acupuncture, general medicine, casting out of demons, paediatrics, pharmaceutics, alchemy for longevity, invigorating the legs and body. But while speaking well of Indian physicians, he says that the best herbs are nearly all to be found in China rather than India.... "In the healing arts of acupuncture and cautery, and the skill of feeling the pulse, China has never been surpassed by any country of Jamboodveepa (the oikoumene); the drug for prolonging life is found only in China.... Is there anyone, in the five parts of India, who does not admire China?" Cf., Needham, *SCC*, vol. I, p. 210n.
9. J. Needham, *SCC*, vol. II, 1956, pp. 425ff.
10. L.A. Waddell, *The Buddhism of Tibet*, pp. 378-79.
11. M.A. Stein, *An Archaeological Tour of Gedrosia*, pp. 86-87 provides a map of ancient Tibet and neighbouring areas. Drusha is a land shown 100 miles above Srinagar and 200 miles west of Khotan. Zahor (?) is shown around Jalandhara, to the west of Sutlej and also about 100 miles west of Kāmarūpa and east of Patna/Nalanda/Rajagṛha/Bodhgayā.
12. Ibid., pp. 72-74.
13. Ibid., pp. 149-51. The initiation price is called dban-gyon, *dakṣiṇā*?
14. Nathan Sivin, *Chinese Alchemy: Preliminary Studies*, Cambridge, Mass., 1968, p. 12 suggests a practical, yet rigorous methodology to crack the research area: "The problem does not differ in kind from that of deciphering the dead terminology of ancient technology...one begins from a basic familiarity with classical Chinese and reads the sources from one period or school together closely and repeatedly, each time

beginning from a new level of understanding, until their content has fallen into place." At least, this will take us one step forward in establishing an inner-consistency of the esoteric or secretive materials dealt with, clouded in riddles and enigmatic terms.

15. Walter, 1980, p. 8, n. 10.
16. Cf., Walter, "The role of alchemy and medicine in Indo-Tibetan Tantrism," Bloomington Indiana University, Ph.D. dissertation, 1980, p. 178, n. 249 for references.
17. Cf., Walter, 1980, n. 241 for references: "Kun-byed is sarvakarmakṛt, that which makes all to act; and according to *Guhyasamāja* tradition, is that combination of unrestrained *bodhicitta* and wind described...*prāṇa bhūtaśca sattvānām vāyvākhyaḥ sarvakarmakṛt* ('that which is called 'wind' is the *prāṇic*-force element of all beings, and the doer of all,'" says Nāgārjuna is his *Guhyasamāja* commentary, the *pañcakrama*). The reference to 'consuming' (*za ba*) the *kun byed* appears as a metaphor for the gradual and moderate controls applied by the yogin in *samādhi* when tackling this powerful force: "The fault of not doing it that way is that the wind swirls, whereupon the heart gets diseased, the body heavy; one is panic-stricken and one's thoughts become tumultuous (i.e., they race). Moreover, if one holds the breath fiercely, a fault occurs in this case: it is taught that upon reverting from that, the *samādhi* is spoiled. When, like an animal, the vital air is not controlled, it is said, 'there is no accomplishment of *samādhi*....' What appears as a somewhat important technical point in the *haṭha yogic* systems of the *Guhyasamāja*, etc., materials is to the Rdzogs-chhen a most fundamental doctrine...*Byan-chub-sems-kun-byed-rgyal-po, Aka Kun-byed-rgyal-po* or simply *Kun-byed*,...the most important texts of this school.... It was considered a heretical concept and actively suppressed at various times...due to the similarity between *kun-byed* and the *prakṛti* of Sāṁkhya as active creators of the universe...the practices of the Rdzogs-chen...would certainly ruffle feathers in any society, at any time."
18. *ṚV*, I.23.19-20.
19. Ibid., V.42.11.
20. Varieties of Immortality: Needham contrasts the Chinese and Western concepts of immortality and distinguishes between *nei tan* and *wai tan*; the former referring to physiological alchemy or the production of medicine of immortality within the body itself by respiratory, gymnastic, sexual, meditational, heliotherapeutic and yogistic exercises; the latter referring to the preparation of laboratory elixirs of longevity or immortality: "In the West there was a rather clear idea of human survival after death which derived from origins both Hebrew and Christian.... The elixir of life, though acculturated to some extent

from the Islamic world, where it had been hardly more at home and certainly derived from further east, was always far less important than the philosopher's stone which would transmute the ignoble metals into gold. From the time of the mystical proto-chemists (or *aurifactors*) of the Hellenistic world onwards, projection by the Stone was primarily for the purpose of acquiring material wealth...with the parallel purpose in mind of purifying the soul of the operator from spiritual dross just as the lead or iron was freed from its base elements and raised to the level of gold. Needham classifies the ancient Alexandrian proto-chemists in the West as *aurifactors*, those who believed that they could imitate gold or make gold from the ignoble metals. He contrasts their techniques with Chinese alchemy (*lien tan shu* or iatro-chemistry) or *macrobiotics*, a belief that it is possible to prepare "with the aid of botany, mineralogy, chemistry and aurifaction, actual substances, drugs or elixirs, which will prolong life, giving longevity (*shou*), or material immortality (*pu ssu*).... The object of the devout Taoist was to transform himself by all kinds of techniques, not only alchemical and pharmaceutical but also dietetic, respiratory, meditational, sexual and heliotherapeutic, into a *hsien*, in other words in immortal, purified, ethereal and free, who could spend the rest of eternity wandering as a wrath through the mountains and forests to enjoy the beauty of Nature without end."

21. J. Needham, "Hygiene and Preventive Medicine," *Clerks and Craftsmen*, p. 342.
22. J. Needham, "Medicine and Chinese Culture," ibid., p. 283.
23. Edgar Thurston, *Castes and Tribes of Southern India*, pp. 32 ff.
24. B. Walker, *The Hindu World*, p. 24.
25. Jagdishchandra Jain, *Life in Ancient India as Depicted in Jaina Canon and Commentaries*, New Delhi, 1984, p. 129.
26. *Niśītha Bhāṣya*, 13.4313; *Uttarādhyayana Ṭīkā*, 4.83; *Dasaveyāliya Cūrṇī*, 1.44; Jagdishchandra Jain, op. cit., p. 129.
27. Cf., A. Waley, "Notes on Chinese Alchemy," *BSOS*, 1930, VI, 1, pp. 1-24; Chinese alchemy has a remarkable parallel. Li Shao-chun, the magician tells the emperor Wu Ti of the Han dynasty: "Sacrifice to the stove *tsao*) and you will be able to summon 'things' (i.e., spirits). Summon spirits and you will be able to change cinnabar into yellow gold. With this yellow gold you make vessels to eat and drink out of. You will then increase your span of life. Having increased your span of life, you will be able to see the *hsien* (Blessed immortals) of P'eng-lai that is in the midst of the sea. Then you may perform the sacrifice *feng* and *shan*, and escape death."
28. Jagdishchandra Jain, op. cit., p. 130; cf., the list of Prītidāna in *Nāyādhammakahāo Ṭīkā*, 1, p. 42a; *Āvaśyaka Cūrṇī*, 147.

29. Is this a reference to the Ṛgvedic riddle, *śaraṇyavana*? This is elsewhere interpreted as a coded phrase composed of morphemes: *kṣāra+ lavaṇa.*
30. Jagdishchandra Jain, op. cit., p. 235.
31. J. Needham, *SCC*, vol. 5, part II, p. 289.
32. Ibid., pp. 292.
33. R.N. Nandi, *Religious Institutions and Cults in the Deccan* (*c.* AD *600-1000*), Delhi, 1973, pp. 114ff. [*tantra* < *tan-* to expand, proliferate; hence "all major rites were intended to deliver increasing quantities of material goods to the performers."]
34. *Jvālinīkalpa*, chaps. 2-9; R.N. Nandi, op. cit., p. 115.
35. *Epigraphica Indica*, Chiṇchaṇi plate inscriptions, 23, no. 25.
36. *AV*, 10.6.2, 4, 34.
37. Ibid., 10.6.5, 23, 27, 34.
38. Ibid., 10.6.10.
39. Ibid., 10.6.12.
40. *Epigraphica Indica*, 30, no. 45, pp. 274-76; R.N. Nandi, op. cit., p. 122.
41. *JASB*, vol. 7, no. 7, July 1911, pp. 444ff.; R.N. Nandi, op. cit., p. 122.
42. *JAHRS*, vol. 14, p. 58; R.N. Nandi, op. cit., p. 123.
43. *Epigraphica Carnatica*, 11, Cd. 774, AD 968.
44. *Epigraphica Indica*, 16, pp. 53ff.; R.N. Nandi, op. cit., p. 147.
45. Iron when placed into a solution of blue vitriol give the appearance of conversion to copper. Similarly copper and arsenic combine to form really an alloy resembling gold.
46. *Arthaśāstra* mentions this as secret practice.
47. *Cilappatikāram*, canto 15, II.115ff.
48. *Annual Report on South Indian Inscriptions*, Appendix C, no. 64, 1923; P.B. Desai, *Jainism in South India and Some Jaina Epigraphs*, Sholapur, 1957, pp. 39ff.
49. Cf., use of citron in making a *rasa-liṅga.*
50. Jas Burgess, *Digambara Jaina Iconography*, Bombay, 1904, pp. 3ff.
51. Desai, op. cit., pp. 171-89, n. 1.
52. B.V. Subbarayappa, and Mira Roy, "Mātṛkābheda-tantram and its Alchemical Ideas," *IJHS*, vol 3, no. 1, pp. 42-49; based on the text translated by Cintāmaṇi Bhattacharya, Calcutta, 1933.
53. The earliest tantric text referring to such a transmutation is *Kubjikā-tantra* (*c.* sixth century AD); cf., Ref. 16, P. Ray, *HCAMI*, p. 115.
54. Cf., Nāgārjuna's *Rasaratnākara* (eighth or ninth century AD); P.C. Ray, *History of Hindu Chemistry*, vol. II, rev. edn., P. Ray, *HCAMI*, pp. 133, 317: "I shall convey to you all that you want to know, namely the remedies for warding off wrinkles, grey hair and other signs of old age. Mineral preparations act with equal efficacy on the metals as on the body (human system)." This is a doctrine central to the use of sal ammonic no metals; the use of *bhasma* as a smear on the body of

adepts; and the use of *sindūra* on the parting of the hair of females. The distinction between symbols and Reality seems to vanish over time, as alchemical ideas evolve.

55. Cf., a cognate tradition: Amoghavajra, a *śramaṇa* (Buddhist priest, *c.* eighth century AD) who travelled to China and Tibet and transmitted tantric doctrines.

9

Apparatus, Terms, and Symbols

Language of alchemy, alchemical apparatus, preparations and symbols
Alchemy uses symbols and terms connoting tension and conflict between chemical substances and during alchemical processes. It is, therefore, necessary to cover some etymological ground to understand the "meaning" of many key terms, in a temporal dimension. Indeed, reconstruction of a plebeian tradition is impossible without recourse to etymological and archaeological aids since the plebeians have not bequeathed "learned" texts. Their "history" may have to be found in the alphabets and language of iconography, for instance and in the folk-traditions. The proto-Indus lapidary may not have been conscious of the chemistry of glazing, but he could lend hardness and colour to clay and faience and produce complicated changes in silicates. He perhaps knew how to part gold and silver and the properties of cinnabar and its potential to modify metal-oxides and -alloys. He knew the use of weights and measures and two-pan balances—a technology which was to play a crucial role in the ultimate evolution of modern chemistry, by introducing the concept of weights of substances before and after a chemical process. The concept of a "balance" and the concomitant concept of "measure" is fundamental in adding a quantitative[1] dimension to a qualitative pseudo-science called alchemy.

Indian alchemy—the child of Lokāyata, Scientific materialism
Debiprasad Chattopadhyaya's brilliant exposition of the *Lokāyata: A Study in Indian Materialism* provides a reconstruction of the belief-system which governed the lives of the plebeians. Citing Needham to reinforce his masterly arguments, Chattopadhyaya notes that magic and science were indistinguishable in early stages because both were "united in a single undifferentiated complex of manual operations;"[2] so too, "Indian Tantrism, because of its rootedness in

the manual operations of agriculture, and in spite of being magic, did also contain the potentialities of later Indian science—particularly the sciences of physiology and alchemy."

The concept of liberation expressed in many tantric texts is not only physical but metallurgical when the combination of mercury and mica (Hara's seed and Gauri's seed) is "destructive of death and poverty." Two thoughts are dominant: death and poverty. Contrarily, the plebeian alchemist's world-view is related to healthy life and a decent economic condition. "(Candali, Dombi, Rajaki, Savari and others) are all female names and they represent some of the lowest castes carrying on the most despised occupations. Again, the Tantras of the Kubjika school 'are said to have originated among the potters, a low-caste Hindu sect, and this is why they are said to have belonged to the *kulali-kamnaya.*' The *Kubjikatantra* prescribed that the venue of the ritual practices should be the house of a potter.... The tantrics proclaimed the essential equality of all men and of all women and, along with it, the rejection of the traditional marriage morals.... It is merely an eloquent protest of a Sahajia poet against the caste system."[3]

Again, reviewing the contribution made by tantrics to proto-science, Chattopadhyaya cites P.C. Ray's *History of Hindu Chemistry* and notes:[4] "The Tantrikas did invent and use a large variety of actual laboratory instruments for their chemical experiments and they gave functional names too these, e.g., Dola Yantram, Svedani Yantram, Patana Yantram, Adhaspatana Yantram, Dheki Yantram, Valuka Yantram, Tiryakpatana Yantram, Vidyādhara Yantram, Dhūpa Yantram, and Koṣṭhi Yantram.... Said the *Rudrayāmalatantra*:[5] I have performed the aforementioned experiments with my own hands and have seen them with my own eyes. They are not recorded from mere hearsay or from the dictation of a teacher. These are being promulgated for the benefit of mankind. Similarly, the *Rasendracintāmaṇi*[6] opened with the following declaration: I shall give publicity only to such processes as I have been able to verify by my own experiments...we find in the texts a conscious acceptance of the materialistic outlook to serve as the theoretical foundation of this science or proto-science.... Said the author of the *Rasārṇava*[7]: As it is used by the best devotees for the highest end, it is called *parada* (quick silver)...a man should preserve that body by means of mercury and medicaments.... The conception of liberation, here, is peculiarly physical...it is this conception of physical immortality that gave the Tantrikas the word for mercury (*parada*).... This conception of physical immortality and its connection with the alchemy of the Tantrikas is, again, strongly reminiscent of ancient Taoism. The Taoists, as Needham showed,[8] were emphasizing the importance of certain techniques like the respiratory technique (*prāṇāyāma*), the gymnastic technique (*āsana*), the sexual technique (*maithuna*), the alchemical and pharmaceutical techniques (*rasāyana*)—and all these for the purpose of attaining a state of *material immortality*.... In short, the proto-materialism of the Tantrikas was the clue to their proto-scientific tendencies."

If the term, *anvīkṣikī* in the context of *Arthaśāstra* (1.2.10) is interpreted not as the science of reasoning,[9] but certain philosophical systems based on reasoning, the threefold classification may be explained: *sāṅkhyam yogo lokāyatam, cetyanvīkṣikī*: Sāṁkhya, Yoga, and Lokāyata are three philosophical systems based on reasoning. This is Kauṭilya's authentication that Lokāyata was a distinct philosophical system founded by Bṛhaspati and later linked with Cārvāka. Lokāyata is a system of reasoning related to worldly affairs. It is proto-materialism, as expounded by Debiprasad Chattopadhyaya, in its socio-political and historical perspective. He also underscores the possibility that the original Sāṁkhya was developed from tantrism as the result of a conscious resistance to the Upaniṣadic idealism. The philosophical system of Lokāyata (exemplified by tantrism) together with Yoga had provided the philosophical basis for the origins and evolution of alchemical traditions of ancient India, exemplified by the streams of alchemical traditions related to external and internal alchemy—internal or external, relative to the alchemist-adept—*siddha* or *yogī*. While the early, proto-historic origins of alchemy are traceable to distillation processes and manual operations of a *caṇḍāḷa*, Indian alchemy seems to have evolved in the historical periods, as the child of Yoga and Lokāyata. This is a hypothesis which will require deeper analysis than has been attempted in the essay. The extent to which the philosophical systems influenced or were influenced by the development of alchemy as a proto-science is a matter for further historical research. It is also clearly perceived that the plebeian-artisan engaged in manual operations is of a class different from the priest- artisan who was smelting *soma-rasa* in the Brāhmaṇa period. The traditions of the historic periods can be delineated with a slightly higher degree of certainty. In sum, more questions are raised than are answered.

"...in the *Arthaśāstra* (1.2.1-12), while classifying the various branches of learning (*vidyā*), Kauṭilya says that the branch of learning known as *anvīkṣikī* comprises Sāṁkhya, Yoga (i.e., Nyāya and Vaiśeṣika) and Lokāyata.... For a clear definition of *anvīkṣikī*, based upon the etymology of the word itself, we may refer to Vātsyāyana, the author of the *Nyāyabhāṣya*. In the commentary of the first *sūtra* (I.1.1), he remarks: 'An inference which is not contradicted by perception and scripture (Āgama) is called *anvīkṣ*, that is, the knowing over again of that which is already known (*ikṣita*) by perception and scripture. This branch of knowledge is called *anvīkṣikī* or *nyāyavidyā* or *nyāyaśāstra*, because it proceeds on the basis of that (namely, *anvīkṣ*).' ...the importance of inference was duly admitted in the system (of Sāṁkhya)...one of (Sāṁkhya's) early texts gives the definition and classification of inference, and recognizes moreover the fact that without the help of inference two of its main principles—the *puruṣa* and the *prakṛti*—would remain unproved, since their perception is not possible (*Sāṁkhyakārikā* of Īśvarakṛṣṇa, v. 6 and Yuktidīpikā thereon)...thus, in short, as far as Kauṭilya's classification is concerned, the Lokāyata too, being a branch of *anvīkṣikī*, should rather be a defender—and not an opponent—of inference."[10]

"Manu, who excommunicates (II.11) men who disregard the Vedas and Dharmasūtras on the strength of reasoning by logic (*hetuśāstra*), admits (VII.43) as legitimate for a king *anvīkṣikī ātmavidyā*, 'the science of the self based on investigation,' and Vātsyāyana claims in his *Nyāyabhāṣya* (p. 3) that this is precisely the character of the Nyāyaśāstra, that, while a doctrine of the self like the Upaniṣads it relies on reasoning, defined as the investigation of that which perception and authority have already conveyed. Against this may be set the fact that in the *Kauṭilīya Arthaśāstra* (p. 7) *anvīkṣikī* is declared to include not only the Sāṁkhya, the Yoga, and the Cārvāka system, under its name of Lokāyata. It has been deduced hence that at 300 BC the traditional date of the *Arthaśāstra*, the Nyāya and Vaiśeṣika were not known as such.... A final hint of the date of the schools is suggested by the fact that Caraka in his medical Saṁhitā (I.1.43 ff.; III.8.24 ff.) gives a sketch of some of the Nyāya principles, not without variation in detail, and of the Vaiśeṣika categories, in such a way as to indicate that he regarded the systems as supplementing each other.... The old Pāli texts ignore the names of Nyāya or Vaiśeṣika.... Of more precision is the Buddhist tradition which asserts that Vaiśeṣika adherents were alive at the time of the Buddhist Council of Kaniṣka, which may be placed at the end of the first century AD."[11]

"The Vedānta view of the human body as composed of three or five elements, and Prabhākara's preference for four are rejected; bodies in this world are of earth only, either womb-born, like viviparous and oviparous animals, or not so born, including on one view plants, as well as insect and such sages as acquire by their merit bodies without physical birth (*Vaiśeṣikasūtra*, IV.2.5-10). As objects (*viṣaya*) other than bodies, earth appears as the whole of inorganic nature; water as the sea, rivers, hail, etc. Fire products are terrestrial, the fuel being earthy in character; celestial, such as lightning; gastric, the fire of digestion; and mineral. Gold cannot be earth because it remains fluid under extreme heat; nor water, for its fluidity is artificial; nor air, because it has colour. It must therefore be fire, earth particles accounting for its absence of light and heat.... (*Vaiśeṣikasūtra*, II.1.1-4; 2.1-5 et seq.) One Mīmāṁsā view makes gold a separate substance, *The Prabhākara School of Pūrva Mīmāṁsā*, by Ganganatha Jha, Allahabad, 1911, p. 94."[12] That gold is treated as a separate substance is extraordinary; so is the observations that gold remains fluid under extreme heat. Both observations are consistent with the characterization of *soma* as a transmutation process and as a *rasa*.

Vaiśeṣikasūtra has perhaps the earliest formulation on inference, defined as *laiṅgikam jñānam*, "knowledge from a mark or sign." The mark is of two types (II.I.8, 10, 15, 16; III.II.6, 7): *dṛṣṭam liṅgam* and *adṛṣṭam* or *samanyato dṛṣṭam liṅgam*. Things stand to each other in real relations; the mark acts inferentially. The *sūtra* IX.II.1 states: *asyedam kāryam kāraṇam saṁyogi virodhi samavāyi ceti laiṅgikam*: "knowledge through an inferential mark is where *this* is (a) effect of, (b) cause of, (c) conjoined with, (d) opposed to, (e) resident in, *that*."

Proto-theories on matter

The following paragraphs, related primarily to the Egypto-Greek alchemical tradition are included for one reason: as additional researches in Indian alchemy proceed, it may be possible to find some parallels and even, links between the Indian tradition and the traditions of these contemporary civilizations in proto-historic periods.

Clearly, ancient alchemy was an empirical science; was there a working hypothesis governing the progress of this science? In the imagery of *yakṣa* and the principal *yakṣa*—Varuṇa—, water is indeed perceived as the prime matter from which all other substances are produced. Vaiśeṣika doctrines postulate distinct entities constituting the universe: earth, water, fire, air, ether, time, space, soul, and *manas.* The first four elements are made up of atoms and exist as aggregates of atoms. They are imperishable, as atoms. Aggregates change, and are subject to birth and decay; atoms do not change, these are indestructible. These are philosophical postulates; the alchemists were workmen who did not always subscribe to these postulates. The priests and workmen differed radically in the processes of reasoning. For the workman involved in manual operations, observation and experimentation were the valid processes.

The metallurgist in primitive societies is a "matter of fire," member of an occult religious society, the secrets of which are transmitted by rites of initiation.[13] The theory is analogous to the theory of universe which preceded the rise of scientific astronomy. The governing doctrine: "rational curiosity as to the working of nature.... The association of gold and silver with the sun and moon is of prehistoric antiquity.... Copper, iron and lead were consistently associated with Venus, Mars and Saturn; Mercury and Jupiter were some reason the planets for which other metals 'competed'... tin, bronze, electrum and quicksilver (which was widely known after 300 BC) alternating as metals to be associated with Mercury and Jupiter. This uncertainty reflects: (1) the imprecise differentiation of the principal alloys, electrum, bronze and (from Roman times) brass, from the metals on which they were based, (2) the imprecise differentiation of tin (and other metals, such as antimony and bismuth) from lead, and (3) the unique character of quicksilver."[14]

Agatharchides (second century BC; name reminds one of Agastya), whose work is not extant, is quoted by Diodorus Siculus (Bk.3;14)[15] that "parting" of gold from metals alloyed with it was accomplished by heating adulterated gold with salt, straw, and other materials. Electrum disappears from the lists of metals in Egypt after the seventh century BC, says Partington (1935:41), but electrum survived on lists elsewhere.

Physica et Mystica is a treatise attributed to Bolos Democritus of

Mende (in the Nile Delta) of *c.* 200 BC Multhauf reviews it based on the edition of Berthelot and Roulle, *AAG*, text: 41-53, French trans. The work is on the art of the jeweller. "After three opening recipes for purple coloration, it is divided into two parts, called gold-making (chrysopoeia) and silver-making or 'the fabrication of asem'. . . genuine goldsmith's recipes."[16] Berthelot's view (1889, 62ff.) was that the emphasis on asem in the Layden Papyrus X indicated a condition which, among the alchemists, made the belief in metallic transmutation possible. Layden Papyrus X appears to use the word "gold" when the reference is only to the colour typifying the metal.[17] Also indicated in the papyrus is that only imitation is involved. The emphasis on imitation, fraudulent in intent, is remarkable.

Multhauf surmises that the Egyptian goldsmith turned to the fabrication of imitation jewellery with his loss of old monopoly and due to the general impoverishment of the temples at a time when the demand for fine metal work was increasing among the Greeks and Romans. Multhauf also believes that the subject matter of the *Physica et Mystica* is so similar to the Layden Papyrus that a common origin may be postulated. The former has 27 recipes compared to the 101 in the Leyden papyrus; but the gold recipes in the papyri were 17 and in the *Physica et Mystica,* there were as many as 13, though much less precisely worded. "The author commonly gives the reader a choice of ingredients, many of which have resisted decipherment into the terms of modern chemistry. Hammer-Jensen has also pointed out that sulphur, which enters into only two of the recipes in the papyrus, is an ingredient of over half of those in the *Physica et Mystica.* She sees the emergence of 'sulphur' as an important ingredient in an otherwise largely unintelligible recipe as critical to the genesis of alchemy."[18]

In the *Physica et Mystica,* the closing sentence to nearly every recipe is translated as follows: One nature rejoices in another nature; one nature triumphs over another nature; one nature masters another nature. A dramatic statement on contrarieties in achieving changes in matter. It is plausible to draw a parallel with the conception of Śakti imageries in the Mother Goddess tradition.

Zosimos of Panopolis (*c.* third century AD) is credited with a collection of fragments from a kind of alchemical encyclopaedia called *Cheirokmeta.* Its features include: "the use of secret words (including the root word, *chemeia* of the term chemistry); the comparison of alchemy with sexual generation; the role of spirits in bringing about changes in matter, and the designation of sulphur, mercury, and arsenic as mineral spirits, and the ferment-like Xerion (which was to become Elixir), whose intervention was supposed to ensure the success of the undertaking."[19]

Maria, the Jewess alchemist, whose name survives in the French *brainmarie* for the water bath, appears to have invented the apparatus which permitted the alchemist to adapt distillation and sublimation to metallurgical or pseudo-metallurgical processes. *Physica et Mystica* lists materials used for colouration: mercury, sulphur and the arsenic sulphides (realgar and orpiment) which are susceptible to distillation or sublimation. Maria thus treats the base metals with these "spirits," or with the divine or sulphur water. Stapleton (1953) refers to the discovery in Cairo of an alchemical tract attributed to Agathodaimon and treats him as a member of Maria's school. Zosimos speaks of him with respect, frequently. Stapleton believes that he may have lived in Harran, in Seleucid Syria, between the fourth and first centuries BC. (Stapleton, 1953, p. 37)

Zosimos's *Cheirokmeta* speaks of "the composition of waters, movement, growth, embodying and disembodying, drawing the spirits from bodies and binding the spirits with bodies...."[20] He mentions the agreement of Agathodaimon on the importance of sulphur. He lists material needed for gold, for yellowing, for purple (iosis). "Theion hudor," translated as either divine water or sulphur water, often seems to play a critical role.[21] He refers to a recipe of Maria with which the philosopher Bolos Democritus agreed: a sandwich of copper and gold is exposed to the fumes of "sulphur water" and gum; a reflux process. Maria is credited with the apparatus. Agathadaimon declares: a stone which is not a stone; a stone in appearance but not in its property of dissolving; it dissolves and becomes a clear water and pure spirit which is the essential nature of stones. Mixed with something (unnamed), pulverized by fire, and evaporated to a paste it becomes a stone (like?) copper burned in its own sulphur. If manipulated wisely, it is leaf-like and many coloured, and upon further treatment with small quantities of liquid it becomes gold.[22] The stone itself is purified by fire; careful attention must be given to the degrees of heat employed. In the operation, colours appear, red, yellow, white, black, and green. The final tincture is purple, of a sweet taste and fragrant odour, its origin in well-tempered earth and soft soil of weight exceeding all else in heaviness. "Important, if vaguely defined, agents in the process are a 'gum' (*kolla*) and 'a fiery poison extracted by fire from the natures,' apparently obtained through distillation." Multhauf adds: copper may be the starting metal; the "single material" of Agathodaimon's stone was realgar (arsenic disulphide). Realgar can be made by fusion with natron (soda) or mercury to yield arsenious oxide, "a stone which is not a stone;" it is indeed a "fiery poison." It can form "a clear water" (solution) and "a pure spirit" (white sublimate). Vegetable oil may be Agathadaimon's gum; mixed what this oil and heated, it yields another sublimate (elemental arsenic) which can be applied to copper in the *kerotakis* and will give it a silvery colour. But this reconstructed process breaks down in the further conversion to gold.

Arsenic compounds yields a variety of colour effects in chemical manipulation. Red realgar can be converted to yellow sulphide, orpiment. This is done by fusion with sulphur. Or red may refer to copper and the yellow to orpiment as starting materials. In either case, if orpiment then is fused with mercury or natron the white sublimated oxide which is "the stone" is obtained. Fused in turn with gum or oil, a black sublimate results, the element itself. Elemental arsenic is a "tincture" capable of giving a silvery colour to copper, an action of which the compounds of arsenic are not capable. If copper is digested in "clear water," a solution of arsenious oxide, the solution turns green; if distilled, the resulting distillate will be blue.[23] Arsenic compounds: realgar, orpiment, "white arsenic" (the oxide) are used in the vaporous as well as the solid form in 10 of the 24 recipes of the *Physica et Mystica. Arsenic compounds are the key, perhaps the "water" that transforms the stone, the alchemist's liṅgam.* The alchemist's focus was on reactive materials which readily vapourized. Maria gave the apparatus (illustrated in Berthelot, 1889, pp. 127-73).

As elaborated in the context of the Indus archaeological finds, it is argued that the Maria's apparatus has been anticipated by the proto-Indus "cult-object," the sublimation apparatus.

Solid, liquid and gaseous states of matter

A vague conception of the gaseous state of matter existed in the term *vāyu* but not as a result of transformation of solids to gaseous state. *Vāyu* may find an analogue in *prāṇa*, the vital breath that sets in motion the five *dhātu*. The transmutation was seen vividly from the solid to a liquid state, say when gold ore is smelted yielding, liquid gold. The ashes were seen as a "powdery" state of reduction beyond which it was not possible to go; hence, the extraordinary importance given to *bhasma* in Indian Siddha/Śaivite traditions which may be broadly grouped as *śramaṇa* or ascetic group of alchemists. Since sal ammoniac, made from reducing goat's skin or animal excrement to ashes, was seen to have potency as a reducing/colouring agent for metals, a parallel application was sought in the use of ashes as a smear for the body (or the use of *sindūra,* red vermilion powder as a mark on a woman's parting of the hair or on her forehead)—perhaps a process of achieving "physical immortality or at least perfection." What fire could not fully consume represented the elemental substance, for example, the ashes of cowdung. *Rasa* and *bhūti*[24]/*bhasma* (ashes[25]) thus become the symbols of agents in the external (workshop, sacrifice) and internal (body, tantra) spaces of the alchemical traditions of ancient India.

Alchemy: An etymological tract

One etymological perspective is that the word *alchemy,* is derived from Arabic *al-kimia* < Greek *chemeia* (*c.* fourth century AD; art of goldsmithy). Greek *cheo,* "I pour" or "cast" connects the process to the ancient practices of melting and pouring of metals.

Another trace links the Greek term to *khemia,* Egypt, assuming this to be the place of its origin. Joseph Needham extends the Egyptian link to China: "In -133 Li Shao-Chun went to the Emperor Han Wu Ti and said, 'If you will sacrifice to the stove' (i.e., support my researches), 'I will demonstrate to you how to make the yellow gold; out of that gold you may make vessels and drink from them to become immortal.' That is the first reference to alchemy in world history. Later on, in +142, you find what is without question the first book on alchemy ever written, *The Kinship of the Three,* which describes the use of chemically transformed substances as elixirs of life. We know that the appearance of alchemy is Islam and Europe dates after that time, because we cannot find it before +eighth century, perhaps not till the +tenth. The origin of the word "alchemy" has been much disputed. It has been suggested that it comes from *khem,* a name for Egypt, said to refer to the black earth of the Nile Valley, but Egyptian alchemy is not ancient. I suggest that the word is really Chinese in origin and comes from the words *lien chin shu,* the art of transmuting gold. This would be pronounced in Cantonese *lien kim shok.* Now it is known that Arabic people and Syrians were trading with China as early as +200, so the Arabs would naturally put the prefix *al* on to it, and get *al-kimm* (actually *al-kimiya*), 'pertaining to the making of gold.' All the greatest alchemists were Taoists."[26]

The parallels of Taoist beliefs with tantric traditions are remarkable and need to be reiterated. In particular, the genii of the Taoist tradition has an extraordinary analogue in the proto-Indic tradition of *yakṣa* as vegetative spirits, their chief Kubera, in particular and his association with gold; this will be elaborated in other chapters.

It is unclear if *kimm, khem, khemia* or Greek *chemeia* is relatable to Egyptian *assem*.

There is an interesting morpheme in the Dravidian languages which may perhaps move the trace further back into the proto-historic periods. The morpheme is: *ce-, cem-*. The *satem-kenṭum* transformations in the Indo-European languages has been well argued by philologists. The proto-Dravidian *ce-, cem-* can, therefore, be linked with the Greek/Arabic *khem-*. The morpheme *ce-, cem-, cempu* denotes (*DEDR*, 1931, 2775): copper, gold, metal vessel, liquid measure and in general, the colour *red*; all these meanings are relatable to the concepts of transmutation, the Greek meanings of pouring or casting, and smelting of metals. It is notable that the Chinese *chin* (gold) or *chin i* (gold juice) is also suggested by Needham, Mahdihassan, Dubs and Schneider as the possible original morphemes from which *chem-* is derived.[27] It is remarkable that *cem-* and *chin-* should denote gold. Dardic *cima, cime*, connotes iron; Sanskrit *cimara* means copper (*CDIAL*, 14496). Red is the colour found on the robe of the statuette of the so-called "priest-king" of the Indus valley civilization: "The figure is draped in an elaborate shawl with corded or rolled-over edge, worn over the left shoulder and under the right arm. This shawl is decorated all over with a design of trefoils in relief interspersed occasionally with small circles, the interiors of which are filled in with a red pigment."[28] Red is the colour of cinnaber, of vermilion or Prākṛta *sindūra* (red lead; lit., of the Indus earth). Gold is *suvarṇam* (lit., of good or bright colour; may connote tawny or reddish-yellow). The other concordant morphemes are: Pāli, Prākṛta: *suvanna*; Dardic: *son, surun*; Sindhi: *sonu*; Gypsy: *sovnakay, somnakay*, gold; the *som-* in Gypsy can be explained by the Ṛgvedic *soma*! Cf., Egyptian *assem*! electrum.

It is remarkable that later-day Nāṭa *siddhas* who attempt to master *vāyu* (the vital wind) also regulate the secretion of *soma* and call the technique *soma rasa.* The "juice" is imbibed to keep the body alive indefinitely [transmuting] the *siddha-deha* into *divya-deha*—an echo of the *amṛtam āyur hiraṇyam* theme.

Alcohol and elixir

The morpheme *kohl* is a very fine powder; it is the black powder used by Indian ladies to blacken round their eyes. Extending the word to various powders and liquids, the generalized term emerged: *al-kohl or alcohol.*[29] *Elixir* is said to be derived from Greek meaning "dry powder;" or from the Arabic root, *kasara,* meaning "to grind," *al-iksir* being "the thing ground," "the powder." There is also a Dravidian morpheme Tulu, *kasaru* which means, "sediment, dross of smelted iron;" Telugu: *gasi,* sediment of ghee or oil; Kannada: *kasa,* sweepings, afterbirth, placenta, *kasaru,* dust and other impurities; Skt.: *kaccara,* dirty, foul; Pāli: *kasaṭa,* nasty; Toda: *kasp,* to break rules of the sacred dairies; Kota: *kacpl* pollution caused by having sexual intercourse on day of god-ceremony. The semantic concordance between the concept of an "elixir of life" and Dravidian morphemes is too remarkable to have been an accident.

Gold as an elixir ingredient

Needham[30] quotes from Li Shih-Chen's (+1518 to +1593) *Pen Tshao Kang Mu* (Great Pharmacopoeia) on the use of gold as an elixir (*chin tan*) ingredient and on the condemnation of the use of poisonous substances by alchemists:

> ...gold was rarely mentioned in ancient medical recipes, but has been the talk of the alchemists. In the *San-shi-liu Shui Fa* (Thirty-Six Methods for Bringing Solids into Aqueous Solutions) of *Huai-nan* (Wang) it is converted into a liquid potion. In Ko Hung's *Pao Phu Tzu* the ingestion of (solid) gold is stated to be as effective as (the drinking of) potable gold (*Nei Phien,* ch. 4, pp. 18a, 20b, etc.)...it can be mixed with the bark of the 'stinking cedar' (*shu* or *chhu*) or solubilised with wine made from the *mu ching* shrub (*vitex negundo,* a medicinal plant) and mag-netite, or ingested with realgar and orpiment. The state of terrestrial immortal (*ti hsien*) can thus be attained. It is also said that cinnabar can be made into 'gold of the sages' (*sheng chin*), which brings about immortality when eaten.... The Pharmacopoeia of Ta Ming, Jih Hua Tzu alleges that (mercury) is not poisonous; the (*Shen Nung*) *Pen* (*Tshao*) *Ching* states that eating (it) over a long period will make a man immortal; Chen Chhuan (author of the early +seventh century pharmacopoeia *Yao Hsing*

Pen Tshao) maintains that (mercury) is the 'mother' (i.e., the basic ingredient) of the 'cyclically-transformed' elixir (*huan tan*); and *Pao Phu Tzu* (i.e., Ko Hung) regards (it) as a prime medicine of longevity. I am not able to tell the number of people who since the Six Dynasties period (+third to +sixth centuries) so coveted life that they took (mercury), but all that happened was that they impaired their health permanently or lost their lives. I need not bother to mention the alchemists, but I cannot bear to see these false statements made in the pharmacopoeias. However, while mercury is not to be taken orally, its use as a medicine must not be ignored.

The reference to mercury as "mother" is an interesting parallel to the association of *sindūra*, red vermilion or cinnabar with "mother goddess" in the Indian tradition. So is the reference to the shrub *vitex negundo* interesting in the context of concordant proto-Indian words for this shrub; *Mahābhārata* refers to it as *sindhu-vara*; Sinhala: *siduvara*. Kannada and Telugu refer to *vavili>? -vara in sindhu-vara*. This is not to be confused with *sindūra*, red lead or cinnabar, mercuric sulphide, which yielded the two wondrous *rasas*: mercury and sulphur which are fundamental in alchemical advances. Shen Kua, is his *Meng Chhi Pi Than* (+1086; ch. 24, p. 7b) refers to mercury compounds and their medical value: "...now cinnabar is an extremely good drug and can be taken even by a newborn baby, but once it has been changed by heat it can kill an (adult) person. If we consider the change and transformation of opposites into one another, since (cinnabar) can be changed into a deadly poison why should it not also be changed into something of extreme benefit?" Needham considers this prophetic and remarkable considering the great use of organo-metallic compounds in modern science, e.g., "mercury is salvarsan or antimony for kala-azar...conviction of Paracelsus centuries later that poisonous action and remedial virtue are intimately bound up with each other, as in the case of arsenic and especially mercury."[31]

In the Jaina canons, *koua*[32] refers to wondrous feats of a juggler[33] who could even taken out fire from his nose. *Koua* includes a number of operations, for example, *homa*, use of sacrificial fire to avert evil; *dhuva*, adding incense to the fire; *avayāsana*, embracing a tree; *bandhana*, typing a talisman; *vinhavana*, giving bath at cemetery or cross-roads to get luck for women or to protect children.[34] Another magical practice relates to *bhuikamma*, besmearing the body with consecrated ashes as a protective charm; at times, damp earth was applied or a piece of thread was tied as a charm. It is *rakkhā poṭṭaliya*, an amulet for a new born babe, a *rakṣā vidhi* described in *Caraka*.[35] "The *Nāyādhammakahāo* refers to the following contrivances: powder prepared from various ingredients causing stiffness (*cunnajoya*), employment of incantations (*mantajoya*), charms causing leprosy and other diseases (*kammanajoya*), causing beauty (*kammājoya*), captivating of heart (*hiyauddāvaṇa*), captivating of body (*kāuddāvaṇa*), subjugation (*ābhiogiya*), fascination (*vaśīkaraṇa*), roots, bulbs, bark, creeper (*vallī*), *kirāta* herb (*siliyā*), tablets (*guliyā*), medicine (*osaha*), and mixture (*bhesajja*)."[36]

If the bones of a recently dead man were placed under the shrine of Āḍambara *yakṣa*, or Rudra or a goddess, the study of scriptures was prohibited according to Jaina custom.[37]

Tegichcaya or *āyuveyya*, medical science, was counted among the nine evil scriptures, *pāvasuya*.[38] It was understandable that the counter-ideology, that is, the ideology counter to the alchemical-scientific tradition had to treat the medical science as an evil scripture. Manu had ordained that all that was knowable had already been known to the Vedic chanter. It was unacceptable, to counter-ideology to permit even the suffix *-veda* to an evil scripture like the *āyurveda*.

An example of the expansion of *dhātu-vāda* of alchemy into ancient medicinal systems may be cited: *Suśruta* relates the *tri-dhātu*, three components of the body, and their balance, to explain a *prameha*, a urine disease: "The bodily principles of *vāyu*, *pittam*, and *kapham* of such a person get mixed with improperly formed chyle of the organism. Thus deranged, they carry down the urinary ducts the deranged fat, etc., of the body and find lodgement at the mouth (neck) of the bladder, whence they are emitted through the urethra, causing disease known by the (generic) name of *prameha*... (the premonitary symptoms are)...burning sensation in the palms of the hand and soles of the feet, heaviness of the body, coldness and slimyness of the skin and limbs, sweetness, lassitude, thirst, a bad-smelling breath, a shortness of breath, etc."[39]

Expanding on this, Obeyesekere[40] explains how the Ayurvedic idea that the body is composed of *dhātus*, of which the most important are blood and semen, is practically universal among the Sinhalese and that the semen is more important than blood...one drop of semen is equal to sixty drops of blood. Suśruta comments:

"A child born of scanty parental sperm becomes an *asekya* and feels no sexual desire (erection) without previously (sucking the genitals and) drinking the semen of another man.... The semen-carrying ducts of an *asekya*, etc., are expanded by the drinking of the semen as above described, which helps the erection of his reproductive organ."[41]

This is an example of the intertwined concepts which can be traced to the use of the morpheme: *dhātu*. In Pāli, the phrase *dhātu-cetiya* refers to a shrine over a relic; *dhātu-ghara* is a house for a relic, a dagoba; *dhātu-vibhāga*, distribution of relics; *dhātu-kuśala*, skilled in the elements; *dhātu-kucchi*, womb.[42] That the morpheme *dhātu*[43] is applied to metallic elements and basic components of the body signifies the unitary doctrine which governed ancient systems of alchemical classification, virtually unifying metallurgy and medicine; forge, crucible and the *kamaṇḍalu*.

The term *yakṣa* (*jakka*) is possibly, semantically linked to *cakka* wheel or Tamil *yakkan* < *iyakkan yakṣa*; Kubera, king of *yakṣas*; *iyakki*, female *yakṣa*, goddess of virtue < (cf. *DEDR*, 469) *iyakku* < *iyaṅku*, movement, act of going, motion, as of stream; to cause to go, to actuate and influence the movements of; *iyaṅkiyar-poruḷ*, living, animate beings or beings which move from place to place < Kota, *iy-*, *ic-* to drive cattle; Kannada: *esagu*, to drive (cf. Tamil: *iyavai*, way, path; *iyavuḷ*, leadership, god, way; *iyal*, dance, to go on foot; *iyavu*, way, leading, proceeding).

The morpheme *yantra* is also traceable to the same semantic radical: *iy-*, to drive, *iyaṅku*, movement. Indeed, it may be stated without any semblance of casuistry that *yantra* and *tantra* are the *yin* and the *yang* of Indian alchemy; one dealt with the manual operations, the other with the extensions of these operations to the body.

In *Ṛgveda*, *yakṣ-* connotes speed, pressing forward, manifestation; and *yantra* means a "controlling device;" extended in *Mahābhārata* as "any implement or contrivance" (cf., *CDIAL*, 10412, Pāli: *yanta*, any mechanism or machine; Prākṛta: *jamta*, machine, oilmill, water-machine; Gypsy: *jandir*, mill; Dardic: *zāl-waṭ*, millstone, Assamese: *zāti*, tripod to support vessel over fire; Bengali: *jāti*, betel-nut, crackers; Sinhala: *yatta*, joiner's plane, *yaturu*, machine, lock. *CDIAL*, 10461, *yāntrika*, relating to machines or instruments, according to Suśruta, Prākṛta: *jamtia*, machine-worker; Lāhṇḍa: *jādri*, miller. *CDIAL*, 10413, *yantraśālā*, millstone room—of great importance in Soma *yajña!*). It is customary for workmen to sing songs while performing manual operations; so does the Vedic artisan: *CDIAL*, 10415, Sanskrit: *yantrasvāra*, mill song; Bhojpuri: *jātasār*, song sung by women while grinding. The famed Yama and Yamī of Ṛgvedic hymns explained in erotic terms may be explained simply by *CDIAL*, 10424, *yamayantra*, double mill (i.e., having two stones?); Dardic: *yamor*, small handmill. The compound *khalla-yantrikā* refers to leather bellows; Nepali: *khalāti*, bellows (< radical, Prākṛta: *khalla*, low, depressed ground, connoting the technique of fixing the bellows). A grinding mill used for bruising or splitting is *dala-yantrikā*. This etymological trace is important in the context of the decipherment elsewhere, of the so-called Indus "cult object" as a sublimation apparatus.

Symbols and associations

Alchemical traditions across civilizations have used metaphors, allegories and symbols to denote alchemical substances and processes. Since the Indus script has not yet been fully deciphered, it may be useful to get a bird's eyeview of the symbols used in contemporary civilizations; particularly, since there is a distinct possibility that some Indus pictorial motifs and script signs may have alchemical significance.

Rasa-ayana

The deification of mercury[44] into a *rasa-liṅga*[45] is relatable to the fact that it was the basis for many elixirs and transmutations.[46] *Parada* or *darada* (denoting the provenance of cinnabar?) or *rasa-rāja* or *rasendra* (*indra* of liquids) or *rasa-nātha* (lord) denoting mercury indicate the fundamental importance of this substance in alchemical lore.[47]

The morpheme *-ayana* in the compound *rasāyana* provides a lead. In the context of the *vrātyas* (lit., "of the *vrata* or rite," cf. *pūrve yajñikāḥ* noted in the *Niruktam*) of antiquity, a *gavām-ayana* rite is important. Shamasastry[48] explains: "The word *ayana* literally means 'going, movement,' and when combined with such words as *gavām*, 'of cows,' and *jyotiṣām*, 'of lights,' it means the 'movement of cows' and the 'movement of (*the havenly*) lights'.... We have already seen how the Vedic poets used to call the first day of their *ṣaḍaha* or six days' period by the name *jyotiṣ*, 'light,' and the second day by the name *go*, 'cow.' It follows, therefore, that the term *gavām-ayana* and *jyotiṣām-ayana* mean 'the march of days'...the term *gavām-ayana* means an intercalary period." Following this brilliant reconstruction of the semantics of *-ayana*, in proto-history, it is reasonable to interpret *rasa-ayana* as the "march of *material essence*," or the gestation of a metal over time, evoking *hiraṇya-garbha*.[49] In this etymological perspective, a Soma *yajña*, for instance, becomes an obstetric action to quicken the process of generation of the perfect metal.[50]

Carakasaṁhitā provides an extensive coverage of *rasāyana* while *Suśrutasaṁhitā* has only four chapters on this. Al-Biruni (973-1048), travelled in India between AD 1017-30. For him, *rasāyana* is an "art which is restricted to certain operations, drugs, and compound medicines, most of which are taken from plants. Its principles restore the health of those who are ill beyond hope, and give back youth to fading old age."[51]

Rasa according to *Suśrutasaṁhitā* is derived from the root *ras*, to move; the *rasa* ceaselessly circulates throughout the organism. This *rasa* yields body's main constituents: *rakta, māṁsa, medas, asthi, majjā*, and *śukra*: blood, flesh, fat, bone, marrow, and semen.[52] *Rasa* is also used to denote the "taste," qualities of natural substances: sweet, sour, salt, pungent, bitter, and astringent.[53]

Rasavāda may itself be interpreted as "a way of life, a mystic doctrine and a means of salvation."[54] In the alchemical tradition, many processes were used: sulphuration, carbonation, reduction and of course, oxidation. The morpheme *rasa* may be interpreted as a "sap, juice, elixir, fluid, quintessence, water, blood, urine, semen and all other liquids, as also substances dissolved in liquids or in their liquid or molten state, e.g., gold, copper, tin; also mixtures of magical drugs and medicines (*auṣadha*)...."[55] "Modes of restoring purity to various inanimate things: From a junction of water and fire arose gold and silver; and they two, therefore, are best purified by the elements, whence they sprang. Vessels of copper, iron, brass, pewter, tin, and lead, may be fitly cleansed with ashes, with acids, or with water." (*Manu*, ch. V, pp. 113-14)

Liṅga iconography

Rasaratna Samuccaya[56] explains the procedure for installing the *rasa-liṅgam:* Make a *liṅga* with three *niṣka* (12 *māṣa*) of gold (*hema patram*), nine *niṣka* of mercury (*rasendra*), and lemon (*amla*) juice. Insert it in a *dolāyantra* smelter and smelt it for one whole day. Install the *liṅga* for *pūjā*. The document extols its potential[57]: worshipping *rasa-liṅga* yields the beneficial effects of prayers to over ten million *liṅgas*...the mere sight of the *liṅga* expiates sins...to touch is to attain liberation (*mukti*)....

The symbolism of *liṅga* in the ancient alchemical tradition may explain the occurrence of this symbol on some early coins. "A Śivaliṅga on a pedestal placed between two different trees in side railings is also represented on the obverse of var. c. of class I coins hailing from Ujjayinī (John Allan, pp. 85-91)...a symbol appearing on some of the uninscribed cast coins described by Allan...a trident with broad flattened prongs...on the obverse of Wema Kadphises' coins, where the king, a Maheśvara by faith, puts offerings in honour of his deity on the sacrificial fire (Whitehead, *PMC*, vol. I, pl. XVII, 36)...Śiva...on coins hailing from Ujjayinī...a staff in the right (hand) and vase in the left...(pl. I, fig. 7)."[58] The symbols identified are: trees, *liṅga*, trident (*śūla*), vase (*kalaśa*).

The source of seman, which was important for physiological alchemists, was *liṅga*. (Cf., arguments tracing the proto-Muṇḍa origins of the morphemes: *liṅga*[59] and *lāṅgula*, plough.) *Liṅga* is a symbol of Indian alchemical traditions; *liṅga* which gets absorbed by the substratum in all streams of Śaiva, Śakti, tantric, etc. doctrines and most vividly in the *rasa-vidyās* which expound on mineral compounds as medicines or as elixirs of immortality or as ingredients for aurifiction.

The origin of the *liṅga* is elucidated in a number of mythologies. *Nārada Pañcarātra* refers to Śiva's semen falling to the ground to become a *liṅga*.[60] *Saura Purāṇa*[61] describes the appearance of the *liṅga* surrounded by flames. Sauptikaparvan of the *Mahābhārata* reports that Aśvatthāmā invokes Śiva and a gold altar with great flames of fire appears.[62] The *Vāyu, Śiva* and *Kūrma* Purāṇas also provide accounts with the imagery of a great cosmic fire, tongues of flames blazing out as the *liṅga* appears. Śiva is a blazing pillar; Gopinatha Rao sees the analogue of the *skambha*, which is intended to beget *hiraṇyagarbha* or *purāṇapuruṣa*. The imagery of *hiraṇyagarbha* in notable; the womb of gold! *ṚV*, IX.61.16: "As *soma* flowed in drops, he caused an immense column of light filling the universe to appear. In a marvellous manner it extended to the sky." Śiva is a *siddha yogī*, *mahā yogī*. He protects cattle (wealth). He heads *gaṇas*. When he discards his *liṅga*, he retires to Mt. Muñjavat to practise *tapas*. *Śiśnadevāḥ* (*ṚV*, VII.21.5) are either phallus worshippers or addicted to sensual enjoyment (Yāska; Sāyaṇa); in either meaning, they are the *yakṣa* types. Rudra, personifying the colour red, precedes Śiva; he is in the league of *bhūta, nāga, vrātya, niṣāda,* thieves, robbers, wood, hills, lonely places; he is of the underworld. He is *muṇḍa* of shaven head (ascetic?), anticipating a practice of the Kāmbojas. If the plebeian alchemical tradition needed a deified symbol, Rudra or his *liṅga* iconic version filled the bill totally.

Maschia and Maschiana, the original human pair in Parsi mythology, sprang from the three *homa* or *haoma* in Heden.[63] A tiny plate of gold, shaped like a fig leaf, called the *tali,* representing the phallus, is tied around a bride's neck at her marriage in many parts of India.[64] Two Mohenjo-daro seals depict a seated personage flanked by kneeling *nāgas.*[65] A number of numismatic and glyptic art examples from ancient India show a snake enclosing a *liṅga* or five-headed snake providing a canopy over the *liṅga.*[66] The *Ṛgveda* represents the rubbing of the two fire-sticks as an act of generation; the apparatus resembles the phallus in the *yoni. Atharvaveda* distinguishes the upper wood as *aśvattha* and the lower as *śamī.*[67] Four entire hymns of the *Ṛgveda* are dedicated to deities who had their own *liṅga* forms; these are treated as riddles.[68] *Ṛgveda* refers to *stambha* pillar and its function to beget *hiraṇyagarbha* or *purāṇa-puruṣa,* the deity of reproduction.[69] This imagery is elaborated in the *Śvetāśvatara Upaniṣad*[70]: "He, the creator and supporter of the gods, Rudra, the great seer, the lord of all, he who formerly gave birth to *hiraṇyagarbha,* may he endow us with good thoughts." The *Matsya Purāṇa* explains in a chapter, *liṅga-lakṣaṇam,* and details the procedures for producing *liṅgas* of metals, crystals, earth, wood etc.[71] *Śatapatha Brāhmaṇa* compares them to Purūravas and Urvaśī.[72] The parallel with human procreation and *araṇi* is drawn in *Bṛhadāraṇyaka Upaniṣad.*[73] Paracelsus, the Greek alchemist (1493-1541) extols the importance of mercury in his famous three hypostatical principles, the doctrine of *tria prima*: that the body is composed of mercury, sulphur and salt. While *iatro-chemistry* of the middle ages was defined as chemistry applied to medicine, Indian alchemists of the second century AD had used chemicals for therapeutics, though an elaborate scientific system had not been documented.

Nathan Sivin[74] categorizes alchemy in China as a qualitative science, together with medicine and astrology; he also sub-divides alchemy as external alchemy carried out in the workshop and internal alchemy practised by adepts in ascetic and mystical sessions, both aiming at religious transcendence combined with physical immortality. A comparable classification of Indian alchemical tradition may be proposed: alchemy performed as a Soma[75] *yajña* on a fire-altar, dealing with a specific substance; and alchemy of a *śramaṇa* drawing parallels between transmutation of base metals and the possibility of achieving physical perfection and immortality defined as "union" or *yoga*. Comparable to the Taoist alchemist's furnace which explains the beginnings of experimental science in China, the Lokāyata alchemist's forge, crucible and *kamaṇḍalu* (which integrate manual operations and abstract theories) may explain the beginnings of experimental sciences in India. Caraka and Suśruta exemplify the need for empiricism and the need to maintain a skeptical attitude toward the ancient authorities or so-called "revealed" truths. A parallel with the Chinese tradition is also found in the master-pupil relationship in the scientific fields, with emphasis not he "secrecy" of oral instruction; "secrecy" insisted upon even by empiricists: Caraka and Suśruta.[76]

Comparable to Christian hermeneutics which prescribed that true understanding is an understanding of the scriptures, the Brāhmaṇas and the Upaniṣads assume that the path to understanding is by "getting within the object," i.e., by unquestioning allegiance to the "revealed truth." Natural sciences, exemplified by Caraka and Suśruta, underscore that understanding comes through "subsuming the object within the operation of a general set of laws."[77] Learning of the Vedas or the alchemical tradition related to *soma* was closed to the masses, i.e., to castes other than Brāhmaṇas. Such a situation led to the Vedic scholars expounding upon or illuminating the Vedic secret doctrine through mythologies. It was possibly such a myth related to the transmutation of base metal into gold, that the *pammenas* had spread to Egyptain and Chinese civilizations.

Akṣa, kamaṇḍalu

Banerjea draws an interesting inference from Varāhamihira's list of qualifications of persons authorized to install specific images: "...these persons 'well-versed in the Vedas.' were the exclusive worshippers of Brahmā...the Vasantgadh (Rajputana) brick temple of the god is as old as the seventh century AD...a standing life-size image of Brahmā with three faces and a nimbus behind him; the figure is two-armed, the hands holding an *akṣamālā*[78] and *kamaṇḍalu*...(*Bṛhatsaṁhitā*, ch. 57, V.41)...the four-faced god holds a ritual water-vessel (*kamaṇḍalu*) in one of his hands and is seated on a lotus...a *brahmacārin* wearing a black antelope skin as his upper garment, his two hands holding a staff and a ritual water-vessel."[79]

One semantic stream links *akṣa* to blue vitriol and the colour green/blue. Why do the icons carry *akṣa* and the *kamaṇḍalu*? The importance of both symbols can be integrated in the context of alchemy. *Rasārṇava* quotes Bhairava: "*Mākṣikā* (copper pyrites), *vimala* (a pyrite), *śilā* (rocks), *chapala* (?sulphur-mineral), *rasaka* (calamine), *saśyaka* (blue vitriol), *darada* (cinnabar), and *srotojana* (stibnite)—these are the eight *mahā-rasas*."[80] Since the personage represented on the icons was an expert on the *rasa-vidyā*, he had to carry the symbols related to some of the *mahā-rasa*. The *akṣa*, vitriol could be used to colour lead ornaments to bedeck the gods.[81] It also imparts colour to quicksilver.[82]

Another semantic stream relates *akṣa* as a recording process in the compound, *akṣa-paṭala*, an office of great importance according to the *Arthaśāstra* (2.7.1-2) and described as a records-cum-audit office of all economic and financial transactions of all departments of government. The apparent importance of *akṣa*, dice in the affairs of the state is a subject for further research.

Alchemical language of icons

The focus on *kamaṇḍalu* in the context of alchemical tradition gains added dimensions when Brahmā is described in later-day icons with four hands: "...his hands are invariably four in number, the attributes in them being a rosary, *śruk, śruva* (sacrificial implements), the Vedas, etc.; he rides on a swan or on a chariot drawn by seven swans; having Sāvitrī on his left and Sarasvatī on his right side.... The later Jaina representations of Brahmā, either as a *yakṣa* attendant of the Jina Śītalanātha or as one of the Dikpālas are endowed with a great deal of hieratism...."[83] What was the Brahmā, as a *yakṣa* carrying in the *kamaṇḍalu*? *Amṛta*? Divine water[84] of alchemy? The Vedas on one of his hands may contain specific processes related to Soma *yajña*? According to *Śatapatha Brāhmaṇa* and *Manu*, the god created waters and deposited in them a seed which became the golden egg incarnating himself as Brahmā, the progenitor. As he moved in *nara* the waters, he was called Nārāyaṇa, a categorical reference to Brahmā the self-existent. He was perhaps perceived as the first alchemist who created the golden egg. The parallels with the Yakṣa cult and the related water-vessel symbolisms are striking, indeed to justify the Jaina tradition of depicting Brahmā as a *yakṣa* or Dikpāla. "...(Brahmā) should be represented with four faces, four arms and as being busy with the performance of the *homa* ceremony.... The colour of Brahmā should be red like the fire."[85] In the Subrahmaṇya-Vaḷḷi marriage, Brahmā with a *śruva* in his hand officiates in ceremonies in front of the fire sculpted as burning in a *kuṇḍa*.[86] An icon of Indra in Cidambaram is also depicted with a *kamaṇḍalu*.[87] So do icons of Agni and Varuṇa.[88]

Another *yakṣa* type, "*dhvaja-gaṇapati* should have four hands, carrying a book, an *akṣamālā*, a *daṇḍa*, and a *kamaṇḍalu*, and be of terrific look."[89] Apart from *Brahmaśāstā*, three of the seven icon types of Subrahmaṇya with four arms carry *kamaṇḍalu*.[90] *Rūpamaṇḍana* an iconographic text prescribes that Kubera should have the elephant for *vāhana*, carry a *gadha*, a purse containing money, a pomegranate fruit[91] and a *kamaṇḍalu*.[92] Of the *nāgas*, the colour of Vāsuki is pearl-white, that of Takṣaka glistening red with his hood marked with *svastika* and all seven forms including Vāsuki and Takṣaka carry in their hands *akṣamālā* and *kamaṇḍalu*.[93]

That *amṛta* is associated with wealth is vividly portrayed in the iconographic tract *Śilparatna*, according to which, Lakṣmī, the goddess of wealth should carry a lotus, a *bilva* fruit, a *śaṅkha* and *amṛta ghaṭa* (pot containing ambrosia).[94] Garuḍa carries a pot of *amṛta* and depicted with a pair of powerful wings of golden yellow colour and bright lustre.[95] The parallel with the bird-shaped fire-altars described in the Śulvasūtra is as vivid as the parallel with the mythological account in the *Mahābhārata* which recounts how Garuḍa proceeds to the capital city of Indra and succeeds in taking possession of the pot of *amṛta* to free his mother Vinata.[96] Dhanvantarin, according to *Viṣṇudharmottara*, an iconographic tract, should be sculpted carrying *amṛta* vessels on both the hands.[97] The term is adopted by later-day physicians who practise *āyurveda*, the medical science of longevity. The morpheme *dhanvan-* is closely allied with wealth and prosperity.

According to *Bṛhatsaṁhitā*, Durgādevī if sculpted with eight hands, should carry a *kamaṇḍalu, dhanuṣ*, book and lotus flower in the left hand and the *bāṇa*, a mirror, an *akṣamālā* on the right hands with the fourth held in Varada pose.[98] Harasiddhi, one of the nine forms of Durgā, as well as Bhadrakālī carries *ḍamarū, kamaṇḍalu, khaḍga* and a drinking vessel.[99] The distinction between *kamaṇḍalu* and a drinking vessel is significant and points to the special contents of the *kamaṇḍalu.*

Of the twelve Ādityas, Sūrya is depicted with *kamaṇḍalu* on the back right hand and *akṣamālā* on the back left hand; with lotuses on both the front hands, according to *Viśvakarmaśāstra.*[100] Among the *navagrahas, bhauma, guru, śukra, śani* carry *kamaṇḍalu* on their left hands.[101]

Svastika

The morpheme *bon* in the Tibetan religion of antiquity (which has striking parallels with Taoism and Tantrism) is derived from *puṇya* by Alexander Cunningham.[102] The term *puṇya* is one of the names of the *seastikas* or worshippers of the mystic fly-foot cross, called in Tibetan *gyun druṇ Punya,* holy man, has a parallel in the term used in Burmese for a monk: *pongyee.*

The fly-foot cross, *svastika,* is a symbol found in Troy and among Teutonic nations of antiquity as the emblem of Thor.[103] The right-handed *svastika* is the form used in Buddhism. Lāmas, "while regarding the symbol as one of good augury, also consider it to typify the continuous moving, or 'the ceaseless becoming,' which is commonly called Life. Cunningham believed it to be a monogram formed from the Aśoka characters for the auspicious words *su+asti,* or 'that which is good.' It was especially associated with the divinity of Fire, as representing the two cross pieces of wood (Sanskrit: *araṇi*) which by friction produce fire. The Jainas, who seem to be an Indian offshoot of Buddhism, appropriate it for the seventh of their mythical saints (Jina Supārśva). The heterodox Tibetans, the Bon, in adopting it have turned the ends in the reverse direction."[104]

Time is cyclical motion, continuous revolution with shifts of the sun in the solstices. May be, the left- and right-handed *svastikas* symbolize reversibility of time or just six-monthly shifts which coincide with the harvests; *poṇkal* in Tamil denotes the harvest festival celebrated when the sun enters the tropic of capricorn and takes a northward course, being the first day of Tai or Saṁkrānti. In Hindu mythology, the rise and fall of each *kalpa* alternates with the rise of good and evil, the churnings of the ocean of milk to gain *amṛta* the elixir of life, of immortality. A concordant morpheme *ṛtu,* may be derived from Tamil *iru-tu,* season of two months; *Ṛgveda* lists six seasons of a year. The same morpheme also means "catamenia," the attainment of puberty and the first menstrual discharge (also called *pūppu* = lit., flowering). That the same morpheme should have been used to connote the seasonal changes and the key stage of biological change in a woman's life is significant in tracing the early man's thought processes: he was constantly drawing parallels between cosmic phenomena governed by time and the transformations in the human body from birth through old age. Such a thought-process contained in itself the seeds of alchemy which could link smelting and transmutation of ore into gold and the attainment of physical immortality through parallel processes.

Incense and other liturgical preparations

It is instructive to review the types of materials used to perform *pūjā* to deities, tantric *sādhanā* or to propitiate the genii, a custom which finds a parallel also among the Taoists. The woods are burned; mixed gums cast in glowing charcoal; incense sticks are allowed to slowly emit the smoke from slow-burning perfumed paste. Camphor (which in Sanskrit is also called *soma!*) is burnt in front of a deity and the flame symbolically touched by the devotees. Paste or ashes are smeared on the bodies of adepts or on the icons. In addition to incense and perfumed flowers, and the use of oils, clarified butter to anoint the icons or to burn cotton-wick lamps, specific leaves of trees or trees themselves, for example, the pipal (*paṇai, aśvattha, bodhi*); wood-apple (Sanskrit: *bilva*; *DEDR*, 5509, Tamil: *veḷḷil, viḷam, viḷavu*; Telugu: *velāga*; Kannada: *beḷāla, bela*); and neem (*DEDR*, 5531, Tamil: *vempu*; Kota: *vep marm*; Tulu: *bevu*; Telugu: *vemu, vepa*) are among the essential ingredients of invocation or propitiation of the gods or genii. That these religious and liturgical material had scientific potential has been elaborated by Needham in the context of Chinese documentation related to fumigants, expellants, control of epidemics and the invention of gun-powder itself. The Indian tradition related to the extensions of liturgy to health and military domains has to be studied further. Another area for further study relates to the possible use of liturgical material as hallucinogens. Perhaps, Indian tradition may parallel the Chinese where "...the incense-burner remained the centre of changes and transformations associated with worship, sacrifice, ascending perfume of sweet savour, fire, combustion, disintegration, transformation, vision, communication with spiritual beings, and assurances of immortality. *Wai tan* and *nei tan* met around the incense-burner." The Indian potter, stone-cutter or *śilpī* and metallurgist of antiquity have indeed been partners in the development of alchemical symbolism with the design of the *pūrṇa-ghaṭa* which held the *amṛta* and the terracotta icons and ornaments for the icons.

Technical terms of siddha alchemical tradition

The *siddhas* of south India are adepts at the use of metaphors and allegories to shroud the medicinal, metallurgical or alchemical terms in secrecy. The process of communication involving such methods became almost an obsession and was carried to its extremes. The following examples are taken from a concordance prepared by R. Manickavāsagam.[105] These terms may provide useful leads to identify some symbols used in old alchemical texts and icons. Some apparent symbolic concordances are underlined: for example, a snake denoting iron; a jackal denoting copper; maiden denoting sulphur; *makara* (crocodile or sea-animal) denoting mercury or its sulphide.

Plants

soma valli	lit., *soma* creeper; *ponnāṇkaṇṇi* (plant, radical *poṉ* means gold)
maka durumam	*arasu, Ficus religiosa,* pipal
kani-c-caaru	(lit., fruit juice) juice of lemon

Minerals, Metals, Pāṣāṇa, Symbols

ahi	iron, snake; *arai-poḍi,* iron powder; *karuṅkol* (lit., black staff); *karuppi* (lit., black lady); *karum-poṉ* (lit., black gold)
asu pati	gold; *āṇi-t-ṭaṅkam, paim-poṉ,* superior gold; *iraṇiyam; kaliyāṇam; kākataṇḍi* (*kākkai poṉ,* lit., crow gold); *cāṇār-kācu (= ṭaṅkam); cirungi;* four types of gold: *hāṭakam, kiḷiccirai, jāta rūpam, jāmbunadam; par-i,* a term used by goldsmiths
aṭṭa dhātu	*velli, pon, cembu, irumbu, veṅgalam, tārā* [? *veḷḷī-yam,* as distinct from *kāriyam* or black lead], *vaṅgam, tuttu-nāgam; ayattirku tāy* = lit., mother of *ayas* (copper); sulphur, *keṇṭakam, atirāgam, antirak-koḍicci, aran peṇḍir* (Śiva's maiden); *Īśvara-nādam; kar-centī; satti, satti-śivam* (also connotes *rasa*)
aparaji	gold; *eymam, eymini, poṉ; candiram*
veḷḷi	silver; *ūdu-vāram*
arava maṇi	*nāga-maṇi, rudrākṣam*

aran̲ bījam	lit., seed of Śiva; *rasa, aran̲ bindu; pāda-rasam, śuklam; ūṟṟik-kāran; cūḍam* [cf., *cūḍa-k-karpūram, rasa-karpūram*]; *teri-muttu.* [An interesting etymon is *makarar=paratar,* it would appear that the reference may be to Bharata's with the *makara-dhvaja*; else, the *parada* may be relatable to *darada* as a region from which cinnabar or mercury is obtained.]
ari kāram	lit., Chinese astringent; *cina-k-kāram, paṭikāram, kṣāra; āṇ-carakku,* lit., male substance, *kṣāra*; five *kṣāras: pañca-k-kāram: cina-k-kāram, veṇ kāram, pūṇkāram, savarkkāram*
veṇ kāram	*vaṇḍil* (lit., bee), borax, *ṭaṅkaṇam* [cf., *cina-k-kāram* and ancient source of borax, Tibet]
pañca-uppu	lit., five salts: *ind-uppu, kal-uppu, kari-uppu, vaḷaiyal-uppu, vey-uppu*
āñcil	*śaṅkha; occiyam*
rasa cuddhi	*īyam, vaṅgam,* lead
īru kaṭṭi	*rasa-karpūram; iviyādam; cūtaka-k-karpūram*
irudi	*pittaḷai*
kaḍuñcāri	*navaccāram; graha-c-cāram* (cf., nine planets); *kānta-catturu* (lit., enemy of sulphur)
kaṇḍar	*turicu = mayil-tuttam* (may be, a reference to the peacock-colour of the copper sulphate; *ceripuk-kaḷimpu*—? copper sulphate—mixed with *keṇṭakam* or sulphur); *kaṇḍar-cembu, kaṇḍar-ravi=turicu-cembu*
karuṅkañcan	*veṅgalam*
cambu	jackal (?*jambu,* cf. *cembu tāmram, ravi,* copper)
śilā cattu	*kal matam; malai vintu; śilā nañju; śilā nātam; śilaikkuḷ tīṭṭu; śilai-t-tīṭṭuu; cīlai yoṟukku; cīlai śroṇitam;* Skt., *śilā jātu*
danuca	*man-o-cilai;* Pārvatī [cf., *pāru, paruntu,* falcon]
cīmai kāṇḍā	
miruga rattam	lit., blood of rhinoceros; *veṇgaiyin picin* (lit., tiger's glue)
garbham	*cembu,* copper
ceppu-k-kuḷicam	*mantra* symbols engraved on copper tablet. [Cf., *gulige* used as a unit of account, possibly denoting a weight of a gold pellet]; *takaḍu-kaṭṭutal,* tying an amulet after invoking *mantras*

Animals

asuvam	horse
oruvai	goat, *āḍu, kār-āḍu, veḷḷāḍi* (lit., white goat)
paḍā muki	elephant, *yāṉai*
kaccapam	tortoise, *āmai; kaḍambak-kūṉaṉ*
kaccam	fish, *mīna*

Constituents of incense, aromatics, anointments or sprinklers (abhiṣeka)

The role of ashes as sal ammoniac has been mentioned in the context of Arabic alchemy which mentions the artificial preparation sal ammoniac from animal hair and animal excrements. It is tempting to view the use of *bhūti* and *bhasma* by *siddhas* and Śaiva believers as a parallel to the "material immortality" or Taoists. The liquid elixir was consumed by Tao adepts; the essence of matter in the form of ashes was anointed on their bodies by *siddhas.* Do these practices connote an elaboration of "material immortality" as an exercise in simulation of "physical immortality and yoga?"

ashes	*DEDR,* 995, Kurku: *ormā,* lampblack; Maltese: *oṭme,* ashes. *DEDR,* 2453, Tamil: *cāmpal,* ashes; Sanskrit (lex.): *bhasma. DEDR,* 2552, Kui: *singa,* charcoal; Kannada: *ijjalu,* charcoal; Tamil: *iru,* black. *DEDR,* 3693, Tamil: *nīru,* ashes, dross of any substance after it has been burned, sacred ashes; Manda: *niy-darambu,* ashes. *DEDR,* 4316, Tamil: *puṛuti,* dust; Telugu: *būḍida,* ashes; Sanskrit: *bhūti,* ashes
aloe	*DEDR,* 13, Tamil: *akil* (drug *agar* obtained). *CDIAL,* 49, Pāli: *akalu;* Arabic: *gharu;* Sanskrit (lex.): *aguru*
asafoetida	Telugu (lex.): *iṅguva;* Hindi: *hiṅg*
balsam	*DEDR,* 1587, Tamil: *kiḷuvai*
basil	*DEDR,* 3357, Tamil: *tuzay, tuḷaci. CDIAL,* 5885, Sanskrit: *tulasī*
bdellium	*guggulu* (cf., Tamil: *kiḷuvai?*)
betal	*DEDR,* 5515, Tamil: *verrilai,* betel pepper; Kota, *vetil,* betel leaf; Tulu: *baccire,* betel leaf (cf., *patchouli;* Sanskrit (lex.): *tāmbūla, nāgavalli*
camphor	Sanskrit (lex.): *karpūra; somaḥ, somasaṁjñam; sitābhraḥ, tārābhraḥ*
citronella	*DEDR,* 1485, Tamil: *kāvaṭṭai;* Kannada: *kāmañci,* lemon grass

clove	Telugu, Sanskrit (lex.): *lavaṅgamu; ākupatri*, the tree
Frankincense	Telugu (lex.): *sāmbrāṇi, guggilamu; kunuru* (Sanskrit), jasminum
samba	*DEDR*, 4987, Tamil: *mullai*. *CDIAL*, 9913, Sanskrit: *mallikā*
musk	Telugu, Sanskrit (lex.): *kastūrī*
patchouli	Tamil: *paccilai*; Sanskrit: *tamālapattra*; Ancient West: *malabathron* (derived from Malayan mints, pogostemon cablin and p.heyneanum)
turmeric	*DEDR*, 220, Kota: *arcn*, saffron (English: turmeric); Toda: *arsn*, saffron, yellow; Kannada: *arisina*, turmeric; Tamil: *aricaṉam*, turmeric
	DEDR, 2608, Kui: *sringa, singa*, turmeric, saffron, yellow; Kui: *hiṅga*, turmeric, saffron, *hiṅgeri*, yellow (cf., Kui: *singa*, charcoal; Hindi: *hiṅg*, asafoetida)
	DEDR, 4635, Tamil: *manual*, turmeric; Kodagu: *mañja*, id.; Tulu: *manjalu*, id., yellow; *manjale*, yellow or tawny-coloured man; Sanskrit (lex.): *haridrā, lasā;* Sanskrit (lex.): *kumkumam, gauram, vāhnikam, kāveram*, sandalwood. *DEDR*, 2448, Tamil: *cāntam*, sandal; *cāntu*, sacred ashes; Malayalam: *cāntu*, compound ointment of sandal, camphor, musk and saffron; *cādu*, to rub into a paste; Sanskrit: *candana*, sandal (tree, paste, wood). *DEDR*, 2449, Tamil: *cāttu*, to put on, adorn; Telugu: *cātu*, to wear caste mark, clothes, etc.
	DEDR, 5520, Tulu: *benna, benga*, sandalwood tree; Tamil: *veṇgai*, East Indian kino tree
	Chinese: *than hsiang, chan than* (remarkable concordance with Sanskrit *candana*), *pai than*

Planets and alchemical associations: metals/symbols

		Associations[106]	
sun	gold[107]	lion	
moon	silver	crab	
mars	iron	scorpion	
venus	copper	bull and scales	
jupiter		tin/bronze electrum	archer and fishes
saturn		lead	(Tamil: *Can-i pāmpiranḍum uḍaṉe)*

		Tevāram 1171, 1: saturn with two snakes; hence snakes may symbolise lead, in the *siddha* alchemical tradition) goat and water-carrier; darkened cubic stone
mercury	mercury	virgin and twins; caduceus; fish

Alchemical concepts and symbols/morphemes

philosopher's stone	*liṅga*
fiery water	six-pointed star (two interlacing triangles)
mother goddess	sulphur, *sindhur*[108]
fire	arrow, lance, hammer, scissors, scythe, sword or a man with a wooden leg
Hermes	Brahmā
spirits	mercury, sulphur, arsenic and sal ammoniac; *rasa, karpūra, bhasma*
bodies	gold, silver, copper, tin, lead and iron
pure substances	gold and silver
colour	*varṇa* [the most devastating equivalence was extending a fourfold classification (of colours of metals) to a hierarchical social organization]
antimony	grey wolf
white sublimate	ascending dove or swan
black or putrefying matter	black crow
earthy matter	toad
mercury and sulphur	winged and wingless lions

Experimental alchemy and "revealed truths"

Driven by a goal to transform base metals into precious metals with or without the aid of an imaginary *philosopher's stone*, many mixtures and compounds were discovered in "laboratory work:" for example, glass, enamel, cloth dyes, metal alloys and medicinal preparations. The Papyrus X of Leiden indicates the Graeco-Egyptian alchemical expertise in processing metallic alloys. The Graeco-Egyptian tradition relates to techniques of distillation, assaying methods, methods for purification of metals, and amalgamation. Egyptian alchemists are credited with the discovery of sal ammoniac. Arabic-speaking alchemists, Geber, Abu Al-Razi are credited with the creation of the first real pharmacy. Abu Mansur, the tenth-century Persian doctor refers to the use of organic materials: e.g., sugar-cane and vegetable acids by Arabs to prepare medicines. Western alchemical tradition of the Middle Ages gets mixed up with magic and mysticism. It was only in the sixteenth century that the impossibility of transmuting metals was established by research and experimental methods of *iatro-chemistry*. Combined with applied, technical chemistry, iatro-chemistry flowered into chemistry as a science. For modern chemistry, the common nature of transmutability of materials is a theoretical premise to be tasted as a practical problem and not an *a priori* "revealed" truth.

Roger Bacon (+1214 to +1292) in his *The Mirror of Alchemy* refers to the "elixir" from mercury and sulfur: "...a material containing pure...mercury mixed, uniformly according to a definite rule and in the necessary proportion with sulfur...." This alchemical tract in effect anticipates the later-day laws of chemistry related to the law of constant composition. Bacon believed that only criterion of knowledge was direct experience, analogous to the Vaiśeṣika doctrine of *dṛṣṭa liṅgam*. In *Opus Majus* (*c.* +1266; Jebb ed., p. 472), Bacon states: "That medicine which will remove all impurities and corruptibilities from the lesser metals will also, in the opinion of the wise, take off so much of the corruptibility of the body that human life may be prolonged for many centuries." Similar ideas can be found in a number of ancient Indian medical texts which in their titles use the term: *rasa-*. The tragic fate of Roger Bacon, Alexander Setonius and other European alchemists may be related to the permitted "white magic" which was Christian alchemy and the forbidden "black magic" of pre-tian "pagans." Medieval alchemy was extraordinary combination of "theoretician and experimenter and practical craftsman, poet and artist, scholar and mystic, theologian and philosopher, and black magician and faithful Christian."[109] Similar was the metallurgical-medical-magico-religious-metaphysical milieu within which Indian alchemical techniques evolved.

Brethren of purity

Maslama al-Majriṭi, i.e., of Madrid is an encyclopaedist (d. *c.* AD 1004 or 1007) reportedly[110] travelled in the East and brought a collection of the famous works of the "Brethren of Purity" devoted to *mineralogy*. The treatise was edited by Dieterici who remarked that the concepts that a mineral had "life," and that it developed or "grew" in the womb of the earth, were conceived on Aristotelian principles, although no specific work of Aristotle about minerals was quoted. He also wrote a book on alchemy, titled *Kanz al-Faḍā'il*, "Treasury of Accomplishment," dated AD 957. In that treatise the doctrine is presented thus: "From the elements which lie like potentialities in the womb of the earth, there are first of all formed, as energies, mercury and sulphur; from those two there are afterwards formed, as entelechies, metals which are good or bad, noble or base, according to circumstances. It is only in consequence of certain injuries undergone that the material does not become silver or gold instead of lead or tin. Alchemy endeavours to repair these injuries (Dieterici, *Die Abhhandlungen der Ikhwaan es-Safaa*, Leipzig, 1886, Vorwort, p. 13 and text, p. 137). The same idea is expressed in the *Cosmography of Quzwini* (ed., Wustenfeld, I, p. 207), and in this work also it is ascribed to Aristotle; the metals in their mines undergo certain injuries which cause their imperfections; e.g., lead is a kind of silver which has three defects—an unpleasant odour, softness, and a disagreeable sound. In this book also, means of getting rid of these defects are suggested." The ideas have a striking parallel with concepts prevalent in India: for example, Brahmanical ideas of "pollution" justifying the social hierarchical classification; *hiranyagarbha* description of gold-bearing womb of the earth or mineral; the *tri-doṣa* or three-defect explanation for diseases and the prescriptions of Āyurveda to remedy these defects or imbalances in the body; the justification for *jāti* or caste as a circumstance caused by birth, a *jāti* which may be noble or base and hence ranked in the "legal" texts.

References

1. The measurement by weighment can also be related to linear measures; cf., Pliny who relates (XXXIII, 61) that from one ounce (30.59 gms.) of gold it was possible to beat 750 and more leaves having a length of side equal to the width of four fingers (1 digitus = .0185 mts., i.e., about .73 ins.)...thus the thinnest leaves were about 1/300 mm. thick, or 13/100,000 inches; so that they were about thirty times as thick as the best gold leaves made in modern times (which are 1/9000 thick). Albert Neuburger, *The Technical Arts and Sciences of the Ancients*, London, 1930, p. 32.
2. D. Chattopadhyaya, *Lokāyata*, p. xxii; Needham, *SCC*, vol. II, pp. 83-

139.

3. D. Chattopadhyaya, *Lokāyata*, pp. 331-32; Bagchi, *Studies in the Tantras*, Calcutta, 1939.
4. D. Chattopadhyaya, *Lokāyata*, pp. 356-58.
5. P.C. Ray, *HHC*, 157.
6. Ibid., II, Intro., lxiv.
7. Ibid., I, Intro., xli.
8. J. Needham, *SCC*, II, 139.
9. *Gautama Dharmasūtra* (XI) refers to *anvīkṣikī* as a science beside the Vedic science (*trayi*) and as a just subject of study for a king. The king has to use reasoning (*tarka*) to arrive at conclusion in law (*nyāya*).
10. Mrinal Kanti Gangopadhyay, *Indian Logic in its Sources on Validity of Inference*, New Delhi, 1984, pp. 30-31.
11. A.B. Keith, *Indian Logic and Atomism, an Exposition of the Nyaya and Vaiseshika Systems*, reprint, New Delhi, 1977, 12-14.
12. A.B. Keith, op. cit., 228-29.
13. Eliade, pp. 8-9, 45-67, 75-88, 94.
14. Multhauf, op. cit., p. 36.
15. In a passage published in translation in Hoover, 1912: 279, n. 8; Multhauf, op. cit., p. 37.
16. R. Multhauf, op. cit., p. 93.
17. *Leyden Papyrus X*, 1889, 30, 37-38 (Recipes 8, 38, 40).
18. R. Multhauf, op. cit., p. 99; Hammer-Jensen, 1921, 41.
19. R. Multhauf, op. cit., pp. 102-3.
20. *AAG*, text, 107; trans., 117; R. Multhauf, op. cit., p. 105.
21. R. Multhauf, op. cit., p. 105; iosis in Greek means: arrow, poison, and rust or verdigris. Gold colouration, the last step in the alchemical synthesis was only its most obvious alchemical signification.
22. Cf., R. Multhauf, op. cit., p. 107; based on Stapleton's summary of a Cairo Arabic manuscript, 1953, pp. 40-43.
23. R. Multhauf, op. cit., p. 108.
24. The compound *vibhūti*, interpreted as "manifestation" extends the concept of *siddhi* or attainment. From being to becoming, the process involved is: *sādhana* or gaining. In the *Ṛgveda* (VI.21.1) the term *vibhūti* means: pervading, mighty, abundant, plentiful. This extends *ṚV*, I.161.1: *bhūti*, growth, prosperity, goodness.
25. Cf., B. Walker, *The Hindu World*, "Ashes. According to alchemical theory some elements of the original cosmic matter are present in all things, but they are concealed by the 'accidents' of their outward form . . . ashes are regarded as a manifestation of primal matter... reduction of anything to ash is a form of purification.... Ashes are referred to as *bhasman* because they are produced by the 'devouring' fire...extensively used in Hindu ritual and occult practice.... Their

application received further support in Ayurveda.... Some ascetics smear their whole body with ashes; others powder their hair with it; many make caste-marks on the forehead and other parts of the body with ashes.... Ashes play a significant role in alchemy since the reduction of substances to their primary elements precedes their use in alchemical experiments. In medieval alchemy ashes from the sacrificial fire, from the *dhūnī* or *jogī*'s fire, from the burning of certain kinds of wood, from cowdung, or from the cremated remains of a corpse, often constituted the basic adhesive ingredient in the preparation of elixirs."

26. J. Needham, "Chinese Science and Technology," *Clerks and Craftsmen*, pp. 76-77. "...technical, speculative and mystical chemistry in Hellenistic Europe (first and second centuries), but it was not alchemy for it did not attempt to make true gold from other substances, only to imitate the metal, and it was not primarily concerned with longevity and material immortality. The later ideas of the 'philosopher's stone' and the 'elixir of life,' though unattainable phantasms, were those which inspired the invention of most of the practical techniques out of which modern chemistry was born.... Actually lin kem shut, but I was speaking from memory. The ancient pronunciation was probably *lien kiem dzhiuet* (Karlgren). Hakka, Korean and Annamese all have *kim* for the main word."
27. Cited in J. Needham, "The Evolution of Oecumenical Science," *Clerks and Craftsmen*, p. 416, 3.
28. E.J.H. Mackay, in John Marshall, *MIG*, p. 356.
29. *ERE*, p. 292.
30. J. Needham, "Elixir Poisoning," *Clerks and Craftsmen*, pp. 325-26.
31. Ibid., p. 327.
32. *Vyavahāra Bhāṣya*, 1, pp. 116af.
33. Cf., Paracelsus, sixteenth century Greek alchemist's views on alchemists: "...They put their fingers among coals, into clay and filth—not into gold rings. They are sooty and black, like smiths and miners, and do not pride themselves upon clean and beautiful faces." A.J. Hopkins, op. cit., p. 205.
34. *Niśīthasūtra* and the *bhāṣya* cited in Jagdishchandra Jain, op. cit., p. 264.
35. *Śarīrasthāna*, VIII.75, pp. 155f.
36. Jagdishchandra Jain, op. cit., p. 265. It is also noted on p. 266, n. 2 that *Āvaśyakacūrṇī*, 161 mentions four great magic arts (*mahāvidyā*): *gaurī*, *gāndhārī*, *rohiṇī*, and *prajapti*; these magic arts figure as goddesses of learning in the sculpture of Deogarh temple in Madhya Pradesh.
37. *Niśīthacūrṇī*, 19.6088-6117; Jagdishchandra Jain, op. cit., p. 275. The same document in 10.2792, p. 43; Jagdishchandra Jain (op. cit., p. 276, n. 5) adds: drinking of fluid gold was considered a remedy for removing poverty. A vague statement, the import of which is unclear, unless a

product of aurifiction bordering on microbiotics was referred to in this statement.

38. *Thānāṅga,* 9.678.
39. *Suśrutasaṁhitā,* ed., and trans., K.L. Bhishagaratna, vol. II, Varanasi, 1963, p. 43.
40. Obeyesekere, p. 213.
41. *Suśrutasaṁhitā,* vol. II, 1963, p. 132.
42. Rhys-Davids, *Pāli-English Dictionary.*
43. *CDIAL,* 6773, *ṚV: dhātu,* substance; *Mahābhārata, Manu:* metal, mineral, ore (esp. of a red colour); lex.: ashes of the dead; Pāli: element, ashes of the dead, relic; Dardic: relic; Prākṛta: *dhāu,* metal, red chalk; Nepali· *dhāu,* ore (esp. of copper); Sinhala: *dā,* relic; Sindhi: *dhāi,* wisp of fibres added from time to time to a rope that is being twisted. *DEDR,* 3159, Tamil: *tātu,* powder, dust, pollen; Toda: *tot,* powdery, soft (of flour or powdered chillies).
44. Cf., M.S. Vats, *EH,* vol. I, p. 312: "Inside the beaker no. 16 (12124) in pl. LXXXII was found a dirty white paste which proved on examination by the Archaeological Chemist in India to be cerussite, a natural carbonate of lead mixed with earth. Pure cerussite is white and he thinks this substance was employed by women as paint for the face...no. 16 (12124) is a broken beaker of turquoise blue colour with traces of a bright frit applied over the glaze. It was found to contain cerussite paint for the face...." Discovery of this carbonate of lead together with cinnabar, sulphide of mercury in Mohenjo-daro indicate their possible use as cosmetics or medicines. If the surmise that cinnabar had been used for the extraction of mercury is valid, the "cult object" can be deciphered as a sublimation apparatus.
45. The morpheme, *liṅga,* is significant and may ultimately explain the "philosopher's *stone*" believed in medieval alchemic beliefs. The Greek word *xerion* (?>Arabic *al-iksir* > *Elixir*) denotes a dry powder used in alchemy and medicine.
46. Cf., *Bṛhadāraṇyaka Upaniṣad:* "I reclaim this spilt semen; let my vigour return; let me glow with strength again; let the fire return to its accustomed place." Cf., B. Walker, *The Hindu World,* pp. 153-54; also, a note on "esoteric chemistry": "Tantrik teachings prescribe various means of regulating the sex act and arresting the *retas.* The technique known as *ūrdhva-retas* 'upward flow,' is concerned with the suppression of ejaculation (*coitus reservatus*), the progress of the semen-power through the stations of the *avadhūtika* (within the spinal column), and its sublimation. By esoteric chemistry of this magical sexual action, the *bindu,* during the climax of the creative moment, is converted into a vital force and given an upward flow. Western scholars have held that the technique is nothing more than a pressure

on the urethra, and the contraction of the anus, combined with certain respiratory methods at the time of ejaculation, resulting not in the 'ascent of the semen' but in its discharge into the bladder, whence it is voided through the urine. The technique was known to the Chinese Taoists and was brought to India from China."

47. Cf., A.J. Hopkins, op. cit., pp. 118-19: "(Of the two spirits, sulphur and mercury), giving tincturing properties to the metals, mercury had long been known. Theophrastus and Dioscorides had prepared the metal and Vitruvius had mentioned the amalgamation process for the recovery of gold enmeshed in fabrics. [The alchemists knew how to prepare mercury from cinnabar by distillation or in the moist way by use of copper or lead.]... Mercury is the feminine, receptive principle, while the active sulphur is masculine." Berthelot, *Collection des anciens alchimistes grecs*, Introduction, p. 257; *La Chimie au moyen age*, II, Traduction, p. 85. Avicenna states that mercury is the mother of the metals...she receives in her womb what is of the same nature as herself.... In Egyptian alchemy, metals are that division of minerals which are fusible.
48. R. Shamasastry, *The Vedic Calendar*, 1912, reprint, New Delhi, 1979, pp. 58ff.
49. Cf., Mircea Eliade, "Alchemy," *ER*, p. 184: "Mineral substances, hidden in the womb of Mother Earth, shared in the sacredness attached to the goddess. Very early we are confronted with the idea that ores 'grow' in the belly of the earth after the manner of embryos. Metallurgy thus takes on the character of obstetrics. The miner and metal-worker intervene in the unfolding of subterranean embryology: they accelerate the rhythm of the growth of ores; they collaborate in the work of nature and assist in giving birth more rapidly...his labours replace the work of time. With the help of fire, metalworkers transform the ores ('the embryos') into metals (the adults)."
50. Cf., Aristotle's concept of entelechy, with its power of reproduction. The metals strive to finish their cycle, tending toward perfection as fire seeks its source, toward the entelechy which is gold. "Following (Aristotle's classification), the alchemist posited a genus mineral of which one species was the metals, having the common element of 'water' or fusibility. Individual metals owe their individuality to the 'distinctive differences' included in grades of fusibility, volatility and colour. The latter tend (and may be aided) to change, but always toward perfection, i.e., to the entelechy gold (which unites the two Aristotelian elements, fire and water) and this is able to reproduce itself, thus transmuting less perfect metals into gold." A.J. Hopkins, op. cit., pp. 26, 30-31E.
51. Sachau, I.188.

52. *Suśrutasaṁhitā,* I.14.13; cf., *Carakasaṁhitā,* VI.15.17.
53. *Carakasaṁhitā,* I.26.9.
54. B. Walker, *The Hindu World,* p. 23.
55. Ibid., p. 23.
56. Ch. 6, 17-18.
57. Ch. 6, 19-21.
58. J.N. Banerjea, *Development of Hindu Iconography,* pp. 114-17.
59. *CDIAL,* 11051-52: *liṅga* characteristic attribute (*Maitrāyaṇī Upaniṣad*), penis, (*Mānava Dharmaśāstra*); influenced by another meaning: *liṅga,* lump, emblem of Śiva, gets the meaning "attribute." Pāli: *liṅga,* mark, penis, vulva; Prākṛta: *liṅga,* sign, penis; Sindhi: *linu,* limb; Western Pahari: *linuni,* tail of sheep or goat (cf., Bengali: *lenga,* naked, lefthanded, *nenara,* lame). Ṛgvedic: *lāṅgāla,* plough > Iranian, *lingor,* plough; this transforms with an initial *n-* in all Dravidian forms (*DEDR,* 2907, Tamil: *nācil;* Kota: *nelg;* Kannada: *negal;* Gadba: *nāṅgal;* plough; Kui: *nangelli,* ploughshare; Konkani: *māṅguli,* penis). F.B.J. Kuiper, *Proto-Munda Words in Sanskrit,* Amsterdam, 1948, p. 127, derives both Indo-Aryan and Dravidian forms from Muṇḍa sources. The semantic collision with "tail" is apparent also in *CDIAL,* 11009: *lāṅgula,* tail; Punjabi: *lāgur,* monkey; Pāli: *naṅguṭṭha,* tail. In the Lakhimpuri dialect of Awadhi, *negulā* is the only boy amongst the girls fed on the ninth day of Aśvin in honour of Devī.
60. *Nārada Pañcarātra,* third *rātra,* ch. 1.
61. Ch. 14.
62. Nanimadhab Chaudhuri, "Liṅga Worship in the Mahābhārata," *IHQ,* vol. XXIV, 1948.
63. Philpot, *The Sacred Tree,* London, 1897, p. 130.
64. E. Thurston, *Castes and Tribes of Southern India,* vol. III, pp. 37 ff.
65. J. Marshall, *MIC,* vol. I, pp. 54, 68; vol. III, pls. CXVI, 29 and CXVIII, 11.
66. J.R. Rivett-Carnac, "The snake symbol in India, especially in connection with the worship of Śiva," *JASB,* 1879, vol. I, pp. 17ff.
67. *ṚV,* III.29.1-6; *AV,* VI.11.1.
68. *ṚV,* IV.13; 14; X.161; 184. Cf., A.K. Chakravorty, "The Liṅga-daivata hymns: A Rigvedic riddle?" in *IHQ,* vol. 38, 1962, pp. 226ff.
69. *ṚV,* X.1-10.
70. III.4; IV.12.
71. Chs. 260ff.
72. III.4.1.22; XI.5.1.15.
73. VI.4.22.
74. Nathan Sivin, ed., *Science and Technology in East Asia,* New York, 1977.
75. It is significant that the planet Mercury, in mythology, is regarded as the son of Soma, by Rohiṇī or by Tārā, wife of Bṛhaspati. Budha,

Mercury, married Ilā, daughter of Manu Vaivasvata. A hymn is ascribed to him. He is also called Tuṅga, Śyāmāṅga. *Ilā* or *Iḍā* is food, a libation of milk. [The Dravidian morpheme *iḷaku* means to become pliable, as melted iron; cf., *DEDR*, 510. The morpheme, Tamil *iḍa* means: to be cracked, split, be torn off as skin; *iḍavan*, clod, lump of earth; Kannada: *iḍi*, to be powdered; Tulu: *iḍe*, split, chasm. The twin morphemes, *iḍa* and *vala*, left and right may be postulated to connote the proto-Indus symbols, the left-and right-handed *svastika* connoting the vernal and autumnal suns.] The Ṛgvedic metaphor may be reconstructed: milk is mixed with the smelted ore. She is the originator of the sacrifice as an institution. Sāyaṇa treats her as the goddess of the earth. She became a man, Su-dyumna due to the intervention of Mitra-Varuṇa. She transmutes again as a woman, and Ilā marries Budha. Some synonyms of *soma*, deity are significantly relatable to smelting processes of a metallurgist: *bhagnātmā*, fractured being; *indu*, drop; *oṣadhi-pati*, lord of herbs; *sitāṁśu*, white-rayed.

76. It is extraordinary that both Caraka and Suśruta do not make any mention of mercury which was a fundamental *rasa* in later-day Āyurveda and Rasāyana in general. Date of the earliest occurrence and use of mercury of cinnabar is of fundamental importance in re-constructing Indian alchemical history. Based on the present archaeological evidence, cinnabar occurs in the Indus civilization, *c.* 2500 BC.
77. W.F. Bynum et al., ed., *Dictionary of the History of Science*, 1981, p. 184.
78. *CDIAL*, 22, *ṚV*, *akṣa*, a dice for gambling; Suśruta: the tree *Elaeocarpus ganitrus*, its seed used for rosaries and also used for dice. Pāli: *akkha*, a die, a small weight; Old Sinhala: *aka*, dice, the tree *Terminalia belerica*. *CDIAL*, 23, Kumaoni: *akhulo*, joint of sugar-cane. *CDIAL*, 24, *akṣa*, blue vitriol; Khotanese: *och*, *oc*, green, blue. *DEDR*, 3198, Gondi: *tāhka*, *Terminalia belerica*; Tamil: *tānri*, id.; Konda: *ṭāṇḍī*, *mrānu*, id.; Telugu: *tādi*, *tāṇḍra*, id.
79. J.N. Banerjea, op. cit., pp. 510ff.
80. VII.2-3; P.C. Ray, *HCAMI*, pp. 137.
81. *Rasārṇava*, XVII.70-74; P.C. Ray, *HCAMI*, p. 140.
82. *Rasahṛdaya* of Bhikṣu Govinda, *paṭala* VIII; P.C. Ray, *HCAMI*, p. 147.
83. J.N. Banerjea, op. cit., pp. 516-18.
84. In the Greek alchemic tradition, there is a reference to "sulphur water," a preparation made by heating raw sulphur with lime (what is now called calcium sulphide, giving off by hydrolysis, the gas hydrogen sulphide; when the gas is passed into metal solutions, varieties of colours are produced). Zosimus adds: "On opening the cover, do not put your nose too close to the mouth of the jar." A.J. Hopkins, op. cit., p. 49.
85. T.A. Gopinatha Rao, *Elements of Hindu Iconography*, vol. II, pp. 341-42.

86. Ibid., vol. II, p. 440.
87. Ibid., p. 521.
88. Ibid., pp. 523, 530.
89. Ibid., vol. I, part Ia, p. 58.
90. Ibid., vol. II, p. 439.
91. Used together with *bilva* in metallurgy; cf., P.C. Ray.
92. T.A. Gopinatha Rao, op. cit., vol. II, p. 537.
93. Ibid., p. 557.
94. Ibid., vol. I, p. 374.
95. Ibid., p. 285.
96. Ibid., p. 284.
97. Ibid., p. 251.
98. Ibid., pp. 202-3.
99. Ibid., p. 349.
100. Ibid., p. 310.
101. Ibid., p. 323.
102. A. Cunningham, *Marco Polo,* I, p. 287; L.A. Waddell, *The Buddhism of Tibet or Lamaism,* p. 30, n. 3.
103. L.A. Waddell, *The Buddhism of Tibet or Lamaism,* p. 389.
104. Ibid., p. 389.
105. R. Manickavāsagam, *Cittargal Paripāṣai Akarāti* (Tamil: Siddha Twilight Language Lexicon), Madras, 1982.
106. Cf., de Bry's title page of Maier's *Viatorium,* Oppenheim, 1618; J. Read, *Prelude to Chemistry,* p. 55, pl. 13.
107. Cf., J. Read, *Prelude to Chemistry,* p. 91; in Basil Valentine's *Last Will and Testament,* gold was represented in more than sixty ways: "To add to the confusion, anagrams, acrostics, and other enigmas were introduced, and various secret alphabets and ciphers came to be used by the alchemists; in some of these, letters and numerals were represented by alchemical and astrological signs. An additional barrier was erected in the shape of an extensive structure of pictorial symbolism and allegorical expression. Ideas processes, even pieces of apparatus, were represented by birds, animals, mythological figures, geometrical designs, and other emblems born of a riotous, extravagant, and superstitious imagination." This quote may as well be applied to the types of symbolisms which run riot in the Brāhmaṇa texts!
108. J. Read, *Prelude to Chemistry,* p. 38. In the royal library of Assur-banipal, king of Assyria in the seventh century BC were found tablets containing chemical terms: *guhlur,* eye-paint (from which "alcohol" is derived; cf., *guggulu* in *Atharvaveda*); *naptu* (from which is derived "naphtha"); and *sindu arqu* (from which "sandarch" is derived). The last term may as well have been derived from *sindhura.* Sandarc (Latin: *sandaraca*) is defined as red colouring (from Greek *sandarake*

realgar, red pigment from realgar), a brittle aromatic translucent resin obtained esp. from the African sandarac tree and used chiefly in making varnish and as incense. A sandarac tree is *Callitris articulata.* Realgar is derived from Arabic *rahj al-ghaar* powder of mine; an orange-red mineral consisting of arsenic sulfide and having a resinous lustre.

109. V.L. Rabinovich, "Alchemy," *The Great Soviet Encyclopedia,* p. 215.
110. "Alchemy (Muhammadan)," in *ERE,* p. 290.

10

Conclusions

Indian alchemical epochs

The fourfold epochs, depicted in a tabular form given below, spanning four millennia should be taken as a preliminary, starting framework, subject to overlaps in dates. The underlying assumption is that the four historical periods represent a *cultural continuum* and are not discrete entities.

For example, just as a Ṛgvedic geometry of Śulbasūtra draws upon the baked-brick technique of the Indus artisan, it is postulated that the Soma *yajña,* central to the Vedic alchemical process draws upon the Indus valley sublimation-distillation and smelting techniques. The yogic, tantric and *siddha* extensions of alchemical thought may be interpreted as manifestations of esoteric alchemy, internalizing the exoteric alchemic practices of the earlier epochs. Coterminous with the progress in alchemical thought, social upheavals are recognized: a rural substratum, emerges as an urban/mercantile civilization (broadly referred to as an industrial culture) in the Indus valley. The proto-*caṇḍāḷa* working on the forge and the crucible, possibly on metal extractions using cinnabar (mercuric-sulphide), and possessing the technical and skill potentials of a proto-alchemist is excluded from the mainstream of society. This exclusion seems to be coterminous with the rise of state power, and the use of gold/silver as currency media. An extraordinary phenomenon of alchemy practised by the royalty-priest consortium is received. The legal declaration and enforcement of a pernicious social order, excluding the *caṇḍāḷa* from the pale of a hierarchically classified four-*varṇa* society carries within itself the seeds of social revolt. The revolt is exemplified by the Tanṭra/ Siddha traditions and is perhaps driven underground, to operate from beer-houses and forests.

Texts	*Dates*	*Key focus*
	[ALCHEMICAL CONCEPT]	Doctrine
[*Religious focii*]	[Political economy]	
Indus valley seals	2500 BC-1700 BC [AURIFACTION]	"Cult object" sublimation apparatus
[Sun, Mother Goddess]	[Mercantile]	Lokāyata
Vedas	1500 BC-600 BC [AURIFACTION]	"Fire-altar" Soma
[Varuṇa, Agni]	[Royalty-priest consortium]	Anti-materialism?
Brāhmaṇas	600 BC-300 BC [INTERNAL ALCHEMY] [AURIFICTION]	*yajña*; yoga Immortality
[Bhakti]	[Hierarchical social classes]	Anti-materialism
Tantras/Caraka	AD 300-1500 [TANTRIC MEDICINE]	Erotic Iconography *siddhi*
[Śiva, Mother Goddess]	[Social revolt]	*bhasma/sindūra* Materialism

Alchemy: the priest-royalty and the plebeian alchemical traditions

Alchemy is not merely the pretension of making gold from base metals, a pseudo-science which evolved under the patronage of the priest-king consortium. This aspect of alchemy is exemplified in the *Śatapatha Brāhmaṇa.* This pretension resulted in the perpetuation of a devastating politico-social order of *varṇas.* The ideology and the class-cleavage resulting from the exclusion of *caṇḍāḷa* from the hierarchically ordered society militated against the broad-based development of sciences based on the *caṇḍāḷa*'s competence in leather-working, stone-cutting, metallurgy and alchemical techniques such as distillation and sublimation. In the proto-Indus, era, there are indications that sulphide ore had been used to extract copper. Marshall[1] observes that the nearest source of copper for Mohenjo-daro might have been copper mines near Ajmer (in Sirohi, Mewar and Jaipur), the Khetri and Singhana mines in particular which have been worked from very ancient times. The copper lumps do not contain tin, but contain a very small quantity of silver indicating the possibility of use of the sulphide ore which abounds in these mine sources. Similarly, the occurrence of cinnabar (mercuric sulphide) in Mohenjo-daro points to the possibility that cinnabar had been subjected to sublimation, to yield mercury.

Alchemy is a search by plebeians, which began in antiquity, for a concept, "the philosopher's stone" or (*tantra*, an extension of material phenomena) which is a general transmutation agent with great potency or *siddhas.* The governing ideology seems to be the possibility of reaching out to the masses with a "universal, affordable remedy" for illnesses. *Yakṣa* is the primordial symbol of "transmutation." These alchemists may be broadly categorised as the Yakṣa-tantra alchemical school, as distinct from the Brāhmaṇa alchemical school. The Yakṣa-tantra alchemical search based primarily on manual operations with metals and other substances, resulted in the accumulation of metallurgical, chemical and medicinal knowledge, despite the ideological and economic obstacles created by the Brāhmaṇa alchemical school.

On a philosophical plane, alchemy is concerned with the nature and transformation of matter. Matter may be inanimate or animate. The search is, in effect, a scientific urge to understand the mysteries of nature and of life. The philosophical under-pinnings link alchemy with magic, religion, mysticism and astrology, the other pseudo-sciences of antiquity. Two broad ideologies operated in ancient India: that of Lokāyata, materialism and what may be called non-materialism (or counter-ideology, to use the phrase of Debiprasad Chattopadhyaya). Lokāyata governed the rituals, symbols, technologies and practices of the Yakṣa-tantra alchemical school. Non-materialism governed the rituals, symbols, technologies and practices of the Brāhmaṇa alchemical school.

One is exemplified by the *siddha* or tantric, an adept of an esoteric cult-group possessing secret knowledge and the "powers." The other is the *āṣāḍha-bhūti*, the swindler, comparable to the "puffer" or the *souffleur*, the exoteric gold-maker of the Greek alchemical tradition; "such uninformed 'labourers in the fire' (who) believed ardently in the possibility of transmutation and sacrificed their own and their patron's resources in their never-ending quest of the Stone."[2] In both traditions, extreme groups existed, those who perform the *mahā*-type of work, the *Great Littany*, etc., which are comparable to the extremism of the Greek alchemical *Great Work* by religion-men and mystics comparable to the European "puffers": Albertus Magnus and Roger Bacon.

The fundamental premises governing the growth of alchemy are the value attached to gold and the possibility of finding a universal medicine to hurdle the economic problems and to combat diseases. The Western tradition is traced to Hermes (Hermetic art, hermetically sealed comparable to the *kampaṭṭam* or *puṭa* type of enclosures or *yantras* in smelting operations). Hermes is the Thrice-great, Hermes Trismegistos and identified with the Egyptian god, Thoth. The Indian analogue is *Trimūrti.* Brahmā is represented in iconography as a *yakṣa*: that he is represented with three faces evokes the Egyptian parallel of Hermes.

The term *rasa* is an abstraction, representing primarily the concept of "essence" or the principle of "liquidity." So is *bhasma* or *bhūti* an abstraction standing for "essence" or the principle of "irreducibility." In Jabir's Islamic alchemy, sulphur and mercury connoted the principles of "combustibility" and "fusibility or metallicity." In the Indian alchemical tradition, these are *upa-rasas,* secondary "liquid principles," secondary to the principal ones, the pure metals. The principle of "purity" was somehow linked to the alchemical foundation, the principle that produced gold. The super-powders such as the *sindūra* or *bhasma* seemed to have connoted the quintessences which had the powers to transmute. The *rasa-liṅga* unites with *śakti* to yield a power that transforms.

It is indeed tough to explain how the concept of "unity," *yoga* or "perfection," *siddhi* which is generally applied to metals got extended to the human bodies. In metallurgy as well as in medicine, the morpheme *dhātu* is used to denote the concept of "irreducibility," the elements which compose a metal-complex or -amalgam or a human-body. If the compound *suda-dohas* of the *Śatapatha Brāhmaṇa* may be interpreted as "pure body" (*suddha* + *dehas*), the problem may perhaps be resolved: just as the metal-complex may be purified to yield the colourful one, the *su-varṇa,* gold, it may be possible to aim for *siddhi* or perfection for the human body also composed of the same *dhātu* or elements. If such a concept of the "unity of matter" may be postulated, it may be possible to explain the ideological conflicts between the Lokāyata and non-materialistic schools of philosophy and contrast the Mother Goddess cults of the substratum with the Brahmanical-sacrificial doctrines which enlarge into metaphysics. The Siddha tradition of alchemy may be compared to the Greek Paracelsus (AD 1493-1541) school of iatro-chemistry, extending alchemy to medicine or diverting alchemy from the gold-making craze to using substances, *carakku,* both female- and male-*carakku* to treat diseases or three *doṣas,* imbalances in the tripartite structure of the body-complex. It is notable that the Paracelsus school uses the theory of *tria prima* or the three hypostatical concepts of sulphur, mercury and salt ("fixity") comparable to the *siddha* concepts of *tiri-kaṭukam* or three types of astringency.

Just as the traditions in contemporary civilizations used allegories, symbols and cryptic expressions to convey or in fact, "hide" the alchemical tenets, Indian alchemical tradition also used comparable techniques to cloud the esoteric practices. One school expemplified by the *Śatapatha Brāhmaṇa,* a compendious alchemical text, says that gods love the mystical. Another school exemplified by the *siddha* texts, says that the techniques should be handled only by an adept and hence, the secret code used.[3] May be, the reasons for the secrecy are traceable to the secrecy shrouding the methods of oral transmission of the Vedic texts. Interpreting *Ṛgveda* as a compendium of traditions related to aurifaction or electrum smelting, it is plausible to hypothesise that the livelihood of the artisan in the Vedic tradition depended on guarding the secret knowledge transmitted to him by his ancestors on the techniques of smelting. May be, he had only vague remembrances of the proto-Indus legacy of making gold beads and lapidary artifacts involving glazing and colouring of earthly substances. As the royal-priestly consortium took roots, the processes of transmutation including aurifiction had to be performed in extreme secrecy, perhaps within the premises of the *antaḥpura,* royal palace where (at least during the *Arthaśāstra* days) both the goldsmiths and Brāhmaṇas under the leadership of the *ṛtvij* and *purohita* lived in the same northern quarters. The journey from the industrial culture of the prato-Indus lapidary continues into the alchemical culture of the Vedic artisan, smelter of gold and silver as precious metals or currency medium, *akṣa,* gold cowrie accumulation to sustain the state power through the treasury.

Within the limited framework of the alchemical tradition, the perspective is clear and unequivocal; there are two distinct streams of alchemical tradition: one running through and traceable to the Yakṣa-Śakti Lokāyata substratum; the other to the Vedic-Brahmanical counter-ideology; and both streams seem to merge into the materialistic, mercantile traditions of the Indus valley civilization of lapidary crafts and metallurgical technologies. The *pāṣaṇḍas* and *caṇḍālas* had known how to extract metals from ores; they also knew how to make alloys, polish[4] minerals, etch[5] beads, make glass, leather,[6] alum, dyes, pigments[7] and fermented liquors. Many *yājikas* were impostors and fakers who pretended to be able to produce gold. Others, such as the *siddhas* or *yogīs*, however, were honest men who performed practical experiments in their quest for attaining "perfection" or *siddhi* or *mokṣa*, the Indian analogues of the Greek "philosopher's stone." The *amṛtam* was never found, but contributions have been made to develop techniques such as distillation, sublimation, smelting, alloying the medicinal preparations.

Some believed that fire and water combined under planetary guidance in the depths of the earth. Levels of impurity resulted in the production of silver or a base metal such as lead.

The task[8] of the Ṛgvedic artisan was to bring together *agni* and *varuṇa*, fire and water in a possible superfine combination with *soma* to yield the *ṛta*, the natural order. How the simple yet grand concept of the nature of matter gets distored into the pseudo-science of alchemy is, in effect, the sad saga of Indian alchemy; sad because manual operations were declared to be impure, low-level activities in a social order; a doctrine which killed many science potentials of a great civilization which was, in early proto-historic phases, governed by a promising Lokāyata world-view.

To quote P.C. Ray, that doyen of the history of science in India: "...it was considered equally undignified to sweat away at the forge like a Cyclops. The arts thus being relegated to the low castes, and the professions made hereditary, and the intellectual portion of the community being thus withdrawn from active participation in the arts, the how and why of phenomenon—the co-ordination of cause and effect—were lost sight of. The spirit of enquiry, gradually died out among a nation, naturally prone to speculation and metaphysical subtleties, and India for once bade adieu to experimental and inductive science."[9]

One example from the Bhakti tradition and the evolution of Sikhism may suffice to indicate the extent to which the social revolt with religious overtones had seeped into the Indian psyche: [Note the alchemical terms highlighted].

Bhairo fifth Guru

By the Guru's grace, obtain thou the True Wealth (*sāch padhārath*). Accepting as true the Lord's well, endure thou it willingly, O man. Rising early every day *in-drink* thou the Lord's elixir (*Rāma rasāyan nit oth pīvoh*), this wise, thou shalt live eternally. With thy tongue, utter (*rasnā kahoh*), thou any God, God, God's name. In the Dark Age (*kaljug*), one is emancipated (*udhār*) only through the name.

Nanak utters the name of the Creator-lord (*brahm bichār*).

The saga of Indian alchemy is thus the saga of a potter-lapidary of the proto-Indus epoch producing material artefacts (including glazed clay or steatite or copper/bronze/gold/silver artefacts) ending up as an "untouchable." What started promisingly, as a pseudo-science concerned with the nature of matter and transformation of matter, with remarkable potentials to advance a scientific temper based on technology ends up in metaphysics and a fatalist world-view based on theories of *karma*, which originally connoted work and in the gambols of metaphysics gets distorted to mean an inexorable process of uncontrollable action and reaction. The metaphysical excursus is also used by the sacerdotal class to justify the pernicious system of *varṇa* and *jāti*. This social or political-economy dimension of alchemy seems to have no parallels in any other civilization.

References

1. Marshall, *MIC*, 1931, pp. 483, 489; Mackay, *FEM*, pp. 479-94.
2. *Chambers Encyclopaedia*, London, 1967, p. 233.
3. *Akattiyar Pūraṇa Cūttiram*, song 216; R. Manickavaasagam, *Padinen cittarkaḷ paripāṣai akarāti* (Dictionary of the "Twilight Language" of 18 Sittars), (Tamil work), Madras, 1982, p. 17: *tāminta cūttirattai-k-koḷiyā tīntāl talai terittu-p-pokumaṭā cattiyamāy-c-cannen naaminda-p-paḍi connom yogi-k-kīvāy*. The import is that the work in song was composed only for the benefit of the Sittar disciples and should not fall into the hands of the "un-initiated," since the process of learning involved many years of dedicated lessons from the "teacher" or *guru*.
4. Polishing of mineral and stone beads was done by garnet and corundum powder; cf., O.N. Bhargava, *Indian Minerals*, 17, 1963.
5. Etching of carnelian beads by the proto-Indus artisan involved a chemical process using soda carbonate. Cf., Vats, *EH*, p. 401.
6. *Mahāvagga* (VIII.3) and *Cullavagga* (IX.1) refer to shoes and bowls studded with *maṇi, valuriya, phaṭika,* and *kāca*. In this context, it may be reasonable to interpret *kāca* as a lump of gold or a gold bead and not as a glass bead, an interpretation given in *Śatapatha Brāhmaṇa*, XIII, 2.6.8. It is notable that stones and gold are linked with leather, a substance handled by a *caṇḍāḷa*; the latter's proficiency in the lapidary craft of making gold beads gains added significance in the context of the alchemical practices of the royal-priestly consortium of the Brāhmaṇa days and the treatment of a *caṇḍāḷa* as an *a-varṇa*.

7. Hematite, bauxite, magnesite and cuprite were used to colour some Indus wares. Cf., P.C. Ray, *HCAMI*, p. 14. Cf., *Viṣṇudharmottaram* (*c.* fifth century AD) (3.40.24-29): Many metals are used are pigments or *raṅga-dravyas: sindūra* (red lead), *haritāla* (yellow pigment), *hiṅgulaka* (vermilion). There is a specific reference to the use of the juice of *sindūra* plant in all the colours. *Mānasollāsa* (twelfth century AD) (3.1.156-57): conch-shell used for white colour; three kinds of red are from *darada* (red lead) for reddish brown, *ālataka* (red sap) for blood red and *gairika* (red chalk) for dark red; for black colour, *kajjala* (soot). S.S. Misra, op. cit., p. 109.
8. The founder of drugs on mountains; *ṚV*, V.85.2.
9. P.C. Ray, *HCAMI*, p. 240.

11

A Survey of Sources for History of Alchemy

Reality of the priestly and plebeian traditions: sources for the historian

Egypto-Greek alchemical traditions use many associations and symbols which may be useful for a historian in interpreting allegorical texts or pictorials.

In a simplified perspective of concordances, between "symbols" and "reality," within a universal alchemical tradition, the oral transmission (to exclusive categories of people) of the *Ṛgveda* tradition exemplified in procedure manuals of the Brāhmaṇas, underscored by the *rahasya* (secret) processes, gains definitive alchemical overtones. Those who added mystical meanings, those who made speculative generalizations in natural philosophy, are, generally, those who have left the legacy of written alchemical works. The artisans who continued with their manual operations and who indeed could have harnessed the science potentials of alchemy had to make do with non-written modes of "documenting" or communicating the core of their works. The icons[1] in stone and clay are one such mode of recording; this renders the process of reconstructing alchemical historical, plebeian reality an extremely challenging task.

The requirements of a true science are that the communication should be simple, intelligible to a layman so that "reality" is not misrepresented; exchange of knowledge should be free; knowledge should be cumulative, continuous and based on experimental observations; all these desiderata are denied in all alchemical traditions, thus negating their science potentials.

1. *Archaeological sources*

In Kulli sites of Makran, southern Baluchistan and the Zhob valley culture (*c.* third millennium BC), numerous clay figurines of women wear oval pendants which resemble cowrie shells. These pendants hang from each of three rows of necklaces, below which are strings made of beads which reach upto the waist. In sites around Zhob river which flows north and northeast into the Indus plain, terracotta figurines have been found with remarkably uniform features which lead Aurel Stein to conjecture that they may represent some tutelary goddess.[2] Mackay conjectures that the Mohenjo-daro statuettes with fan-shaped head-dress and pannier-like projections (which might have been used as lamps) indicate a connection with the Mother Goddess cult.[3] "As household deities they were preserved perhaps in a niche in the wall in almost every house in the ancient Indus valley cities ... a conventionalized *liṅga* in yellow sandstone at Harappa with finely cut coils and necklaces may have had a *yoni* base, and six occurred in an earthenware jar with some small pieces of shell, a unicorn seal, stone pestles and a stone palette. Some miniature conical baetyls have a sort of ring round the body which has been regarded as a possible *yoni*."[4]

Saraswatī civilization

The Goddess cult is less defined in the archaeological finds of the Indus civilizations than in Mesopotamia or Egypt or even in Iran, Elam, Palestine, and Anatolia. It is unclear if the Ahura Mithras and Anahita—Father and Mother symbols of nature—of Achaemenian Iran (*c.* second millennium BC) are comparable to Mitra-Varuṇa and Aditi (?or the womb of *ṛta*, ?mother of Varuṇa; "she is what has been born and what will be born"[5]—*ṚV*, I.8, 9, 10) in the Ṛgvedic text. *Taittirīya Āraṇyaka* (X.1.7) treats the Goddess Umā, as the daughter of the sun. In a vague conceptualization of goddess as resource, *Śatapatha Brāhmaṇa* states that, "Agni took her (Lakṣmī's) food; Soma, kingly authority; Varuṇa, imperial authority; Mitra, marital energy; Indra, force; Bṛhaspati, priestly glory; Savitṛ, dominion; Pūṣan, splendour; Saraswatī, nourishment,"[6] If the dried bed of Hakra or Ghaggar in Rajasthan is identified with Saraswatī of antiquity, the concept of Mother Goddess as a river-goddess may perhaps, symbolize the principal economic resource, the fertilizing waters of antiquity [cf., her association with Brahmā, represented in iconography as a *yakṣa* type].

The Khafaje symbols on a vase, of a goddess, the waters and other alchemical symbols may be hazily, vaguely related to this Goddess cult (Earth-mother), geophysical framework. Perhaps, the reconstruction of the reality of plebeian beliefs in antiquity may have to start from the traditions of *jātras* and the fierce *grāma devatās* (village tutelary deities) such as Mahā Māī (Great Mother), Śītalā (chilling the small-pox), Māriamma (mother of seasons), Manasā (snake-mother) and those *yakhiṇīs* with abodes in trees.

2. *Anthropological sources*

Customs such the Mātaṅgī and Baṅgāramma Mother Goddess cults and settling scores between *mādigas* (a *caṇḍāḷa* class) and the Brāhmaṇas are of extraordinary importance in an anthropological perspective which may yield some clues as to the origins of the *caṇḍāḷa* as category "excluded from the social structure," who plays a key role in the Indian alchemical tradition as a counterfoil to the Brāhmaṇa. Such customs may symbolize a social revolt of antiquity as classes struggled to gain control of mineral resources, gold and silver, in particular which had gained economic exchange value.

[A Brāhmaṇa could indeed have derived great profit by consulting and collaborating with the true artisans instead of engaging in the great *yajñas* and the history of sciences in India might have been vastly different. That he broke away from *caṇḍāḷa* is the central enigma of Indian alchemy, perhaps of India's social history. But it said that, it is not in the domain of history to speculate or ask, "what if" questions. But then, history has to be humanized too, by underscoring the foibles of metaphysical masks.]

3. *Textual sources: manuscripts*

Indian alchemical texts are many and varied; many have not been studied at all. There are many texts of the Siddha tradition in the Oriental Manuscripts Library in Madras. A note is included on the Indo-Tibetan alchemy and medicine and related source material. There are many manuscripts of the Arabic alchemical tradition in Hyderabad and other places in India. In this context, it may be relevant to summarize a note by H.E. Stapleton (late Principal of Presidency College, Calcutta) dated 19 April 1936 addressed to George Sarton, editor of *ISIS* (vol. XXVI, 1, no. 71, December 1936, pp. 127-31): Stapleton's search for alchemical manuscripts in India is mentioned in a "Note on the Arabic MSS. on alchemy in the Asafiyah Library, Hyderabad," *Archeion*, 14, 57-61; *ISIS* 19, 431. In 1935, he found "62 volumes of alchemical treatises in Arabic in that library, apart from 26 volumes of Persian treatises, 3 Urdu ones and

4 printed (modern) works in Arabic.... The total number of Arabic treatises had risen to 300 . . . (included were) alchemical views of Khalid ibn Yazid (AD 720) . . . treatises in the Rampur library . . . 10 alchemical MSS. in the rooms of the Asiatic Society of Bengal . . . (including) *Kitab-ilal* of Balinas and Ar-Razi's *Sirr al-asrar* . . . small number of alchemical MSS. in Khuda Bakhsh Library at Bankipore, Patna . . . (including) Al-jildaki's works . . . and two by Ibn Sina . . . (at Rampur) . . . 45 volumes labelled *Kimiya* containing treatises in Arabic...of Qadi Sayyid Abd al-Jabbar al Hamadani (AD 1086)...copy of a *Risalah* on *kimiya* of Aristotle for Alexander, which is stated to have been translated from Greek into Syriac by Yazdin, the Christian Wazir of Kisra (? Khusraw Parviz, AD 590-627)...and translated from Syriac into Arabic for Al-Mansur (AD 754-75). *Adhdhakhirat al-Iskandariyah,* said to have been written by Hermes, and discovered by Balinas. The latter gave it to Aristotle (!), who dedicated it to Alexander. It was then engraved on thick plates of gold, which were placed in a chest of gold enclosed in another chest and concealed in the wall of a church at Amuriyah.[7] Here it was discovered when Al-Mu'tasim (who died in AD 841) captured the town, and it was then translated from Greek into Arabic. The story is perhaps given some verisimilitude by the discovery of the inscribed gold plates, in three languages, of Xerxes, recently found at Persepolis. Another copy of this treatise is in the A.S.B. Library...Khalid (who was born in AD 672) derived some of his alchemical knowledge from a monk called Mariyanos...Jabir appears to have been the private (court) alchemist of Ja'far as-Sadiq...an authentic copy of the actual *Kitab ar-Rahmah* of Jabir (in the Asafiyah library...) found under Jabir's pillow, when he died in AD 815.... The more I think, however, of the amount of work that has still to be done, the more idiotic I feel at ever having ventured to begin this enquiry at all...."

This impassioned note by Stapleton was written in 1936 and his statements about the amount of work that awaits the science historian are valid even today. Only, the resource base has widened beyond Arabic into Tibetan and Tamil and significant insights have been provided by brilliant expositions on Lokāyata (cf., Debiprasad Chattopadhyaya), and on Chinese (cf., Needham) and Greek (cf., Hopkins) alchemical legacies which provide leads to unravel the Indian alchemical traditions and its science potentials, inhibited in a socio-political context.

Bibliographical notes in Walter's dissertation

The following notes are entirely based on the references used in Michael Lee Walter's Ph.D. dissertation, "The role of alchemy and medicine in Indo-Tibetan tantrism," 1980 (University Microfilms International, reference 8024583). The objective of this bibliographical note is to indicate the extent of work that needs to be done in the subject area of Indian alchemical traditions and science potentials. The rationale for this extensive extract from Walter's path-breaking dissertation is that it costs US $50 to get a copy of the dissertation and the material he has collected are invaluable for a student of alchemy in particular and ancient social history of India, in general.

Secrecy

The Egyptian priesthood, according to Zosimos, a third century alchemist, was prohibited from writing down anything concerning metallurgical matters.[8] This is important because of the virtual unanimity of scholarly opinion tracing Greek alchemical traditions to Egyptain heretic orders though no alchemical text from the latters' hands is extant. Similar problems of lost Sanskrit alchemical works are well-known.[9]

Andre-Jean Festugiere, *La Ravelation d'Hermes Trismegiste*, Paris, 1949-54 in his supplement to vol. I, mentions that "Nagarjuna (according to an article of Palmyr Cordier, q.v.) also had inscribed a medical formula on a pillar. Of course, this is not technically the same as concealing it within a pillar intentionally."[10] *Gter ma* in Tibetan, is one revelatory procedure. Another procedure involves vision, called *dgons gter.*

Gnosticism and Tantrism

On both doctrinal and practical points, many similarities have been noticed between Gnosticism and Tantrism. Guiseppe Tucci, *Tibetan Painted Scrolls*, vol. I, Rome, 1952, 210f.; W.Y. Evans-Wentz, *Tibet's Great Yogi Milrepa*, London, 1928, pp. 8-12; Helmut Hoffman, *Tibet: A Handbook*, Bloomington, Indiana, n.d.; idem, *The Religions of Tibet*, London, 1961, 51f.; Mircea Eliade, *Yoga: Immortality and Freedom*, New York, 1969; Edward Conze, "Buddhism and Gnosis," in *Further Buddhist Studies; Selected Essays of Edward Conze*, pp. 15-32, London, 1975. The role of Gnosticism in alchemy is in H.J. Sheppard, "Gnosticism and Alchemy," *Ambix*, VI, 1957-58, pp. 86-101; idem, "The redemption theme and Hellenistic alchemy," *Ambix*, VII, 1959, pp. 42-46 also including a recapitulation of Father Andre Jean Festugiere's classic work, *La revelation d'Hermes Trismegiste*, Paris, 1950-54 on common points in Hermetic and Gnostic literature.

In Buddhist *sādhanās* and tantric exegetical works, a reflex of the Hellenistic alchemy's criterion of identity between microcosm and macrocosm is recurrent: e.g., *lus ni gzal yas khan du gyur/sans rgyas kun gyi yan dag rten*, "the body shall become a palace, an immaculate receptacle for all the Buddhas," says Tson-kha-pa, cf., Alex Wayman, *The Buddhist Tantras: Light on Indo-Tibetan Esotericism*, New York, 1973, p. 83, cf., also "Macrocosm and Microcosm" in J. Woodroffe, *Introduction to Tantra Śāstra*, fifth edn., Madras, 1969. Tantric and Gnostic schemes both use, on their path of purification, the physical world to overcome the physical world. "Tantric and Gnostic practice both require the commitment of the adherent in a battle with the forces of Matter and mortality."[11]

H.J. Sheppard, "Gnosticism and Alchemy," *Ambix*, VI, 1957-58, pp. 86-101 refers to tensions between "practical" alchemy and religious Gnosticism and concludes that ultimately, Gnostic soteriology came to dominate and then replace interest in applied alchemy. "The picture is quite clear in India, where even the earliest Tantric literature [the *Mañjuśrīmūlakalpa* and the *Guhyasamājatantra* (*c.* third-sixth centuries AD; a Buddhist work in written form), for example] is specialized in content and purpose. Such factors as these must also be taken into account when one attempts to define an esoteric tradition as being 'this' or 'that' based on the study of a small number of texts."[12] For the time of the composition of *Guhyasamājatantra*, cf., Bhattacharyya, "Tāntrika Culture among the Buddhists," *The Cultural Heritage of India*, vol. IV, p. 263; Maurice Winternitz, "Notes on the *Guhyasamājatantra* and the Age of the Tantras," *IHQ*, IX, 1933, pp. 1-10; Alex Wayman, *Yoga of the Guhyasamājatantra.* The Arcane Lore of Forty Verses, a Buddhist tantra commentary, Delhi, 1978, p. 97.

Limitations of Ray's work

"Ray's *History of Chemistry in Ancient and Medieval India* and the works of Berthelot are, indeed, 'classics' in their fields...lacking any sensitivity to the religious dimensions of the works with which they dealt, and paying scant regard[13] to the cultural milieus in which they functioned. They, like many others, have assumed that texts largely composed of formulae and lacking in doctrinal content reflect the secular nature of the subject matter. Is it not just as reasonable to assume that, like the highly technical yogic and meditational manuals of various traditions, they are merely expanding on practices which presuppose a spiritual preparation and orientation?... Cf., C.S. Narayanaswami Aiyar, 1925, pp. 597-614; Bhudev Mookerji, *Rasajalanidhi*, a five volume compendium of recipes and advice culled from many alchemical works as well as oral teachings from his *rasācārya*, alchemical teacher."[14]

Tantrism, medicine and pharmacology

The *Gso-dpyad-tshogs-kyi-man-nag-rin-chen-'khruns-dpe'-bstan-pa* is a medical text of great rarity, "believed to date from the time of Khrisron-lde-btsan himself; in the colophon we read that this work was composed by the Indian scholar Śāntigarbha and the seven royal physicians to the Tibetan court after they had discussed medical matters...according to its reproduction on p. 583 of *Three Tibetan Medical Texts from the Library of Ri-bo-che Rje-drun Rin-po-che of Padma-bkod*, Tibetan Nyingmapa Monastery, Camp no. 5, Arunachal Pradesh, 1973."[15]

On pharmacological traditions in India, cf., A.K. Ghosh, "European Interest in Botanical Studies in India from Medieval times," in D.M. Bose et al., eds., *A Concise History of Science in India*, New Delhi, 1971, pp. 400-402. On Tibetan medicine, cf., Joseph Rehmann, *Besch-reibung einer Thibetānischen Handapotheke, ein Beitrag zur Kenntnis Arzneykunde Asiens*, St. Petersburg, 1811. A forthcoming article by Christopher I. Beckwith in the *Journal of the American Oriental Society*, "The Introduction of Greek Medicine in Tibet in the Seventh and Eighth Centuries."[16]

C.J. Meulenbeld, *The Mādhavanidāna and Its Chief Commentary*, chaps. 1-10, Leiden, 1974. He merely lists the most important and plausible alternatives, in descending order of preference while interpreting the Tantric terminology, *sandhābhāṣā*. "For now we must be content with some more 'standard' approach, relying (unfortunately) on standard Ayurvedic studies whose applicability to Tantric contexts is yet untested."[17]

Śaivite influence in Tibet

Many Tibetan alchemical works are non-Buddhist, in particular Śaivite, cf., the colophons of two versions of the *Sarveśvara-rasāyana roga-hara śarīra pustaka nāma/ Thams-cad-kyi-dban-phyug-bcud-len-nad-thams-cad-joms-sin-lus-kyi-stobs-rgyas-par-byed-pa-zes-bya-ba,* from the Bstan-'gyur. In the Snarthan edition as printed by Ray (p. 451) we read: *dban-phyug gis bstan pa'i rin po che'i bcud len grub par rdzogs so.* Here is finished the text on acquiring the precious elixir, as taught by Īśvara. "Inasmuch as Īśvara is an epithet of Śiva, this is a text either revealed by Śiva or taught by one of his followers. The edition utilized by Berthold Laufer in his translation and study [at the conclusion of Henrich Laufer's *Beitrage zur Kenntnis der tibetischen Medicin,* Berlin and Leipzig, 1900, pp. 84ff.] contains this additional statement in its colophon: 'Der Yogin Civadāca aus Haridhobar and der aus Udyāna haben die Schrift in Bhootra ubersetzt.' Explicitly Śaivite materials are also found in VyaaDi-pa's *Rasaśāstra Siddhināma/Dnul-chu-grub-pa'i-bstan-bcos* (Book no. of the Sde-dge Bstan-' gyur)."[18] This Vyāḍi-pa text is suspiciously similar in places to two alchemical texts from Peking Tanjur and perhaps may be traced to a common root. The Peking Tanjur texts are: *Gser-'gyur-gyi-bstan-bcos-bsdus-pa/Rasāyana-Śāstra-uddhṛti* and *Gser-'gyur-gyi-rtsi/Dhātuvāda,* Suzuki edition, nos. 5803 and 3236 respectively.[19]

On the "Bower Manuscript," cf., Georg Buhler, "The New Sanskrit MS. from Mingai," *Weiner Zeitschrft fur die Kunde des Morgenlandes,* V, 1891, pp. 103-10; and A.F.R. Hoernle, "On the date of the Bower Manuscript," *JRASB,* LX, 1891, pp. 79-96.

Alchemy and tantra

"Nearly all large alchemical texts in Brahmanic and Buddhist traditions are either Tantras or chapters within them, or Tantric commentarial literature,"[20] cf., Ray, p. 128 for a list of representative tantric works. The largest Tibetan works on alchemy yet discovered are from Bo-don-pa's exegeses on the Kālacakratantra system: the *Dus-'khor-nas-gsuns-pa'i-gser-'gyur-dan-bcud-len-la-sogs-pa'i-sbyor-ba-bsad-pa,* the *Bcud-len-gyi-mannag-bsad-pa,* and the *Gser-'gyur-dan-bcud-len-la-sogs-pa'i-sbyor-ba-bsad-pa,* totalling 330 pages, are found in volumes two and nine of his published collected works [*Encyclopaedia Tibetica: the Collected Works of Bo-don Pan-chen Phyogs-las-rnam-rgyal,* edited by S.T. Kazi, New Delhi, 1970.]

Mircea Eliade, *The Forge and the Crucible, the Origins and Structures of Alchemy,* New York, 1971, p. 129: "...both Tantrist and alchemist strive to dominate 'matter.' They do not withdraw from the world as do the ascetic and metaphysician, but dream of conquering it and changing its ontological regime."

Sanskrit *vidhyādhara* is a knowledge holder; Tibetan synonym, *rig 'dzin*, magician. In tantric contexts, the term may denote a group of spirits or human beings with magical powers; they form a retinue of Śiva, Vajrapāṇi or to Padmasambhava. Jean Przyluski has noted a probable Indian influence in Hermetic philosophy concerned with the question of the *vidyādhara* in "Les Vidyārāja; contribution a l'historie de la magie dans les sects Mahāyānistes," *Bulletin de l'Ecole francaise d' extreme Orient*, XXIII, 1923, pp. 301-18; see especially pp. 317-18. According to him and Jean Filliozat, *Le Kumāra-tantra de Rāvan.a et les texts parallels indiens, tibetains, chinois, cambodgien et arabe*, Cahiers de la Societe Asiatique, Premiere Serie, tome IV, Paris, 1937, p. 148 and to judge by many tantric *sādhanās*, *vidyādharas* more often than not are "deified magicians with tremendous powers...."[21]

Mercury: transmutation and medicine

The references to "elixir" in dealing with a particular drug may indeed be "medical hyperbole": an Indian practice which goes back to the *mantric* medicine of the *Atharvaveda* and the Soma hymns of the *Ṛgveda*; cf., Henry R. Zimmer, *Hindu Medicine*, Baltimore, 1948, pp. 29-31.

Examples of the works in mercurial medicine (*rasa-cikitsā*; though transmutation or physical immortality are not the stated goal in such works, supranatural results are mentioned; hence, these may be brought within a broad definition of alchemy) are: *Dnul-chu-rjen-par-za-ba'i-thabs* of the First Dalai Lama, Dge-'dun-grub-pa (b. 1391) [Tohoku Catalogue number 5542] and the *Bcud-len-gyi-ril-bu-sgrubs-nas-spyod-tshul* by the recent Dge-lugs-pa scholar Dnul-chu Dharmabhadra (1772-1851) [on pp. 419-25 of the *Collected Works (Gsun 'bum) of Dnul-chu Dharmabhadra*, vol. II, New Delhi, 1973].

Rasa-rasāyanasiddhi is mentioned in Benoytosh Bhattacharya, ed., *Sādhanamālā*, Gaekwad's Oriental Series, nos. 26 and 41, Baroda, 1925-28, p. 250.

Recipes for mercurial elixirs are very common in Tibet, "at all times and in all traditions...." The two principal Sanskrit terms for alchemy are *rasāyana* (Tibetan *bcud kyi len* or *bcud kyis len*) and *dhātuvāda*. The former, the earlier formulations, originally applied to the use of elixirs for longevity made of vegetable products;[22] it is even referred to in the *Yogasūtras* of Patañjali (composed AD 300-

500), according to the unanimous opinion of its commentators; cf., Pensa, Corrado, "On the Purification Concept in Indian Tradition, with Special Reference to Yoga," *East and West*, XIX, 1964, pp. 194-228. The latter refers almost exclusively to metallic transmutation, stemming from its original meaning "chemistry and metallurgy" [Ray, p. 239]. Two points need to be made about these terms. *Rasāyana* as an organised practice is best known to us an one of the eight branches (*aṣṭāṅgas*) of traditional Ayurvedic practice. It deals with regeneratives and restoratives, "elixirs" in the popular sense of the word, in such works as the *Caraka* and *Suśruta* Saṁhitās... historical relationship between it used in early yogic and medical literature...certainly deserves a detailed study. The only two essays which attempt to relate these two conceptions of *rasāyana* in a cogent manner are Arion Rosu's "Considerations sur une technique du Rasāyana Āyurvedique," *Indo-Iranian Journal*, XVII, 1975, pp. 1-29; and P. Ray, "Origin[23] and Tradition of Alchemy," *IJHS*, II, 1967, pp. 1-21.

Dhātuvādī: one able to create wealth!

"*Dhātuvāda*, unlike *rasāyana*, has no calque in Tibetan it would presumably be *khams kyi smra ba* and *gser 'gyur rtsi*...as an equivalent is certainly a random translation, as is *Mahāvyutpatti* #3754, where *dhātuvādī*, 'an alchemist,' is rendered by *nor bsgyur mkhan*, 'one able to create wealth.' Viduśekhara Bhattacharya long ago noted this discrepancy, adding that *gser 'gyur rtsi* would be *suvarṇa parivartana rasa* ["Sanskrit Treatises on Dhātuvāda or Alchemy as translated into Tibetan," *Ācharyya Ray Commemoration Volume*, Calcutta, 1932, pp. 121-35; p. 13 esp.]. This lack of consistency in dealing with the old Indian term for metallic alchemy would seem to allow us to conclude that no organized body of knowledge identified with *dhātuvāda* reached the Tibetans, who consistently use *boud len* when referring to metallic, non-metallic, and 'tonic.' This is rather surprising, considering the large number of contacts and influences of Indian chemistry and medicine in Tibetan civilization."[24]

According to P. Ray, 1956, p. 71, there is only one recipe containing mercury in the *Aṣṭāṅgahṛdaya* of Vāgbhaṭa (ninth century AD), which along with the *Caraka* and *Suśruta* Saṁhitās constitute the *bṛhattrayī*, the "three greats" of Indian medicine.

For a discussion of the *dhātu* concept in Indian medicine, cf., Johannes Nobel, *Ein alter medizinischer Sanskrit-text und Seine Deutung*

[Supplement no. 11 of the *JAOS*, appended to vol. LXXI/3, 1951, p. 35; pp. 7-12 esp. *Vajrakāya, vajra* body is the reward for the successful alchemist in the *dhātuvāda.* V. Bhattacharya, "Sanskrit Treatises on Dhātuvāda or Alchemy as translated into Tibetan," *Acharya Prafulla Chandra Ray Commemoration Volume,* Calcutta, 1932, p. 135; recipe in the *Rasārṇavatantra: kṣīra-hārasca jīrṇante vajrakāyo bhavennaraḥ;* cf., P.C Ray's edn., 1908, 257. *Bāhyantara-amṛta-kalpa/ Phyinan-bdud-rtsi-bcud-len-gdams-pa* of the Tāntrika and alchemist VyaaDi-pa [Peking Bstan-'gyur, vol. 69, p. 215], best known for his metallic and mercurial recipes; include the spiritual bases of psychophysical experiences (in diagnosis).

About O.P. Jaggi,[25] "The author presents chapter's subtitle physiology of *kuṇḍalinīyoga,* the *āsanas* of *haṭhayoga,* and the literature and equipment of tantric alchemists, among other subjects. Unfortunately, he brings forth utterly no new data, does not attempt a synthesis of what is already known, and nowhere even tries to define tantric medicine. He apparently assumes that we already know what it is.... Let us set forth a few traits which distinguish Tantric medicine: (1) Its practice within ritual contexts; (2) its use to prolong and strengthen the ascetic's life in connection with his religious practices; (3) its use to achieve supernatural powers (*siddhis*) in the same connection. Thus, we see that it is distinct from a strictly alchemical practice in that it does not directly seek an elixir of life rendering true immortality or a substance which transmutes base metals into nobler ones. Nevertheless, it is based on the same principles as alchemy."[26]

One Vāgbhaṭa

The edition of Paṇḍita Śrīdharmānandāśrama, Delhi, 1977 of Vāgbhaṭa's *Rasaratna Samuccaya* has a colophon on each *adhyāya* of the text attesting to its authorship by Vāgbhaṭācārya, son of Siṁhagupta the glorious lord of medicine. Jolly fixes a later date for this Vāgbhaṭa II: thirteenth to fourteenth centuries. [Julius Jolly, *Medicin,* Grundiss der Indo-Arischen Philologie und Altertumskunde, band III, heft 2, Strassburg, 1901, pp. 29.] "This is later than the flowering of mercurial alchemy, but no scholar has as yet undertaken any explanation of the hiatus here."[27]

The two-Vāgbhaṭa theory has been criticized [without reconciling the two works so different in orientation] by Dinesh C. Bhattacharya, "Date and Works of Vāgbhaṭa the Physician," *Annals of the Bhandarkar*

Oriental Research Institute, vol. XXVII, 1947, pp. 112-27.

A single author theory is ascribed to by Walter (in lieu of any more thorough research), stating that this would at least bring into agreement dates for the flourishing of Indian (and Indo-Tibetan) alchemy and the birth of the medical system which most clearly shows its impact.

South Indian Siddha: Integration of tantrism, mercurial medicine, and chemistry

Another mercurial medicine work, focusing on pharmaceutical use of mercury is *Ānandakandam*. A study and precise translation of portions of this work is in: B. Rama Rao, "Ānandakandam: A Mediaeval Treatise of South India," *BIHM*, vol. I, nos. 1-2, 1971, pp. 7-16; vol. II, no. 3, pp. 121-29. This work and *Rasaratna Samuccaya* may contain references to transmutation; this needs further research.

Siddha system has remained popular in south India and for centuries combined mercurial medicine and chemistry to a degree not achieved in either Ayurvedic, alchemical, or Rasacikitsā teachings...none of its major texts (which number in the hundreds) in various south Indian languages and scripts have been translated...traces its origins and traditions back to the *siddhas*, i.e., perfected tantric yogins. "So permeated by alchemical notions is this school that the primary qualification for a *siddha* physician is that he be a tantric practitioner and an alchemist, or the son of an alchemist. Thus, this highly organized school of therapeutics based upon metallic medicinal compounds and alchemical procedures is the only tradition in India or Tibet which may be referred to without qualification as practising 'tantric alchemy' and 'tantric medicine' to the exclusion of everything else."[28] All the following articles have been published in *BIHM*. P. Ray, and D.N. Bose, et al. devote a total of four pages only to this school!

P. Gurusiromani, "A Short Note on History of Siddha Medicine," vol. II, no. 2, 1972, 78f.; K. Palanichamy, tr., "Siddhas—Their Attainments and Their Role in Medicine" (extract from *Cyclopaedic Dictionary*), vol. III, no. 2, 1973, pp. 71-73; idem, "Basic Principles of Siddha Medicine," vol. II, no. 2, pp. 80-82; D.V. Subba Reddy, "History of Siddha Medicine: Need for Further Detailed Studies," vol. III, no. 4, pp. 182-85.

Folklore

Kathāsaritsāgara, a collection of tales and *Mānasollāsa* (sixteenth century), an encyclopaedia, are popular works which contain references to alchemical procedures.[29] There are also biographies (actually hagiographies) of *mahāsiddhas* in Tibet usually carrying the title such as *Sgrub-thob-brgyad-bcu-rtsa-bzi'i-rnam-thar.* The most famous *mahāsiddhas* in tantrism are the immortals, usually enumerated as eighty-four; included in their ranks are alchemists Cārpaṭi, Nāgārjuna, and Govinda. Overlapping with this conception, Nāthas are "believed to be immortal demigods and preachers of the sect for all ages; ...they are still living in the Himalayan region; sometimes they are regarded as the guardian spirits of Himalayan peaks."[30]

Purification

Pañcabhūta viśuddhi or simply, *bhūta viśuddhi* is a fivefold purification dealing with "subtle elements" (*pañcatanmātrāṇi* or *de tsam lna* in both Hindu and Buddhist tantrism) of the yogin's body with its abstract constituents: earth (solidity), water (liquidity), fire (warmth, "liveliness"), air (gaseousness), and ether (any hollow within body). These are brought into correspondence with other groupings such as *pañcajānāni, pañca-skandhāḥ, pañca-indriyāṇi, pañca-mahā-bhūtāni,* and *pañca-kulāni* based on the pervasive influence of *pañca-tathāgatāḥ.* Hindu tantrism tends to resolve these elements into *Prakṛti* (the personification of the material basis of all existence) or some manifestation thereof.[31] This schema is adapted in the yogic alchemical context: cf., Corrado Pensa, "On the purification concept in Indian tradition, with special reference to Yoga," *East and West,* XIX, 1964, pp. 194-228. Terminology used are: "purification," "desiccation," "reduction," and "oxidation."[32] In an agonizing search for truth, artificial means to lengthen life provide a greater opportunity to continue the search. Nātha *siddha*: "For *mukti* worth the name...the body must be preserved and perfected, and liberation is thus attainable only through perfection and preservation of the body by the application of the *rasa*...."[33]

Doctrines

Countering the Mādhyamika school of logical argumentation, the Vijñānavāda school asserted that consciousness is real while objects are illusory; both schools accept that only knowledge will free us from worldly illusion. Asaṅga (*c.* AD 375-430) is the founder of the Vijñānavāda school and also considered the founder of

Buddhist tantrism. To him is also attributed the authorship of *Guhyasamājatantra* which has been refuted by Wayman, 1973, p. 15 (op. cit.) and in *Yoga of the Guhyasamājatantra*. The Arcane Lore of Forty Verses, a Buddhist tantra commentary, p. 97.

P.C. Ray,[34] ed., *śloka* 18: *karma yogena devesi prāpyate piṇḍa-dhāraṇam/rasaśca pavanaśca iti karmayogo dvidhā smṛtaḥ*: "Through *karmayoga* (i.e., the Great Work), oh Goddess, preservation of the body is attained: that Great work is known to be of two parts: *rasa* (mercury) and *pavana* (*prāṇa*)."

Layers of ascending realities are posited;[35] in each layer, beings reside who transmit knowledge or aid in removing obstacles. Cf., Lindsay, op. cit., 1970, pp. 325, 336f. on the role of the Gnostic *daimones*; the Goddess Prajñāpāramitā and the "Glorious Yakṣiṇī of the Bodhi Tree" (*śrīvaṭayakṣiṇī*) reveal recipes to the Buddhist Nāgārjuna in his *Rasaratnākara*, Ray, 316f.[36] There is no Hermes-Thoth (Graeco-Egyptian deity, revealer of all traditional sciences and alchemic teacher) in Hindu tantrism. The closest comparison is with Śiva in Hindu alchemical tantras. Tibet has a figure comparable to Hermes: *Padmasambhava* (lit., born of a lotus, Brahmā). He is an esoteric adept, a revealer of traditional wisdom, he is deified but does not lone his historical role as a teacher and founder of an important movement. He is the second Buddha (*sans-rgyas gnis pa*), a historical person to a sect which worships him, the Rnin-ma-pa. "Indian alchemy really flourished only within the lineages and sub-culture of *siddha*-yogins who lived aloof from society and mixed Hinduism and Buddhism—basically in their Tantric forms—at will."[37] Secrecy is fundamental, in "initiation" or communicating essentials from teacher to pupil: Padmasambhava secretly instructed khri-sron-Ide-btsan and his other spiritual sons at night in the temples at Bsam-yas.[38]

In Rnin-ma and Bon yogic and ritual literature, the doctrine of the transmutation of elements is applied; the goal is for the yogin to become immortal. A distinctive feature that pervades the meditational and ritual systems is: extraction of the "essences" of substances.[39] An example cited clearly overlaps the traditional Ayurvedic concept of *rasāyana*; this is from the second most important Tibetan medical text: "Preventing illness in the body and doing away with old age by virtue of obtaining essences: these bring about an increase in one's powers and life expectancy. On this point: what is known as *rasāyana* is the extracting of the essences of things in a pure state (*dan du*) in order to lengthen one's lifetime; (such essences are those of) rock, earth, wood, vegetable matter, grasses and juices." [*Cha-lag-bco-brgyad*, p. 18.] Walter adds: "However, extracting essences from plants and rocks is not taught in Ayurveda, although there are similar conceptions [Bose et al., p. 242]. To explain this tantric use of *rasāyana* we thus venture the speculation that the Tibetan calque *bcud kyi/kyis len* represents a popular Indian etymology not utilized in Ayurvedic circles but within tantric sects. 'To obtain essences' requires *rasa* and *āyanam*, an incorrectly formed past passive participle of *āyam-* or *āyat-* (these verbs have approximately equal meanings), 'to arrive, to come, reach; to grasp, possess.'[40] Such a derivation would explain this consistent interpretation on *bcud len* in Tibetan tantric materials, when mercurial alchemy is not being referred to, as an 'extraction' or 'obtaining' of essence."[41]

Biographical Notes in P.C. Ray's Work[42]

Vedic period

"*Soma*, the fermented juice from the stems of *soma* plant, had been highly extolled and even worshipped or invoked as the representation of divine power. It was, however, largely used during the religious rituals. Among other fermented liquors, there is a mention of *madhu*, a drink supplied at feasts, and *sura*, which was probably a kind of beer brewed from barley grain. Curds or fermented milk also constituted an important article of diet." (p. 36)

"In the *White Yajurveda* we find, however, mention of six metals. It tells of *ayas* (gold), *hiraṇya* (silver), *loha* (copper), *śyāma* (iron), *sīsa* (lead), and *trapu* (tin). The *Atharvaveda*, on the other hand, names gold as *harita* (yellow), silver as *rajata* (white), and copper as *lohita* (red).

"The *Atharvaveda* consists mostly of charms, spells, incantations, magic, sorcery, demonology and witchcraft. It also deals with plants and vegetable products as helpful agents in the treatment of diseases and for the prolongation of life. In one hymn it refers to the *soma* plant as follows:

> The strength of this *amrita* (ambrosia) do we give this man to drink. Moreover, I prepare a remedy that he may live a hundred years! (pp. 36-37)

"...In the *Atharvaveda* the hymns for the cure of diseases and of possessions by demons of disease are known as *bhaiṣajyāni,* while those which have for their object the prolongation of life and preservation of youth and health are known as *āyuṣyani*—a term which later on gave place to *rasāyana* the Sanskrit equivalent of alchemy. As illustrations, we shall quote here two such hymns under the latter heading, which are in the form of invocations to pearl and shell and to gold respectively.

> Born in the Heavens, bron in the sea, brought on from the river (Sindhu), this shell, born of gold, is our life-prolonging amulet.
>
> The bone of the gods turned into pearls; that, animated, dwells in waters. That do I fasten upon thee unto life, lustre, strength and longevity, unto a life lasting a hundred autumns. May the (amulet) of pearl protect thee!
>
> The gold which is born from fire, the immortal they bestowed upon the mortals. He knows this, deserves it; of old age dies he who wears it.
>
> The gold, (endowed by) the sun with beautiful colour, which the men of yore, rich in descendants, did desire, may it gleaming envelope thee in lustre! Long-lived becomes he who wears it.

"While gold was regarded as the elixir of life, lead was looked upon as the dispeller of sorcery. Thus a hymn tells us:

> To the lead Varuna gives blessings, to the lead Agni gives help. Indra gave me the lead; unfailingly dispels sorcery.

"Thus we find that the origin of alchemical notions gathered round gold, lead, *soma* juice and other medicinal plants as early as the age of the *Atharvaveda* in India. And as the Vedas, the sacred scriptures of the ancient Hindus, enjoyed a very high canonical sanctity and were viewed more as revelations than as human compositions, there is no wonder that medicine and, for that matter, chemical knowledge as well in ancient India have seldom been able to shake themselves completely free from the influence of magic, religion and alchemy as auxiliaries. For, chemistry in ancient India, possibly more so than in Europe, was evolved chiefly as a handmaid of medicine and, somewhat later on, as adjunct to the Tantric cult. The efficacy of the drug alone was by no means considered sufficient unless backed by the kindly interpretation of the deities.

"Hence both medicine and chemistry, particularly in their alchemical aspects, followed the course of religious practices in their development. In fact, at no time they were free from theological tinge or urge. It had been a usual practice for the early workers and writers, while discussing theories or describing processes of chemical operations, to ascribe to origin thereof to their favourite gods and goddesses, or to start with a prayer to the presiding deity of the branch of knowledge concerned. Each element and phenomenon of nature, as well as the properties of each substance, were associated with their respective divinities responsible for their manifestation. The presentation of subject matter in many writings and works of Ayurvedic and Tantric period will be found to have been made in the shape of a dialogue between the god Siva or Hara and his consort Parvati or Gouri. Where the authors of the works were Buddhist by religion, we meet with the name of a Buddha, a Tathagata or an Avalokiteswara being invoked as the revealer of all knowledge." (pp. 37-39)

Ayurvedic period: chemistry in Kauṭilya

"...there is a passage in *Samyuttanikaya* (pt. III, p. 152) where Buddha is described to refer incidentally to a number of vegetable substances used by the dyers or painters for preparing dyes and colours. These are: (a) resin (*rajana*), (b) lac (*lakha*), (c) turmeric (*halidda*), (d) indigo (*nīli*), and (e) maddar (*manjatthi*).

"The earliest and most authentic record of informations relating to the knowledge of chemistry, metallurgy and medicine of these early days is found in the *Arthaśāstra* (Treatise on Polity) of Kauṭilya.... A very comprehensive account of ores, minerals and metals with their extraction and working, as well as alloys, is found in the *Arthaśāstra*...

> Gold ores: 'These are obtained from plains or slopes of mountains, and are either yellow, or reddish yellow, or as red as copper in colour.... They are heavy. There is a sandy layer within them and they contain globular masses; when roasted they do not split but emit much foam and smoke. (This indicates the presence of organic matter.) They are used to form amalgams with copper and silver.' That is they are made use of in converting copper or silver into gold. This furnishes evidence of the practice of alchemy in Kauṭilya's time. (82) (pp. 49-50)
>
> ...Lead ores: 'Lead ores have the colour of *kakamechaka* (*solanum indicum*), pigeon, or cow's bile, are marked with white lines and possess smell like raw meat.' (83)...Iron ores: 'These are of orange colour, or pale red, or of the colour of the flower of *sinduvara* (*Vitex trifolia*). (83)...'
> The superintendent of mines should possess knowledge of the science dealing with copper and other minerals; he should have experience *in*

the art of distillation and condensation of mercury and of testing gems. Aided by experts in mineralogy and provided with mining labourers and necessary instruments he should examine mines which, on account of their containing mineral excrement, crucibles, charcoal and ashes, may appear to have been exploited, or which may be newly discovered on plains or mountain slopes possessing mineral ores, the richness of which can be ascertained by *weight, depth of colour, piercing smell and taste.* The superintendent of metals (*lohadhyakshah*) shall carry on the manufacture of copper, lead, tin, brass (*arakuta*), bronze (*kamsya*), sulphide of arsenit (*haritala*), and also of commodities from them. (84) (p. 51)

'...metals are rendered soft when they are treated with the ashes of certain plants and cereals, or with the milk of both cow and sheep. Brittle metals are rendered soft when thrice soaked in a mixture made up of honey, sheep's milk, sesamum oil, clarified butter, jaggery, ferment (*kinva*) and mushroom.' (83). A rather detailed description of the properties of gold and silver, and of their working has been given by Kautilya. 'Gold may be obtained *either pure or amalgamated with mercury or silver, or alloyed with other impurities as mine gold.*' (85). 'That which is of the colour of the petals of lotus, ductile, glossy, incapable of making any continuous sound, and glittering is the best. That which is reddish yellow is of middle quality; and that which is red is of low quality.' (85). 'Impure gold is of whitish colour. *It shall be fused with lead four times the quantity of impurity. When gold is rendered brittle owing to its contamination with lead, it shall be heated with cow-dung, when it splits into pieces owing to hardness. It shall be drenched (after heating) into oil mixed with cow-dung.*' (86). 'Mine gold, which is brittle owing to its contamination with lead, shall be heated wrapped with cloth and hammered on a wooden anvil. Or, it may be drenched in a mixture of mushroom and *vajrakhand* (*Euphorbia antiquorun*).' (86)...'Impure silver should be heated with lead of one-fourth the quantity of impurity.' (86). This indicates that the knowledge of purification of gold and silver by alloying with lead was known in Kautilya's time. This is comparable to the modern process of cupellation. '*When from one to sixteen kakanis of gold in a pure specimen of the metal (of sixteen mashakas) are replaced by from one to sixteen kakanis of copper so that the copper is inseparably alloyed with the whole mass of the remaining quantity of the gold, the sixteen varieties of the standard of the purity of gold will be obtained.*' This may be compared to the modern system of expressing the standard of purity of gold by *carat* numbers. Description is also given for testing the purity of gold by means of touchstone. (pp. 52-53)

Ayurvedic period—Caraka and Suśruta

"According to Caraka medicines are classified under two main heads: one increases the strength and vitality of people, already healthy (vital *elixir*), the other cures diseases (cf., *āyuṣyani* and *bhaiṣajyāni* of *Atharvaveda*). The former, which promotes longevity, retentive memory, health, vitality, etc., is called *rasāyana*, and may, therefore, be regarded as part of alchemy." (p. 63)

"Susruta has dealt mostly with vegetable drugs. There is, however, on *sloka* in which the six metals, viz., tin, lead, copper, silver, *krishna loha* (iron) and gold, and their calces are also recommended for use as drugs. Among the minerals Susruta has made use of sulphate of copper, sulphate of iron, alum-earth, red ochre, realgar, etc., as medicaments for external application." (p. 65)

Tantric period (from c. AD 700 to 1300)

"Indian alchemy very largely derived its colour, flavour and in fact, its nourishment from the Tantric cult. In almost every country the progress of chemistry can be traced to medicine and a belief in the artificial gold-making or the transmutation of the base metals into gold, as well as to the search after the *vital elixir of life* or the *philosopher's stone*. In India, however, these ends have played a secondary part and, in fact, as means to a still higher end, i.e., religious worship, and performance of religious rites. It is well-known that the Indian life in all its aspects, social, political and intellectual, had been at all times under the mighty sway of religion. Medicine and alchemy too, along with the other branches of science, had their origin and growth with this end in view, as necessary aids and helping agents to spiritual pursuit." (p. 113)

"...but their are evidences that alchemical knowledge was widely cultivated in India even before the Tantric age. The *Vasavadatta* and *Dasakumaracharita* in the sixth century allude to the preparation of a mass of fixed or coagulated mercury (*paradapindadraba—Vasavadatta*); of a chemical powder capable of producing deep sleep or stupor by its inhalation (*yogachurna—Dasakumaracharita*); of a chemically prepared wick for producing light without fire (*yogabartika—Dasakumaracharita*); and of a powder which acts as an anaesthetic and paralyses sensory and motor nerves (*stambhana-churnam—Vasavadatta*)." (p. 115)

"...a tantra belonging to the extinct school of Kubjikamata and named *Kubjikatantra* in the valuable manuscript collections of the

Maharaja of Nepal. This was written in Gupta character and copied about the sixth century AD. In one place of this tantra we come across a passage in which Siva himself speaks of *parada* (mercury) as his generative principle and eulogises its efficacy when killed six times. In this tantra we find allusions to the transmutation of copper into gold with the aid of mercury, as also to other alchemical processes.

"...during the period of its decline Buddhism imbibed many of the superstitious beliefs and corrupt rites of effete and popular Brahminical religion.... What is it that made the tantras the repositories of chemical knowledge? In contrast to the highly philosophical religion of the Upanishads accessible only to the upper intellectual classes of the society and according to which salvation or the highest end of life is attained only by right conduct through numerous births and re-births, Tantras offer an easy liberation for all even in this life by enjoining certain rites and ceremonies. Therefore, the ascetic who aspires after liberation in this life must preserve his body for the fulfillment of these rites and ceremonies. According to the tantras, preservation of the body is achieved by the use of mercury, medicaments and breathing exercises. Tantras, therefore, deal with medicinal preparations consisting mostly of mercury, calculated to make the body undecaying and immortal for the emancipation of a man while alive. In all the tantric treatises the word *rasa* has been used to mean mercury. Thus they came to be the repositories of many chemical informations and alchemical recipes." (p. 116)

"...in the tantric treatise *Rasahridaya* speaks of *rasasiddhas* (alchemists) as those who, without quitting their bodies, have attained to new ones through the influence of Hara and Gouri (mercury and mica). By the science of mercury is to be understood not only a branch of chemistry alone, but it is also to be applied to salvation according to the tantric treatises. Mercury, according to *Rasarnava*, can improve not only the quality of metals (i.e., convert the base metals into gold), but can make the body undecaying and imperishable. *Rasarnava* is believed to be a tantric work of the twelfth century AD, which throws a flood of light on the chemical knowledge of the Indians in those days...." (pp. 118-19)

"...to trace some of the tantric treatises from their Tibetan translations recorded in the great Tibetan scriptures, Kanjur (*Kang-gyur*) and Tanjur (*Stan-gyur*), the Tibetan equivalent of the Buddhist

Tripitika.... Some parts of Tanjur are believed to date back to the seventh century AD...divided into two main classes: *Rgyud*, corresponding to the Sanskrit tantra and *Mdo* or *Do*, corresponding to the Sanskrit *sūtra* (science and literature).... Hungarian scholar, Csoma de Koros...has made mention of a work on preparing quicksilver, described as the most powerful agent for subduing every sickness and for improving the vigour of the body, as well as of a work on turning base metals into gold (i.e., on alchemy)." (p. 123)

Rasaratnākara of Nāgārjuna

I shall now speak of the purification of important *rasas* (minerals).

"What wonder is it that *rājavarta* (lapis lazuli) digested with the juice of *Albizzia lebbek* converts silver of the weight of one *gunja* (*rati*—a kind of seed weighing 1.9 grains approx.) into one hundred times its weight of gold of the lustre of the rising sun?" (1)

"What wonder is it that yellow sulphur, purified with the juice of *Butea monosperma*, converts silver into gold when roasted thrice over the fire of cow-dung cakes?" (2)

"What wonder is it that calamine...roasted thrice with copper converts the latter into gold?" (3)

"Calamine, a zinc mineral, when roasted with copper in the presence of reducing organic matters, is likely to give rise to brass, which was possibly passed as artificially prepared gold." (p. 129)

"What wonder is it that cinnabar digested several times with the milk of the ewe and the acids (vegetable acids) imparts to silver the lustre of gold glowing as saffron?" (4)

"Digestion of minerals is to be effected in the decoction of *Dolichos biflorus, Paspalum scrobiculatum*, the urine of man and acid juices of (the fruit of) *rattan (Calamus rotang)* and afterwards with the addition of alkalies (soda, borax, etc.). The operation of roasting is to be performed thrice." (5)

"What wonder is it that the pyrites macerated in the juice of *Musa sapientum* and in castor oil and clarified butter, and placed inside the bulb of *Amorphophalus campanulatus* and roasted (in a closed crucible) undergoes perfect purification?" (6)

"The process is likely to lead to the production of metallic copper from pyrites." (p. 130)

"Mercury is to be rubbed with its equal weight of gold and then (the *amalgam*) further admixed with sulphur, borax, etc. The mixture is then to be transferred to a crucible and its lid put on, and then submitted to gentle roasting. By partaking of this elixir (i.e., the sublimate) the devotee acquires a body not liable to decay." (30-32)

"I shall now describe the *garbha yantram*...for reducing *pistika* (a cake of mercury and sulphur) to ashes. Make a clay crucible, 4 digits in length and 3 digits in width, with the mouth rounded. Take 20 parts of salt and one of bdellium and pound them finely, adding water frequently; smear the crucible with this mixture. Make a fire of paddy husks and apply gentle heat." (84-86) (p. 132)

Chemistry in Rasārṇava

"The killing of *metals vida.—'Hear attentively as I shall now speak of the killing of metals. There is no such elephant of a metal which cannot be killed by the lion of sulphur.'*" (VII.138-42, p. 138)

"Killing of gold: Saltpetre, green vitriol, sea-salt, rock-salt, mustard, borax, sal ammoniac, camphor, the pyrites—all these are to be taken in equal parts. The crucible is to be smeared with the milky juice of *Euphorbia neriifolia* and *Asclepias gigantea*; then having added the powder of the aforesaid *vida*, the gold is to be killed, my beloved!" (XI.83-86, p. 139)

Chemistry in *Dhātuvāda* (translated from the Tibetan Xylograph by Pandit Vidushekhara Bhattacharya)

"In the Himalayas there is a very good and well-known plant called *kustha* (*Costus speciosa—ru.rta*), from the leaf of which drops towards the earth (*sa.phyogs*) a fluid having a colour like bright gold. This and the ashes of pure lead (*za.ne.dkar.po*), and quicksilver when, according to the instruction given, come into contact with the copper mixed with silver, they turn into gold." (12) (p. 146)

Chemistry in Rasaprakāśasudhākara of Yaśodhara

"*Hemakriyā* or process for the fabrication of gold: I shall now speak of some curiosities of metals, partly from my own experience and partly from the classics on the subject. Calamine, cinnabar, copper pyrites and realgar are to be rubbed with the milky juice of *Euphorbia neriifolia* for seven days together and then to be digested another three days. Melted copper or silver or lead, being alloyed with the aforesaid mixture, acquires the power of converting hundred times its weight of base metals into gold." (pp. 153-54)

Chemistry in Rasaratnasamuccaya

"By partaking of mercury, men are freed from a multitude of

diseases, arising out of the sins of former existence—of this there is no doubt." (26) (p. 165)

"Project into melted gold its own weight of the ash of mercury; (when cooled) powder it and rub it with lemon juice and cinnabar, and roast it in a covered crucible twelve times. The gold thus acquires the colour of saffron." (15-16) (p. 180)

Chemistry in Dhātukriyā or Dhātumañjarī (Rudrayāmalatantra)

"One part of gold and four parts of zinc are to be melted together and the alloy roasted in a closed crucible...the process repeated with the addition of alkalies...gold of a reddish-yellow colour will thus be generated." (11-17) (p. 198)

"By using the augmented (weight increased by the addition of inferior metals) *gold as a means of exchange one can amass wealth.*" (52) (p. 199)

References

1. To quote Lacroix, in the context of a fourteenth century status of St. Marcellus of Notre-Dame, "those wonderful Gothic monuments in which the statuary has represented a mass of figures, sacred and profane, real and imaginary, and which give one the impression of being a book of alchemy, with a chisel upon stone," J. Read, *Prelude to Chemistry*, 1969, p. 113.
2. M.A. Stein, *An Archaeological Tour in Waziristan and Northern Baluchistan, MASI*, no. 37, 1929, pp. 38, 42, 60, 75; pls. IX, XII, XVI. Cf., Piggott, *Prehistoric India*, 1950, p. 60.
3. E. Mackay, *FEM*, vol. I, pp. 260ff.
4. E.O. James, *Mother Goddess Cults*, pp. 34, 36; E. Mackay, *FEM*, vol. I, p. 259; Vats, *EH*, vol. I, p. 370.
5. There is a remarkable parallel to this concept of "born and unborn" in an inscription at Gal-lena wihaara, in the north-western province of Srilanka, recording the dedication of a cave; H. Parker, *Ancient Ceylon*, New Delhi, 1909, reprint, 1981, p. 446; inscription no. 68 on p. 447, fig. 153 Facsimiles of Inscriptions. The inscription has five-pronged base with a *svastika* rising from the middle prong and reads: *devānapiya mahā rāja gāmaṇi abhayasa puta tisayasa mahā leṇa* (cave) *agatānāgattasa cāt* (*u*) *disa sagasa.* "The Great cave of Tissa the Noble (tissa + aya), son of the great king Gāmaṇi Abhaya, beloved of the gods; to the community of the four quarters, present or future." This is a definitive echo of the proto-Indus pictorial motif of the *svastika* and the sign with five-

prongs, like a harrow; or vertical, like the English alphabet E.

6. *Śatapatha Brāhmaṇa*, XI.4.3.
7. Can this practice of hiding alchemical texts also vouched in the Tibetan alchemical tradition explain why many temple icons were disfigured—possibly in search of hidden alchemical manuals?
8. Jack Lindsay, *The Origins of Alchemy in Graeco-Roman Egypt*, New York, 1970. An outstanding study.
9. One procedure to maintain secrecy is to hide a secret text within a pillar. The legend is that the pillar will break open and the secrets will reveal themselves when a "deserving" pupil comes along. (Cf., the interesting legend of Hiraṇyākṣa, golden eye, *daitya* twin-brother of Hiraṇya-kacipu, golden dress, killed by the Boar and Man-lion incarnations respectively; note the golden connotations in morphemes and the parallels with pictorial motifs on proto-Indus seals.)
10. M.L. Walter, p. 26; a scholarly explanation of the gter ma system of hiding texts in a temple pillar to be received by a disciple; it will split open at the moment of their greatest usefulness. Cf., *Hindu Iconography. Cult Symbols carried on Multiple Hands of Icons.* Multiple hands may be an artistic freedom to ensure that all key symbols are portrayed on the carrier. The so-called esoteric, erotic sculptures on the temples of India are vividly tantric/alchemical allegories, or "sculpted" metaphors.
11. M.L. Walter, op. cit., p. 69, n. 17.
12. Ibid., p. 6, n. 3.
13. This is a sweeping statement, no borne out by the great work of P.C. Ray; cf., the sample quote in the concluding part of this essay.
14. M.L. Walter, op. cit., p. 7, n. 6.
15. Ibid., p. 86, n. 94. Stablein, "A medical-cultural system among the Tibetan and Newar Buddhists: Ceremonial Medicine," *Kailash*, I, 3, 1973, pp. 193-203.
16. M.L. Walter, op. cit., p. 8, n. 9; this was written in 1980.
17. Ibid., p. 213, n. 187.
18. Ibid., p. 8, n. 10.
19. Ibid., p. 65, n. 2.
20. Ibid., p. 10, n. 1.
21. Ibid., p. 81, n. 77.
22. Cf., the use by *siddhas* of south India, of *tiri-kaṭukam,* three astringents: *cukku, miḷagu, tippili.* Longevity and good-health are two phases of the transient problem of a *doṣa*?
23. Cf., P.C. Ray, p. 140: The etymology for *rasāyana* in the standard Ayurvedic works is "the method (*ayanam*, past passive participle of i- 'to go') or *rasa* (the nutritive fluid within the human body);" like-wise, in metallic alchemical works it is the method of mercury (*rasa*)

as the magical nutritive fluid which pervades nature and in Hindu tantras is often referred to as "Śiva's semen" or as representing Śiva himself.

24. M.L. Walter, op. cit., p. 65, nn. 3 and 4.
25. O.P. Jaggi, *Yogic and Tantric Medicine, History of Science and Technology,* vol. V, Delhi, 1973.
26. M.L. Walter, op. cit., p. 139.
27. Ibid., p. 67, n. 7.
28. Ibid., pp. 11-12, n. 10.
29. C.H. Tawney, tr., *The Ocean of Story*; being C.H. Tawney's translation of Somadeva's *Kathāsaritsāgara* (or *Ocean of Streams of Story*), London, 1925-28; cf., two tales in vol. III, pp. 161-63 and 252-56; Gajanan K. Shrigondekar, ed., *Mānasollāsa,* Gaekwad's Oriental Series, vol. XXVIII< Baroda; cf., review by "U.N.G.," in *IHQ*, vol. II, 1926, pp. 207-9; and the notice in Mauritz Winternitz, *A History of Indian Literature,* vol. III, part 2, Delhi, 1967, first edn. English tr., p. 613.
30. Cf., Shashibhushan Dasgupta, *Obscure Religious Cults,* Calcutta, 1969, p. 207.
31. Cf., Shashibhusan Dasgupta, *An Introduction to Tantric Buddhism,* Calcutta, 1974, p.p 85.
32. M.L. Walter, op. cit., p. 70, n. 23.
33. Shashibhusan Dasgupta, *Obscure Religious Cults,* p. 253, quoting the *Sarvadarśanasaṁgraha,* vv. 18-22.
34. *Rasārṇavam,* in *Bibliotheca Indica,* NS, nos. 1193, 1220, 1238, Calcutta, 1910, p. 3.
35. M.L. Walter, op. cit., p. 21.
36. Ibid., p. 73, n. 40.
37. Ibid., p. 73, n. 43.
38. Cf., O-rgyan, *Btsun-mo,* pp. 133f. with Eva M. Dargyay, *The Rise of Esoteric Buddhism in Tibet,* Delhi, 1977, p. 33.
39. M.L. Walter, op. cit., p. 28, n. 61.
40. V.S. Apte, *The Practical Sanskrit-English Dictionary,* Poona, 1957, p. 348.
41. M.L. Walter, op. cit., p. 78, n. 61.
42. All references in this section are from: P.C. Ray, ed., *History of Chemistry in Ancient and Medieval India (HCAMI)* (incorporating *The History of Hindu Chemistry* by Acharya Prafulla Chandra Ray).

Bibliography

The bibliography is organized in three sub-sections:

a. Works cited in Walter's dissertation (tantric alchemy);
b. Works on science and technology, including metallurgy; and
c. Works on alchemy, medicine and natural sciences

a. *Works cited in Walter's dissertation*

Bagchi, Prabodh Chandra, *Studies in the Tantras,* part I (no more published), Calcutta, University of Calcutta, 1939.

Bagchi, Sitansusekhar, ed., *Suvarṇa-prabhāsasūtra,* Darbhanga, Mithila Institute, 1967, Buddhist Sanskrit Texts, no. 8.

Bhattacharya, Vidushekhara, "Sanskrit Treatises on Dhātuvāda or Alchemy as translated into Tibetan," *Acharya Prafull Chandra Ray Commemoration Volume,* Calcutta, Calcutta Oriental Press, 1932.

Bhattacharyya, Dinesh C., "Date and Works of Vāgbhaṭa the Physician," *Annals of the Bhandarkar Oriental Research Institute,* XXVII, 1947, pp. 112-27.

Cha-lag-bco-brgyad, Lokesh Chandra, ed., *Yuuthok's Treatise on Tibetan Medicine,* New Delhi, International Academy of Indian Culture, 1968. Satapitaka Series, Indo-Asian Literatures, vol. 72. [An error-filled edition of G. yu-thog-yon-tan-mgon-po's classic.]

Das, Sarat Chandra, *A Tibetan-English Dictionary with Sanskrit Synonyms,* Delhi, Motilal Banarsidass, 1970. [Unaltered reprint of the 1902 edition.]

Dash, Bhagwan, *Tibetan Medicine: with Special Reference to Yoga Sataka,* Dharmashala, Library of Tibetan Works and Archives, 1967.

Dpal-Idan-tshul-khrims, *G'yun-drun-bon-gyi-bstan-'byun; a Detailed History of the Bon Religion with a Survey of Bonpo Monasteries in Tibet,* Dolanji, Tibetan Bonpo Monastic Centre, 1972.

Dutt, Uday Chand, *The Materia Medica of the Hindus,* Calcutta, Madan Gopal Dass, 1922.

Dymock, William, Warden, C.J.H., and Hooper, David, *Pharmacographia Indica.* A history of the principal drugs of vegetable origin met within British India, London, Kegan Paul, Trench and Trubner, 1890-93.

Finot, Louis, *Les lapidaries Indian,* Paris, Librarie Emile Bouillon, 1896, Bibliotheque de l'Ecole des Hautes Etudes, Sciences philologiques et historiques, cent-onzieme fascicule.

Francke, A.H., *Antiquities of Indian Tibet,* New Delhi, S. Chand & Co., 1972, Archaeological Survey of India, New Imperial Series, vol. XXXVIII.

—, gzer-myig, "A Book of the Tibetan Bon-pos," *Asia Major,* I, 1924, pp. 243-346; III, 1926, pp. 321-29; IV, 1927, pp. 161-239 and 481-580; V, 1928, pp. 1-40; and VI, 1930, pp. 299-314.

Garbe, Richard, *Die indischen Minerallen, ihre Namen und die ihnen zugeschriebenen Krafte,* Leipzig, Verlag von S. Hirzel, 1882.

Govinda, Lama Angarika, *Foundations of Tibetan Mysticism,* New York, Samuel Weiser, 1971.

Hoffman, Helmut, translation of *Die Religionen Tibets; Bon und Lamaismus in ihrer geschichtlichen Entwicklung,* Freiburg, 1956.

—, *Quellen zur Geschichte der tibetischen Bon-Religion,* Wiesbaden, Franz Steiner Verlag, 1950.

Kvaern, Per, "Aspects of the Origin of the Buddhist Tradition in Tibet," *Numen,* XIX, 1972, pp. 22-40.

—, "The canon of the Tibetan bon-pos," *Indo-Iranian Journal,* XVI, 1974, pp. 34-40.

Lessing, Ferdinand K., and Wayman, Alex, *Mkhas Grub Rje's Fundamentals of the Buddhist Tantras,* The Hague and Paris, Mouton, 1968, Indo-Iranian Monographs, vol. VIII.

Li An-che, "Rnin-ma-pa: The Early form of Lamaism," *JRAS,* 1948, pp. 142-63.

Lokesh Chandra, ed., *Jam-dpal, an Illustrated Tibeto-Mongolian Materia Medica of Ayurveda,* New Delhi, International Academy of Indian Culture, 1971, Satapitaka Series, Indo-Asian Literatures, vol. 82. [Reproduction of 'Jam-dpal-rdo-rje's *Gso-byed-bdud-rtsi'i-'khrul-med-nos-'dzin-bzo-rig-me-lon-du-rnam-par-sar-pa-mdzes-mtshar-mig.*]

Mahaa, *Bye-brag-tu-rtogs-a-chen-po. Mahāvyutpatti,* Tokyo, Suzuki Research Foundation, 1965. [Reprint of the 1916 Sakaki Ryozaburo edition, with the index of Kyoo Nishio, published originally in 1924.]

Mallmann, Marie-Therese de, *Etude iconographique sur Manjusri*, Paris, Ecole Francaise d' Extreme-orient, 1964, Publications de l'Ecole Francaise d' Extreme-orient, vol. LV.

Mojumder, Atindra, *The Caryāpadas*, sec. rev. edn., Calcutta, Naya Prakash, 1973.

Nebesky-Wojkowitz, Rene de, *Oracles and Demons of Tibet; The Cult and Iconography of the Tibetan Protective Deities*, Graz, Akademische Druck-u, Verlagsanstalt, 1975. [A reprint with an added introduction by Per Kvaerne, of the original 1956 edn.]

Nobel, Johannes, *Ein Alter Medizinischer Sanskrit-text und seine Deutung*, Supplement no. 11 to the *JAOS*, appended to vol. LXXI, 1951.

Rosu, Arion, "Considerations sur une technique du Rasāyana Ayurvedique," *Indo-Iranian Journal*, XVII, 1975, pp. 1-29.

Singh, Thakur Balwant, *Glossary of Vegetable Drugs in Bṛhattrayī*, Varanasi, The Chowkhamba Sanskrit Series Office, 1972, The Chowkhamba Sanskrit Series, vol. LXXXVII.

Snellgrove, David L., *Hevajra Tantra: A Critical Study*, London, Oxford University Press, 1959, London Oriental Series, vol. 6.

Suzuki, D.T., *Studies in the Lankavatara Sutra*, London, Routledge & Kegan Paul, 1930; reprint, New Delhi, Munshiram Manoharlal Publishers, 1998.

Tāranātha, *Five Historical Works of Tāranātha*, Arunachal Pradesh, Tibetan Nyingmapa Monastery, Camp no. 5, 1974.

Thomas, F.W., *Tibetan Literary Texts and Documents Concerning Chinese Turkestan*, London, Luzac & Co., 1935-63, Oriental Translation Fund of the Royal Asiatic Society, New Series, vol. XL.

Vaidya, P.L., ed., *Saddharma Laṅkāvatārasūtram*, Darbhanga, Mithila Institute, 1963, Buddhist Sanskrit Text Series, no. 3.

Vimalamitra, *Skyabs-'gro-yan-lag-drug-pa*, Tibetan Tripitaka (Bstan-'gyur), Tokyo, Suzuki Research Institute, 1956.

Vostrikov, Andrej Ivanovic, *Tibetan Historical Literature*, translated from the Russian by Harish Chandra Gupta, Calcutta, Indian Studies, Past and Present, 1970, Soviet Indology Series, no. 4. [Translation of *Tibetskaja Istoriceskaja Literature*, originally published in 1962.]

VyaaDi-pa, *Phy-nan-bdud-rtsi-bcud-len-gdams-pa*, Tibetan Tripitaka (Bstan-gyur), vol. 69, Tokyo, Suzuki Research Institute, 1956.

Wayman, Alex, "Studies in Yama and Maara," *Indo-Iranian Journal* III/1, 1959, pp. 44-73 and III/2, 1959, pp. 112-31.

b. *Works on Science and Technology, including Metallurgy*

Agrawal, D.P., "Metal Technology of the Harappans," in *FIC*.
Aitchison, Leslie, *A History of Metals*, 2 vols., London, 1960.
Aiyappan, A., "Pottery braziers of Mohenjo-daro," *Man*, 39, 1939, 71-74.
Alberuni's India, tr. by E.C. Sachau, reprint, New Delhi, 1983.
Allchin, B., and Allchin, F.R., *The Rise of Civilization in India and Pakistan*, New Delhi, 1983.
Allchin, F.R., *Piklihal Excavations*, Hyderabad, Government of Andhra Pradesh, 1960, Andhra Pradesh Government Archaeol. Series 1.
Atharvaveda, tr., W.D. Whitney, 2 vols., reprint, Delhi, 1962.
Bagchi, P.C., "Evolution of the Tantras," *The Cultural Heritage of India*, vol. IV, Calcutta, 1956, p. 111.
—, "The Cult of the Buddhist Siddhacharyas," *The Cultural Heritage of India*, vol. IV, Calcutta, 1956, p. 273.
Banerjee, M.N., "On Metals and Metallurgy in Ancient India," *IHQ*, III, 1, 1927, pp. 121-33; 4, 1927, pp. 793-802.
Banerjee, N.R., *The Iron Age in India*, Munshiram Manoharlal Publishers, New Delhi, 1965.
Bernal, J.D., *Science in History*, 4 vols. (first pub. 1954), revised edition, Harmondsworth, Penguin Books, 1969.
Besterman, T., *A World Bibliography of Oriental Bibliographies*, Oxford, Blackwell, 1975.
Bharadwaj, H.C., "Aspects of Early Iron Technology in India," in *RIA*.
—, *Aspects of Ancient Indian Technology*, Delhi, Motilal Banarsidass, 1979.
Bhattacharya, B., *Two Vajrayana Works*, Baroda, 1929.
—, *Guhyasamajatantra*, Baroda, M.S. University of Baroda, Gaekwad's Oriental Series, 1931.
—, *Sakti Sangraha Tantra*, 3 vols., Baroda, M.S. University of Baroda, Gaekwad's Oriental Series, LXI, XCI, CIV, 3 vols., 1932, 1941, 1947.
—, *Buddhist Esoterism*, London, Oxford University Press, 1932.
Blunt, E.A.H., *The Caste System of Northern India*, London, Oxford University Press, 1931.
Bose, N.K., "Some Aspects of Caste in Bengal," in Milton Singer, ed., *Traditional India: Structure and Change*, Philadelphia, American Folklore Society, 1959.
Bose, D.M., Sen, S.N., and Subbarayappa, B.V., *A Concise History of*

Science in India, New Delhi, 1971.

Briggs, G.W., *Gorakhanath and the Kanpatha Yogis*, Calcutta, 1938.

British Journal for the History of Science, Newsletter, no. 1, 1980, Chalfont St. Giles.

Bromage, B., *Tibetan Yoga*, London, 1959.

Bynum, W.F., Browne, E.J., and Porter, R.S., eds., *Dictionary of the History of Science*, London, Macmillan, 1981.

Campbell, J., *The Mystics, Ascetics and Saints of India*, London, 1903.

Carrington, H., *Hindu Magic*, London, 1909.

Chakravarti, C., "Antiquity of Tantrism," *IHQ*, VI, 1, 1930, pp. 114-26.

—, "The Cult of the Baro Bhaiya of Eastern Bengal," *JRASB*, XXVI, 1930, pp. 379-88.

—, "The Soma or Sauma Sect of the Saivas," *IHQ*, VIII, 1, 1932, pp. 221-23.

—, *Tantras: Studies on Their Religion and Literature*, Calcutta, 1963.

Chattopadhyaya, Debiprasad, *Lokāyata: A Study in Ancient Indian Materialism*, New Delhi, 1959, sixth reprint, 1985.

—, *Science and Society in Ancient India*, Calcutta, 1977, reprint, 1979.

—, *What is Living and What is Dead in Indian Philosophy*? New Delhi, 1976.

—, *History of Science and Technology in Ancient India*, Calcutta, 1986.

Coomaraswamy, Ananda K., *Yakṣas*, pts. I and II, first published 1928; reprint, second edn., New Delhi, Munshiram Manoharlal Publishers, 2002.

Corsi, P., and Weindling, P., eds., *Information Sources in the History of Science and Medicine*, London, Butterworth Scientific, 1983.

Cowell, Edward B., tr., Mādhava's *Sarvadarśana Saṁgraha*, seventh reprint, Varanasi, 1978, with a section on the mercurial school of Indian philosophy.

Dare, Paul, *Indian Underworld, Indian Saints, Sorcerers and Superstitions*, London, 1938.

Dasgupta, Shashibhushan, *Obscure Religious Cults*, third edn., Calcutta, 1976.

—, *An Introduction to Tantric Buddhism*, Calcutta, 1958.

Deshpande, M.N., "Archaeological Sources for the Reconstruction of the History of Sciences of India," *IJHS*, vol. 6, 1971, pp. 1-22.

Dharampal, S., *Indian Science and Technology in Eighteenth Century. Some Contemporary European Accounts*, Delhi, Impex India, 1971.

Dikshit, S.K., *The Mother Goddess*, Delhi, 1960.

Dutt, N.K., *Origin and Growth of Caste in India*, vol. I, London, Kegan Paul, Trench and Trubner, 1931; vol. II, Calcutta, K.L. Mukhopadhyaya, 1965.

Filliozat, J., *The Classical Doctrine of Indian Medicine*, New Delhi, Munshiram Manoharlal Publishers, 1964.

Forbes, R.T., *A Short History of the Art of Distillation*, Leiden, E.J. Brill, 1948.

—, *Metallurgy in Antiquity: a Notebook for Archaeologists and Technologists*, Leiden, E.J. Brill, 1950.

—, *Studies in Ancient Technology*, vol. 9, Leiden, E.J. Brill, 1964.

Gopal, S., "Social set-up of science and technology in Mughal India," *IJHS*, vol. 4, 1969, pp. 52-58.

Govind, V., "Some Aspects of Glass Manufacturing in Ancient India," *IJHS*, vol. 5, 1970, pp. 281-308.

Jacolliot, L., *Occult Science in India and Among the Ancients*, London, 1930.

Jaggi, O.P., *History of Science and Technology in India*, 15 vols., Delhi, Atma Ram & Sons, 1969-80.

Kalia D.R., and Jain, M.K., *A Bibliography of Bibliographies on India*, Delhi, Concept Publishing Co., 1957.

Karpinski, L.C., "Hindu Science," *American Mathematical Monthly*, XXVI, 1919, p. 289.

Kosambi, D.D., *The Culture and Civilization of Ancient India*, London, 1965.

Lahiri, D., "Mineralogy in Ancient India," *IJHS*, vol. 3, 1968, pp. 1-8.

Lal, B.B., "History of Technology in Ancient and Mediaeval India," in *SHSIA*, 1968, pp. 87-88.

Lamberg-Karlovsky, C.C., and Sabloff, J.A., "Archaeology and Metallurgical Technology in Prehistoric Afghanistan, India and Pakistan," in *American Anthropologist*, Beloit, vol. 69; 1967, pp. 145-62.

Laurence, L.W. de, *The Great Book of Magical Art and East Indian Occultism and the Book of Secret Hindu Ceremonial and Talismanic Magic*, fourteenth edn., Chicago, 1939.

Liang, Chou Yi, "Tantrism in China," *Harvard Journal of Asiatic Studies*, VIII, 1945, 241-332.

Mackay, E.J.H., *Early Indus Civilization*, revised and enlarged edn., New Delhi, 1976.

—, *Further Excavations at Mohenjodaro*, 2 vols., Delhi, 1938; reprint, New Delhi, Munshiram Manoharlal Publishers, 1998.

Mahadevan, I., *The Indus Script: Text, Concordance and Tables*, MASI, no. 77, New Delhi, 1977.
—, "The Cult object on Unicorn Seals: A Sacred Filter" in Noboru Karashima, ed., *Indus Valley to Mekong Delta: Explorations in Epigraphy*, Madras, New Era Publications, 1985, pp. 219-68.
Mahar, J.M., *India. A Critical Bibliography*, Tucson, University of Arizona Press, 1964.
Manchanda, O., *A Study of the Harappan Pottery*, New Delhi, Oriental Publishers, 1972.
Marshall, J., ed., *Mohenjodaro and the Indus Civilizations*, 2 vols., London, 1931.
—, *Taxila*, 3 vols., Cambridge, 1951.
Mehta, D.D., *The Positive Sciences in the Vedas*, New Delhi, 1961.
Needham, Joseph, *Science and Civilization in China*, several volumes published so far, Cambridge, Cambridge University Press, 1954.
—, *Clerks and Craftsmen in China and the West*, Cambridge, Cambridge University Press, 1970.
—, *The Grand Titration: Science and Society in East and West*, London, 1969, second impression, 1979.
Neogi, P., *Copper in Ancient India*, Bulletin 1, Indian Association for the Cultivation of Science, Calcutta, 1918.
—*Iron in Ancient India*, Bulletin 12, Indian Association for the Cultivation of Science, Calcutta, 1914.
Oman, J.C., *The Mystics, Ascetics and Saints of India: A Study of Sadhu-ism*, London, 1905.
—, *Cults, Customs and Superstitions of India*, London, 1908.
Paddayya, K., "On the Form and Function of Perforated Pottery of the Deccan Neolithic Culture," *Man*, Journal of the Royal Anthropological Society, London, vol. 4, 1969, pp. 450-53.
Piggott, Stuart, *Prehistoric India*, Harmondsworth, 1950.
Pingree, D., "Census of the Exact Sciences in Sanskrit," *Memoirs of the American Philosophical Society*, vol. 81, pp. 1-60; vol. 86, pp. 1-147; vol. 111, pp. 1-208, 1970-76.
Raghavan, V., *Yantras or Mechanical Contrivances in Ancient India*, Bangalore, 1952.
Rahman, P., *Bibliography of Source Materical on History of Science and Technology in Mediaeval India*, New Delhi, Indian National Science Academy, 1975.
Rashid, A., *Society and Culture in Medieval India*, Calcutta, K.L. Mukhopadhyaya, 1969.

Raychaudhuri, S.P., *Agriculture in Ancient India*, New Delhi, Indian Council of Agricultural Research, 1964.

Renou, Louis, *Religions of Ancient India*, London, 1953; reprint, New Delhi, 1998.

Rickard, T.A., *Man and Metals: A History of Mining in Relation to the Development of Civilizations*, 2 vols., New York, 1932.

Sankalia, H.D., *Some Aspects of Prehistoric Technology in India*, New Delhi, Indian National Science Academy, 1970.

—, *Prehistory and Protohistory in India and Pakistan*, Bombay, 1963.

Sarkar, B.K., *Hindu Achievements in the Exact Science*, New York and Calcutta, Longmans Green, 1918.

Sarton, George, *Introduction to the History of Science*, 3 vols., Washington, D.C., 1927-48, chap. 5.

Satchidananda Murty, K., *Nāgārjuna*, New Delhi, 1971.

Seal, B.N., *The Positive Sciences of the Ancient Hindus*, London, 1915; reprinted, New Delhi, 1958.

Sen, S.N., "The Impetus Theory of the Vaisesikas," *IJHS*, vol. 1, 1966, pp. 34-45.

—, "Scientific Works in Sanskrit, translated into Foreign Languages and vice-versa in the 18th and 19th century AD," *IJHS*, vol. 7, 1972, pp. 44-70.

Sikdar, J.C., "Jaina Atomic Theory," *IJHS*, vol. 5, 1970, pp. 199-218.

Sivin, Nathan, *Science and Technology in East Asia*, New York, Science History Publications, 1977.

Stein, M., Aurel, *An Archaeological Tour in Gedrosia* (*MASI*, 43), Calcutta, 1931.

Studies in History and Philosophy of Science, vol. 1, no. 1, 1970, London. Hist. Abs. 1977.

Subbarao, B., *The Personality of India*, sec. edn., Baroda, 1958.

Thapar, B.K., "Kalibangan: A Harappan Metropolis beyond the Indus Valley," in *ACI*, pp. 196-202.

Thibaut, G., *Mathematics in the Making in Ancient India*, ed. by D. Chattopadhyaya, Calcutta, 1984.

Tripathi, Vibha, "Introduction of Iron in India—A Chronological Perspective," in *RCIA*.

Tucci, Guiseppe, "Animadversions Indicae," *JASB*, 26, 1930, pp. 125-60.

Tylecote, R.F., *Metallurgy in Archaeology*, London, 1962.

Vats, M.S., *Excavations at Harappa*, 2 vols., Delhi, 1940; reprint, New Delhi, Munshiram Manoharlal Publishers, 1998.

Walker, B., *Hindu World: An Encyclopedic Survey of Hinduism*, 2 vols., London, George Allen and Unwin, 1968; reprint, New Delhi, Munshiram Manoharlal Publishers, 1990.

Wheeler, M., *Civilization of the Indus Valley and Beyond*, London, 1966.

—, *Early India and Pakistan*, London, 1959; rev. edn., 1968.

—, *Five Thousand Years of Pakistan. An Archaeological Outline*, London, 1950.

—, *The Indus Civilization*, third ed., Cambridge, 1979.

Winter, H.J.J., *Eastern Science. An Outline of its Scope and Contributions.* The Wisdom of the East Series, ed., J.L. Cranmer-Byng, London, John Murray, 1952.

Wood, E., *The Occult Training of the Hindus*, London, 1931.

Zvelebil, Kamil V., *The Poets of Powers*, London, 1973 (on Tamil Siddhas).

c. *Works on alchemy, medicine and natural sciences*

Acharya, Jadavji Trikamji, ed., *Rasasanketa-kalika* of Chamunda, Ayurvidya Granthamala, 6, Bombay, 1912.

—, *Rasasāra of Govindacharya*, Ayurvidya Granthamala, 2, Bombay, 1912.

Ainslie, A., *Materia Medica of Hindustan*, 1826.

Aiyar, A.K.Y.N., *Agricultural and Allied Arts in Vedic India*, Bangalore, Bangalore Press, 1949.

Alchemical Society Journal, vols. 1-3, AMS Press, reprint of 1915 edn.

Allchin, F.R., "India: the Ancient Home of Distillation?" *Man*, vol. 14, 1979, pp. 55-63.

Ambix. The Journal of the Society for the History of Alchemy and Chemistry, 1937, Index to vols. 1-17 (1937-70); 18-27 (1971-80).

Askari, S.H., "Medicines and Hospitals in Muslim India," *JBRS*, Patna, 1957, 43, pp. 7-21.

Bernal, J.D., "Comparative Macro-biotics," *Science in Traditional China*, Cambridge, Mass., 1981, pp. 57-84.

Bhattacharya, Chintamani, ed., *Matrika-bheda-tantrum*, Calcutta Sanskrit Series, no. 8, Calcutta, 1958.

Bhushan, H.G. Tatta, *Kāmaratna Tantra*, Shillong, 1928.

Bodding, O., *Studies in Santal Medicine and Connected Folklore*, pt. I: The Santals and Disease; pt. II: Santal Medicine; pt. III: How the Santals live, Memories of Asiatic Society of Bengal, X, nos. 1, 2, 3, 1925, p. 502.

Browne, E.G., *Arabian Medicine*, sec. edn., Cambridge, Cambridge University Press, 1962, first edn., 1921.

Burckhardt, Titus, *Alchemy: Science of the Cosmos, Science of the Soul*, Baltimore, 1971.

Burkhill, J.H., *Chapters on the History of Botany in India*, Delhi, Government of India Press, 1965.

Butler, A.R., and Needham, J., "An Experimental Comparison of the East Asiosopan, Hellenistic and Indian (Gandhāran) stills in Relation to Distillation of Ethanol and Acetic Acid," *Ambix*, vol. 27, 1980, pp. 69-76.

Castiglion, Arturo, *A History of Medicine*, tr. from Italian and ed. by B. Krumbhaar, New York, Alfred Knopf, 1941.

—, *Cauda Pavonis: the Alchemy and Literature Newsletter*, no. 1, 1977, Las Cruces, New Mexico, Association for the Study of Alchemy and Literature.

—, *Centaurus. International Magazine for the History of Science, Medicine and Technology*, vol. 1, no. 1, 1950, Copenhagen, Hist. Abs. 1963.

Chakravarty, C.A., *A Comparative Study of Hindu Meteria Medica*, 1929.

Chattopadhyaya, Aparna, "Some Rules for Public Health in Kautilya," *Nāgārjuna*, 11, 1967, pp. 158-61.

—, "Some Greek impressions about Indian Medical System," *Journal of Research in Indian Medicine*, 2, 1968, pp. 256-63.

—, "Hygienic Principles in the Regulation of Food Habits in the Dharma Sutras," *Nāgārjuna*, 11, 1968, pp. 294-99.

—, "A Note on the Hygienic Principles in the Manu Smrti," *Nāgārjuna*, 12, 1969, pp. 294-99.

Chevers, N., "Surgeons in India—Past and Present," *Calcutta Review*, vol. 23, no. 45, 1854, pp. 217-54.

Chikashige, Masumi, *Alchemy and Other Chemical Achievements of the Ancient Orient*, Tokyo, 1936, reprint, New York, AMS Press.

Chopra, R.N., *Glossary of Indian Medicinal Plants*, New Delhi, Publications and Information Directorate, 1969.

Clymer, Reuben S., *Alchemy and the Alchemists*, 3 vols., reprint of 1907 edn., AMS Press, New York.

Coedes, George, "Les hopitaux de Jayavarman VII," *Bulletin de l'ecole francaise d'extreme Orient*, 1940, 40: 344ff.

Coudert, A., *Alchemy: The Philosopher's Stone*, London, Wildwood House, Sydney, Bookwise, Boulder, 1980.

Crosland, Maurice, *Historical Studies in the Language of Chemistry*, London, 1962.

Cummings, Richard, *The Alchemists: Fathers of Practical Chemistry*, New York, D. Mckay, 1966.

Current Work in the History of Medicine. An International Bibliography, vol. 1, 1954, London, Wellcome Institute for the History of Medicine.

Debus, Allen G., "Alchemy and the Historian of Science," *History of Science*, 6, 1967, pp. 128-38.

—, "The Chemical Philosophers: Chemical Medicine from Paracelsus to van Helmont," *History of Science*, 12, 1974, pp. 235-59.

Dobb, Betty J., *The Foundations of Newton's Alchemy*, Cambridge, 1975.

Dub, Homer H., "The Beginnings of Alchemy," *ISIS*, 38, November 1947, pp. 62-86.

Dutt, U.C., *The Materia Medica of the Hindus*, compiled from Sanskrit Medical Works, with a glossary of Indian plants by G. King, Calcutta, Thacker Spink, 1877; reprint, 1971.

Dymock, W., Warden, C.J.H., and Hopper, W., *Pharmacographia India. A History of the Principal Drugs of Vegetable Origin, Met. with in British India*, 3 vols., London, Kegan Paul, 1890-93, reprinted, Dehradun, 1972.

Edgerton, F., ed., *The Elephant Lore of the Hindus*, The elephant sport (*Matanga-lila*) of Nilakantha (tr.), New Haven, Conn., Yale University Press, 1931.

Eliade, Mircea, *Metallurgy, Magic and Alchemy*, Paris, 1938.

—, *Sacred and the Profane: The Nature of Religion*, New York, Harvest Book, 1959.

—, *Shamanism: Archaic Techniques of Ecstasy*, New York, Pantheon, 1964.

—, *Yoga: Immortality and Freedom*, sec. edn., Princeton, 1969.

—, *Forge and the Crucible: The Origins and Structure of Alchemy*, sec. edn., Chicago, 1978.

Fenner, Edward Todd, *Rasāyanasiddhi: Medicine and Alchemy in the Buddhist Tantras*, Madison, Wisconsin, 1983 (with a translation of the alchemical section of *Vimalaprabhā*, a commentary on the *Kālacakratantra*).

Gupta, S.P., *Psychopathology in Indian Medicine (Ayurveda) with Special Reference to its Philosophical Bases*, Aligarh, Ajaya Publishers, 1977.

Hartmann, Franz, *Alchemy*, Holmes Publishers, 1984.

Hehir, P., *The Medical Profession in India*, London, Oxford Medical Publications, 1923, 1977.

Heym, Gerard, "Al-Razi and Alchemy," *Ambix*, 1, March 1938, pp. 184-191.

Hoernle, A.F.R., ed., *Suśrutasaṁhitā*, Calcutta, 1897.

—, *Studies in the Medicine of Ancient India*, vol. 1, Osteology, Oxford, Clarendon Press, 1907.

—, *The Bower Manuscript, Archaeological Survey of India Reports*, vol. 22, Calcutta, 1893-1912.

Hogart, Ron C., ed., *Alchemy: A Comprehensive Bibliography of the Manly P. Hall Collection of Books and Manuscripts*, 1985, Philos. Res.

Holmyard, Eric John, *Makers of Chemistry*, Oxford, Clarendon Press, 1931.

—, "Alchemy in Mediaeval Islam," *Endeavour*, 14 July 1955, pp. 117-25.

—, *Alchemy*, Baltimore, 1957.

Hopkins, A.J., *Alchemy: Child of Greek Philosophy*, 1943; reprint, New York, AMS Press, 1967.

Iyer, Vīrarāghava K.C., "The Study of Alchemy," *P.C. Ray Commemoration Volume*, Calcutta, 1958.

Jaggi, O.P., "Indigenous Systems of Medicine during British Supremacy in India," *Studies in History of Medicine*, vol. 1, 1977, pp. 320-47.

Jolly, Julius, *Indian Medicine*, English translation from German by C.G. Kashikar, New Delhi, Munshiram Manoharlal Publishers, 1994.

Jung, C.G., *Psychology and Alchemy*, tr., R.F.C. Hull, Princeton, 1953.

Kapil, R.N., "Biology in Ancient and Medieval India," *IJHS*, vol. 5, 1970, pp. 112-40.

Karambelkar, V.W., *The Atharvavedic Civilization*, Nagpur, 1959.

Kashikar, C.G., "Pottery in the Vedic Literature," *IJHS*, vol. 4, 1969, 15-26.

Keswani, N.H., "Medical Education in India since Ancient Times," in O'Malley, C.D.O., ed., *The History of Medical Education*, Berkeley, University of California Press, 1970.

Kishore, J., "About Entry of Homoeopathy into India," *BHM*, vol. 3, 1973, 76-78.

Kunte, A.M., *The Aṣṭāṅgahṛdayasaṁhitā*, Bombay, 1891.

Kutumbiah, P., *Ancient Indian Medicine*, Bombay, Orient Longman, 1962.

—, "The Pulse in Indian Medicine," *IJHM*, vol. 12, 1967, pp. 11-14.

—, "The Siddha and Rasa-siddha Schools of Indian Medicine," *IJHM*, vol. 18, 1973, pp. 21-33.

Leslie, Charles, ed., *Asian Medical Systems: A Comparative Study*, Berkeley, 1976. (A.L. Basham's survey of the social history of medicine during the classical period, "The Practice of Medicine in Ancient and Mediaeval India," 18-43.) Leslie's essay on modernization of Ayurvedic institutions through the nineteenth and twentieth centuries, "Ambiguities of Revivalism in Modern India," pp. 356-67.

Mahdihassan, H., "The Earliest Distillation Units in Indo-Pakistan," *Pakistan Archaeology*, 8, 1972, pp. 159-68.

—, "Medicine and Alchemy in Indian Culture," *Scientia* (Extract from the IX, X, XI, XII), 1-6 issues, 1973.

—, *Indian Alchemy: or Rasāyana in the light of Asceticism and Geriatrics*, Delhi, Vikas Publications, 1979.

—, "The Tradition of Alchemy in India," *American Journal of Chinese Medicine*, vol. 9, no. 1, 1981, pp. 23-33.

—, "Cinnabar-gold as the best Alchemical Drug of Longevity, called Makaradhwaja in India," *American Journal of Chinese Medicine*, 13, 1-4, 1985, pp. 93-108.

Maheshwari, P., and Singh, V., *Dictionary of Economic Plants in India*, Delhi, Indian Council of Agricultural Research, 1965.

Majumdar, A.K., *Charaka and His Successors in Hindu Medicine*, 1901.

Majumdar, G.P., *Vanaspati: Plants and Plant Life as in Indian Treatises and Traditions*, Calcutta, Calcutta University Press, 1927.

Mathur, R.B., "Hungry Mercury: its Scientific Character and uses," *Nāgārjuna*, 3, 10, 1960, p. 915.

—, "Mercurial Samskaras: their Scientific Background," *Nāgārjuna*, 6, 8, 1963, p. 607; 10, p. 55.

McDonald, D., *Surgeons Twoe and a Barber. Being Some Account of the Life and Work of the Indian Medical Service (1600-1947)*, London, Heinemann, 1950.

Meyer, J.J., *Trilogie altindischer Machte und Feste der Vegetation*, 284 pp. Kaama +267pp. Bali + 399pp. Indra, Zurich, Neihans, 1937.

Ministry of Health, Government of India, *Report on the Committee on Indigenous Systems of Medicines*, New Delhi, 1948.

Mitra, Rajendralal, "Spirituous Drinks in Ancient India," *Journal of the Asiatic Society of Bengal*, 43, 1873, pp. 1-23.

Montgomery, J.W., "Cross, Constellation and Crucible: Luthern

Astrology and Alchemy in the Age of Reformation," *Ambix*, 11, 1963, pp. 650-86.

Moore, F., *A History of Chemistry*, New York, McGraw-Hill, 1918.

Mukhopadhyaya, G.N., *History of Indian Medicine*, 3 vols., Calcutta, 1923-29; reprint, New Delhi, Munshiram Manoharlal Publishers, 1994.

Multhauf, Robert P., *The Origins of Chemistry*, London, 1966.

—, "Alchemy," *Encyclopaedia Britannica*, vol. 1, fifteenth edn., Chicago, 1983.

Muthu, D.C., *The Antiquity of Hindu Medicine and Civilization*, London, 1930.

Narayanaswami Aiyar, C.S., "Ancient Indian Chemistry and Alchemy of the Chemico-Philosophical Siddhānta System of the Indian Mystics," *Proceedings and Transactions of the Third Oriental Conference*, 1924, Madras, 1925, pp. 597-614.

Nasr, Hossein, "Alchemy and Other Occult Sciences," *Islamic Science: An Illustrated Study*, Westerham, England, 1976, pp. 193-208.

Needham, Joseph, *Refiner's Fire: the Enigma of Alchemy in East and West*, London, 1971.

Neelamegham, A., *Development of Medical Societies and Medical Periodicals in India*, 1780 to 1920, Calcutta, Oxford Book and Stationery Company, 1963.

Om Prakash, *Food and Drinks in Ancient India*, New Delhi, Munshiram Manoharlal Publishers, 1961.

Paracelsus, *Alchemical Medicine*, Holmes Publishers, 1986.

Patrington, J.R., "Chinese Alchemy," *Nature* (London), CXII, 1927, 11; CXXVIII, 1931, 1074-75.

—, "Relationship between Chinese and Arabic Alchemy," *Nature* (London), CXX, 1927, 158.

—, *A Short History of Chemistry*, sec. edn., London, Macmillan, 1951.

—, *A History of Chemistry*, 4 vols., London, 1961-70.

Patterson, T.J.S., "The Transmission of Indian Surgical Techniques to Europe at the End of the Eighteenth Century," *Proceedings of XXIII International Congress of the History of Medicine*, vol. 1, 1974, pp. 694-96.

Patvardhan, R.V., "Rasavidyā or Alchemy in Ancient India," *Proceeding and Transactions of the First Oriental Conference*, 1919, 1, CLV, Poona, 1920, 2 vols.

Pritchard, Alan, *Alchemy: A Bibliography of English Language Writings*, London, Methuen, 1980.

—, *Proceedings of the Charaka Club*, vols. 1-11, 1902-47, New York.

Ray, P., "The Theory of Chemical Combination in Ancient Indian Philosophies," *IJHS*, vol. 1, 1966, pp. 1-14.

—, "Origin and Tradition of Alchemy," *IJHS*, vol. 2, 1967, pp. 1-21.

—, "Medicine—as it evolved in Ancient and Mediaeval India," *IJHS*, vol. 5, 1970, pp. 86-100.

—, and Gupta, H.N., *Carakasaṁhitā (a Scientific Synopsis)*, New Delhi, National Institute of Sciences of India, 1965.

Ray, Prafulla Chandra, *History of Hindu Chemistry*, first published—vol. I, 1902-3; vol. II, 1909, The Bengal Chemical and Pharmaceutical Works Limited, Calcutta.

—, and Kaviratna, Harish Chandra, eds., *Rasārṇava*, Bibliotheca Indica Series, no. 174, Asiatic Society, Calcutta, 1910.

Ray, Priyadaranjan, ed., *History of Chemistry in Ancient and Mediaeval India*, Indian Chemical Society, Calcutta, 1956.

Redgrove, H.S., *Alchemy, Ancient and Modern*, 1980.

Reed, John, *Prelude to Chemistry*, London, 1937.

—, *Through Alchemy to Chemistry*, London, 1957.

Reichen, Charles A., *A History of Chemistry*, New York, Hawthorne Books, 1963.

Roy, B.C., *Food and Drink in Ancient Bengal*, Calcutta, 1959.

Roy, K.K., "Early Relations between the British and Indian Medical Systems," *Proceedings of XXIII International Congress of the History of Medicine*, vol. 1, 1974, pp. 697-703.

Roy, M., "Anatomy in Indic Literature," *IJHS*, vol. 2, 1967, 35-46.

—, "Rasārṇavakalpa of the Rudrayāmalatantra," *IJHS*, vol. 2, 1967, 137.

Royle, J.F., *An Essay on the Antiquity of Hindu Medicine*, London, 1837.

Sarman, Yadava, ed., *Rasendra-cūḍāmaṇi* of Somadeva, Lahore, Motilal Banarsidass, 1932.

Sastri, B., *The Medical Lore of the Ancient Hindus*, 1901.

Sastri, D., "The Lokāyatikas and the Kapālikas," *IHQ*, VII, 1, 1931, pp. 125-27.

Schmidt, T., *The Eighty-five Siddhas*, Stockholm, 1958.

Scott, H.H., *A History of Tropical Medicine*, sec. edn. with Appendix, 2 vols., London, Edward Arnold, 1942.

Seal, S.C., "A Short History of Public Health in India," *IJHS*, vol. 16, 1971, 25-41.

Sengupta, Upendra, ed., *Rasendrasāra-saṁgraha* of Gopal Krishna